Becoming a Group Leader

Nina W. Brown
Old Dominion University

Merrill
is an imprint of

Upper Saddle River, New Jersey
Columbus, Ohio

This book is dedicated to the special people in my life: Wil, Toni, Mike, Linda, Billy, Joey, Samantha, Christopher, Nick, Emma, Chris, and Jill; and to my friends and colleagues who value group work as much as I do.

Library of Congress Cataloging in Publication Data
Brown, Nina W.
  Becoming a group leader / Nina W. Brown.
    p. cm.
  ISBN-13: 978-0-205-50328-5
  ISBN-10: 0-205-50328-4
  1. Group relations training.   2. Leadership—Study and teaching.   3. Group psychotherapy.   I. Title.
  HM1086.B76 2009
  303.3′4071—dc22   2008032843

Vice President and Executive Publisher: Jeffery W. Johnston
Publisher: Kevin M. Davis
Editor: Meredith D. Fossel
Editorial Assistant: Nancy J. Holstein
Senior Project Manager: Mary M. Irvin
Senior Managing Editor: Pamela D. Bennett
Senior Art Director: Diane C. Lorenzo
Cover Designer: Ali Mohrman
Cover Image: Jupiter Images
Operations Specialist: Susan Hannahs
Director of Marketing: Quinn Perkson
Marketing Coordinator: Brian Mounts

This book was set in Adobe Garamond by GGS Book Services. It was printed and bound by Hamilton Printing Company. The cover was printed by Phoenix Color Corp.

Pearson Education Ltd., London
Pearson Education Singapore Pte. Ltd.
Pearson Education Canada, Inc.
Pearson Education—Japan
Pearson Education Australia, Limited

Pearson Education North Asia, Ltd., Hong Kong
Pearson Educación de Mexico, S.A. de C.V.
Pearson Education Malaysia Pte. Ltd.
Pearson Education Upper Saddle River, New Jersey

Merrill
is an imprint of

10 9 8 7 6 5 4 3 2 1
ISBN 13: 978-0-205-50328-5
ISBN 10:   0-205-50328-4

Preface

The six primary goals for this book are built around a learning group leadership model of knowledge, being, and doing.

- Integrate the cognitive and affective components for learning group leadership that can be applied to clinical and nonclinical groups.
- Provide a conceptual roadmap and guidance for developing the art and science of group leadership.
- Stimulate critical thinking about the tasks and responsibilities of group leaders.
- Develop clinical judgment.
- Explore the tasks for the group leader's personal development.
- Describe practical strategies that can be used for all types of groups.

Central to the purpose for learning group leadership are the identification and constructive use of group dynamics. The group leader does not encounter these in isolation, but that is how they are often presented—separate from each other, where most of the complexity is lost or lessened.

Basic information and fundamentals about groups and group leadership are discussed with examples: how to create a group, stages of group development, therapeutic factors, and difficult member behaviors. There is an emphasis on practical information for what a group leader can and is expected to do, the importance of the developed and developing self of group leaders, and the clinical use of the self.

All of the major topics generally covered for group counseling have illustrations, vignettes, and exercises. In addition, the following unique topics are integrated into the discussion.

- A model for becoming a group leader
- Developing the leader's self to promote emotional presence, reduction of self-absorption and faulty beliefs, and a deeper and more profound understanding of group dynamics
- An in situ (real-time) ethical decision-making model
- Skills to develop the therapeutic relationship
- Managing transference and resistance
- Group process and process commentary

- Reconceptualizing difficult groups and difficult members, and intervention strategies
- Use of creative and expressive techniques
- New trend toward integrative group counseling/therapy
- Group-level dynamics and interventions

The approach in this book focuses on the beginning group leader and provides guidance on how to use an integrative theory and practice. Provided are descriptions of unfolding individual and group dynamics that contribute to an understanding of the complexity when deciding on strategies for analyses and interventions. Information is given to help beginning group leaders understand their unique experience and to help them know when and how to intervene, how to tune in to the needs of the group and individual members, and how to effectively use group-level dynamics. For example, the book discusses these topics:

- A cognitive and affective understanding of group forces
- Developing the inner self of the group leader
- How the group leader contributes to the functioning of the group
- The importance of empathic responding
- How to manage and contain difficult feelings
- Conducting the critical first and last sessions
- Recognizing countertransference
- Strategies for promoting growth and development for group members

Some material that could not be included in the book is presented in the electronic Instructor's Manual. Topics in the electronic manual include:

- Test items for each chapter
- Guidelines and evaluation forms for journal entries and leader critiques
- Transparencies for major chapter topics
- Assessment form for reflection and integrative paper
- A sample syllabus
- Sample assessment forms: Likert scale, Semantic differential
- Tips for facilitating nonclinical groups

Acknowledgments and Dedication

A never-ending, fascinating, unfolding, and dynamic process is how I would describe my journey toward understanding enough about groups and how to teach the subject. Considerable valuable help was provided me in this journey, and I appreciate very much all contributions. Colleagues, some of whom came before me, and who advanced understanding by sharing their experiences, research, and insight through professional journals, books, and conference presentations are to be recognized and thanked. Members of the Mid-Atlantic Group Psychotherapy Society who taught and encouraged me receive my heartfelt appreciation. Special thanks to MAGPS members George Saiger, M.D.; Beryce MacLennan, Ph.D.; John Dluhy, M.D.; Mary Dluhy, M.S.W.; Tom Wessel, Ph.D.; Barry Buktaman, M.D.; and Louisa Swartz, M.S.W. Additional thanks and appreciation go to the many members of the American Group Psychotherapy Association who welcomed and encouraged me, especially Hylene Dublin, M.S.W.; Howard Kiebel, M.D.; Scott Rutan, Ph.D.; and Gary Burlingame, Ph.D.

My learning was also increased with the interactions and professional contributions from colleagues in the Association for Specialists in Group Work, and Division 49 (Group Psychology and Group Psychotherapy) of the American Psychological Association.

Preparation of this book was facilitated with the help of many people, and my appreciation and thanks are extended to them: my graduate assistants Lindsay Meyers and Betty Davis, two editors Ginny Blandford and Meredith Fossel, and to my contributing author for the electronic instructor's manual, Mike Hauser, MA. Your help enabled me to complete this task.

I would also like to thank the following reviewers for their insights and helpful suggestions: Heather Barker, University of New Hampshire; Fred Bemak, George Mason University; Fred O. Bradley, Kansas State University; Matthew R. Buckley, Delta State University; Dianne Gossett, Troy University; Aaron W. Hughey, Western Kentucky University; Noreen Mokuau, University of Hawaii; Verl T. Pope, Southeast Missouri State University; Tammy Shafer, Western Kentucky University; Jeannine Studer, University of Tennessee; Linwood G. Vereen, Idaho State University; and Manuel X. Zamarripa, University of Texas at Brownsville.

Finally, I want to acknowledge the importance of my family in production of this book. They have a major impact on my life, keep me focused on the important relationships in life, and promote creative thought and effort on my part. Their love and affection are sustaining and affirming. Special thanks go to my husband Wil; my children Toni, Mike, and Linda; and my grandchildren Billy, Joey, Samantha, Christopher, Nicholas, and Emma.

Author Biography

Dr. Nina W. Brown is the author of 18 published books, 5 of which are on group: *Teaching Group Dynamics, Group Counseling for Elementary and Middle School Children, Expressive Processes in Group Counseling, Psychoeducational Groups* (Editions 1 and 2), and *Creating High Performance Classroom Groups.* She also authored a curriculum for the American Group Psychotherapy Association on training leaders of psychoeducational groups. Her published books on narcissism include *Children of the Self-Absorbed* (Editions 1 and 2), *Working With the Self-Absorbed, Whose Life Is It Anyway?, Coping with Your Partner's Jealousy,* and *Loving the Self-Absorbed.* She received her doctorate form the College of William and Mary, and is employed as a counselor educator at Old Dominion University in Norfolk, Virginia. Dr. Brown was designated as a Fellow of the American Group Psychotherapy Association, is a member and on the editorial board of the Association for Specialists in Group Work, and is a member of Division 49 of the American Psychological Association. She is a Licensed Professional Counselor in Virginia, and a Nationally Certified Counselor. Nina resides with her husband in Virginia Beach, Virginia.

Brief Contents

Contents

CHAPTER 8
The Group Leader's Personal Development 174

CHAPTER 9
Building a Therapeutic Self 197

CHAPTER 10
Educational and Skills Training Groups 220

CHAPTER 11
Psychoeducational and Task Groups 249

Chapter 1

Becoming an Effective Group Leader

Major Topics

1. Characteristics and skills of effective group leaders.
2. A knowledge, self, tasks, and techniques and skills model for learning group leadership skills.
3. Types of groups.
4. Classification and descriptions for major theories used with groups.
5. An integrative theory used for this book.

Introduction

Group leadership is complex, incorporating numerous factors, skills, characteristics, and attributes. It is significantly more challenging than other forms of counseling because of these complexities, and because of the numbers of stranger participants, and the additional knowledge needed about group dynamics and other such group-related topics. The group leader is expected to assist each individual group member to grow, learn, develop, and change through effective group facilitation and directing. This expectation holds whether the group has five members, as in some counseling groups, or 35 members, as in educational or task groups.

This book presents the basic knowledge needed for becoming an effective group leader, a rationale and guide for the group leader's personal development, descriptions and examples of different types of groups used in varying settings for a range of target audiences, and suggested skills and techniques to facilitate groups. The textbook focuses on the art and science of group leadership, with each chapter covering one of these two components. For example, the text discusses specific topics related to groups and group leaders, such as group developmental stages (the science). Other topics are discussed that are more abstract and complex because these also need and rely on the inner resources and development of the group leader, such as group process commentary (the art). They provide the group leader with the expertise and knowledge to decide when and how to intervene, to motivate members when the group becomes reluctant to face the challenges of difficult members and difficult groups, to use constructively emotional intensity and conflict, and to prevent the negative impact of the leader's countertransference on members and/or the group as a whole.

Learning to be a group leader is a continual, never-ending process. The most effective group leaders are those who are open to growth and development. There is always more to learn, more skills to develop, and new understandings to integrate into your existing knowledge. All these factors combine to refine your expertise as a group leader. It is important to note that effective group leaders have more than a set of mastered skills that work in every situation and can be used when needed; they also develop both the art and science of leadership. The major intent of this book is to guide you through the process of learning both the art and the science for leading groups, and the basics needed to become an effective group leader. The information presented will help you sort through some of the ambiguity and uncertainty about groups and become more confident about your knowledge and skills. But this is only a beginning. I encourage you to get supervised experience in leading groups and to continue your personal development.

Following are examples for three common group situations that group leaders will face. Read these and try to formulate what you would say or do if you were the group leader.

Vignette: How Shall We Begin?

This is the first group session, introductions are over, and you have reviewed the rules and group goals. When you are finished, all group members turn to you and fall silent.

Vignette: You Don't Understand

Two group members have engaged in a lively discussion about religious beliefs. Other members seem to be taking sides. The leader intervenes with a comment about how diverse opinions and ideas should be tolerated in the group. Immediately, one of the two members in the discussion tells the leader that she is distant, aloof, uncaring, and guarded in disclosing her feelings, although she is pushing members to do so. Other members chime in with agreements.

Vignette: We're Not Through

It is nearing the end of the session, but group members are involved in an emotionally intense interaction. The leader intervenes to begin the process for ending the session by empathizing with the feelings expressed by members, noting the importance of the topic, saying that the topic will continue to be explored in the group. The leader also points out the time left for the session, and that it is helpful to lessen the emotional intensity at this time. The members agree with what the leader says and there are sighs of relief, but the members then return to the intense topic.

A leader could make many possible responses and/or interventions that would be positive for the growth and development of the group and its members. There are also responses and interventions that would be less helpful, that would criticize group members, promote resistance and defensiveness, and create other negative outcomes. The material presented in this book will guide you to formulate the best responses.

The Leader Is a Critical Component

A major premise for being an effective group leader is that the leader is the critical component in the group. In fact, much of the success for group members depends on the leader. This in no way diminishes the group members' responsibility for their own personal progress. However, the leader acts as a facilitator, guide, model, instructor, mediator, and coordinator, and therefore has the major responsibility for the group's outcome (DeLucia-Waack & Kalodner, 2005; Morran, Stockton, & Whittingham, 2004; Riva, Wachtel, & Lasky, 2004).

Numerous factors appear to influence outcomes, such as leader self-disclosure (Dies, 1977), leader experience (Heikkinen, 1975), leader–group interaction (MacLennan, 1975), and leader personality (Kellerman, 1979). Although research findings support the idea that the leader is a vital component for successful group outcomes, exactly which leader characteristics are most influential has not yet been determined by empirical evidence.

Leading a group or even learning about becoming a group leader can feel overwhelming and daunting when you realize just how complex a task that can be, and when that realization is coupled with the desire to not make mistakes (do it right) it becomes almost paralyzing. It would be helpful if there were a guide with step-by-step instructions on what to do and say, exact or even approximate actions for every contingency in the group, and evidence that these interventions would produce the desired result. Unfortunately, nothing like this exists today and is likely to never be developed because of the unique and ever-changing dynamics for each group. The best that can be offered is a guide to learning group leadership that can be adapted for different types of groups, various leadership styles, and numerous issues, concerns, and problems.

Attributes of Effective Leaders

Effective group leaders have certain basic relationship attributes generally agreed to be important in developing rapport. They also excel at the therapeutic relationship, facilitating members' self-disclosure, fostering the emergence of therapeutic factors, and possessing the capacity to capitalize on group process. These attributes are both part of the person's personality and can be further developed. The relationship attributes include warmth, caring, acceptance, respect, tolerance, genuineness (Dies, 1994), cultural and diversity sensitivity, and tolerance and respect (Gladding, 2003); a willingness to engage in self-exploration to reduce negative countertransference (Rutan & Stone, 2001); healthy adult narcissism with empathy, creativity, and wisdom (Brown, 2006); and tolerance of ambiguity and the ability to contain and manage personal anxiety. It is also important for effective group leaders to develop a personal leadership style.

Personal Leadership Styles

Leadership style refers to the manner in which the leader conducts or facilitates the group. Capuzzi and Gross (1998) propose that developing your personal leadership style is an "integrative, sequential and creative endeavor" (p. 51) whose end result is unique but one that "encourages emotional, cognitive and behavioral changes" (p. 51) for group members. Corey (2000) writes, "Leaders bring to every group their personal qualities, values and life experiences" (p. 28), and that effectiveness is tied to the group's perceptions of what you demonstrate rather than what you say. Who you are ends up being more influential on group members than your actions or your words.

Leadership styles can be categorized in a variety of ways, but most are described around where the power and control are invested.

- *Leader invested*—Authoritarian (Lewin, 1944); leader centered (Gladding, 1991); charismatic (Rutan & Rice, 1981)
- *Group invested*—Laissez-faire (Lewin, 1944); group centered (Gladding, 1991)
- *Both leader and group invested*—Democratic (Lewin, 1944)

These examples apply to all types of groups, but the type of group and members' needs should play major roles in the decision about the best style for a particular group. This means that group leaders should adjust their styles when leading different types of groups, and not expect that any one style will fit all groups. For example, the authoritarian style is a directive-driven style with many instructions, directions, and the like. It can be a bit rigid, but this style could be just what is needed for groups with adolescents, whereas that style most likely would not be well received for a task group of adult professionals. Group leaders find it advantageous to be flexible and adjust their leadership to the type of group they are leading and the collective needs of group members rather than having a "one style fits all" group perspective. For example, a group leader may use an authoritarian style in the beginning when members need more direct structuring, move to the democratic style when members show that they want and can handle more independence, and the laissez-faire style when the group is in the third stage of development where they are working more on their own.

Another important consideration is the effect of leader style on group outcomes, but this is difficult to determine because there are too many intangibles. Each member is different and brings numerous intangibles to the group that affect perceptions and reactions to the leader's style. For example, if the leader has a democratic style, and a member is from a culture that vests authority in the leader, this person may not view this leader's style as positive. Further, although skills play an important role, it is the therapist's developed inner self that contributes significantly to the therapeutic part of group. Who you are is more important than what you do for the group. This is why there is considerable attention and emphasis is given to personal growth for the leader in this book.

The Art and Science of Leadership

The art and science of leadership incorporate basic knowledge, the leader's needed inner development, and the skills and techniques needed for facilitation. The science component emphasizes knowledge, leader tasks, and skills. The art component focuses on the leader's personal qualities, attitudes, and inner experiencing as guides for understanding the group and its members, the decision-making process for interventions, and the potential forces that could have negative impact. Both components interact in complex ways and are important and necessary for becoming an effective group leader. The model used in this book capitalizes on the art as well as science components and has four categories: the knowledge base, the self of the group leader, leadership tasks, and techniques and skills. These four categories recognize the complexities inherent in every type of group, and are designed to provide the necessary information and conditions for developing leadership competencies.

Knowledge Base

Knowledge factors are critical to structuring the group and facilitating the emergence of constructive group processes. These factors provide the frame for defining the group and its work, contributing to the development of trust and safety in the group, highlighting the leader's competence for understanding and intervening, and for keeping the group focused. The knowledge factors have generally been researched and are accepted as fundamental and basic for effective group leadership, whether with children, adolescents, or adults, or whether the group is focused on cognitive, affective, or developmental concerns. Table 1.1 presents an overview of the major knowledge factors.

Creating a group involves planning, screening, and attending to environmental concerns that help structure the group. Considerable thought, time, and effort can be expended for these tasks, and the group leader has to know what to do, and what is essential for effective functioning for the group. Planning is discussed in Chapter 6.

Group dynamics are the helping and restraining forces impacting the group (Lewin, 1944). Considerable research on dynamics shows that the group leader has to observe and know their importance for intervention. The basic group dynamics are presented in Chapter 2.

The importance of *group norms and group climate* and how the group leader helps shape these were documented in the work done by Sherif (1936) and Agazarian (1997). The norms and climate can play major roles in the extent to which members feel included or excluded and determine what feelings are appropriate to express and when and the self-disclosures that will be tolerated. The leader can influence the norms and climate, but much of this is subtle and nonconscious and group members are very influential. The group leader must understand how norms are established, and intervene to ensure that the group norms and climate are facilitative. More information about group norms and climate is presented in Chapter 5.

Cultural and diversity issues and concerns are recognized as important and critical (Salvendy, 1999). It has become increasingly accepted that group leaders play a central role in the group's effectiveness, and that they must become more sensitive and clinically competent in cultural and diversity issues and concerns to facilitate the inclusion and treatment of all group members. This information is presented in Chapter 2.

Table 1.1 Knowledge Factors	
	Creating a group
	Group dynamics
	Shaping group norms and the group climate
	Cultural and diversity issues and concerns
	Group therapeutic factors
	Ethics
	Stages of group development
	Process and process commentary

There is also considerable evidence that *therapeutic factors* facilitate the growth and development of group members. Although the group leader and members may have different perspectives for the relative importance for each of the 11 factors, they still agree on their positive contributions to the group and to the individual members (Yalom, 2005). Chapter 2 addresses these factors.

It is crucial and important for group leaders to have a comprehensive understanding of the code of *ethics* for their mental health profession. There are numerous ethical considerations that affect groups somewhat differently than therapy with individuals (e.g., confidentiality), and group leaders are well advised to remain aware of these as part of clinical and risk management. Attention should also be given to state and federal laws, and to professional standards of practice.

Chapter 4 presents models of ethical decision making, and introduces a model focused on real-time ethical decision making for groups. Current models assume time for consultation outside the sessions, while there can also be immediate situations within a session that call for a decision involving ethical issues. Specific and sequential steps are described for pre-group preparation, real time or *in situ* decisions, and post-session review and reflection. Additional discussion focuses on ethical issues as they apply to groups.

Group development stages are accepted as substantiated, and that all groups pass through some of the stages, especially the beginning stage and the ending stage. Group leaders will find it helpful to know what behaviors members will exhibit in each of the stages to be prepared to intervene appropriately. This information is also helpful to better understand the needs of the group and its members. Chapter 5 focuses on group stages.

Process and process commentary involve art as well as science factors. The knowledge portion includes what group dynamics to observe, what the group is avoiding, and other such information. Teaching members to accept and constructively use process commentary is also a part of knowledge. This topic is addressed in more detail in Chapter 7.

Group leaders will find it extremely helpful to know about the *intangibles* that will affect individual members and the group as a whole. Intangibles include the impact of family-of-origin events on development, transference, and other past events that continue to affect the person in direct and indirect ways. This information is presented in Chapters 13 and 14.

The Self of the Group Leader

The self of the group leader refers to the importance of the group leader's personal development, and how the self of the leader can significantly impact the group's functioning, progress, cohesiveness, and individual members' growth and development. Although skills and information from texts, lectures, demonstrations, supervision, and other resources play an important role in becoming an effective leader, personal development contributes significantly to your expertise as a group leader and to the therapeutic part of group. Self factors are listed in Table 1.2.

Core attributes of genuineness, caring, warmth, positive regard, and being nonjudgmental are accepted as core conditions for counseling (Rogers, 1951). These attributes place the attention, focus, and welfare of the group member at the center of the group leader's emphasis. The therapeutic relationship can reduce resistance and defensiveness, increase commitment and participation, and foster appropriate self-disclosure. This information is presented in Chapter 7.

Tolerance of ambiguity and uncertainty is central for the group leader and is to be expected at the beginning of every group. Group members can be extremely anxious and fearful for

Table 1.2
Personal Development (Self)
Factors

Core attributes of genuineness, caring and the like.
Tolerance of ambiguity and uncertainty
Reduction of self-absorption and increase of self-reflection
Awareness of potential countertransference and other intangible forces
The capacity to be empathic
Understanding what difficult behavior for the group and for individuals is intended to communicate
The capacity and ability to be emotionally present

these and other reasons. The group leader not only has to manage and contain his or her personal anxiety; he or she has to model how to do this for group members. Suggestions are given in Chapters 7, 8, and 9.

Self-reflection is the group leader's act of using personal experiencing as a source of information about the group and its members. Because group leaders can function as containers for members' anxieties, fears, hopes, wishes, and so on, the leader's inner experiencing can be a reflection of what is taking place in the group at that time. When used in this way, group leaders can identify the group's need or actions of which they may be unaware, and keep the group's progress moving forward, or even make a giant leap in its understanding. This can expedite making group process commentary.

Self-absorption occurs when leaders' thoughts, feelings, actions toward the group, and so on are focused on their own personal needs, concerns, and issues. This can happen when a leader becomes angry when challenged by a group member. Self-absorbed behaviors and attitudes are a reflection of the leader's personal line of self-development that can range from extremely unhealthy and pathological to the ideal of healthy adult narcissism with an appropriate focus on self-care (Kohut, 1977). Both self-reflection and self-absorption are described further in Chapter 9.

Intangibles, such as countertransference and undeveloped narcissism, are leader self factors that can negatively impact the group; their potential presence must be recognized and monitored to prevent this from happening. Group leaders can make constructive use of their countertransference when they are willing to identify it and accept its presence, because these unconscious feelings may have some parts that are functioning as containers for what group members are experiencing in the group at that time (Rutan & Stone, 2001). The leader's personal development can be enhanced when he or she works to understand how family-of-origin experiences and other past experiences helped shape and form him or her. Personal development can continue to have an unconscious impact on a leader's perceptions, reactions, functioning, and well-being, as well as his or her relationships with others, such as group members. The nature and impact of intangibles as part of personal development are discussed in Chapters 8 and 9.

The capacity *to be empathic* is closely related to the extent of self-development and healthy adult narcissism a person possesses. This is distinguished from giving reflective or sympathic responses that are sometimes confused with being empathic. To be empathic, you have to open yourself to experiencing what the other person is experiencing without losing the realization of being separate and distinct from the other person (Rogers, 1951). True empathy means that you do not become enmeshed in, overwhelmed by, or mired in the other person's feelings.

However, you do feel what the other person is feeling. The importance of empathy, its development, the necessity for sufficient psychological boundary strength, and its application and helpfulness in groups are discussed in several chapters.

Difficult groups and difficult member behavior can occur in any group, and how it is handled can depend heavily on the leader's personal development. Group leaders have to come to understand that the difficulties are a form of communication, and it is their responsibility to try to translate this into more useable information. It is important that group leaders not take these challenges personally, blame the group member, allow the group to scapegoat them, and other such negative responses. It calls for a high level of personal understanding of oneself to understand the possible communication and to effectively and constructively intervene when these behaviors occur. These topics are discussed in Chapters 13 and 14.

It is essential that the group leader *be emotionally present* when in the group. This promotes feelings of safety and trust for group members that they will be heard and understood and that the leader will take care of them. Emotional presence allows the leader to be immediate, to tune into the process, and to understand the indirect communication from members, such as feelings they are finding it difficult to express. Chapter 8 presents information and strategies to accomplish this development.

Leadership Tasks

Table 1.3 presents the important tasks for a group leader, tasks where the leader has a major responsibility for and a major impact on the effectiveness and functioning of the group. The completion of these tasks allows the establishment of a safe place to do the work of the group, provides guidance for how the work can be efficiently accomplished, fosters the emergence of therapeutic factors, and sets the tone and atmosphere for how the group will function. Group members need to feel supported, that they can and will achieve their realistic personal goals and the group's goals, and that their input and participation are valued. Other members can contribute, but the leader is the critical element and bears the major responsibility to carry out these tasks.

Planning for all types of groups is critical to the functioning of the group, and even when the leader has facilitated similar groups before, it is still important to plan the new group to incorporate lessons learned from previous experiences. Planning also includes screening, which is advised for all groups. There are some groups for which screening may not be possible. For example, in an educational group held in a school setting where all children in

Table 1.3 Leadership Tasks	
	Planning
	Structuring
	Directing
	Facilitating
	Establishing trust and safety
	Group process commentary
	Conflict resolution and intervention
	Repairing empathic failures

the class have to participate. However, group leaders should formulate screening questions and criteria to use when screening is possible. Planning is discussed in Chapter 6.

Structuring group sessions is also a major group leader responsibility, and althogh this can be part of planning, it is also subject to modifications when events so dictate. For example, a group leader may use member check-in to start the group but will need to modify this if a member is in crisis. It can be helpful for group leaders to have some consistent actions as part of the structure for sessions, such as checking in on progress, asking if there is unfinished business from the previous session, and summarizing at the end of the session. This can reduce ambiguity and uncertainty for group members. This topic is discussed in Chapters 5, 9, and 10.

Directing is a leader task that can be very helpful in some situations when not overdone so that it becomes more dictating than directing. Think of directing as guiding group members in self-exploration to promote understanding and formulation of action plans for needed changes or enhancements. This can be particularly useful when members are experiencing emotional intensity, and the leaders provide the direction for using the emotional intensity in constructive ways rather than leaving the member to flounder or become mired in the emotions. This topic is discussed in several chapters related to the various types of groups, target audiences, and focus for the group.

Facilitating the group is a very complex and important leader task. Members can assume some responsibility for their performance, growth, and development, and can be expected to reach out to other members to give assistance, empathy, and support. However, the major responsibility still lies with the leader.

All groups require facilitation, but the quality and kind of facilitation can differ among the different types of groups. For example, a 1-session task group requires a different type of facilitation than does a 12-session counseling group.

Establishing trust and safety is a critical leader task so that members will not feel in danger when they express their thoughts, feelings, and ideas, and disclose their guilt and shame. All members will be part of establishing trust and safety, but the leader bears the major responsibility for this task.

As already stated, it is not unusual for members to feel anxious and fearful in the beginning of the group as they are unsure about their acceptance and approval by other members and by the leader. Until their anxiousness and fearfulness are reduced to acceptable limits, group members will limit their participation and the group will not progress toward its identified goal. This topic is discussed in several chapters, and most extensively in Chapter 5.

Group process commentary is used to help the group understand its actions or inactions, especially when either of these seems to be interfering with the group's progress. For example, when group members are fearful of the potential destructiveness to relationships that conflict can bring, they will unconsciously collaborate to ensure that conflict does not emerge in the group. If the leader were to bring this to the group's attention with a group process comment, and the members have been taught to accept and use it, then it is very likely that they would explore their fears and reluctance to allow conflict to emerge, be recognized, and possibly resolved. Group process commentary is presented in Chapters 12 and 14.

Conflict resolution and intervention should be part of every group leader's expertise. The development of expertise begins with identifying, understanding, accepting, and, when necessary, changing your perception and reaction to conflict. Group members need to have a leader who can model constructive responses to conflict, and who does not fear that conflict will always, or mostly, be destructive to relationships.

Group leaders, like group members, learned their perceptions and reactions to any hint of conflict from their family-of-origin experiences, and through relationships and interactions with others throughout their lives. This is one reason why group leaders should have this issue or concern addressed as part of their personal development. Whereas conflict resolution strategies can be taught and learned, the more emotional and unconscious perceptions and reactions to conflict have to be addressed through other means, such as exploring one's personal self-development.

Repairing empathic failures is also a leader task and responsibility. Group members can learn to do this, and will be of assistance, but it is the group leader who will model identification and process for repair. This is one way that members can learn.

Kohut (1977) pointed out the importance of empathic responding on the early development of the child; how everyone is empathically failed throughout life, and how some of these failures are very injurious to the person, leading to lowered self-esteem, mistrust of others, and failure to thrive psychologically. Kohut stated that it is the role of the therapist to repair some of these empathic failures as part of the healing process. It is extremely helpful when the group leader can recognize empathic failures, no matter how insignificant they seem to be or if the empathically failed person minimizes these, as this recognition makes the person feel heard, valued, and supported. Repairing empathic failures is presented in several chapters, but is explored in more detail in Chapters 6, 8, 11 and 12.

Techniques and Skills

The basic relating attributes and communication skills are also fundamental for group leadership. Added to these are group level intervention skills, exercises and other activities, and techniques associated with particular theories such as "I've got a secret," which is associated with Gestalt Therapy. Theories are discussed later in the chapter. The skills and techniques discussed here are used in all types of groups, and are not associated with specific theories. Readers are encouraged to have a thorough knowledge of techniques and skills associated with their theory of choice. The basic relating attributes and communication skills are presented in Chapter 7.

Group-level intervention skills refer to the ability to act in support and encouragement of the entire group, not just for an individual member, or subgroups within the group. An example of a group-level intervention skill would be group process commentary. This set of skills calls for a high degree of knowledge and understanding on the part of the group leader, and confidence in his or her analysis of what the group is doing, or needs.

Intervening at the group level shows the group that there are unacknowledged similarities among group members that would be helpful to verbalize and explore. Anything that reduces isolation, alienation, and the feeling of being different is also helpful in encouraging group cohesion—one of the therapeutic factors for groups. This level of intervention is also helpful to show members what is being avoided, minimized, discounted, or ignored that could be very important for further growth and development. Group-level interventions are presented in Chapter 14.

Exercises, role-play, and other strategies are helpful for a variety of groups and target audiences and can help promote learning and retention. These can be nonthreatening ways to help group members identify and accept parts of self that could be perceived as flawed and shameful, show new ways of perceiving, practice new skills such as those for relating and communicating, and just to have fun and relieve tension. There are many valuable and therapeutically valid reasons for using these techniques.

Leaders are cautioned to be aware of the possibility of overusing some techniques, exercises, and activities, as these can lose their potency when used too often with a particular group. Further, they can be too structuring and prevent members from self-selecting what to explore that would be meaningful for them.

Perceptual Shifts

Leading groups calls for many of the characteristics and skills used with other modes of counseling, but demands different expertise from the skills needed when working with individuals, families, and couples. Some major perceptual shifts include the following:

- Focus on the group as a whole
- Observe and understand interactions among and between members
- Identify similarities among members
- Use group dynamics effectively
- Foster the emergence of therapeutic factors
- Make group process commentary
- Understand that the leader cannot be perceived as having favorites or showing favoritism
- Recognize the impact of the various cultural and diversity factors present in the group even when all members appear to be from the same culture or diversity is not apparent

The most important shift you must make is to *focus on the group as a whole.* The leader must be aware of the entire group as an entity as well as the specific needs of the individual group members. It can be easier to give attention to one person than it is to attend to an individual while remaining aware of other members' experiencing at the same time.

Observe interactions among group members to *understand their characteristic behavior outside the group* (Yalom, 2005), to provide clues about their unresolved family-of-origin issues and other concerns, and to better understand if they are projecting or using transference. These interactions help the leader make decisions about when or if to intervene.

A major leader task and contribution is to *identify and emphasize similarities* among members. Group members usually focus on differences among themselves in the beginning of group, and a focus on similarities facilitates the emergence of the therapeutic factor of universality. This, in turn, contributes to establishing trust and safety in the group.

The effective use of *group dynamics* cannot be overemphasized, as these are a major source of information about members' issues and the process taking place in the group. The perceptual shift has to be to focus on the individuals and on the group as a whole. This perceptual shift enhances the group leader's ability to identify what group members feel and think is important, where and how an intervention could be helpful, and to make group process commentary. The energy and direction for the group rests primarily in the dynamics taking place in the group.

There is considerable documentation about the value of *therapeutic factors,* some of which can be experienced only, or best, in the group setting. The group leader can encourage and foster the emergence of therapeutic factors when there is a conscious effort to do so.

Group process commentary is a complex group-level intervention that identifies what the group as a whole is emphasizing, ignoring or suppressing, doing or not doing. It is used to increase the group's awareness, and is the leader's responsibility. The perceptual shift from the individual and the ability to identify group themes and metaphors help the group to move, deepen the experiencing, and become more aware that individual behavior contributes to and is reflective of the group's needs and desires.

Group leaders have to stay alert to the possibility that they may, nonconsciously or unconsciously, *show favoritism.* For example, some group members are more likeable than others, there is the possibility that the leader's unresolved issues and concerns are leading to becoming attracted to the member, and so on. There are many reasons why favoritism can become a concern, and the leader should be alert for this. Members can become angry or jealous, feel rejected, become resentful, and/or experience a whole host of negative feelings that can be difficult to overcome or resolve.

The *impact of culture* in and on the group should not be minimized, and group leaders need to understand that culture and diversity factors affect not only that particular person but also other group members, the leader, and the group process.

Types of Groups

Six types of groups are presented in more detail in later chapters. Groups presented are educational, task, skills training, psychoeducational, and clinical groups. Five other types of groups are briefly described in this chapter as well: training, support, self-help, process, and e-groups.

Educational groups focus on teaching and learning new material, and are very much like a class in organization and presentation. Examples of educational groups are groups for educational planning, career exploration, leisure, and groups for professionals that focus on work-related development topics. Educational groups are presented in Chapter 10.

Task groups are usually associated with the business and professional worlds where the focus is on building and maintaining productivity, increasing expertise, and developing relationships and communication for working groups, units, departments, and teams. The emphasis in task groups is on constructive relationships and managing tasks. Examples include team development, project management, and leadership training. Task groups are presented in Chapter 11.

Skills training groups focus on the acquisition of new skills for learning, working, and relating. A specific set of behaviors related to the needed skill is presented and practiced with feedback. Examples of skills training groups are study skills, parenting skills, time management, social skills, and communication skills. Skills training groups are presented in Chapter 10.

Psychoeducational groups are a blend of educational and counseling groups where the dissemination of information can be as important as the exploration of feelings. These groups are being used more extensively with all target audiences in a variety of settings. Examples of psychoeducational groups include groups for people with medical illnesses, psychiatric and emotional disturbances, chemical dependency, and caregivers for people with disabilities. Chapter 11 discusses psychoeducational groups in detail.

The groups described to this point have some common characteristics.

- All group members are attending for essentially the same reason, issue, or concern.
- The focus for the group is usually narrow with a specific body of knowledge to be disseminated.
- The group is time-bound and of short duration.

- Cognitive material is generally emphasized, or is equal to the affective component.
- Some groups can have a large number of participants.
- The leader is very active.
- Group sessions are generally structured.
- Considerable use is made of exercises and other such activities.

Clinical groups can be more problem centered and incorporate emotional intensity as part of the group process. The defining boundary between these groups has become more vague and ambiguous as techniques, strategies, foci, and other group factors are increasingly used for both types.

Counseling groups are defined here as groups that, although problem centered, have a wellness perspective as basic. Group members are perceived as active participants with many strengths that can be used; the issue, problem, or concern is transitory, a part of life's transitions and/or development; and increasing interpersonal efficacy is an important component. Examples of counseling groups include grief and loss with an absence of complicated mourning, emotional regulation and control, relationship building, and other life transitions.

Therapy and psychotherapy groups usually have character change as a goal. These groups are focused on assisting group members to overcome deep-seated, long-standing, and usually not very well-known or understood feelings, thoughts, and behaviors that are negatively affecting their lives. An important element for these groups will be on family-of-origin and other past experiences that are continuing to impact the person's well-being and functioning. These groups provide members encouragement, resources, and understanding, and teach coping skills to address adverse situations and conditions. Examples for therapy and psychotherapy groups are addictions treatment, psychiatric and emotional disturbances, and deep-seated medical illnesses that have a mental health component such as eating disorders. Clinical groups are presented in Chapter 12.

Other Types of Groups

There are many other types of groups than the ones just described. Five such groups will be presented here, but not elaborated on in later chapters. These groups are training groups for mental health professionals, support groups, self-help groups, process groups, and e-groups.

Training groups for mental health professionals generally have two goals: attaining personal growth, and cognitive information about groups. The personal growth component is designed to make participants more aware of conscious and unconscious unresolved issues and concerns that may emerge as countertransference; to observe personal and others' relationship attributes; to practice effective ways to relate and communicate in groups; and to build sensitivity to others' issues. The cognitive component is designed to reduce some of the anxiety, uncertainty, and ambiguity about groups and to introduce group members to group process.

Support groups are organized around a specific issue, concern, or condition. A leader guides and directs the sessions, helps organize and present the material, and helps determine who serves as gatekeeper for the group. Support groups can be closed groups, but most are open ended where new members come in and others leave the group. The primary purposes for support groups are to provide encouragement and support for group members, to educate members and help with coping attitudes and skills, and to provide social support .

Self-help groups are designed for members to provide mutual assistance and support, and are not dependent on the leader for organization and facilitation. Peer assistance and facilitation are common, and there may not be a formal leader for the group. Instead, members may rotate the responsibilities for leadership. Self-help groups may seek outside experts to provide needed knowledge and to answer questions about treatment provided by other means. Information and guidance are the mainstays for these groups.

Process groups deal with members' inner worlds, unresolved issues, unfinished business, and interpersonal relationships by using the here-and-now interactions and relationships in the group for exploration. Members' actions, verbalizations, and feelings provide the material for exploration, and the opportunity to see others' self-exploration promotes universality and allows for reflected learning. These groups provide a venue that can enhance awareness of the impact of what members are doing, saying, and feeling at a particular time. In addition, they provide validation, confrontation, feedback, and exploration of triggered responses to produce considerable learning and understanding. Leaders of process groups use the here-and-now experiencing in the group as material for exploration, and members do not have to disclose past experiences. The relationships between and among members and between members and the leader form the basis for what takes place in the sessions. This does not preclude members' disclosing family-of-origin and other important past experiences, but this is not a requirement for important work to take place.

E-groups are also termed cybergroups, e-therapy, virtual groups, and electronically linked groups. They use the resources of television, the Internet, and other such communication devices to deliver group experiences, such as education team development, and therapy at a distance where some, or all, of the members and/or the leader are not physically present. Businesses and corporations make more extensive use of these resources, but providers of mental health services are increasing their use for this mode of delivery.

Advantages of e-groups include more effective use of time, reduced travel, participants feel safer, and it can be easier to record and have a record of sessions. Limitations include a lack of security, and confidentiality and privacy issues (unless communications are encrypted). In addition, group leaders have less information about members and the group because they cannot see or sense the group as a whole; screening for inclusion in the group may be severely limited; the possibility of technical failure of equipment exists; and the legalities to practice across state lines are still murky.

Despite their limitations, there are numerous possible benefits for e-groups.

- People in remote or rural areas can access services.
- Task groups for businesses and corporations can be more cost-effective.
- Teams that are separated geographically can maintain contact and work collaboratively.
- Members can be less inhibited and thereby be more revealing.
- Group meetings can be scheduled at any time, making them more convenient for members.

We are just beginning to answer many of the issues and concerns about e-groups, conduct studies on their efficacy, and develop guidelines, principles, and ethics that are acceptable to professional organizations. Many resources are available to help group leaders of e-groups, and many more are becoming available every day.

Theories and Their Applications

Theories provide a framework for how clients are perceived, what issues and problems are or can be addressed, and the focus for sessions. Although the processes and the philosophies underlying these are much more complex and abstract, the essentials for the framework are discussed in the following sections. It can be important to work within a particular theoretical orientation, as there is usually some evidence for the basic assumptions and procedures used to attain the therapeutic goals.

It is difficult to categorize theories applying to group because the majority focus on individuals and give little or no attention to group factors. Most often, the group factors are discussed in isolation as if they were important, but not integrated into the theory. The systems-centered theories of Agazarian (1997) and Bion (1961) are notable exceptions, as both approaches provide substantial attention to group and individual factors.

Table 1.4 presents an overview of a classification for many existing theories as a means to conceptualize their best uses in group. The categories are information dissemination and skills acquisition, symptom relief, supportive and interpersonal effectiveness, and self-development and self-understanding.

Information Dissemination and Skills Acquisition

The major theories that fall into this category are theories related to learning, teaching, and retention. Learning theories address the many factors related to learning and retention—individual factors, methods of instruction and learning, meaningfulness of material, and transfer of

Table 1.4
Classification of Major Theories

Information Dissemination and Skills Acquisition

Learning theories: behavioral, social interdependence

Symptom Relief

Behavioral therapy	Cognitive-behavioral therapy
Dialectical behavioral therapy	Rational-emotive therapy
Reality therapy	

Supportive and Interpersonal Effectiveness

Client-centered theory	Relational theory
Feminist theory	

Self-development and Self-understanding

Object-relations	Self-psychology	Modern analytic
Gestalt	Adlerian	Jungian
Psychodynamic	Interpersonal	Existential

learning. Behavioral learning theories emphasize the impact of group reinforcers and rewards for learning. Skinner (1968) emphasized contingencies, Bandura (1977) highlighted imitation, and Thibaut and Kelley (1959) focused on the balance of rewards and costs in social exchange among interdependent individuals for an explanation of effective learning. Techniques used include schedules of reinforcement, contingency management, cooperative learning, and other behavioral theories techniques.

Symptom Relief

These theories have a narrow focus, specifying the particular behavior that is to be changed. The approaches tend to use cognitively oriented techniques where exploration of feelings is minimized. Group leaders tend to work with individuals in the group setting and make little or no use of group-level factors in sessions. There is considerable use of forms, scales, and behavioral observations; sessions usually have a formally prescribed structured format; and there is less emphasis on affect, although this is not omitted.

The aspects of these theories that are most appealing are that the behavior to be changed is narrowly defined, is constantly and consistently worked on, and the results are observable and in some cases measurable. Both the leader and the members understand the scope of the therapeutic work, and expectations fit within this scope.

Theories categorized as symptom relief are behavioral therapy, cognitive-behavioral therapy, dialectical behavioral therapy, reality therapy, and rational-emotive therapy. Each will be presented listing some theorists associated with the class of theory, the major goals, distinguishing key concepts, and associated techniques and strategies.

Behavioral Therapy. Major goals for behavioral therapy (Bandura, 1977; Meichenbaum, 1986; Skinner, 1953) include learning new behaviors and unlearning maladaptive behaviors. Distinguishing key concepts focus on defining observable behavior, developing specific and concrete goals, and using the scientific method. Numerous techniques have been developed for this theory that are now used as parts of other therapies, such as self-management and self-control, self-efficacy, participant modeling, systematic desensitization, token economy, flooding, aversion therapy, and assertiveness training (Nystul, 2006).

Cognitive-Behavioral Therapy (CBT). This theory or therapy is a blend or combination of cognitive therapy as developed by Beck with behavioral techniques. The major goals for CBT are to correct cognitive distortions (Beck & Weishaar, 2005), change problematic behaviors, and reduce systematic bias individuals may have in information processing (Nystul, 2006). Distinguishing key concepts include conducting a behavioral assessment, collaboratively setting specific and concrete goals, narrowly focusing on cognitive distortions that are leading to problematic behaviors, and objectively evaluating the outcomes for therapy. Techniques and strategies include behavioral rehearsal, skills training, redefining, decentering, reattribution, identifying automatic thoughts, core beliefs, imagery, and homework.

Dialectical Behavioral Therapy. This approach (Linehan, 2001) uses behavioral and cognitive theories together with dialectical perspectives and Zen concepts. The major goals for dialectical behavioral therapy are to improve skills for a satisfying life, improve emotional regulation and interpersonal effectiveness, and increase tolerance for distress in life. The distinguishing key concepts include having individual as well as group sessions for clients, utilizing Zen concepts for becoming more reality focused, understanding the holistic and interrelated nature for functioning, teaching interpersonal effectiveness, developing distress tolerance skills, and reducing and managing emotional intensity. Techniques include teaching mindfulness, emotional regulation and control, how to relate and communicate more effectively, and how to contain and manage personal stress.

Reality Therapy. Emphasized in this therapy (Glasser, 1965) are responsibility, a success identity, the concept of positive addiction, and choice theory. The major goals for reality therapy are developing a success identity through accepting responsibility for one's actions (Nystul, 2006); teaching clients to make choices that respect the rights of others but that also meet their needs; and understanding that labeling behaviors as mental disorders is unnecessary. Techniques revolve around an eight-step approach developed by Glasser: create the relationship, focus on current behavior, evaluate one's personal behavior, develop a realistic plan of action, get a commitment, refuse to accept excuses for noncompliance or nonperformance, refuse to use punishment, and refuse to give up.

Rational-Emotive Therapy. The major premise for this theory (Ellis, 1993) is that irrational thoughts create self-defeating, emotionally disturbing reactions. To understand this, one must understand the interrelationship between thinking, feeling, and behavior. A distinguishing concept is the A-B-C-D-E acronym that stands for an activating event, the person's belief system or cognitive reaction to A, the emotional consequence, the disputing of self-defeating thoughts, and the effect of implementing D. The major goals for therapy are to revise self-defeating thoughts to gain more realistic perceptions and reactions to life. Techniques include cognitive restructuring of irrational and illogical thoughts, humor, imagery, shame-attacking exercises, and the techniques and strategies used in behavioral therapy.

Supportive and Interpersonal Effectiveness

Classified under this category are client-centered, feminist, and relational theories. These theoretical approaches deal with the concepts of self with others in the world, focus more on feelings, teach relating and communication skills, build emotional awareness and sensitivity, provide a guide to developing problem-solving skills that involve self and others, reduce loneliness and alienation, and provide support and encouragement.

Client-Centered Theory. Also known as person-centered therapy (Rogers, 1951), this theory uses a phenomenological perspective as a means to understand the other person. Three core conditions for successful therapy were identified: counselor congruence, empathic understanding, and positive regard. The client participates in his or her own therapy, and the counselor is a guide. The group leader (counselor) should try to enter the internal reference of the client or group member as this is the best source of information about what that person is experiencing. The goals for therapy are to help move the person from dependence to independence, to become better integrated, and to be centered in the present instead of the past or the future. Rogers minimized the use of specific techniques and emphasized the importance of the therapeutic relationship. Listening and empathic responding are the main techniques used in this theory.

Feminist Theory. Feminist theory perceives the inner strength, resiliency of the human spirit, and the desire and drive for freedom and equality to be inherent for all people, but that socio-political forces have worked to prevent women from becoming self-actualized and attaining these admirable outcomes (Elliott, 1999; Enns, 1993; Evans, Seem, & Kincade, 2005; Kottler, 2002). Goals for therapy include increasing awareness of gender-role stereotyping and developing strategies to overcome this, and demonstrating how egalitarian relationships and mutual respect promote more satisfying and enduring relationships. Many of the principles are taken from relational theory, as discussed in the next section. Techniques use an integrative approach that includes applying feminist principles to family therapy and career counseling, to existential therapy to explore the meaning and purpose for one's life, and to cognitive-behavioral techniques, bibliotherapy, gay and lesbian issues, and political advocacy.

Relational Theory. Relational theory was developed by the Stone Center's Jean Baker Miller Training Institute and emphasizes human connection as critical, crucial, and important (Jordan, Walker, & Hartling, 2004). This theory integrates principles from human development, psychodynamic theory, and feminist therapy to form a new therapy model for understanding the complexity of connections, transforming disconnections, and building satisfying, enduring, and meaningful relationships. Techniques rely more on relationship and self attributes of the group leader, emphasizing authenticity and empathic responding as modeling for establishing connections among people. Members become empowered, less disconnected, and more connected; experience the supportiveness and power of connection; and learn new ways to relate.

Self-Development and Self-Understanding

This group of theories focuses on fostering a deep understanding of self, and characterological change. Topics addressed include understanding the course of personal development, character and personality deficits, and lack of sufficient completion of expected developmental tasks; promoting changes in ways of relating and behaving; increasing meaningful connections to others; increasing understanding of and sensitivity to others; and providing other life enrichments. The primary goal is to develop a more integrated, personally effective self. Factors considered important in therapy are exploring of the family-of-origin experiences and other past experiences that shaped the person, providing the corrective emotional experience; repairing empathic failures; rediscovering disowned parts of self; and consciously exploring unconscious material. Techniques used include dream analysis, free association, imagery, games and other exercises, and analysis of transference in the therapist–client relationship.

Theories included in this category include object-relations (Kernberg, 1965; Klein, 1952; Mahler, 1968; Winnicott, 1989), self-psychology (Kohut, 1977), modern analytic (Whitaker & Lieberman, 1964), Gestalt (Perls, 1969), Adlerian (Adler, 1969), Jungian (Jung , 1959), psychodynamic (Rutan & Stone, 2001), interpersonal (Sullivan, 1968), and existential (Yalom, 1980). Brief descriptions follow for interpersonal, Gestalt, and existential theories.

Interpersonal. Yalom and Leszcz (2005) describe an interpersonal group psychotherapy approach that is widely recognized as clinically sound. It emphasizes the here-and-now experiencing and interpersonal feedback loop that gives members new information to promote insight and change. The goals for therapy are to foster interpersonal relationships among members and with the leader that are substantial, genuine, and allow for healing. Attention is also given to the corrective emotional experience to allow validation of feelings that were previously dismissed, minimized, or ignored. Techniques associated with other theories are used, but attention remains on the quality of relationships as they affect the self, first proposed by Harry Stack Sullivan.

Gestalt. Gestalt therapy has the goals of discovering previously disowned parts of self, and of repairing the fragmented self. The group leader is very active in challenging, directing, encouraging, and supporting self-exploration. Techniques are termed games and these are frequently used to produce new personal understanding and learning. Games include Top Dog–Under Dog, Playing the Projection, and I've Got a Secret. The method of dream analysis used with this theoretical approach has the dreamer playing each item in the dream to discern the masked message; the thought is that each part of the dream reflects a part of the dreamer, some of which may be disowned or fragmented.

Existential. Human conditions such as freedom and will, responsibility, existential anxiety, and death are constants for life and these form the central topics for exploration in this approach to therapy. These human conditions cannot be resolved, except for the moment, and will continue to reemerge throughout one's life to be addressed in different ways. The questions and dilemmas do not change, but the answers do as people grow and change. No techniques are associated with this theoretical perspective, and group leaders will freely use techniques and strategies from other theories.

Integrative Group Theories. Three theories describe integration of general systems theory with group processes and treatment. The basic work of the group leader is to define and understand the group as a system, to work with transactions occurring across boundaries, and to teach members to create boundaries that are permeable enough for transactions and for defense. The focus on the group as a whole should reflect individual members' needs, fears, wants, desires, fantasies, and so on. Techniques used focus on group-level leader interventions that bring important behaviors and issues to members' attention.

Systems-centered therapy for groups (Agazarian, 1997) defines living human systems as existing in a hierarchy of input and output, opening and closing their boundaries, remaining stable by integrating similarities, becoming closed to differences, changing by integrating differences, being goal directed, and being self-correcting. The group leader manages the work of the group by defining the function, energy, and structure the group is displaying; recognizing when members have created a subgroup and directing the communication toward the goals for the group; managing permeability of boundaries; weakening the restraining forces; and redirecting the efforts toward work goals.

Tavistock (Bion, 1961) is a model for group work that has the group as a whole as a basic premise. The leader functions as a consultant to the group and provides interventions for the group to consider. The leader does not respond to or direct individual members—all interventions are at the group level. Other premises of this approach are that the primary task for the group is to survive, the members are used by the group to accomplish its work and task attainment, the behavior of any group member at a particular time is to express both individual and group needs and so on; the group is always focused on itself, and members grow and develop individually through understanding the group process. Bion also proposed that the group's survival assumptions fall into one of three categories that can change through the group's development: dependency, fight or flight, and pairing.

Group dynamics theory was developed by Lewin (1948) as a conceptual system to identify and explain all of the influences on the group. He also created the field theory analysis that focuses on identifying the helping and restraining forces that impact the group at any particular time. Rutan and Stone (2001) propose that this perspective views the group as a totality, and as a social field in which the elements of leadership, status, roles, structure, climate, standards, pressure, and communication interact (p. 30). Techniques are adapted from many other theoretical perspectives and include dream analysis, affect exploration, identification of resistance and defenses, empathic responding, empathic failure and repair, and translating the group members' communication to and about the leader and other group members.

Theory for This Book

The material presented in this book is an integration of concepts and practices of several theories to provide a unifying perspective to leading a group. The following primary elements form the core for what is presented in this book.

- The group is an entity to be considered in addition to the individual members.
- The therapeutic relationship and collaborative goal setting are critical.
- Personal development of the group leader provides the foundation for effective interventions.
- Behaviors and patterns of relating for individual members in the group reflect their behaviors outside the group.
- The self of the group leader is an important component for effective group leadership.
- There is a strong emphasis on here-and-now experiencing and interpersonal learning.
- Group leaders intentionally foster the emergence and use of group therapeutic factors.
- Cultural and diversity concerns are an integral part of group leadership.
- Ethical standards are at the forefront of all group work.

The interpersonal theory of Harry Stack Sullivan is a major theoretical contributor to the integrative theory used for this book. It emphasizes the relationships that take place in the group as a fruitful source for interpersonal learning and change (Yalom, with Leszcz, 2005). These in-group relationships can be a means for understanding the impact and influence of family-of-origin and other past experiences on the growth and development of the individual group members and on the leader, as well as being a reflection of their relationships outside the group.

Another major contributor is Lewin's group dynamics theory as described by Rutan and Stone (2001). Lewin's theory emphasizes the group as a whole and recognizes the dynamic forces that continually exert their influences on the group and its members. Self-psychology and object-relations theories contribute their understanding of how psychological growth and development occur, and the importance of empathy and the group leader's attention to empathic failures in the group to help overcome earlier lapses in empathic responding. These early lapses in empathic responding can negatively impact individuals and cause deficits in self-esteem, self-confidence, and self-efficacy; can result in attitudes and behaviors that are troubling to relationships; and may result in undeveloped narcissism.

The structure and guidance provided by the cognitive and behavioral theories give ideas for strategies for treatment, foster the progress for the group and for individual members, and suggest techniques that keep the group focused. The specifics provided by these theories are very helpful for group treatment.

Theories that are being assimilated and used regardless of theoretical perspective, and are part of the integrative theory, include the psychodynamic and psychoanalytic concepts of transference, countertransference, resistance, and defenses; the importance of empathy and establishing the therapeutic alliance, and the personhood of the therapist from Rogers's client-centered theory; and the presence and pervasiveness of existential concerns throughout one's life from existential theory.

Personal Development Exercises

Chapters 7 and 8 focus on the personal development of the group leader. Chapters 1–6 have personal development exercises that can be completed outside the class or group, and then discussed in the group or class. These and other such exercises can be compiled to form a Book of Self, and if each exercise is accompanied by a short essay about the exercise and feelings aroused or associated with it, you will end up with a product that can be very informative.

The exercises are designed to be easy to complete, have few materials, ask for relatively nonthreatening information, but at the same time provide new information or rediscover forgotten personal material. When the exercises are used as part of a class or group, the process fosters disclosure about more meaningful information; can highlight similarities among group members; encourages interactions and connections among group members; and reveals an underlying focus for the session.

Summary

1. The art and science of group leadership is complex and incorporates numerous factors, skills, characteristics, abstract concepts, and attributes. Among the challenges are group variables, individual member variables, and leader variables.

2. The model used to describe learning to be a group leader involves four major aspects: knowledge base, self of the group leader, leadership tasks, and techniques and skills.

3. Groups differ from other forms of counseling in significant ways and the group leader needs to make some perceptual shifts in how the group is viewed, how members are attended to, how interventions are made, and the use of the leader's self.

4. Numerous types of groups are formed to meet various goals. Educational groups, task groups, and skills training groups have a strong emphasis on cognitive learning and tend to deemphasize the affective component, past experiences, and family-of-origin factors. Psychoeducational groups are a blend of cognitive and affective emphases, and tend to blend the two. Counseling and therapy/psychotherapy groups emphasize developmental concerns and changes. These groups tend to emphasize affective concerns, and to incorporate exploration of past experiences and family-of-origin factors.

5. Theories form a framework for the therapeutic process and for leader interventions. Five categories of theories were presented: information dissemination and skills acquisition, symptom relief, supportive and interpersonal effectiveness, and self-development and self-understanding. This book uses an integrative theoretical perspective for groups.

Chapter Activities

1. Form small groups and discuss previous group experiences and leader characteristics. These groups need not be counseling groups; they can be groups in a social club, church, or other religious setting, or any kind of group. Discuss what was positive about the leaders, and what was not. As a class, have each group report on the discussions.

2. Brainstorm and list the ways that group counseling differs from individual and family counseling in terms of goals, methods, and counselor tasks.

3. Divide into small groups and select one theory to explore. Describe how a group leader using that theory would conduct a group for either children, adolescents, or adults. Groups may want to use additional resources for this activity.

Personal Development Exercise: Construct a collage that describes you as you are today. Use symbols for your physical self, emotional self, relational self, spiritual self, self-sufficiency, and other personality characteristics. Write a summary paragraph about the current "you."

Chapter 2

Group Dynamics and Therapeutic Factors

Major Topics

1. Description of group dynamics.
2. Sample vignettes with possible interventions for six dynamics.
3. Definitions and descriptions for therapeutic factors.
4. Definitions, descriptions, and importance of therapeutic factors.
5. How to recognize therapeutic factors.
6. How to encourage the emergence of therapeutic factors.

Introduction

There are numerous variables that comprise the processes of change for group members. Some are internal and unique for the individual group member, while others seem to be related to elements of the group experience. Facilitating positive changes by using the resources of the group is a major task for the group leader, whether the desired or needed change is learning a new skill, or better communication skills, working through loss and grief, or building a stronger and more resilient self.

Group dynamics and therapeutic factors are central to group resources for facilitating change. Both are present in all types of groups and can be capitalized on for the benefit and growth of group members. Group leaders who are knowledgeable about the value and uses for group dynamics, and who understand how to recognize and encourage the emergence of therapeutic factors in the group, are in the position to deepen and enrich the group experience. Group members can support and encourage each other's personal growth and development by constructive use of these whole-group factors. This chapter explains the value and uses for group dynamics and therapeutic factors, and suggests specific strategies for identification and interventions.

Group Dynamics

The term *group dynamics* refers to the movement and changes for members, their interactions and relationships, constructive forces such as therapeutic factors, counterproductive forces such as possible leader countertransference, and understanding the group as a whole. The leader who can tune in to these dynamics, understand what they mean, and communicate and use them as indicators for interventions can facilitate members' growth, development, and self-understanding. These dynamics can be used for more effective teaching and members' learning, as a means for fostering connections and reducing alienation and isolation, and to contribute to accomplishing the goals for the group.

Group dynamics is described in various ways. Lewin (1948) was the first to describe group dynamics as including everything that goes on in a small group—the climate and its processes, and their influences on interactions and outcomes. Bion (1959), from the Tavistock Institute in London, simply describes group dynamics as the influence of groups on their members. Durkin (1964) perceived group dynamics as a social field that was composed of interactions among leadership, status, roles, structure, climate, standards, pressure, and communication. Jacobs, Harvill, and Masson (1988) define group dynamics as the forces operating in a group. Forsyth (1999) describes it as the scientific study of groups and a general term for group processes. According to Kline (2005), it is as group process and group structure, and Yalom (2006) sees group dynamics as the inferential and invisible constructs that affect the overall functioning of the group.

The common unifying thread for all descriptions is to understand the ever-moving, shifting and changing, visible and hidden experiencing taking place in the here-and-now life of the group session, and over the life of the group. These visible and hidden experiences provide valuable information about and for individual members and for the group as a whole. This information gives the leader cues as to what group norms are being established, where interventions would be helpful, needs for the group and for individual members, empathic failures and the need for repair of these, and is a basis for understanding group process and how to make group process commentary. Basic dynamics to observe include the following:

- Inclusion and exclusion
- Relating styles
- Shifts in the level of participation
- Nonverbal communication
- Counterproductive behaviors
- Feeling expression
- Verbal communication patterns
- Conflict and conflict management
- Resistance

Inclusion and Exclusion

How group members are included or excluded can be important to observe as these play important roles for members' participation and the development of group cohesion. They also impact the development of trust and safety in the group. Group members who are included are listened to and responded to when they speak; their suggestions and input receive careful consideration by other group members; they are more apt to volunteer and be active participants; their input is solicited by other members; and they exhibit other such inclusion behaviors. Excluded members can experience the opposite attitudes and behaviors. For example, when excluded members speak, other members do not listen at all or they only partially listen; they change the topic instead of responding to the person; they show nonverbal signs of impatience or disinterest; they tell the excluded member what he or she should or ought to do or think; or they just ignore him or her. The group sends clear signals that the excluded member is not welcome.

It then becomes the leader's responsibility and task to try to get the excluded member included as a viable member of the group. The leader can point out lapses, such as not being responded to, and encourage group members to be respectful and tolerant of differing perspectives. Another strategy would be for the leader to fill in, such as responding or redirecting the focus back to the excluded member when topics are changed; soliciting input from the ignored members; encouraging empathic responses by members to each other; and so on. Leaders can model the desired behavior and some members will imitate that behavior.

Relating Styles

Observe relating styles because these behaviors in the group reflect behavior outside the group and can provide clues for possible relationship problems and strengths. Two basic styles are the extroverted and the introverted, with many subcategories. The *extroverted* styles are outgoing, active, and energetic and can be overwhelming and intrusive at times. Some subcategories for this style are power seeking, control needy, and self-absorbed. Members who use this style for relating can also be charming, initiate contact and connections, and reach out to others easily and frequently.

The *introverted* styles are cautious, wary, and reserved and can be perceived as aloof, snooty, and uninvolved at times. They tend to take more time to warm up to contact and connections, resist being pushed or pulled into relationships, and can be quiet and passive. Subcategories for this style are seductive, independence seeking, and reflective. Their reticence and reserve are often misunderstood by others and can lead them to be excluded.

Leaders can appreciate the positive aspects for each style and highlight these in the group. For example, the tendency of the extroverted style to talk a lot could be commented on as getting the group or session started, bringing in other members' perspectives, or other positive aspects of the style. For instance, the leader could comment on his or her tendency to not speak until reflecing on the topic and its meaning. Leaders of nonclinical groups may not use what is observed about relating styles for group members directly in the group, unless relating and relationship issues are a focus for that group, but there are numerous ways to use this information indirectly.

Shifts in the Level of Participation

Shifts are generally signals for individual members and for the group as a whole, and can be especially noteworthy after a pattern of participation has been established and observed. Changes, such as becoming quiet after being actively engaged and talking, increased tension or feelings, talking more than usual, abrupt changes in topic, discussing out-of-group topics, telling jokes that are inappropriate for the task of the group, and becoming aggressive or attacking are examples of shifts that could be important. The group leader has to be aware of the shift and understand what it may be signaling.

The first step for observing shifts in level of participation is the awareness of the usual pattern for participating, and what the difference is at this point. When the shift was noticed, and when it occurred can be reflected on by the leader because the shift may occur without conscious awareness at that point, and it is only later that the leader becomes aware of it. The next step would be to reflect on what was taking place at the time of the shift. That is the area of sensitivity, resistance, or avoidance. The leader can choose whether or not to bring this to the group's or member's attention, to just note it for future reference, to make a group process comment, or to intervene in other ways. The task for the group, the stage of group development, and other such variables are integral parts of the decision as to what would be best to do. For example, in a very short-term group that is in the beginning stage of development, it would not be helpful to make a group process comment as members would likely not be ready to accept it.

Nonverbal Communication

The vast majority of the real content for messages is in the nonverbal portion called *metacommunication*. Generally, the nonverbal communication is from the unconscious or the nonconscious, the part that is just below the level of conscious awareness. Thus, the person can unintentionally communicate the real message, which can be at odds with the verbal message. For example, a member can deny being upset, but his voice tone, tense body posture, and clenched fists send a very different nonverbal message.

It is important to observe and understand the nonverbal communication for group members to accurately identify what they are experiencing at the moment, to gain information about needed interventions, and to help make visible real messages when nonverbal communication is at variance with verbal communication.

Observe clusters of gestures, voice tone, and facial expression to get an accurate reading of what the person is experiencing. Try not to stare when you are observing an individual as this can be intimidating, scary, or disconcerting for some people. You may want to do additional reading on this topic because what is presented here is too brief for a full understanding.

Clusters of gestures are more accurate than any single one gesture in isolation. It is best to not try to analyze or interpret single gestures. Gestures such as arm and hand positions and movements; leg positions and movements; and posture including standing, sitting, and walking, are examples of what to observe.

Voice tone can provide a lot of information about the person's inner experiencing. For example, I have a male colleague with a very deep voice, and when he is irritated, his voice sounds even deeper and resonating. He doesn't even have to admit being irritated as his voice tone conveys it. If you listen carefully when members speak, you can hear possible nervousness, excitement, pain, anger, and other emotions. This can be especially informative in a session where a sensitive topic is introduced.

Facial expression is usually informative, but may be less so where individuals have learned how to control their expressions to avoid revealing their real feelings or thoughts. Actors and actresses, poker players, and therapists do this, but there are still clues. Pay particular attention to eye contact or lack of contact; shifting eyes, especially if there are other signs of fear or distress; smiles that are more like grimaces than mirth or pleasure; an expressionless face; and parts of the face hidden with hands or objects. Even people who try to hide their real feelings will sometimes be unable to do so and others, who are not trying to hide their feelings, can be very informative by their facial expressions.

Counterproductive Behaviors

These counterproductive behaviors are not problem behaviors, such as monopolizing, but they are actions that can negatively affect the group's functioning and progress. Leaders will want to observe these so that they can intervene, if needed, and model more constructive behavior. Also, leaders should observe how these behaviors impact the group, and how they are tolerated and managed by group members. Examples of counterproductive behaviors are categorized as follows:

Social convention counterproductive behaviors include
- rushing to soothe and reassure other members to reduce their affect
- giving less than genuine responses in order to be polite
- holding back on expression of thoughts, ideas, and feelings for fear of offending

Group insensitivity counterproductive behaviors include
- arriving late, especially on more than one occasion, and returning late from breaks
- leaving early
- holding side conversations when others are talking
- not responding or not responding directly to others
- missing sessions and premature termination from the group

Feeling Expression

Observe what feelings are expressed openly, those that members seem to have difficulty expressing or are avoiding and how these are expressed, and the level of acceptance of the feelings by the group. For example, members may easily express dissatisfaction and irritation, but seem to have more difficulty expressing appreciation or approval. This can be true for individual members, or for the group as a whole. There are even some groups where members are unable to directly express their feelings. In these instances, members may have to be taught feeling words and given permission to express their feelings.

It can be important to note how the group receives expressions of feelings because this is a part of establishing the norms and culture for the group. Unconscious messages are sent about what the group expects, wants suppressed, or may absolutely reject. For example, social convention plays a major role in feeling expression, leading to some feelings that can be experienced but not openly expressed. Thus, when someone breaks this unspoken taboo, that member may be excluded, attacked, or reacted to in other negative ways. The group can exert enormous pressure on its members to conform, and this can retard progress.

Verbal Communication Patterns

Notice the individual's and the group's verbal communication patterns. While a particular verbal communication may be important, the patterns are much more revealing of held opinions, suppressed feelings, and the main group issue. Observe behavior such as the following:

- Is there member-to-member interaction, or do members direct their communication to and through the leader?
- Do members talk to the group rather than to specific group members?
- Are one or more members excluded from verbal interactions—is their input not being solicited or is it ignored?
- When members are cranky, snap at each other, or appear to be disgruntled, is this a way to prevent challenging the leader, or establishing connections among members?
- Does one particular member seem to attract or be the target for many expressed negative feelings?
- Do members talk outside the group topics as a means to avoid talking about in-group relationships and issues?
- When members become anxious, do they ask the leader lots of questions, or express frustration and confusion?

Leaders can get clues about members' safety needs and how well these are being met or not met; whether the group wants to challenge the leader but is doing so in indirect ways; if a member is assuming the role of scapegoat; when sensitive topics are being avoided and what the sensitivity may be about; and members' perceptions about authority figures. These all provide clues about how and when to intervene.

One of the most important outcomes for observing communication patterns is the identification of empathic failures, giving the leader an opportunity to repair these in the session and as promptly as possible. It is always helpful to repair empathic failures at a later time, but it is most effective to do so as soon as the failure occurs. Empathic failure, identification, and repair will be discussed in more detail later in the book.

Conflict and Conflict Management

These topics are presented in more detail in Chapter 14, and suggestions are given there for constructive use of conflict. This discussion focuses on observing conflict and how it is managed by the group, rather than focusing on individual members.

The background for observing conflict relies on the leader's perceptions about conflict, the extent to which the leader can tolerate conflict, and an understanding of how it can be constructively and effectively used. Group members have their own unique perceptions and tolerance levels, but will unconsciously take their cues from the leader's conscious and unconscious perceptions and tolerance for conflict. This background is discussed in the chapters on personal development.

Observe if members recognize conflicts, the extent to which conflicts are openly expressed, and what the group does when conflict emerges. Conflict of some sort is always to be expected in every group, and is one of the defining characteristics of stage 2 in group development.

The most effective uses for conflict are to demonstrate how to express differences so that the relationship is maintained, and to constructively work through them for the benefit and satisfaction of all who are involved.

Usual group responses to conflict include the following:

- Denying that conflict exists
- Suppressing intense feelings that may be aroused
- Ignoring the conflict; for example, changing the topic or asking a question
- Attacking members in the conflict, or the leader, or other members
- Redirecting the focus or emphasis
- Soothing the participants in the conflict
- Becoming silent and withdrawn

Conflict can be used to disguise a more sensitive topic, as an indirect way of expressing displeasure and disappointment, to keep from experiencing intimacy, as a coverup for shame, and so on. The conflict itself may be important information, or it can carry other unknown or feared information.

Resistance

Resistance is always present in some form, and can also be informative when recognized by the group leader. Members can gain considerable personal information when they explore their resistance, but few nonclinical groups get to the point where members feel sufficiently safe and trusting for this kind of personal work. However, resistance is still worthwhile to observe, and can provide the leader with clues for possible interventions, changes, or adaptations.

There can be individual resistance and whole-group resistance. Because nonclinical groups are usually not designed to capitalize on individual resistance, leaders can simply note these when they are observed, but not bring them to the person's attention. Group-level resistance (Brown, 2007), however, may be used constructively in some instances. For example, in a group on relationships, if members resist making meaningful connections with each other, the group's goal would be helped by bringing this to the group's attention.

The capability of recognizing group-level resistance develops over time and with experience. The leader learns to pay attention to collective group member behaviors, and to what is ignored or avoided. Avoidance is one key sign of resistance. Observe the group for the following:

- Are members avoiding conflict, soothing over disagreements, and the like?
- Do members deny having different opinions, thoughts, and ideas from those of the leader?
- Is there nonverbal communication that suggests members fear becoming connected or too close to each other?
- Is the group overly polite or very cranky?
- Do group members insist on talking about things unrelated to the purpose for the group?
- Does the group tolerate or encourage counterproductive or problem behaviors such as continual tardiness of one or more members, or monopolizing behavior?

How and when to bring this group-level resistance to the attention of group members is discussed in the chapter on group process commentary.

Sample Possible Leader Interventions

Following are some sample possible interventions for several observed group dynamics. These are presented with the assumption that the groups are short term, are focused, and are non-clinical. Clinical groups have other possible interventions because they have more time to develop the therapeutic alliance, establish safety and trust, and allow therapeutic factors to emerge, and for the group leader to observe individual and group patterns over time. Sample interventions are presented for inclusion and exclusion, relating styles, shifts in the level of participation, empathic failures as a communication pattern, feeling expression, and example counterproductive behaviors.

Vignette: Inclusion and Exclusion

The group of adolescents has met for three of the eight scheduled sessions focusing on study skills. The group is composed of 10 males, who were all identified by their teachers and counselors as underachievers. The leader notices that two group members seldom volunteer input, and that their input is not sought by other members. This is in contrast to the remaining group members. It is now the fourth session, the discussion is lively, but these members are silent. They look interested, but their opinions are not sought.

Possible Intervention. The leader can directly solicit input from every member by saying that it is important to hear from everyone, and then respond to the input by noting its positive points. If a member wants to pass, the leader can ask if he or she would report on the feelings, thoughts, or ideas experienced at that time.

Vignette: Relating Styles

Eric is an active participator in the group—eagerly volunteering input, talking frequently and loudly, having something to say about everything—but does not respond to other members' input.

Possible Intervention. The leader can ask Eric to respond directly to a member immediately after that member has said something. The request could be phrased, "Eric, I think it would be helpful to _____ if you would tell him or her what you experienced as he or she was speaking." Making this request to Eric and to other group members will help members begin to interact and relate in more constructive ways.

Vignette: Shifts in the Level of Participation

The leader notices that group members are entering the room quietly where, in the previous four sessions, they were talking to each other and even joking as they entered the group room. When the session begins, the leader poses the goal for the session and invites input.

Members either nod or say nothing. The leader decides to move forward, but the same kind of behavior continues.

Possible Leader Intervention. The leader can openly speak of the differences in the group's behavior and invite members to talk about what is, or may be, producing the behavior. There are numerous possibilities for the change, such as conflict between two or more members that occurred outside the group, a shared secret that members are keeping from the leader, or a reluctance to disagree or challenge the leader.

Vignette: Empathic Failures

The leader has noticed the following over several sessions.
1. When members made emotional disclosures, other members did not respond to him or her.
2. There were two to three rather abrupt changes of topic during sessions.
3. Members talked freely about outside-the-group topics, but became silent when the leader tried to have them become more present-centered.
4. Disclosure by a member was responded to by personal stories from other members.
5. There were several instances of advice giving.

Possible Leader Intervention. The leader can tell the group that several empathic failures may have occurred (did occur), report on each of the listed observations, and tell the group that it would be more constructive and helpful if members would first respond directly and empathically to each other. (Please note that the leader should use specific observable incidents for examples of empathic failures.)

Vignette: Feeling Expression

The group members tend to intellectualize and to talk about their feelings indirectly, but do not openly identify or express their feelings.

Possible Leader Intervention. Wait until they once again engage in intellectualizing or indirect expression. Block the intellectualizing, and tell them what was observed. Then ask members to report on the feelings they are experiencing in the moment.

Vignette: Example Counterproductive Behaviors

From the beginning of the group, members do much advice giving, expressing these as should, ought, and what the speaker would do.

Possible Leader Intervention. The leader can wait for two or three sessions to see if the behavior is reduced or eliminated. Whenever the leader decides to intervene, he or she can say that it would be more helpful and constructive to respond empathically, try and understand what that member is experiencing, and that situations and people differ so that what works for one person may not work for another.

Therapeutic Factors

The importance of factors conducive to promoting therapeutic progress, healing, and change for group members has received attention in the literature (Colijn, Hoencamp, Snijders, Van Der Spek, & Duivenvoorden, 1991; Corsini & Rosenberg, 1955; Crouch, Bloch, & Wanlass, 1994; Dies, 1997; Fuhriman, 1997; Fuhriman & Burlingame, 1994; Kivlighan, Coleman, & Anderson, 2000; Kivlighan & Goldfine, 1991; Kivlighan & Holmes, 2004; Kivlighan & Mullison, 1988; MacKenzie, 1997; MacNair-Semands & Lese, 2000; Tschuschke & Dies, 1994; Yalom, 1995).What has emerged from these studies and reviews is confirmation of the impact of behaviors and attitudes that are clustered as categories for therapeutic, and curative change; that some are common and valued for all types of groups, whereas some differ in their importance and value depending on the type of population; and that there are few guidelines for leaders on how to foster and encourage the emergence of these factors.

These factors have been given various titles, but can be generally categorized as Yalom (1995) presented them. These 12 factors are:

- Universality
- Existential factors
- Instillation of hope
- Altruism
- Family of origin issues
- Corrective emotional experience
- Catharsis
- Interpersonal learning
- Socializing techniques
- Imitative behavior
- Guidance
- Group cohesiveness

The relative importance of these factors differs for various types of groups. Group structure characteristics such as duration of the group, number of participants, and the focus for the group determine the importance and emergence of therapeutic factors. For example, task groups do not have a focus, goal, or emphasis that would highlight and encourage the emergence and exploration for the corrective recapitulation of the primary family group. The therapeutic factors are described in more detail in the following sections.

Universality

Universality highlights similarities among group members. When group members find one or more members with whom they can identify, that identification reduces feelings of alienation and isolation, promotes feelings of belonging and inclusion, and reduces fears. An added benefit, as Agazarian (1997) points out, is that groups become cohesive around similarities and stay disconnected and detached around differences.

The tendencies of many group members and some leaders are to stay focused on visible differences and to highlight these. It can be helpful for some members to have their visible differences acknowledged at some point. Visible differences in gender, age, race/ethnicity, disability, and so on are important to these members and they want to know that they are being seen as they are. However, the leader must take care to not rush to highlight these visible differences for the following reasons:

- The desire to have one's visible differences highlighted does not apply to all members who are visually different.
- The group can get misdirected into a prolonged discussion about the impact of these differences and lose its focus.
- Members may assume the leader's stance and highlight differences instead of searching for similarities.
- The difference that is very important to the person can be minimized with protestations such as "We all have some disability."

It could be more helpful for the group if the leader would remember the benefits for members perceiving similarities, and to identify and highlight these. Members who have a strong need to have their differences recognized will bring this to the group's attention. The leader then has an opening to address these and other differences that exist in the group.

What may be of more importance for universality are other not so visible similarities such as past experiences, values, emotional reactions, needs, desires, and fantasies. Any of these, when made visible, can help forge connections at a deeper and more meaningful level.

Clinical Vignette: Fostering Universality

Ten adult men and women assigned to a group for people arrested for driving under the influence of alcohol or drugs (DUI) have been meeting for 5 weeks in a 15-week program. Members displayed considerable resistance and resentment for several sessions. Most members did not feel that they needed the group or the program, and attended only because they would lose their driver's licenses if they did not attend. They resisted all attempts the leader made to introduce universality about something other than the DUI, and some even maintained that the cops and machines that led to their convictions were erroneous.

It is the beginning of the sixth session and a member becomes angry about something the leader says, and tells him that he (the leader) is doing the same thing that his father always did—putting him down. The member goes on to say more about his father's emotional abuse. Other members begin to relate their stories about parental emotional abuse and neglect. Some abusers were mothers and some were fathers. The leader does not intervene and lets members tell their stories until almost everyone has contributed. He then points out the similarities of experiences, invites the members who have not yet spoken to speak of their experiences with their parents, which they do. The leader then reinforces the notion of similarities, and the possible sensitivity to perceived comments as put-downs because of these past experiences. The group members begin to explore this possible sensitivity as a trigger for some excessive drinking or using drugs. Members interact with each other without prompting; demonstrate sympathy, understanding, and even some empathy for each other; and the session becomes very productive.

Existential Factors

Yalom (1995) cites existential factors as therapeutic for group members. He and others write about existential factors emerging during the life span of the group, sometimes in an obvious way and sometimes in indirect and disguised ways. Yalom (1995) explores existential factors in therapy more extensively in his book *Existential Psychotherapy.* The discussion in this chapter will not be as extensive and you are encouraged to read Yalom's book and others listed at the back of this book for a more in-depth understanding of existential factors in the therapeutic setting.

The focus here is to highlight the overt and covert ways in which existential factors may be present in the group so that group leaders can begin to be more aware of their presence. Also discussed are some therapeutic benefits of these factors and suggestions for strategies a group leader can use to help members capitalize on these benefits.

It may be helpful to begin by describing what are existential factors: meaning and purpose in life, pain and suffering, isolation and alienation, freedom and responsibility, anxiety, and the inevitability of death.

Some members enter group with issues around *meaning and purpose* in their lives. They say that they feel empty and unfulfilled. They may be successful in their jobs or careers, have families and other support systems, and participate in numerous activities. From the outside they have full lives, but they report that much of what they do seems meaningless.

Feeling empty and unfulfilled is not depression, although a depressed person may also report these feelings. Members with these issues claim that there does not seem to be sufficient reason for what they do, and that what they do leaves them feeling like there is something missing. They may say that they are going through the motions and not deriving any satisfaction or benefit. There is an underlying assumption in what they say that others have meaning and purpose in their lives, but this has managed to elude them.

There may be other members in the group who are *not* searching for meaning and purpose in their lives. These members do not feel that particular deficit, although they have other problems and issues. Some may have strong religious beliefs that guide, direct, and provide meaning and purpose. They cannot imagine living any other way and may not understand why someone is searching for meaning and purpose. Some may feel so strongly that they rush to give advice and try to convince the searchers that if they would only do what is suggested or follow the example, then there would be meaning and purpose in their lives. It can be tricky for the group leader to block this advice giving, especially in early stages of the group.

Emptiness is difficult to describe but easy to understand, especially if you have ever felt that way. It differs from numbness, loneliness, and depression because it is not accompanied by the feelings associated with them. For example, associated with numbness are knowing what other states are like, its temporary nature, its use as defense against pain from loss and grief, its uniqueness for the person, and its temporariness. Associated with loneliness are longing, feelings that may be intense such as dejection, and the desire to be included. Associated with depression are feelings of worthlessness, hopelessness, despair, and helplessness.

Emptiness, on the other hand, has nothing as its primary state. There seems to be nothing at the core of the person and he or she feels hollow, has a hole, is unable to feel intensely. Have you ever tried to describe nothing? It can only be described in reference to something—that is, by an absence of something.

Persons who feel empty may use a variety of means to try and fill up the "hole." Activities, drugs, alcohol, and other self-defeating acts are their ways of trying to feel less empty. They derive little pleasure from these acts and realize that they are not fulfilling their intended purpose.

The group leader's task is to block other group members from giving advice on how to feel less empty. Another task is to guide the members in accepting that they are the only ones who can determine what is meaningful and purposeful for them.

One of the first things almost every group member seeks and wants is relief from *pain and suffering*. A quick fix would be very much appreciated. However, this is not possible and most members will be content to have some hope that one day there will be relief.

The existential piece is that pain and suffering is a human condition and, although some relief is possible for some people at some time, there will continue to be pain and suffering throughout one's life. Spending time and effort avoiding pain is counterproductive as there appears to be no way you can fully escape from it. It can be helpful, hopeful, and relieving to understand that pain and suffering are universal, even though the situations differ. It is also helpful to begin to understand that this is part of the human condition—that is, it happens to everyone at some time.

Members spend considerable time and effort denying, repressing, and rationalizing their pain. They fear that if they allow themselves to fully experience it, they will become overwhelmed or destroyed. Even worse, they may fear that others will find them weird or crazy, and will reject them. Thus, they do not speak of their pain, nor do they admit the extent to which they are experiencing pain. Even members who appear to be talking about their pain may be trying to deflect attention from the real pain by getting involved in a less agonizing painful experience. The real source for the pain cannot be tolerated by them. Pointing out the universality, providing hope for relief, and making members aware that pain and suffering are human conditions are part of the leader's responsibility.

Humans appear to need significant connections to other humans. When these connections are not made, are disrupted, or severed, we tap into the existential concerns of being isolated and alienated. *Isolation and alienation* occur when we do not feel we can connect with others. Something within makes us feel that we are different and does not allow us to reach out to others. Or, we feel that we are being excluded and not being welcomed to connect. Either way, the lack of meaningful human connections is troubling.

There are many life situations that can produce the feelings of isolation and alienation such as the following:

- The death of a loved one
- Rejection by a significant person in your life
- Being excluded by others
- Not building support systems
- Becoming estranged from family and friends
- Lack of social skills
- Self-absorption

Whatever brought on the feelings of being isolated or alienated, the results are the same: disconnection with other humans.

Group members may have considerable feelings of isolation and alienation in the beginning of group because they do not know if they will be included or excluded from the group. It is the leader's job to help group members overcome these feelings.

The existential issues around isolation and alienation take time to emerge. Members have to feel safe before they admit that they do not feel connected with others at a very deep level. They will be reluctant to admit that they want and need to feel connected at a meaningful level. If they present with life circumstances that are conducive to isolation and alienation, such as the death of a loved one, it can be easier for them to admit that they are "walled off."

These feelings are also a part of the human condition. There are times when, no matter how hard you or others try, you cannot make the wanted or needed connections. The group leader has the task of helping members understand how they are contributing to this state, that it is to be experienced not denied, and that there are ways to reach out to others and develop the connections.

The ability to make personal choices, to decide for oneself, and to develop to one's capacity is one way of conceptualizing *freedom*. This is what is understood by the phrase "the freedom to be." The other side of freedom is *responsibility*. We cannot be authentic humans without also assuming responsibility. These, too, are human conditions. Many members arrive in group not fully understanding that they have choices, how to make choices, and the responsibility carried by making choices.

To gain a deeper understanding of personal choice making, consider this. Although you have had numerous opportunities to make choices in your life, in many circumstances other people intervened to direct or even select the choice for you. Even when you could have made a conscious choice, you did not.

Group members may carry some resentment because they do not feel they were allowed to make choices. Some may blame others for the choices they did make and the results or outcomes. Still other members may not even have considered that they had choices. Whereas one task for the group leader is to guide members in understanding what choices they have, another primary task is recognizing when this is an issue for members. Helping members recognize that they do have the freedom to be and developing progress toward self-actualization can do much to promote this therapeutic factor.

One of the more terrifying things we face is the awareness of our *death*. Ceasing to be is so upsetting that we will do almost anything to keep from accepting that one day we will cease to exist. Regardless of faith, belief, and the assurances of some religions, at our core is the *anxiety* that results from not knowing or understanding what death is or really means. We can believe in an afterlife, but we cannot know that it exists or what it means for us as we exist today. Thus, we go out of our way to avoid even the thought of death.

However much we try to avoid the idea of death, it still appears in the group—sometimes directly as when a group member or a member's close family member dies, or even when a celebrity dies. The topic of death can emerge unexpectedly at almost any time. Members go out of their way to deny the emergence of this existential factor because it produces terror.

Following are some behaviors and attitudes typically displayed by group members that can indicate existential concerns. Even though existential concerns are part of the human condition, their impact on members still causes distress. The group leader's task is to help identify the existential issues as separate or part of the psychological issues and to guide members in understanding that these are not solvable, and that solutions are only for the present.

- Evading responsibility
- Blaming others for evoking feelings, etc.
- Not making decisions

- Refusing to participate
- Canceling sessions and/or absenteeism
- Using inappropriate humor
- Not recognizing or accepting problems and personal responsibility
- Withholding information
- Breaking confidentiality
- Wanting to be rescued
- Insisting on predictability and always knowing what to expect
- Feeling lonely and alienated in life
- Failing to contribute to sessions as a pattern of behavior
- Expressing hopelessness
- Refusing to be engaged
- Not connecting to others for fear of being rejected
- Thinking of oneself as "special"
- Putting up physical and emotional barriers that prevent connecting to others
- Ignoring others or being ignored
- Feeling that one is different from other members, and so are excluded by them
- Feeling alienated or being alienated by members
- Being "dead" in the group
- Choosing or deciding not to work because of the potential ending of the session or of the group
- Refraining from emotionally investing in the group
- Blocking, repressing, or denying feelings
- Exhibiting self-destructive behaviors (e.g., unsafe sex or alcohol or drug abuse)
- Intellectualizing
- Avoiding of "death" topics

Fostering the Emergence of Hope and Altruism in the Group

Hope and altruism are 2 of the 12 curative or therapeutic factors found to be significant in helping members get better by improving feelings of emotional and psychological well-being, increasing satisfaction with personal progress and with the group, promoting optimism, and increasing self-confidence in one's ability to grow, develop, and cope (Yalom, 1995). Although these factors are seen as important, there is little guidance provided to show leaders how to foster and encourage their emergence in the group. For example, leading clinicians and authors of group counseling/therapy resources give little attention to these factors and even less guidance for the leader (Agazarian, 1997; Brabender, 2002; Corey & Corey, 1997; Gazda, Ginter, & Horne, 2001; Gladding, 2003; Ivey & Ivey, 2003; Kline, 2003; Kottler, 2001; Posthuma, 2002; Rutan & Stone, 2001). The following sections provide definitions for hope and altruism, a summary of some literature about their importance for individuals and for groups, and strategies to emphasize and highlight the factors thereby encouraging their emergence. Central to this presentation is the assumption that the primary responsibility for encouraging the emergence of these therapeutic factors rests with the group leader.

Hope. Hope is defined here as the individual's inner encouragement and support (Brown, 2002). Hope is unique for each group member, and members may not even be able to describe what can trigger their hopefulness. Hope does not deny or minimize the reality of the individual's experiencing or predicament, nor does it seek to perceive these through "rose-colored glasses" (Davis, 1999; Elliott, 1997; Hopper, 2001; Snyder, Cheaveus, & Sympsons, 1997; Vallant, 2000). Hafen, Karren, Frandsen, and Smith (1996) define hope as "a wealth of optimism, a want of fear" (p. 443), and as one of the strongest influences on health and the human body. Yalom (1995) seems to equate hope with encouragement, especially seeing the progress other members make, and knowing that their situation can change for the better.

Frank (1978) studied how infusing an attitude of hope contributes to the process of healing. At a Veterans Administration hospital a program was developed where the entire health professional staff worked together to effect changes. Before this program the hospital was described as "a dreary warehouse where patients were stored for years." The program examined all treatment plans, and reevaluated and made changes. Efforts to reestablish ties with family members and others in the community were initiated and group activities were sponsored to boost morale and reduce feelings of isolation among patients.

Most patients had been hospitalized from 3 to 10 years. Within 3 months the discharge rate rose to 70%. Forty percent of those released became self-supporting, indicating that they were not only physically healthier but also psychologically better adjusted.

Altruism. Altruism is defined as a concern for the welfare of others that is selfless. That is, the giver does not expect gratitude, liking, joining, or reciprocity. The concern is a gift with no strings attached (Brown, 2002). Members reach out to each other without hidden agendas, manipulative intent, or as a way of bolstering their self-esteem. Although helping another person can bring the giver satisfaction, pleasure, and a feeling of being valued, the giver is willing to give freely with no expectations. The personal benefits are a bonus, not the reason for giving. Hafen et al. (1996) note that altruism has been termed as one of the healthiest characteristics that humans can possess. There are studies linking altruism to health, counteracting stress, and bolstering the immune system.

Positive psychology is an emerging field of study that pays considerable attention to intraindividual subjective qualities, such as meaning and purpose in life, hope, and altruism. There is evidence that many of the factors such as faith, optimism, and hope affect physical health (Salovey, Rothman, Detweiler, & Steward, 2000), relationships (Ryan & Deci, 2000), give meaning and purpose for life (Myers, 2000), and enhance the quality of one's life (Fredrickson, 2001; Peterson, 2000; Taylor, Kemeny, Reed, Bowers, & Gruenwald, 2000). Luks (1988) studied the effects of regular volunteer activities on 1,700 women and found that they reported relief of physical ailments (e.g., headaches, loss of voice, pain due to lupus and multiple sclerosis, and depression). Approximately 90% rated their health as better than or as good as others their age. Sobel (1993) studied 2,700 residents of Tecumseh, Michigan, and found that men who volunteer for community organizations are two and a half times less likely to die from all causes of disease than those who don't get involved in volunteer work.

Strategies for Encouraging Hope. Many group members come to group in a state of hopelessness and despair, and having unrealistic expectations for what being in a group can accomplish for them. It is not unusual for members to expect the leader and the group to "fix" whatever they perceive as needing fixing, or to have a mind-set that trying to do anything about their situation is futile and hopeless. The group leader can be instrumental in turning their despair into hope.

The foundation for encouraging hope is the leader's beliefs and attitudes about members and the efficacy of group counseling/therapy. Members will be susceptible to "catching" the leader's unconscious perceptions and feelings, interpreting and incorporating these according to their personal needs, and using them as a guide to concluding that there is hope, or that it is hopeless. Following are some examples for encouraging hope. Presented first is the option or goal, followed with a specific leader strategy or strategies.

1. Have a realistic belief about what can be achieved.

   EXAMPLE: Long-term goals can be broken down into short-term goals and progress monitored so that members can begin to recognize progress. Change is possible, but takes time and effort.

2. Explore with members their beliefs about what can be achieved. This can assist them to be realistic about their expectations and goals.

   EXAMPLE: Focus their thoughts on what they can accomplish that does not involve change on the part of another person.

3. Concentrate on positive aspects, underused or unrecognized inner resources, personal strengths members have, and possible coping strategies.

   EXAMPLE: Identify one or more strengths each member brings to the group, or to his or her situation. Highlight a possible strength embedded in the self, or in criticism by others.

4. Build on, highlight, and emphasize whatever is positive in the session.

   EXAMPLE: When members reach out to each other, give support and encouragement and use that opportunity to comment, praise, or explain how that was helpful.

5. Give members a reason to continue to struggle.

   EXAMPLE: Show your faith in their ability to learn other coping strategies. Empower them to take charge of their growth and development and provide opportunities for them to note how others were successful. This is a place where bibliotherapy could be helpful.

6. Emphasize positive coping strategies.

   EXAMPLE: Members can share personal coping strategies, and the leader can explore with other members how it is possible for them to adapt a particular strategy to meet their personal needs. The leader can propose or suggest strategies that have worked for others.

There are some possible leader behaviors that will not be helpful and should be avoided. This can be difficult for the leader because members have individualistic perceptions, past experiences, and transference. That is, the leader may not intend to do what is perceived as such by a member, but because of one or more of these individual factors, it can be perceived differently than intended. For example, leaders are well advised to not criticize members for such things as an inability to take specific actions; most leaders try to refrain from criticizing members at all.

Another attitude or behavior to avoid is being overly demanding. There can be a fine line between encouragement and support, and that of being overly demanding. What can be difficult for a leader to know and understand is where the line is for each member, and how members react and personalize things from the leader's interactions with other members.

Most of what has been discussed to this point are internal states of the leader, and attention to possible internal states of members. We now turn to actions leaders can use.

1. Call attention to any slight improvement for feelings, attitudes, and behaviors. It can be important for all members to increase their awareness of progress, either personally or for another member. Yalom (1995) reports on research that lists "seeing others get better" as one means to instill hope. It is possible that members are so mired in their misery that they lack conscious awareness of a slight improvement.

2. Help members formulate a course of action that has reasonable possibilities for success. Members are likely to be stuck and even depressed about their situations so that they cannot begin to see how to take action, much less know what action to take.

3. Identify members' underused or overlooked inner resources. These are not always evident on first glance. The leader must listen to members recount past events and experiences; stay aware of their possible inner resources as members reveal these in the group through their actions, interactions, and responses; and seek to capitalize on these.

   EXAMPLE: Observe what members say and do that reveal an inner resource that may be overlooked by the person, such as determination, living up to his or her principles, or being guided by a freely chosen set of values. Sometimes, just hearing another person name a strength you have is encouraging and can promote hope.

4. The value of empathic responses cannot be overemphasized. Many, if not all, group members will have experienced numerous empathic failures throughout their lives. The group leader has many opportunities to make empathic responses, and then in turn can help promote hope, especially hope that one is valued and understood.

Fostering Altruism Among Members. Leaders may need to become more familiar with recognizing altruistic acts to better identify them in the group. But first, the leader may have to explain the benefits of altruism for members, such as reducing loneliness and improving health. The mind–body connection seems to be strong, and this needs to be explained to group members. Further, members may need reminding of just what altruism is, giving the gift of helping others without expecting rewards either tangible or intangible. Other actions leaders can take include the following:

1. Model tolerance and respect.

   EXAMPLE: Do not always express your differing opinion or perspective. Because you are the leader, some members take this as you telling them they are wrong, shameful, or bad. Instead, reflect back to members their feelings about their values, perspectives, and beliefs without judgment either verbally or nonverbally. This of course does not imply agreement or approval, it just conveys tolerance and respect. Nor does it mean that leaders should remain mute about illegal or abusive acts.

2. Teach members to accept caring acts.

   EXAMPLE: Some members are suspicious of any caring act because of past experiences where these led to manipulation, rejection, or betrayal. To them, caring comes with hidden strings attached. Leaders can point out when members are supportive of each other, make appreciative comments, or provide encouragement. You cannot know if these are hidden "strings," but if you've emphasized altruistic acts and their benefits, many members will try to practice them.

3. Encourage members to verbally express positive feelings to and about each other.

   EXAMPLE: The group is a place where members can practice openly verbalizing positive feelings about each other. These may be compliments, but members should be encouraged to take responsibility for their feelings and try and refrain from insincere flattery. This means, for example, that when a member is appreciative of some supportive and kind words expressed toward him or her, he or she does not label the other person as wonderful, supportive, and so on. Rather, the receiver can say that he or she is appreciative and values or feels cared for by the words.

4. Suggest that members practice kind acts both in and out of the group.

   EXAMPLE: Have members give examples of small acts of kindness that they received and appreciated. Further, members could brainstorm ideas for these acts, carry out one or more of them as homework, and report back to the group on the impact and effect on them and the other person.

5. Develop a list of books that feature altruism and suggest that members read one or more of them.

   EXAMPLE: Members and the leader could develop a list of possible civic and community activities where members could volunteer. The effects of volunteering on members could be reported to the group.

Members and group leaders can face much confusion when trying to identify therapeutic factors as they appear in the group. Some are more easily identified by behavior, such as cohesion and universality, but others are more difficult, such as the corrective recapitulation of family of origin. The next sections focus on describing member behaviors that reflect family of origin and how these get played out or manifested for members and for the leader. The chapter also offers suggestions for promoting the corrective emotional experience, catharsis, interpersonal learning, and socialization techniques.

Family-of-Origin Factors

Families are where members receive the foundation for their growth and development. The interaction of genetic predispositions, environment, and basic personality are significant factors, with family falling under environmental factors. The individual's position and role in the family, how they were interacted with, the relationships with parents and siblings, and early relationship deprivations all have an impact on their growth and development.

The importance of experiences in the family of origin cannot be underestimated and group leaders need to learn how to understand what impact family of origin has had on each member, and to take steps to foster the corrective experience. (Rutan & Stone, 2000; Yalom, 1995) A basic premise is that relationships among members and with the leader mirror the quality and kind of relationships members have outside the group, including past and present relationships with family of origin. Observation of ways and patterns members relate within the group provides clues for their other relationships, and helps the leader identify transference and projection (Tschuschke & Dies, 1994).

The first discussion presents some behaviors, attitudes, and feelings that are related to family of origin: parental relationships, sibling relationships, seduction, and competition. These are not exhaustive but can serve as guides to understand what may be taking place for members and for the group as a whole. Transference is discussed because that is one way to recognize members' family of origin as they experienced it. Suggestions and examples for providing the corrective emotional experience are also presented.

Indices of Parental Relationships. Table 2.1 presents some behavioral and attitudinal manifestations of relationships with parents, and Table 2.2 presents some indicators of relationships with siblings. All are associated with perceptions and reactions to the leader. If leaders are alert, they will pay careful attention to how members treat the leader and other members, how they confirm members' expectations, when they disappoint members, and when they are misunderstood by members. What leaders will not know at this point is whether it is a maternal transference or a paternal transference.

The behaviors and attitudes listed in Table 2.1 can be categorized as dependency, power and control, and affection. *Dependency*, for this discussion, refers to an individual relying on, expecting, demanding, or manipulating others to take care of him or her because the person is too helpless to assume that responsibility. This is usually learned behavior that began in childhood and persists even when the person becomes an adult. Leaders will note dependency needs when the following persist for several sessions. Please remember that some of these behaviors and attitudes are expected from all members in the beginning group stage. However, most members stop these behaviors.

Table 2.1 Behaviors and Attitudes Reflective of Relationships with Parents	Perceiving the leader as a powerful authority figure
	Thinking that the leader has "the answer"
	Becoming profoundly disappointed when the leader fails to meet expectations
	Fearing being found inadequate or wrong by the leader
	Identifying strongly with the leader
	Wanting the leader to consider them as "special"
	Perceiving the leader as criticizing, punitive, blaming
	Wanting to do it "right" to win the leader's approval
	Seeking an alliance with the leader
	Questioning the leader's competence or abilities
	Seeking advice, support, or directions from the leader
	Wanting the leader to take care of them

Table 2.2 Manifestations of Relationships with Siblings	Competing with other group members for the leader's attention
	Perceiving members as "putting them down"
	Tattling
	Colluding with other members to keep secrets from the leader
	Rescuing
	Protecting
	Becoming irritated at members when they do things such as sitting in their chair, picking up a personal possession, monopolizing, playing one-upmanship, or saying what they should or ought to do

Some examples of manifestation of dependency needs follow:

- Asking many questions for several sessions about roles or leader expectations
- Acting confused
- Expressing frustration about the ambiguity of leader expectations
- Trying to win the leader's approval
- Continually asking the leader for advice, support, directions, and so on
- Trying to be "special"

The *power and control* category could also be termed *defiance of authority*. The behaviors and attitudes in this category all represent rebellion against being controlled, manipulated, or put in a subordinate position, such as the parent–child relationship. The authoritarian or controlling parent may have been dictatorial or manipulative. Either way, the child was expected to meet the parent's needs and was allowed little or no personal control. Thus, this person grew up reacting to authority figures as if the person in authority were the parent who was trying to control or manipulate him or her. Power, control, defiance, and manipulation avoidance behaviors can be inferred when a member exhibits the following:

- Becomes deeply disappointed in the leader
- Perceives the leader as punitive, blaming, and so on
- Constantly questions the leader's competence
- Reacts as if the leader is personally criticizing him or her
- Considers the leader to be "all-knowing"
- Frequently challenges or attacks the leader
- Resists developing a therapeutic relationship with the leader

Need for affection is akin to dependency. It is a separate category here to highlight the seemingly positive behaviors that are, in reality, a reflection of behavior in the family of origin. The member with affection needs has an overwhelming need to be liked and approved of, but not so much helplessness is involved as it is with dependency. The intensity of this need should not be underestimated, as it generally permeates the person's being. He or she becomes hypersensitive to the slightest verbal and nonverbal hint of criticism or disapproval and goes to extraordinary lengths to win the leader's approval.

As a group leader, notice consistent patterns of behavior that suggest the member is fearful of being perceived inadequate by the leader, strongly identifies with the leader, is concerned with "doing it right," and forms, or tries to form an alliance with the leader. Group leaders should note the following member behaviors as these can be reflective of sibling relationships:

- Is territorial
- Plays one-upmanship
- Tattles
- Is judgmental
- Seems jealous
- Acts more needy
- "Acts out" to get leader's attention
- Becomes sullen or withdrawn
- Is easily irritated at a particular member
- Seems very protective of a particular member

Promoting the Corrective Emotional Experience

The theoretical framework of the group leader will determine how he or she will choose to work with the information about members' issues around family of origin. This discussion presents some interventions and options that can be used to provide the corrective experience. The corrective experience is what makes for a group therapeutic factor.

There are numerous interventions and options whose choice will depend on the leader, the needs for a particular member, and the needs for the entire group. This is where a leader's expertise is essential: to select from a wide array of choices and to be able to select immediately. The impact is greater when the intervention is present centered. Following are some choices for leaders:

- Do nothing.
- Identify the goal of the behavior out loud for the member.
- Meet the need underlying the goal.
- Infuse objective reality.
- Relate behavior and goal to current experiencing and relationships for the member.
- Make a group process comment.

A leader can absorb the information and do nothing. It may not be the best time in the life of the group to make an intervention, the member may not be at a point where he or she is ready to hear and use the information, or it would be disruptive to something more urgent taking place in the group. *Doing nothing* does not mean ignoring the behavior, goal, or family-of-origin issues. It is an active choice. The member is not punished, denigrated, or shamed for what was said or done. The authority figure did not become angry, upset, sad, blaming, and so on.

Another option is to *identify the goal of the behavior* for the member. Sometimes, just bringing this to someone's attention is sufficient to get him or her thinking about associations with possible family-of-origin issues. Creating awareness of the behavior or goal can also be a first step. When members are faced with accepting that this is their behavior and a possible goal, the leader can then begin to help them make associations and direct their focus to family-of-origin issues.

It could be helpful to the member for the leader to meet the need underlying the goal. For example, if the goal is to gain attention, a leader could provide some attention. This action by the leader could be one of the few times the member is able to get his or her need met right off the bat. This empathic response is a corrective emotional experience.

Infusing objective reality refers to the leader pointing out possible transference and projections, other members agreeing what happened, and the collective experience differing from what the member responded to or did. Not only was the member's behavior off target, it was a clear reflection of previously identified family-of-origin issues. This intervention would be most helpful if used after a therapeutic relationship was established, and when the member had identified some unresolved issues related to family of origin. Using the intervention before these two conditions are in place will probably be counterproductive.

Related to the previous option, but less threatening, is to *associate* the member's behavior and goal in the group *with current experiencing and relationships.* This can be particularly effective when the current relationships mirror family-of-origin issues, or there are continuing family relationships that can be highlighted. Beginning with the present can be preliminary to exploring the past. For example, if the member tends to try and rescue others to prevent them from experiencing intense emotions, the leader could describe the behavior, encourage members in the group to respond with their reactions, and connect this to family-of-origin experiences.

The final choice discussed here is for the leader to make a *group process comment.* This choice would be used when there are considerable commonalties among group members for the behavior and goals. Note that members do not need to have common family-of-origin issues. What is common are the behaviors and goals. What produces the commentary is the behavior and impact on relationships in the group. Associated with this current experiencing is the family-of-origin issues that may be different for each member. Group process commentary would identify the seductive, competitive, rivalrous, and other such behaviors taking place in the group for all members, not just a few.

Clinical Vignette: Disguised Group Members' Needs

All group members have reported on family-of-origin experiences where they repeatedly felt neglected and marginalized in getting their needs met. The reasons range from parental emotional abuse, to absent parents due to military service or employment, to the birth of siblings, to maternal depression. The group process comment could be something like, "Group members are wondering if I and other members are willing to give attention to their needs, and are asking for this in disguised ways, such as being silent, starting disagreements, interrupting each other, challenging me, and so on. It would be more constructive to directly ask for what you want from me and other members."

The Group Leader's Family-of-Origin Experiences. Other reasons for the group leader's personal development and work on family-of-origin issues include understanding his or her personal issues to be better able to recognize group members' transference, and to identify how transference is contributing to certain behaviors and attitudes. This can be very confusing for the beginning group leader.

How do you detect transference? It is unconscious, buried in past relationships with family and others. Positive and negative attributes are involved, but it does not have to be real and can be around an imaginary event or misperception of an event, and is not limited to the parental relationship. Adding to the complexity is that transference is dynamic, ever shifting in order to remain unknown to the person. That is, the unconscious works to keep the material unconscious. Yet, all the leader has to work with are members' behaviors, patterns of interactions and communication, and the leader's knowledge, understanding, feelings, and past experiences.

The impact of early experiences on an individual is considerable. Regardless of what theoretical approach the leader favors, he or she can still be faced with the outcomes of these early experiences for group members. As the group leader, you should be familiar with physical, psychological, and emotional growth and development theories. What is even more important is for you to know something about each member's early experiences. You should know some of the relationships from the past that are significant. Because members repress and deny threatening material, you cannot know all there is to know, even when members cooperate. Some of the most significant material remains in the unconscious. However, even limited information can be valuable in identifying potential transference.

Unfinished business and issues with parents are also important. These tend to emerge during the course of therapy, and group leaders need to be patient and not try to rush the process. After all, you are asking members to experience pain and that is not comfortable. No wonder they resist. Pay attention to members' behavior toward each other in the group. These behaviors provide cues to their roles in their families of origin, other significant relationships, and unfinished business.

Leaders will have numerous opportunities to highlight possible transference. Once begun, members become more sensitive to their possible personal transference and will begin to wonder out loud if their reactions and responses are more connected to past relationships than present ones. Members will begin to explore why they become angry in certain situations, can be hurt by remarks, immediately become defensive, feel guilty or shamed, and so on.

Further exploration of the impact of transference on current relationships outside the group is another positive outcome.

Catharsis

Emotional venting is one way to describe catharsis. Tension and anxiety from suppressed and denied feelings are relieved. There are times when just speaking of feelings that are being held in is sufficient, but Yalom (1995) notes that this is of limited value if some intrapersonal learning does not accompany the catharsis. Beck (2000) says, "Intense negative emotion is painful and may be dysfunctional if it interferes with the patient's capacity to think clearly, solve problems, act effectively, or gain satisfaction" (p. 94). When intense emotions are suppressed, repressed, or denied, this can only impair the person's capacities even further without understanding the unconscious impact.

However, some people have difficulty expressing emotions, and even more are fearful of expressing intense negative ones. Verderber and Verderber (1992) list five barriers or constraints that prevent people from expressing their emotions: insufficient vocabulary; a reluctance, resistance, or fear that doing so will reveal too much about them; fear that the reactions of others will trigger their guilt; fear that others will be harmed; and cultural determinants and expectations that discourage open expression of feelings.

Then there are people whose family-of-origin experiences have taught them that they are safer when their emotions are not expressed, and are suppressed. This seems to happen in substance-abusing households and in narcissistic families (Donaldson-Pressman & Pressman, 1994). The authors go on to point out, "The skill of appropriate communication of feelings becomes a monumental task" (p. 25). For these members, just speaking of their feelings at all is cathartic and an intense emotional venting is unlikely. Group leaders need to be aware of the effort it takes for some members to identify a feeling, and then openly express it.

In some instances it may be necessary for the group leader to teach members how to distinguish between thoughts and feelings, and how to identify and name an immediate feeling, levels of feelings, and appropriate ways to express these feelings. One way that some members can lack access to their feelings, or defend against experiencing them, is to stay in the cognitive realm where their thoughts take priority, such as intellectualizing.

Interpersonal Learning

Members can and do learn from each other, and can experiment with new behavior in the group that can lead to improved relationships outside the group. How members relate to the leader and other group members mirrors how they relate to people outside the group, especially those who are in close or intimate relationships with them. For example, if a member is tentative at expressing displeasure in the group, he or she exhibits the behavior outside the group. The person is also tentative with others in letting them know when they are displeased. The in-group behavior differs in quality and intensity, but is basically the same.

It is helpful for leaders to observe and understand all the following about their groups:

- Which members each member responds to
- Which members are ignored and by whom
- Who is supportive of other members
- The rescuer and who they rescue
- The soother and who they soothe
- How envy and jealously are expressed or manifested
- How each member handles conflict
- Members responses to conflict
- Differences in feelings that are expressed to different members
- The members who use sarcasm and other indirect ways to express hostility
- How accepting members are of differences of opinion, values, perspectives, and so on
- Competitive behaviors
- Seductive behaviors

- Power and control behaviors
- Affection and approval needs
- Projections

What members do, what they do not do, who they seem to avoid, what they deny doing or feeling, who they respond to positively or negatively are all reflective of their behaviors and attitudes outside the group. This is one reason why focusing on the here and now can produce changes for the there and then. Members may be confused or resist working on relationships in the group because they do not understand how it can benefit their out-of-group relationships. A group leader can expect to be challenged on this point.

When challenged, a group leader need only illustrate how mirroring behavior works by describing members' behavior in the group and its impact on relationships, and asking if this is how they relate to someone outside the group. Most of the time the members are willing to admit that they do similar things in relationships outside the group. Members who challenge the leader, especially if they do so early in the life of the group, tend to challenge authority figures outside the group, assert their need for control and dominance, or react in other similar ways. So all behavior is of importance.

Once members accept that how they are relating to each other mirrors their pattern of behaving in other relationships outside the group, they begin to be more open to accepting feedback on others' perception of them. They may even invite it, as this feedback can be valuable information that is helpful in other relationships. They are more receptive to practicing new behaviors in the group when the group feels safe. It is less risky than practicing with someone in an outside relationship.

Group experiences can be a rich source for interpersonal learning when the opportunity presents itself, and is used to constructively explore the following:

- How members are perceived by others
- Underused or unrealized inner resources
- Communication and relating behaviors and attitudes
- Feelings and other reactions aroused in other group members
- Resistance, transference, and projections
- How to capitalize on one's strengths, and reduce or eliminate undesirable behaviors and attitudes

Yalom (1995) describes the "mechanics of interpersonal learning" as the following sequence.

1. Feelings are expressed.
2. Reality is tested.
3. Dissonance occurs between personal experiencing and reality.
4. There is increased awareness of denied, suppressed, and repressed feelings.
5. The person's concept of self becomes more congruent.
6. There is increased ability to tolerate acceptance and positive regard.
7. The cycle is repeated and more learning occurs.

The sequence begins with the individual expressing feelings, usually personal in nature, and related to the person's beliefs, attitudes, values, behaviors, and so on. The feelings may be either negative or positive, and can be very intense or just mild. They may trigger responses from fellow group members. This is where the leader's expertise is needed to guide members in expressing their reactions and feelings in a manner that the receiver can hear and accept. The leader will want to block inappropriate ways of expression that will only produce defensiveness and distract from further and productive exploration by the speaker.

The reactions of fellow group members can be a form of reality testing. The speaker has access to other perspectives, which may differ from the speaker's. It can be helpful for the leader to encourage members to respond in the here and now on their experiencing or feelings as they listen to one another. These responses are opportunities for reality checks, especially when there is consensual validation for what was done or said.

Dissonance between what the speaker thinks and feels and what others hear can open the door to important interpersonal learning by providing differing perspectives, or by helping the speaker understand that what was said, what was meant, and what was heard and understood are vastly different. Following are two vignettes to illustrate reality checks and dissonance.

Clinical Vignette: Confrontation About Dissonance

The group of young adults have met for several sessions and have become wary of one member who makes off-the-wall comments, announcing that she is sensitive and does not want to be challenged or attacked, and phrasing her responses to others in such a way that any response or explanation from them would result in her charging that they were defensive or attacking. She is also inconsistent in many remarks, taking one position this minute and another position the next.

In this particular session she does the latter, and the leader intervenes and describes the inconsistency. She immediately denies being inconsistent, even in the face of the leader using direct quotes of what she said. Other members agree with the leader's quotes, and validate that she has indeed said this. The leader invites her to examine the possible effects of being inconsistent on relationships in and outside the group.

Clinical Vignette: Unclear Communication

Clair, who had considerable tragedy in her life, announced at the first group session that she was willing to listen to others, but would not share her feelings at all (this is a direct quote). She explained that she considered her feelings to be private, and she intended to keep them so. The leader did not challenge this at that time, feeling that the therapeutic relationship had not been established, and wanting to honor the rule that members were in charge of deciding what, how much, and when to self-disclose.

Several meetings later, Rose begins to challenge Claire by telling her that she, Rose, is interested in Claire's thoughts and feelings about what is taking place in the group, but does not want to push her to disclose these. Claire responds that she is willing to do this, thinks she had been doing so, and does not understand why Rose is challenging her. Rose then says that she was very aware and respectful of Claire's statement at the first session about not sharing her feelings. Claire looks surprised, and says that she was upset about being misunderstood. What she meant in the first session was that she did not want to talk about her life events, secrets, and so on, but was willing to speak of her feelings and experiencing in the group sessions. This exchange leeds to an exploration of how Claire feels she is constantly being misunderstood, and that she may not be communicating her meaning and intent clearly so that others can understand. Other group members can identify with not being clear in their communication, and feeling misunderstood.

When a person is receptive, his or her concept of self can become more congruent in the sense that he or she can perceive a part of self that was seen by others but not by himself or herself. This revealed part of self then becomes a part of the self that is seen by self and by others.

It is crucial that this sequence be guided with sensitivity and caring as you are opening the person up to unknown, and maybe even unacceptable parts of self. But the outcome can be that the person becomes better able to tolerate acceptance and positive regard where before the person was wary and skeptical, expecting criticism and blame. This step completes the sequence, and the cycle can begin again.

Socializing Techniques

One very helpful benefit for group participation is learning socializing techniques to help reduce or eliminate isolation and alienation. There are many reasons for people feeling a lack of connectedness to other people, such as the following:

- Grieving over the loss of a significant person in their lives
- Feeling different, weird, or inadequate
- Moving to a new city or neighborhood
- Being unable to form and maintain lasting and meaningful relationships
- Failing to develop social skills
- Being unable to trust others because of past experiences

All types of groups can provide some measure of this therapeutic factor even if it is only an opportunity to meet and interact with people in a structured setting. Groups that have a focus on teaching communication, relating, or social skills have the greatest impact, and longer term counseling and therapy groups have numerous opportunities to indirectly explore socializing techniques.

The relating and communication skills modeled by the leader are indirect ways to teach social skills. For example, showing group members the value of attending, acceptance, respect, and positive regard is much more powerful than just speaking about these. The membership skills that are taught and practiced in the group are also helpful. Skills such as taking responsibility for personal feelings, communicating directly and specifically, and expressing feelings are examples of group membership skills that are also helpful for encouraging the emergence of this therapeutic factor.

Another positive outcome can be helping members understand the elements of meaningful and satisfying relationships, and demonstrating the impact of these relationships on group members. Elements that can be highlighted and emphasized include:

- Mutual respect and caring
- Trust and safety
- Sensitivity and genuineness

- Spontaneity and play
- Interdependence and autonomy
- Emotional awareness and expression

Members can become more aware of their characteristic relating style, the reception and impact this style has on others, and practice new behaviors that are more constructive. Leaders need to recognize and reinforce behaviors that demonstrate that members have learned and are practicing effective socializing techniques. This too can be influential in modeling behavior for others, and is reinforcing.

Imitative Behavior

Group members will pay close attention to what the group leader does, as this is a more valid source of information about feelings and perceptions than what the group leader says. Members can learn from the modeling behavior of the group leader, and also from that of other members. It is important for the group leader to have a heightened awareness of what he or she is doing, what the behavior reflects about his or her inner state, and what is being communicated to group members. Members learn from observing the group leader, and this learning can be from intentional or unintentional, conscious or unconscious leader behaviors. This is why the personal development of the group leader is critical to prevent unintentional behavior that the leader does not want or intend to be imitated. Some examples of group leader behaviors and their unintentional communication follow.

Chapters 6, 7, and 8 emphasize the personal development of the group leaders, as this is what allows the leader to model desired behaviors. These modeled relating and communication

Behavior	Communication
Empathic failures without repair	It's acceptable to ignore others' feelings, or to minimize their concerns.
Soothing intense feelings	Others' pain cannot be tolerated; move away from it to prevent "catching" their feelings.
Ignoring or minimizing conflict	Conflict is destructive, cannot be managed or handled constructively, has only negative effects on relationships, and must be avoided at all costs.
Not disclosing feelings in a session	Avoid openness, acceptance of personal feelings, and appropriate expression of these feelings.
Handing tissues to teary members	Stop crying because I can't handle your distress.
Failure to confront	Confrontation is dangerous and to be avoided.
Ignoring a member's distress	Intense feelings are uncomfortable for me, and my needs are more important than yours.
Overuse of exercises and other activities	Don't get close to each other, don't get too deep, as the leader may not be able to manage that. Stay busy so as to not reflect on what you are experiencing.

behaviors become an integral part of the person, and are not "put on" for the group session. The genuineness then communicates itself, and group members can see and feel this.

Let's not neglect the positive aspects of members' imitative behavior, as this too can be helpful. Members can learn from other group members things like the following:

- Experiencing positive outcomes for experimenting with new behaviors when this is reported to the group
- Seeing other members get better
- Observing how other members are more effective at communicating their thoughts, feelings, ideas, needs, and so on
- Seeing that catharsis can facilitate healing, growing, and understanding of oneself
- Appropriate ways to express difficult feelings
- The pleasure and benefits of altruistic acts

Guidance

Imparting information is an important therapeutic factor, and a primary objective for educational, task, skills training, and psychoeducational groups. However, it is also a part of other types of groups and should not be neglected. Information can be helpful to clarify misconceptions, correct errors of fact, understand a process such as application for a position, learn where other needed information is located, attain new knowledge, and assist in decision making.

Less helpful is information that is disguised advice as to what a person should or ought to do or think. While knowing another member's perspective can be helpful at times, it is not helpful when it is accompanied by an unspoken demand to comply with it. This is an act the group leader must block in a way that supports both the giver and the receiver. After all, the giver is usually trying to be helpful, although there can be occasions when that person is trying to show off, or demonstrate how he or she is superior.

The group leader is not immune to giving advice, and should be careful when doing so because the leader's advice carries power and authority conferred by the position. The leader is generally perceived as more knowledgeable, competent, and capable, leading to greater unqualified acceptance of what he or she suggests or tells members to do. Refraining from advice giving can be particularly difficult for group leaders when they do have more knowledge and insight about the topic. However, leaders should also remember that information dissemination is not advice, it is factual and the member is free to accept or reject it.

Further, there are numerous ways to aid group members in getting needed information, and suggestions are provided in Chapters 6, 10 and 11.

Group Cohesiveness

Group cohesiveness is a very valuable therapeutic factor as well as a group stage that is characterized by productivity. The group is working effectively and efficiently on group and individual goals, members are appreciative of the resources of the group, interpersonal learning is facilitated as members feel safe and are more trusting, and they are taking more risks and responsibility for their growth and development. Group leaders are less active during this phase. However, this does not mean that the group leader remains detached from what is taking place. The group leader still has important tasks for this stage of group development so that it is also a therapeutic factor. Major leader tasks include the following:

- Empowering group members to become independent and to take charge of their personal progress
- Recognizing when conflict is being suppressed or ignored to maintain harmony in the group, and to bring this to the group's attention
- Highlighting members' progress and growth
- Maintaining an emotional presence as a means of identifying unspoken emotional intensity and aiding in its expression
- Reminding members of effective communication, such as empathic responses
- Suggesting how resistance and defenses can be explored
- Assisting members in recognizing when transference, projections, and/or projective identifications may be present
- Making group process commentary

Do short term non-clinical groups experience group cohesiveness? They certainly can be productive, members can grow and develop, and they can have valuable interactions. These non-clinical groups generally have a specific but narrow goal that is focused on prescribed learning. There is generally a significant educational component that emphasizes facts, and the affective and personal development component becomes secondary. This teaching–learning emphasis reduces the amount of time that can be spent on developing relationships among group members, hearing personal history, exploring unresolved family of origin issues and other unfinished business, and practicing new relating behaviors in the group. These are actions that can give members confidence and a willingness to explore difficult personal concerns in the group, which is a characteristic of group cohesiveness. This level of group cohesiveness needs time to develop, and many short-term and non-clinical groups are time bound where the duration and goal do not permit the deep and extensive level of group cohesiveness to emerge.

However, some group cohesiveness is possible where the group feels and is productive, and members are interacting with each other. The group leader can foster this level of cohesiveness by attending to the following:

- Taking time for member introductions where important personal information is disclosed that can allow members-to-make connections, to see similarities, and to begin to feel safe in the group
- Fostering member-to-member interactions instead of mainly leader responses. Try asking members to respond first such as saying, "Has anyone had a similar thought, feeling, or experience?" or "It could be helpful to (Name) if you would tell him what came to your mind as he was speaking."
- Empowering members to take charge of their self-disclosure, deciding what, when, and if to disclose, and refrain from pushing for disclosure
- Providing a group climate and norms where emotional expression is encouraged and facilitated
- Having a proper balance for the cognitive and affective group components

Summary

1. The term *group dynamics* describes the helping forces, the restraining forces, and all influences on the group and its members. Learning to recognize these dynamics as they emerge in the group can provide the group leader with valuable information about the group as a whole, individual members' needs, and suggestions for interventions.

2. Research has provided evidence on the efficacy of therapeutic factors, and most are expected to emerge in almost every type of group. Group leaders are expected to help foster the emergence and constructive use of these factors. Suggestions are provided on how they can be encouraged and used.

Chapter Activities

1. Form small groups and have members identify 8 to 10 similarities among themselves that are not characteristics such as age, gender, and educational level. Then as a class have the small groups report on their lists.

2. Prepare a list of therapeutic factors before class with enough copies for each class member. Ask them to rank each factor in order of importance for them as group members, with the most important factor being 1.

Personal Development Exercise: Develop a list of 10–15 personal strengths, your talents, and competencies. Write a sentence about each that describes your feeling about it. For example, if one item were organizational skills, you would describe one or more of your feeling about this skill.

Chapter 3

Cultural and Diversity Factors

Major Topics

1. Cultural and diversity factors in groups.
2. Developing the leader's sensitivity to cultural and diversity factors.
3. Leader strategies to attend to culture and diversity factors in the group.

Introduction

Salvendy (1999) presents some compelling reasons why therapists need to know and stay aware of cultural and diversity factors for their clients. He asserts that race and ethnic characteristics affect the following for the client:

- Diagnosis
- Assignment to a particular mode of therapy
- Transference
- Countertransference
- Establishment of the authentic relationship.

Research conducted by Whaley and Geller (2007) provides evidence that reinforces the need for knowledge and understanding of cultural factors as part of clinical judgment. They found in their analyses that African American psychiatric patients with a differential diagnosis of affective disorder and schizophrenia were misdiagnosed most of the time as schizophrenic (Strakowski et al., 1997), that race differences remain when diagnostic accuracy is controlled (Pavkov, Lewis, & Lyons, 1989; Strakowski et al., 1997), and that flawed clinical judgment occurs as a result of unawareness of cultural differences in presentation of symptoms (Neighbors, Jackson, Campbell, & Williams, 1989).

Unconscious bias and stereotyping lead to the tendency to be unintentionally insensitive, which can affect the therapeutic relationship, and the establishment of trust and safety for the group and its members; to fail to be appropriately empathic to members who are culturally different; and other such acts that impede the client's growth, development, and healing. The unconscious nature of bias and stereotyping makes them especially difficult to address because the person who holds these attitudes may be unaware of their existence. Developing cultural sensitivity and competence begins with becoming aware of one's thoughts, behaviors, and attitudes that are culturally insensitive, biased, prejudiced, and/or stereotypical. Read the following statements and silently reflect on your agreement or disagreement with them.

1. Status and achievement of White Americans are a result of their personal efforts.
2. People of color receive status and achievements as a result of affirmative action.
3. It is unintentional racism to say to someone that you don't think of them as _____ (White, Black, Hispanic, and so on).
4. Language supports a belief system of who is superior, afforded status, and worthy of deference, or who is denied status and marginalized.
5. Many people have negative beliefs about people of color.
6. Women are devalued in our society.

(References for each statement are as follows: 1. Carter, 1995; McIntosh, 1992: 2. Carter, 1995; McIntosh, 1992: 3. Ridley, 1995; 4. Morrison, 1992: 5. Dovidio and Gaetner, 2000; Steele, 1997: 6. Morrison, 1992)

Now reflect on your honesty in admitting your first thoughts and feelings when reading the statements. If you are like most everyone else, you were socialized to be polite and courteous, you want to think of yourself as open and tolerant of all people, and you tend to deny and repress the automatic feelings and thoughts that were triggered. You may even feel some embarrassment at having intolerant feelings and thoughts that you consider unacceptable, biased, and stereotypical. What research has shown is that many people do retain these thoughts about others. There seems to be a tendency to categorize, to predict behavior and character, and we unconsciously react to others on the basis of these even when we think we are reacting differently.

This chapter's goal is to increase awareness of the roles that cultural and diversity factors play in the group, how group leaders can develop more sensitivity to the impact these factors have on individual members' development and responses in the group, and to suggest leader strategies. We begin with some definitions for concepts and constructs: culture, ethnic groups, race, acculturation, prejudice, stereotyping, multiple identities, and privilege.

Definitions

Culture is defined by Theodorson and Theodorson (1969) as a social group that contains and transmits memories and values from one generation to the next. Sue, Akutsu, and Higashi (1987) expand this definition to include knowledge, beliefs, art, morals, law, behavioral patterns, and customs and habits that are the group's traditional ideas and values. Thus, in the United States as in other countries with diverse populations, there is the greater American culture, but there are also a multitude of subcultures, and group members can be a member of each, any, or all of these.

Ethnic groups, often mistakenly called racial groups, refer to minority groups that have a set of commonly-held characteristics (Salvendy, 1999). Theodorson and Theodorson (1969) propose the following characteristics for members of ethnic groups:

- Identification as different from those in the larger society
- Have distinctive customs
- Feel that they are very different as a group
- Have common features and traits among themselves
- Share religious beliefs
- Participate in mutual social activities
- Have a sense of identity affected by acculturation and marginalization

Race is defined here as a group of people united or classified together on the basis of common history, nationality, or geographic distribution, having a human genetic variation marked by specific physical characteristics common to that group. Race has become more difficult to describe and define with the advent of DNA testing, which tends to show that the variations among humans are minor; migration and intermarriage have led to individuals with multiple racial identities; and that simply using race for categorization can lead to misidentification. Further, some individuals do not wish to be categorized as belonging to a single race as that denies their other ancestry.

Acculturation is described by Alvidreq, Azocar, and Miranda (1996) as a process of psychological and social changes that occur when an individual or group is in contact with another culture, such as what happens with immigrants to the United States. The extent and level of acculturation can be seen in the following:

- Use of language, especially the language of the dominant culture
- Values incorporated from the larger culture that replace or coexist with previous values
- Beliefs about self and others
- Attitudes
- Psychological frame of reference, such as thoughts about therapy, self-disclosure, and so on
- Relational and communication skills
- Preferences, such as television programming, food, music, leisure-time activities, observance of holidays, and so on
- Cultural self-identity

Prejudice is an irrational pattern of hostility, hatred, or suspicion for a group of people. Overgeneralizations are made on the basis of incomplete or inaccurate information, leading to misperceptions that negatively influence interpersonal relations. Differences are perceived as dangerous or inferior and allow the holder of the prejudice to be contemptuous and to display a superior attitude toward the person or group. The irrational nature of prejudice makes it difficult to address.

Stereotyping is categorizing people, and permits exaggerated or even erroneous beliefs about certain categories of people. Individuals so categorized are reacted to in terms of the erroneous beliefs about the category, not as individuals, and without acknowledgment of any exceptions to the beliefs.

Multiple identities can be overlooked, and thus misunderstood as the tendency seems to be to focus on only one aspect of the person, such as skin color, which permits categorizing on the basis of perceived race. However, humans are much more complex than can be understood from a single categorization. Multiple identities refers to the person's membership or characteristics. Some identities that can be combined in various ways include age, gender, disability or none, sexual orientation, socioeconomic status, education and profession, religion or spiritual orientation, and occupation.

Privilege is an often-overlooked cultural and diversity factor. Peggy McIntosh (1988) provides a working definition that speaks of an invisible package of unearned assets that can be counted on to support one's position in society, or in the particular setting. The person who is privileged usually doesn't perceive the privilege, denies that it exists, makes unconscious use of it, and may recognize that others do experience discrimination, but does not see their own advantage(s). The power and authority position of the group leader can have unacknowledged privilege associated with the status. Lott (2002) speaks of this as unearned advantage and conferred dominance; it can have an impact on the group if unrecognized.

Diversity refers to the visible and invisible characteristics that are a function of time, genetics, life circumstance, and/or personal choice, and which can contribute to perceptions and reactions of self and of others. These are characteristics such as age, gender, sexual orientation, religion, and disability. They are also characteristics that can arouse conscious and unconscious prejudice and bias.

Culture and Diversity Awareness

Culture and diversity factors have considerable influence on human development. Roles, gender and sexual identity, class and status, race and ethnic identity, and other self-factors are all impacted by family of origin, the community, and the larger culture. Group leaders must be especially aware of and sensitive to these factors.

It is impossible to learn and understand all the relevant aspects and nuances of the culture and diversity components for every group member. For example, suppose you had a group with three Native Americans from different tribes. You could not assume that their cultures were all alike because there are over 513 Native American nations in the United States, and each nation has several tribes. Even if you studied one or more tribes in depth, you could not be sure that the cultural components were similar for all three members. The magnitude of the task of becoming culturally knowledgeable about even one culture is discussed in recent articles in the February 2006 edition of the American Psychological Association's newsletter featuring Asian American psychology. Articles presented information about risk factors for mental illness and seeking treatment (Meyers, 2006); difficulties encountered because of having two cultural identities and multiple racial identities (Tracey, 2006); the need to understand more about the variety of Asian American cultures (Munsey, 2006); and cognitive differences between East Asians and Westerners (Winerman, 2006).

There is literature available on a considerable variety of topics: multiracial (Devan, 2001), cross-cultural (Sharma, 2004), and ethnocultural (Salvendy, 1999). There is also literature that focuses on specific racial/ethnic groups; for example, Chicanas (Gloria, 1999), Asians (Cheung & Chan, 2002), Mexican Americans (Baca & Koss-Chioino, 1997), Native Americans (Colmant & Merta, 1999), and African American women (Jackson & Greene, 2000).

Multicultural Competency Models Components

Fowers and Davidov (2006) categorize the multicultural conceptualization and research models to date as having three components: knowledge, awareness, and skills. Professional organizations, such as the Association for Specialists in Group Work, the American Counseling Association, and the American Psychological Association, have adopted guidelines for multicultural competencies expected of mental health professionals. Arredondo et al. (1996) developed and presented guidelines that are organized by characteristics and dimensions. The characteristics are cultural self-awareness, awareness of other cultures, and appropriate intervention strategies. The dimensions are attitudes and beliefs, knowledge, and skills. Whaley and Davis (2007) propose that cultural competence and evidence-based practice be integrated, and advocate a culture-specific approach for treatment.

There are considerable articles and books available on these topics, but few provide specific information on how to use cultural competency in the group. The three-component model proposed by Fowers and Davidov (2007) helps frame the understandings that group leaders will need. This chapter focuses on defining the three factors as knowledge of individual development and cultural influences on growth, awareness of cultural factors that can be important when leading groups, and skills that demonstrate cultural competency.

Knowledge

Knowledge of individual development and cultural influences on growth begins with self-knowledge and understanding. A good start is to examine the cultural and diversity factors presented in Table 3.1 as they relate to you. A good exercise would be to quickly write down all the associations that come to mind when each of these components is considered. Do so without evaluating or changing what emerges as you think of the component. An in-depth exploration of your current thoughts and how they developed; the influences of your cultural environment and the larger community, nation, and world; and the impact of these during your developing years would provide you with considerable knowledge and understanding. This process would also help you gain a deeper understanding of how others may have developed and been influenced, and how the outcomes were different from yours.

Knowledge is also gained from other sources, such as books, articles, the Internet, consultants, and so on. These can give you information about other cultures, provide an understanding of diversity factors on individuals, and raise your sensitivity to these issues.

Awareness

There is considerable awareness that group leaders need to develop, both about themselves and about the impact of their cultural competence on group members. Sue et al., (2007) describe several personal awarenesses that are important for the group leader while facilitating the group.

- Awareness of oneself as a racial/cultural person
- Awareness of personal biases, prejudices, stereotypes, and assumptions that will impact relationships, such as that of the group leader with group members
- Awareness of the cultural differences that can impact group members

- Awareness of the limitations of your knowledge and understanding of culture and diversity, especially as these relate to the group
- Conscious attention to personal verbal and nonverbal communication and the impact of these
- Attention to the impact of cultural differences, verbal and nonverbal communication, and their impact among group members

How does one develop awareness? Awareness can be developed through instruction, self-exploration, meaningful contact with others who are different in culture and diversity, and with a conviction that accepting others is therapeutically sound and productive. It can be helpful to begin with an understanding of some significant group member factors that interrelate with culture and diversity.

Skills

Cultural and diversity competency *skills* are difficult to define and describe because they are the usual core counseling relational attributes and communication skills with a culture and diversity sensitivity overlay, and because they are mostly negative in the sense of what *not* to do. Further, these skills depend on awareness and knowledge, as well as continual self-examination. When you then add personal characteristics and experiences, the skill set is more confounded. It can be important for group leaders to recognize these difficulties, as they may have groups with members who have varied cultures, or some members with multiple identities.

This chapter describes the value for cultural and diversity concerns; examples for how these impact the individual, the leader, and the group's work; developmental needs for leaders; and strategies for use in groups. Many skills needed are the same as those used in basic group leadership, but are used with a heightened awareness that culture and diversity are important personal aspects for individual group members, and can affect their responsiveness to learning, growing, developing, healing, and even how they respond to the leader and to other members.

Basic attributes for cultural and diversity competencies include openness, acceptance, tolerance, and respect. It is assumed that the sensitive group leader will be aware of the possible impact of culture and diversity on members and on the group, seek out knowledge about these factors for the particular target audience, and have some education and training that incorporates culture and diversity. Self-awareness about the impact of one's personal cultural and diversity characteristics is also a part of the basic assumptions. The following attributes grow from awareness, knowledge, and personal development.

- Openness to experiencing the varied impacts of culture and diversity on the individual member with sensitivity to recognize the positive and negative aspects for that member
- Acceptance of differences as worthwhile and valid, of group members as they present themselves, and of the developmental aspects for the cultural and diversity influences for group members
- Tolerance for these differences that does not carry an evaluative aspect of their being good or bad, or of being right or wrong. Personal values and reactions are muted for therapeutic concerns

- Respect for the validity of differences in perspectives, worldview, and even values. Noticing differences, respecting these, and an ability to maintain one's personal perspectives without feeling diminished, or of needing to have others also accept them conveys respect.

There are communication skills that can also be important: active listening and responding, clarification, frequent check-ins, appropriate self-disclosure and probing, verbal recognition of meaningful differences, and linking to highlight commonalties.

- Active listening and responding conveys that the person was heard and understood. While empathic responding is best, that is not always possible but, at a minimum, group leaders can seek to provide active listening and responding.
- Clarification can be helpful, both giving and requesting it. Don't always assume that others understand, or that you, as the group leader, understand what is meant. Notice nonverbal cues that may signal a lack of understanding for group members. Ask if some additional information is needed, provide information to the members and for the benefit of other group members, and be sensitive to possible misunderstandings.
- Frequent check-ins with all group members to determine levels of understanding can help members to feel valued and understood. Don't single out the "different" member(s) for check-ins; do it for all group members, but if there are members with cultural and/or diversity differences, use the check-in more often with all group members.
- Appropriate self-disclosure and probing means that the group leader openly acknowledges confusion, lack of knowledge, and even misunderstanding, and ask questions to remedy these. Openly acknowledge that your experiences could be different, and that you want more information about their experiences to increase your understanding.
- Verbal recognition of meaningful differences can only be helpful after trust and safety are established in the group, and the meaningful differences are not surface ones or inferred. Speaking of differences too soon in the group's life can keep universality from forming, allows members to feel excluded, and sets a group climate that is unintentional.
- Linking to highlight commonalties promotes inclusion, universality, and an understanding of meaningful connections. Experiences differ for each member, but there are other commonalities regardless of culture and diversity differences. Skillful group leaders recognize how linking can promote group cohesion.

Significant Member Factors

Tables 3.1, 3.2, and 3.3 present categories with a few examples that are unique and descriptive for each group member. Each interrelates and interacts with the others. The categories include cultural and diversity factors, personality and ability characteristics, and self, family-of-origin, and past experiences factors. These examples are presented so that group leaders will not lose sight of understanding the whole person, and that members should be understood in terms of a variety of characteristics, not just for cultural and diversity concerns, although they are significant.

Table 3.1 presents cultural and diversity factors. Culture refers to the culture of origin for the individual, but this can get complicated when the individual has migrated to another country or region. It becomes very complex because the adopted culture has helped shape and form

Table 3.1

Examples of Cultural and Diversity Factors

Socioeconomic status	Racial designation, identity, and discrimination
Social class and status	Role of the family, social group, or tribe
Gender role and expectations	Religion
Expression of thoughts, ideas, and feelings	Role and reactions to authority
Individualism vs. collectivism	Language and language use
How respect is shown	Multiple racial and other identities
Ethnic identity	Disabilities
Sexual identity	

the individual, and it can be a mistake to assume that the culture from the country of origin, or the particular region of a country, should be the only consideration (Sue, 2006). There are 11 examples of *cultural factors*, each of which can affect individuals in different ways. These can be very strong determinants of how group members behave, and how they expect to be treated.

Diversity factors can also be of importance. They can contribute to the extent to which members are excluded, rejected, or included. Members may be related to as different because of visible or hidden characteristics that produce bias, stereotyping, and discrimination. And diversity factors can shape the experiences that help form the person. It is interesting to note that diversity factors are generally described in terms of how members are reacted to in negative ways; they never seem to have positive connotations.

When both cultural and diversity factors are significant for a group member, or for the group, the group leader has to be especially sensitive to their implications for the person, for possible interventions, and for the extent to which members can and will participate. It is a mistake to respond to members in terms of only one of their cultural or diversity characteristics, or to make assumptions of how these have affected individual members. Group leaders must take care to not think of members only in terms of culture and diversity.

Table 3.2 presents some general personality and ability characteristics that have been shown to be cross-cultural (Paunonen, 1996 et al., Williams & Best, 1983). Whereas some are influenced by the richness or impoverishment of the environment, others seem to be inborn and capable of only modest or no modification. For example, academic ability is influenced by the environment, but native intellectual ability is less likely to be as influenced. There is little empirical information available on the positive and negative impact of these kinds of characteristics on the individual, or sufficient information on how behavior reflects many of them.

Table 3.2

Examples of Personality and Ability Characteristics

Intellectual and academic ability	Creativity, imagination, and the like
Extroversion-introversion	Ambition, perseverance, and determination
Learning style	

Information about these characteristics could be important to the group leader, and when assessment is conducted as part of screening, gathering information about these characteristics could be a part of that process. The resulting information could provide the group leader with valuable information about the group member, help form realistic expectations for participation and understanding, and suggest possibilities for interventions.

Table 3.3 shows examples for self characteristics and family-of-origin and past experiences. The core self of the individual refers to the person's self-perception of his or her efficacy, worth, and value, and the degree of emotional and other *self characteristics* development. Some personal characteristics are known to the person, others are seen only by other individuals, and yet other personal characteristics remain hidden from both the person and others. These are cross-cultural characteristics that impact all external experiences interacting with innate individual characteristics.

Family-of-origin experiences are also cross-cultural and include the quality and kind of experiences encountered in one's family of origin. The earliest relationships that helped form self-perceptions of ability, worth, efficacy, and the like are significant components of self-development. Although some groups, such as psychoeducational groups, tend to not focus on or emphasize family of origin experiences, these still have an enormous impact on the development of the person. In counseling and psychotherapy groups these variables are an integral part of understanding the members.

Past experiences play an important role in forming the person and contribute significantly to reactions, thoughts, perceptions of self and of others, the quality of relationships, current reactions and relationships, and so on. These are especially strong contributors to the ability and facility to initiate, establish, and maintain meaningful and satisfying relationships.

Table 3.3
Examples of Self Characteristics and Family-of-Origin, and Past Experiences Factors

Self Characteristics

Self-confidence	Self-esteem
Self-efficacy	Level of self-absorption
Emotional regulation and control	

Family-of-Origin Experiences

Acceptance and approval	Empathic responding
Parental messages about worth, value	Sibling relationships
Parental disorders and stress	Childhood trauma
Parental narcissism	

Past Experiences with Relationships

Acceptance-rejection	Trust-betrayal
Safety-danger	Nurturing-cold
Valued-devalued	Meaningful-meaningless
Enduring-transitory	Intimate-surface

Steps to Develop Greater Awareness and Sensitivity

Although the complexity of culture, diversity, and other concerns can be daunting, developing sensitivity to cultural and diversity concerns can be accomplished. I propose four steps:

- Understanding the visible differences
- Recognizing that there are hidden differences that may be significant and that making these visible can be helpful
- Engaging in leader self-preparation with attention to specific leader tasks
- Using the strategies designed to promote knowledge, understanding, and sensitivity

Visible differences are usually the first to be noticed and highlighted. Some cultural and diversity characteristics can be easily identified because of their prominence and visibility. Examples of these are age, gender, race/ethnicity, and overt physical disabilities. But, even some of these can be misleading, and group leaders should take care to not make too many assumptions based on visible characteristics.

Further, some group members may prefer that their visible differences not be emphasized, whereas others want some acknowledgment of them. Group leaders need to carefully examine their personal reactions to visible differences to be fully accepting and empathic. There are numerous unconscious biases and prejudices that have potential for negatively affecting the therapeutic relationship.

Indirect or hidden differences are cultural and/or diversity factors that are important for that person, but may not be readily apparent when you look at the person. For example, it is not apparent what religion, if any, is important for a person unless he or she is wearing a symbol that identifies it as such. Other less visible differences are sexual preference or orientation; values, such as the role of the family; and meaning attribution for experiences such as being self-induced, brought on by fate, or random.

A difference may be important for one person but not for another with the same or similar difference. So, it is essential that a group leader not make assumptions. It is much more helpful to ask—to let the person reveal, in his or her own time and way, its presence and importance. Group leaders must be sensitive to possibilities that there are hidden and indirect differences, but not jump to conclusions about them and their influences on group members.

Leader's self-preparation and tasks are essential parts of cultural and diversity sensitivity and competence. Group leaders need to engage in self-examination about all of the following:

- Preconceived assumptions about culture and diversity
- Possible stereotypes they may have
- Conscious and unconscious biases and prejudices
- Unconscious assumptions about the value and worth of others' differences
- Meaning attribution for their experiences

In addition, it would be helpful for group leaders to learn about other cultures, the impact of diversity factors on individuals, and to seek out resources to be available for consultation.

A significant part of the leader's preparation and training for cultural and diversity sensitivity is an understanding of his or her own culture and its impact on forming the leader's beliefs, attitudes, values, and behavior. This self-exploration can help increase awareness of how different cultures produce different effects, which can lead to greater appreciation and acceptance. Another helpful action is to receive instruction and experiences that provide cognitive and affective learning about various cultures and diversity, and how to work therapeutically with these differences. It can be most helpful to build personal cultural and diversity contacts and networks as both enriching for you personally, and as consultation resources.

All of this preparation is done without knowing what cultures and/or diversity will be encountered in future group leadership experiences. The desired and possible outcomes for the preparation are supportive of the leader's tasks for the following:

- Promoting feelings of safety for all members
- Increasing inclusion of those who are culturally different
- Demonstrating and modeling respect, caring, and concern
- Reducing feelings of alienation, isolation, or of being different
- Increasing the emergence for the therapeutic factor of universality

It can be helpful to keep in mind that the leader has the primary responsibility for facilitating change without offending the cultural and diversity sensitivities of group members, to protect the "different" group member from insensitivity and bias wherever possible in the group, to promote inclusion, and to model tolerance and acceptance.

Leader Strategies

Preparation for the leader can do much to help reduce culture shock, and the leader who has an openness to learning about other cultures and diversity is well on the way to developing cultural and diversity sensitivity and competence. There are some specific leader strategies that can help demonstrate this sensitivity and competence, convey respect and positive regard, and reduce feelings of being different or alien. Such strategies include:

- Limit information
- Check for clarity and understanding
- Use open-ended questions
- Use simple words
- Ask them for information
- Understand cultural taboos and sensitivities
- Find a cultural or diversity mentor
- Pay attention to culturally derived customs such as greetings, use of time, formalities, and nonverbal gestures

Limiting information to that which members can absorb is fundamental for nonclinical groups, but can be particularly important for those who are culturally different, or whose native or usual language is not Standard English, such as group members born in the United States where English is not the language of choice at home. This simply means that the leader should pay attention to the amount of material that is presented, and attend to the members' capacities for absorbing the information.

Checks for clarity and understanding can help guide the leader in knowing what information is being absorbed and understood, and what is not. This is a good and necessary step for all groups, but can be particularly helpful when one or more group members are from a different culture. Terms, concepts, and ideas can be misunderstood or imperfectly understood, especially when trying to absorb new information. Frequent checking with the entire group is a good idea.

Open-ended questions permit responses that can be more informative and revealing. The answers are richer and can disclose much more about the responder that can be helpful to group leaders who want to tailor the group experiences for individual members. Closed questions reduce the amount of information, and do not provide clues for extensions and explorations because the answers to these effectively end data gathering.

Leaders should use *simple words* to increase the receivers' understanding, reduce frustration, and to keep communication clearer and unambiguous. The material presented needs to be reviewed for jargon and difficult and complex concepts; and descriptions, illustrations, explanations, and the like should be substituted. Leaders may not know the educational level or academic abilities of group members in advance, must plan that group members are unfamiliar with the material, and should present it in as simple a way as possible. Doing so may be especially important when the native language of one or more members is something other than English.

It can be helpful to ask culturally different group members for *information* that would assist the leader to be respectful of them, but does not highlight their differences. Each person is unique and different so that it is best to remember that some members will want their differences openly acknowledged, whereas others will want to blend in and not stand out. Restrict any probing for information to those times when it appears that you are not understanding, or are misunderstanding, their input. These members should not become the focus of the group, and peppered with questions because they are different.

Understand cultural taboos and sensitivities because they are means for unintentional offenses and insults. Each culture has these and, unconsciously or consciously, they affect individuals. Some examples follow about how customary actions in the United States can be offensive to people from other cultures (Acuff, 1993).

- Asking personal questions about private lives (Belgium)
- Discussing religion or social conditions (Hungary)
- Refering to yourself as an American (Brazil)
- Making the okay sign with the thumb and index finger forming a circle (Brazil)
- Showing the sole of the shoe or foot (Indonesia, Middle East)
- Touching people on the head (Singapore)
- Giving compliments (South Korea)

Where possible, it can be extremely helpful to find a *cultural mentor*—someone from the same nation, country, region, tribe, and so on as the group member. This can be difficult to do, but there are alternatives to locating a mentor. There can be people in the community who are somewhat knowledgeable about the culture, such as university professors who majored in that language and culture or who are from that culture, retired military and spouses who lived there and learned about it, and others. It also may be possible to get a cultural mentor via the Internet. In all instances, the leader must be careful to maintain confidentiality when consulting with a cultural mentor.

Attend to culturally derived customs because group members have probably internalized and are unconsciously acting on them, or they are part of the members' conscious expectations. Customs, when different, can be a source for unintentional offense and insults. Examples include greetings, use of time, formalities (also termed role orderliness and conformity), and nonverbal gestures.

Learn the various customs for greetings, the expectations for how these are initiated, and what is respectful. Who is supposed to initiate the greeting? This is not consistent across regions in the United States for native-born citizens, and when you add the cultural overlay of other countries and cultural expectations to these, you can have even more options. For example, I once asked my class of graduate students about initiating greetings. We then had a lively discussion about how these differences led to feelings of being offended for newcomers to the area, how expectations differed, and how these differences were never discussed elsewhere. This is a relatively minor point, but could be very important when the leader first meets group members and unintentionally offends by the way he or she greets the members.

Use of time also varies, and can be a source of confusion and misunderstanding. Some may even be offended on occasion. Some cultures have a flexible perception about time, and consider that there are no firm boundaries. Here in the United States we've come to expect firm time boundaries for the greater culture. The expectations are to arrive on or near the designated time and even the designated day, and to respect the agreed or posted ending time. It can be disconcerting to those who have a more flexible perception of time, as they unconsciously think that others share this perception, and they continue to arrive late or not at all believing that this is acceptable. It can be difficult to adjust, and group leaders need to be aware of the cultural differences for use of time.

Formalities convey respect and should not be ignored or overlooked. They can be especially important for building trust and safety in the group, as group leaders don't need the added unspoken resistance that could result when members are offended and feel disrespected. You can begin to appreciate the importance of formalities if you stop and recall when your expectations were ignored or overlooked. Most likely you suppressed your feelings and tried to move on. However, it is those little offenses that color our perceptions and reactions, and the same will happen for your group members. You may think that group members should know that you have good intentions, but they may or may not believe this, and still have negative feelings when their expectations of formalities are not met.

Examples of formalities include who is greeted first (Greece), handing out of business cards (Japanese), flowery language (Middle East), ritualistic manners (Korea), and who is empowered to make promises and decisions (China).

Nonverbal communications are a virtual minefield for offending and miscommunicating. In terms of culture and diversity, "nonverbal communication is critical in decoding rites, gestures, forms of politeness, the concept of 'face,' silence, and pauses" (Acuff, 1993). Thus, a group leader has to be knowledgeable of the meanings of nonverbal communication not only in the larger society but also in many U.S. subcultures as well as cultures from other countries.

Simple acts, such as handshakes, breaking a silence or not allowing enough time for someone to respond, and personal physical space can offer opportunities for misunderstandings. It is important that you become aware of your nonverbal communication, and learn something about nonverbal communication for other cultures.

A Leader Strategy for Handling Incidents

Given the complexity and pervasiveness of cultural and diversity factors, group leaders must be prepared to have incidents arise in group sessions. These can be biased, stereotypical, or prejudicial comments, insensitive comments and questions, and discriminatory statements. Collins and Pieterse (2007) provide the basics for a procedure that can be used or adapted that is derived from their critical incident analysis based training (CIABT). The basic procedure is a "reflective examination of the incident," explored on the cognitive and affective levels designed to promote transformational learning. The goal is to have group members increase their knowledge and awareness of their beliefs and attitudes, increase awareness and understanding of the impact of the incident and the implications on the person, and to do so in a nonthreatening way that is affirming to all involved, including the leader.

What usually happens is that a comment is made, a question asked, or some other action that signals discrimination, bias, racism, or stereotyping. The incident produces the typical reactions—awkwardness, uncertainty, denial, a need to appear aware, and the experience of being silenced. Awkwardness results from the awareness that something offensive to someone has occurred, and social convention dictates that it should not be acknowledged as that would not be polite and courteous. Uncertainty occurs because group members, and sometimes the group leader, are in doubt as to what to do: Let it go or acknowledge it. If addressed, sometimes the member will deny that the comment has any importance or impact and not be willing to admit that it was hurtful or offensive. Other members can also deny that they were affected in any way, and the speaker can become defensive, saying that any hurt or offense was unintentional. The receiver then is in the position of having to sit with their distress, the speaker can feel blamed and is resentful of having the possible impact of the remark pointed out, and other group members become very uncomfortable. This could be an opportunity for more open discussion, or could be so uncomfortable that everyone wants to get away from the topic. However, the member who was hurt or offended continues to sit with these feelings.

Some group members may have a need to be perceived as aware, or to think of themselves as aware, caring, unbiased, and so on. These people will rush to rescue the receiver and to smooth over the incident. The experience of being silenced happens to both the sender and the receiver. The sender can easily get an idea that the group is not accepting of the comment or other action, and that he or she is unacceptable. Therefore, other such beliefs and attitudes can be suppressed rather than being explored with the possibility of transformation to something more tolerant and accepting. The receiver can be silenced by receiving too much comforting, not enough support or empathy, or by not receiving any empathy at all.

Barriers that can affect group members' responses and actions include the following in addition to the socialization barriers:

- Blame—toward the victim, society, the culture, and/or the self
- A need for approval and liking that reduces genuineness and self-disclosure
- Self-absorption where there is lack of empathy, and self is the center

- Fear of destruction if one's real attitudes and feelings were to be expressed
- Fear of abandonment for being different, or for having a different perspective
- Despair, hopelessness, and helplessness to effect changes that would reduce or eliminate discrimination, stereotyping, and so on

Basic Critical Incident Analysis Based Training

The four steps proposed by Collins and Pieterse (2007) are acknowledgment, confrontation, reflection, and commitment. *Acknowledgment* that something important occurred is a necessary first step to bring the incident to the attention of the group. This involves a certain amount of risk, as it will be an uncomfortable topic that many would just as soon dismiss. *Confrontation* is the agreement of group members to analyze the incident, explore their feelings and attitudes, and to express their negative effect triggered by the incident and the discussion. This can be a challenging step because there are many potential pitfalls for the group and the members. The group leader's expertise is of vital importance for this step. *Reflection* focuses on understanding causes for the incident, patterns of behavior and interactions, and the impact on all involved, the participants and the observers. It is through this step that group members can begin to understand their reactions and the impact of these on others, cultural and diversity misconceptions and prejudice, and can begin to explore other reactions and alternatives. The final step is *commitment*, which involves acknowledging the need to understand better, appreciate and respect others, and commit to being open around this topic.

The CIABT procedure has many positive aspects, and would be very useful with groups that have attained cohesion, or are the end of stage 2. It demands a great deal of self-awareness, risk taking, and genuineness, characteristics that will not be present for some group members or for some groups. They will have to be built before this procedure can be safely undertaken. It probably would not be advisable to undertake CIABT in the first stage of group, or before the group leader has established trust and confidence in group members for his or her competence.

Building on the CIABT Procedure

What I propose here is that there be additional steps that build on the CIABT procedure. The additional steps are part of a decision-making model that is preliminary to the first step in the CIABT procedure, that of acknowledgment. These preliminary steps are part of the cultural competence of the group leader:

1. Recognition
2. Internal processing of event
3. Observation of impact on the sender and the receiver
4. Verbal and nonverbal reactions of other group members
5. Stage of group development
6. Decision process about possible intervention
7. Procedure if the decision is to have an immediate intervention

The group leader needs to *recognize* the incident or event as microaggression, bias, stereo-typing, or racially or otherwise biased. The group leader has to be sensitive to these incidents as they are not always blatant, can be overlooked or minimized as unimportant, or could be overreactions. The leader's internal reactions and the impact on him or her is a valuable source of information as to the severity of the incident, what the receiver or other members may be experiencing, and a clue for intervention.

It is critical that the group leader *observe the impact* on the sender and on the receiver. Most often, the sender is unaware that the incident has occurred, can feel that he or she is only expressing what others are thinking and feeling, and is insensitive to the impact on the receiver. Many times the sender was not targeting another group member, and this can be even harder to deal with effectively.

Observe the impact on other group members. They too are impacted in some way. Be sure to observe their verbal and nonverbal behavior as both are part of the messages. Notice changes in behavior, indices of awkwardness, a need to change topics or smooth over the incident, shifting body and eye positions, and other such signals.

The stage of group development will be very important in the decision-making process. As noted before, if the group is in stage 1, sufficient trust and safety may not have been established so that members will feel free to openly express their genuine thoughts, ideas, and feelings, or to be receptive to exploring the sensitive topic as outlined in the CIABT procedure. If the group is in the early part of stage 2, the leader may find it difficult to proceed as members are seeking independence from the leader, and the leader's intervention could be perceived as punishing, defensive, and the like, where members will then shut down, or considerable conflict could emerge among them and with the leader. It's already uncomfortable enough without adding an issue that does not have to be addressed at this point. If the group is in the latter part of stage 2 moving to the cohesive stage, this could signal that it could handle the sensitivity about the incident.

The decision-making process would involve the leader's internally working through questions such as the following:

- What is the severity of the incident on the members' and the group's progress?
- Are the group members emotionally able to handle a confrontation or an exploration of the incident? Are they emotionally fragile, or strong?
- Would it be best to address this immediately, or to delay until the group is more firmly established and cohesive?
- Would an intervention silence one or more group members?
- How can I, the group leader, be supportive of members and encourage open and honest expression of thoughts, feelings, and ideas; affirm acceptance and tolerance; reduce discomfort; and block attacks, scapegoating, rescuing, rationalizing, and other defenses?

If the decision is to have an immediate intervention, the following can be used as a guide:

- Sensitively and tactfully state what the incident was, its impact on you the leader, and possible impact on relations in the group.
- Empathize with both the sender and the receiver. What message about self and others did the sender seem to mean to send, and what message was projected to be received by the receiver?
- Ask other group members to speak openly of their reactions, thoughts, feelings, and the like.

- Do not allow the incident to be laughed away, minimized, or dismissed as trivial or minor.
- Block apologies; the receiver should not be put in a position of taking care of the sender of the offense even if this was unintentional. It would be more helpful if the receiver were to state his or her reactions, and so on and other group members do the same. Apologies can be offered later if so desired. Sometimes understanding is more affirming than an apology.
- Use the incident as a metaphor for interpersonal relations in the group, such as inclusion versus exclusion, safety versus danger, group members' similarities versus their differences.

Summary

1. Cultural and diversity factors are extremely important, and group leaders are encouraged to develop the needed knowledge, sensitivity, and competencies that will recognize and respect these factors. Presented in this chapter were a rationale for cultural and diversity competence, strategies that group leaders can use for their personal development and for facilitating groups where these factors appear, and a process to use when incidents occur in the group. Group leaders are encouraged to keep their minds open to the many possibilities that cultural and diversity factors bring to the group, and to capitalize on these for the benefit of all group members.

2. It is helpful for group leaders to do and be the following:
   - Don't generalize about members within an ethnic/racial population, as there is considerable variation among members of the same population.
   - Communicate respect and acceptance for group members in a way that they can understand.
   - Build basic trust, mutual understanding, and respect among group members before using an intervention around cultural and diversity factors.
   - Demonstrate empathy, tolerance, cultural and diversity sensitivity, and appropriate self-disclosure.
   - Develop credibility by conceptualizing a member's problems in a manner congruent with his or her culture, but only after ensuring what the member's culture is.
   - Continue to develop personal cultural and diversity competence.

Chapter Activities

Following are two group scenes. Assume that the group has been meeting for some time, and that some measure of cohesion has developed. Decide for each if it is an incident that should be immediately addressed in the group, and describe what you would do or say as the leader for either decision.

1. An African American woman turns to another member with whom she had an earlier disagreement and asks him if he self-identifies as Jewish. (He had told the group that he was adopted by Jewish parents earlier.) He refuses to respond.

2. The group is meeting after a tragic event has occured in the community where an undocumented immigrant from Colombia rear-ended a car stopped at a stoplight, killing both young women in the car. The newspaper reported that he had a blood-alcohol level over double that for a DUI offense. Group members are discussing the tragedy, with some members incensed about the immigrant's illegal status. One group member announces that she is part Hispanic, although that cannot be determined from her appearance.

Personal Development Exercise: Draw a scene or abstraction that depicts all of your cultural and/or diversity characteristics. Write a short explanation of your drawing.

Chapter 4

Ethics, Professional Standards, and Legal Concerns

Major Topics

1. Overview of ethical decision-making models.
2. An in situ ethical decision-making model.
3. Examples of ethical dilemmas.
4. Major ethical principles applied to group work:
   a. Professional preparation
   b. Relationship standards and ethics
   c. Privacy and confidentiality
   d. Technology and documentation
   e. Professional boundaries
   f. Professional practice
   g. Duties to report, warn, and protect

Introduction

Ethics and professional standards are the rules of conduct governing the members of a professional organization that define the system of moral principles and define good or right behavior. Legal concerns refer to the federal, state, and local laws that apply to professions. All mental health professionals have ethical standards that they are expected to know and abide by, as these standards guide counselors and protect clients. Professionals are also expected to be familiar with the federal, state, and local laws that relate to their practice and professional performance. However, little is provided in the literature that focuses on ethics for groups. The information presented in this chapter was developed from the ethical standards for the American Group Psychotherapy Association (AGPA), the National Organization for Human Services (NOHS),

Table 4.1
Categorized Ethics, Legal, and Professional Standards

Relationship	**Professional Boundaries**
Informed consent	Dual relationships
Do no harm	Sexual relationships
Freedom to exit	**Professional Practice**
Impairment	Screening
Privacy	Standards and qualifications
Confidentiality	Use of techniques
Privilege	Use of technology
HIPAA	
Records, documentation	
Technology	
Duties to Warn	
Risk management	
Abuse: elder, children	
Domestic violence	
Crimes	
AIDS/HIV	
Colleagues' unprofessional conduct	
Suicide or homicide	

the American Psychological Association (APA), the Association for Specialists in Group Work (ASGW) of the American Counseling Association (ACA), and the National Association of Social Workers (NASW). The focus here is on the general ethics common across professions that guide ethically and professionally responsible group leaders. Table 4.1 shows categories for ethics, legal, and professional standards.

We begin by presenting ethical decision-making models, an in situ ethical decision-making model for use with groups, categories and descriptions for ethical principals and standards of practice that seem most applicable to groups, and suggestions for responsible and professional protection for group leaders.

Ethical Decision-Making Models

Table 4.2 presents an overview of five decision-making models from the literature. Models presented have between 4 (Nystul, 2006) to 10 steps (Welfel, 2002). All models have the following in common: identifying the problem, consulting, and generating a course of action. Hill and colleagues (1995) and Nystul (2006) do not specifically list referring to ethics, standards, or laws as a step, although this is certainly implied. All describe a systematic process to guide the thinking about an ethical dilemma. Basically, these decision-making processes involve the following steps used in general decision making (Johnson & Johnson, 2006).

- Identifying the problem or issue
- Gathering information about the existence of the problem or issue
- Formulating and considering alternative solutions
- Deciding on a solution
- Implementing the solution
- Evaluating the outcomes of implementation

Corey, Corey, and Callanan (2003) add the steps of reviewing ethics, knowing laws and regulations, and consulting to the basic decision model, but omit the evaluating step. Forester-Miller and Davis (1996) add applying the ACA's code to their steps, omit consulting, and list evaluating prior to implementing. Hill et al. (1995) use all the steps in the basic model, but include consulting and reflecting steps. Welfel (2002) begins the process with developing ethical sensitivity, adds the steps of referring to professional standards and laws, searching out ethics scholarship, consulting with supervisor and peers, and informing supervisor and taking action. Nystul (2006) has only four steps in his model, but adds addressing contextual issues such as culture and personal bias. He also proposes two different consultations when needed, one with a legal consultant and one with a supervisor.

All such models omit specific references to potential impact on the client, and in the case of groups or families, on others who are present when the decision is implemented. Further, no mention is made of the current physical, mental, and/or emotional state of the counselor or group leader, of monitoring countertransference as part of decision making, or who should be primary as the recipient—for example, the presenting client or group member, the agency, the court, or the general public could all be potentially impacted or harmed.

Barnett, Rosenthal, and Koocher (2007) provide a helpful list of questions to ask yourself when facing an ethical dilemma.

- Will the client be helped?
- Will anyone be harmed? This can be especially important when leading a group because the decision made will affect all group members.
- Who has my obligation or allegiance in the current situation?
- Will my decision lead to greater dependency on me?
- Is what I propose to do consistent with how others treat their clients?
- Is there a possibility that I am impaired? (Insufficient attention to my health, emotional, and/or cognitive well-being)

Table 4.2
Ethical Decision-Making Models

Ethical Decision-Making Models

Hill, Glaser, & Harden (1995)

1. Recognize problem
2. Define problem
3. Consult
4. Develop solutions
5. Consult if needed
6. Choose a solution
7. Review process
8. Implement plan and evaluate
9. Reflect

Forester-Miller & Davis (1996)

1. Identify problem
2. Apply ACA code
3. Determine nature of dilemma
4. Generate potential actions
5. Consider consequences
6. Evaluate course of action
7. Implement plan and evaluate
8. Reflect

Welfel (2002)

1. Develop ethical sensitivity
2. Define dilemma and options
3. Refer to professional standards
4. Examine relevant laws and regulations
5. Search out ethics scholarship
6. Apply ethical principle to situation
7. Consult with supervisor and peers
8. Deliberate and decide
9. Inform supervisor and take action
10. Reflect

Corey, Corey, & Callanan (2003)

1. Identify problem
2. Identify potential issues
3. Review ethics
4. Know laws and regulations
5. Consult

Table 4.2
Ethical Decision-Making Models
(*Continued*)

6. Consider possible actions and recourse
7. List possible consequences
8. Decide

Ethical–legal Decision-Making Models

Nystul (2006)

1. Determine issue
2. Address contextual issues such as culture and personal bias
3. Formulate an ethical–legal course of action
   - legal consultation
   - supervisor consultation
4. Implement action plan

In Situ Ethical Decision-Making Model

Although all of these models have merit, another deficit is that none address real-time ethical decision making that is likely to occur during group sessions. A model that does address real-time decision making was proposed by Stephenson and Staal (2007). They developed the model for application in operational psychology, a subdivision of military psychology. According to the authors, operational psychology is "the use of psychological principles and skills to improve a commander's decision making as it pertains to combat (or related operations)" (p. 61). They are referring to the support and services psychologists provide for direct action support during combat operations, intelligence collection activities, military strategy development, information operations, psychological operations, indirect assessment and profiling, and interrogation and detention operations. Using psychological services under combat conditions, or even preparing for them, can produce complex ethical dilemmas.

Stephenson and Staal's model shares some of the same characteristics as are encountered in group therapy, and their naturalistic decision making (NDM) model provides some suggestions for the in situ model. Both approaches recognize the contributions from Orasanu and Connolly (1995), who defined eight factors that describe naturalistic decision making.

- *Ill-structured problems*—the problem is not clear and unambiguous.
- *Uncertain dynamic environment*—the group is dynamic, members' emotional states shift and change during the course of a group session, and the impact of the dilemma and/or the possible decision is in doubt.
- *Shifting, ill-defined, or competing goals*—who is the primary client, how can the group be saved from harm, is the best thing the right thing to do under the circumstances, are all questions that make the goal hard to pin down.
- *Action and feedback loops*— the support and input of supervisors, other professionals, and even reference sources are not available at the moment.

- *Time stress*—many of these decisions cannot be delayed for consultation and research, and/or the messages sent to all group members may be difficult to overcome, or can become impaired with a delay.
- *High stakes*—the consequences for the decision are urgent and important.
- *Multiple players*—there are numerous others that may be affected by the decision, such as other group members, family members, other professionals, the court, and even the public at large.
- *The organizational goals and norms*—these are factors in the decision-making process and these can be complex and complicating to an already complex matter. Instant decisions have to be made about whose goals and norms receive priority in the current situation.

Also embedded in Stephenson and Staal's (2007) model are the steps from Klein's (1999) recognition-primed decision (RPD) model: situation recognition, serial option evaluation, and mental stimulation. Situation recognition refers to categorizing the ethical dilemma as typical or novel. If typical, then the person should have a set of options that have been thought through and decisions about what to do finalized. If the situation is novel, the person moves to the serial option evaluation, that of generating alternative actions. Mental stimulation refers to the thought processes that assess the probability of success or failure for the different alternatives. What is very helpful is the proposed evaluation of alternatives across four dimensions—safety, legality, ethics, and effectiveness.

Incorporating these concepts, thoughts, and suggestions leads to the in situ real-time decision-making model process that includes the following assumptions:

- Identification of a problem emerging during the session that may have ethical and/or legal ramifications.
- An immediate response or action is needed and/or therapeutically desirable.
- The group leader's response or other action may affect more than one group member and/or the viability of the group as a whole can be affected by the response or action, or the lack of either.

There are three steps listed for most other models that cannot be implemented for real-time ethical decision making. These can be used when the action or response can be delayed, and the delay is therapeutically responsible.

1. Review ethics, laws, and professional standards.
2. Consult experts, supervisor, and colleagues.
3. Review process for possible actions prior to implementation.

There are two major sections to the process—preparation and real-time process.

I. Preparation—a part of training, and with frequent review and update.
   1. Federal laws, such as HIPAA
   2. State laws and professional regulations for counselors
   3. The professional organization's code of ethics and standards of practice

    4. The institution's policies, procedures, and the like, such as schools, agencies, and hospitals

    5. An ethical decision-making process

II. Real-Time Process—all described steps are performed mentally, except step 8

    1. Notice or identify problem that emerged in the group.

    2. Relate the appropriate ethical or professional standard, or a law to the problem.

    3. Review potential responses and/or actions.

    4. Associate each potential response and/or action with the applicable ethic, law, or standard including an option of no response.

    5. List pros and cons for each potential response or action.

      a. Evaluate each option's adherence to the ethic, standard, or law.

      b. Judge the possible impact or outcome for the individual member.

      c. Judge the possible impact or outcome for other group members.

      d. Judge the possible impact or outcome for the viability and functioning of the group.

    6. Monitor countertransference and personal motive(s).

    7. Select a response or action that fulfills the following:

      a. It is ethically responsible, or legally sound, and meets professional standards.

      b. It does not appear to be harmful to the group member, or other group members or to the group as a whole.

      c. The response or action is therapeutically helpful.

      d. The response or action can be implemented.

    8. Implement the selected response.

    9. Monitor reactions of all group members.

   10. After the session, write case notes that describe the decision-making process you used, and the outcomes or reactions.

Preparation cannot be overemphasized. Group leaders should be knowledgeable about the ethics, laws, and professional standards that affect their group work so that they do not have to research these when situations occur in the group that demand an immediate response. Although there are many steps in the real-time decision-making process, they can be accomplished because, you can think very fast. It is essential that group leaders monitor their countertransference and/or personal motives when pondering which alternative to select. The guiding principles are to do no harm, and to be clinically and therapeutically responsible.

Examples of Ethical Dilemmas

Following are four group situations that present ethical dilemmas. Read these and apply any one ethical decision model, then discuss the choices and the application of the model. Suggested applications for the in situ model to these dilemmas are presented at the end of the chapter.

1. *The group for children had met for four sessions when the group leader brought a new member in and introduced him to the group. As part of the introduction, the leader told group members that the new member was depressed because of his father's leaving the family. The group leader obtained this information during the screening process and had suggested that he tell this to the group. The new member said that he would think about it, and matters were left there. He did not give the group leader his decision.*

2. *Five therapists from a mental health agency went to lunch at a restaurant, and began discussing some cases they had that were presenting difficulties. They were careful to not use names of clients. One therapist who was leading a group of young adults being treated for alcohol abuse described one group member who was extremely resistant. Another therapist remarked that she knew the person as she had done the intake on him.*

3. *The leader of an adolescent group comprised of court-mandated attendees tried hard to encourage group interaction and participation, but members continued to resist. One member in particular was sullenly silent during sessions, even when he was invited to provide input. His behavior was affecting other members, and during the current session they were very open and vocal about their displeasure. He finally stood up and angrily said that he was leaving the group. The group leader proposed that he stay and try to work things out with the other group members, but he left the room. The leader reported the event to the court.*

4. *The group leader personally benefited from the empty chair technique demonstrated in one of his graduate counseling classes, and decided to use it in his group.*

Professional Preparation and Competence

Professional preparation requires successful completion of prescribed coursework in a formal academic program, such as counseling, psychology, social work and psychiatry, practica, and supervised internship and residency programs at a minimum. Specialties require coursework and supervised practice beyond the minimum. It is ethically responsible to practice within the scope of your competence, which is based on knowledge, skills, supervised practice, and the context within which you work.

Bennett et al. (2006) specify areas of competence for practice as emotional competence, competence with diverse populations, and conscientious further education. Emotional competence refers to the therapist's emotional and psychological state. Personal problems, compassion fatigue, and burnout can lead to using impaired clinical judgment, disrespecting clients, neglecting symptoms, and other such reduction of competence. Competence with diverse populations is self-explanatory, but needs emphasizing because the importance of cultural and diversity factors for therapeutic effectiveness continues to be highlighted in the research. Conscientious further education can be accomplished in a variety of ways, and most licenses require a minimum number of continuing education or educational credits each year for license maintenance. Reading the professional literature, attending workshops, and enrolling in formal training programs are examples of how professional preparation can be maintained.

Relationship Standards and Ethics

Informed consent refers to providing group members with sufficient information so that they are able to evaluate the personal risks and benefits for the proposed group. Group members have a right to know this information in advance of participation. Basic information needed for informed consent includes the following:

1. Purpose and goals for the group
2. Techniques to be used
3. General procedures
4. Potential risks and gains for participation
5. The group leader's credentials
6. Screening procedures when these are used
7. Consent forms and treatment plans (Burlingame, Fuhriman, & Johnson, 2001)

This information can be provided in writing, such as a brochure or as part of the consent form, or verbally such as during the screening process. The information is also provided to parents and/or guardians of children and adolescents who must give legal consent for participation, and this must be completed prior to the group's beginning.

When possible, pregroup preparation sessions should be held to detail expectations, techniques that will be used, the ethical and legal responsibilities of the group leader, documentation and needs for reporting, and the limits of confidentiality. Pregroup sessions have been shown to be valuable in helping reduce group members' fears and anxieties, and providing safety for the group and its members.

Freedom to exit gives members the right to leave the group at any time. It is assurance that they will not be forced to remain in the group against their will. This seems reasonable, and group leaders want to provide this option. However, there are penalties for some group members that can make leaving the group not a viable choice. Examples include court-mandated participation, training groups that are part of educational and degree programs, and task groups for the work environment. Yes, members can leave, but the consequences may be so negative that they feel forced to remain. Group leaders need to understand and practice freedom to exit, to not try to force members to remain in the group, and to let it be the member's decision to remain or to leave.

Impairment is anything, such as a condition or disease, that interferes with the group leader's ability to provide professional and responsible treatment. An impaired group leader puts members and the group at risk of being harmed, and of failing to receive proper care and treatment. For example, alcohol abuse can lead to impaired cognitive functioning and judgment. This impairment can cause the group leader to miss or misinterpret clues and signs for intervention, or when a group member is experiencing unspoken or suppressed emotional distress, or fail to make effective interventions in other group situations. There are other conditions and diseases that lead to impaired cognitive functioning where the results would also be detrimental to the group.

The group leader has an ethical responsibility to monitor his or her physical, mental, and emotional condition and actions for signs of impairment, and to take action to address these, including self-reporting to the supervisor or licensing board. Failure to do so can lead to being less effective as a group leader or even doing harmful things, and failing to take needed actions that would benefit group members.

Do no harm sounds simple, but may be more difficult to effect. Lack of knowledge about group members prior to the group's beginning, and the inability to screen members can leave the group leader without sufficient information to plan activities that are best for group members. This void is why certain activities, such as imagery and movement or touching exercises, are not recommended in this book. Nonclinical groups may have members whose past experiences or other characteristics would cause them to feel anxious or threatened by activities like these, and they could be potentially harmful. The need to not harm is also why group leaders need to be therapeutically neutral in nonverbal communication, probing, and in responding. The latter can be especially important until more is known about group members. Group leaders are unlikely to intentionally harm group members, but there is a vast territory for unintentional harm.

Privacy and Confidentiality

Confidentiality is always of concern, particularly in nonclinical groups with a high degree of information dissemination. Leaders cannot guarantee that personal disclosures will be kept confidential by all members, but can request this, and speak of the leader's intentions. In addition, there can be legal requirements for reporting that the leader must obey, and these should be revealed to group members prior to the group's beginning. Leaders are also advised to become knowledgeable about the federal HIPAA regulations about reporting and exchange of treatment information, including group members' access to reports and case notes about them and the group. These regulations describe what information can be shared with others, under what conditions, and need for consent; how the information can be conveyed; and other restrictions and limitations. There can be state and local laws that also affect confidentiality, as well as agency or institutional policies. Leaders should be aware of all requirements, limitations, and the like that affect confidentiality.

Group leaders must remain sensitive to the needs and limitations for confidentiality, and specifically address these at the beginning of the group. Some nonclinical groups may have more relaxed guidelines for maintaining confidentiality because they are more focused on cognitive material, and there is less revealing of members' sensitive personal information, such as what can be expected for educational and skills training groups. Group members can be asked to keep personal information disclosed in the group confidential, but are free to disclose the process, materials, and cognitive information.

Privileged communications refers to the extent of privacy in the therapeutic relationship, and the limited right to withhold information from the court. Attorneys and clergy have privileged communication rights with their clients in every state. Some states have laws that protect social workers, sexual assault counselors, domestic abuse counselors, and journalists in keeping their sources confidential. Group leaders need to check the laws in their states, and to know their rights and responsibilities, such as if there is a requirement to respond to a subpoena for records without proper consent, or a court order. Generally, the client has to give consent for release of records, except under narrowly defined circumstances.

The Health Insurance Portability and Accountability Act (HIPAA) of 1996 sets standards for transactions and code sets, unique identifiers, and privacy and security for personal health information. The standards delineate what health information may be transmitted, in what form, and to whom. Also covered is the security of this information including how it is kept, stored, transmitted, and accessed in electronic form. It includes any protected health information, such as billing records, insurance reimbursements, health care claims, eligibility and coordination of benefits as well as case notes, recordings, and other forms of record keeping and documentation. Protection of privacy is the guiding principle.

HIPAA requires special confidentiality treatment for counseling minors, substance abuse records, group and family counseling, counseling public offenders, and deceased clients. *Counseling minors* requires parental/guardian permission, but the laws and standards for adult confidentiality also usually apply to minors.Consult your state laws for applicability to minors in your state, and be familiar with the Family Educational Rights and Privacy Act (FERPA) of 1974, and with the school board policies of the district when working with children in schools.

Substance abuse treatment records have rigid requirements for confidentiality if the treatment was part of a federally assisted program. (Wheeler & Betram, 2008). Consult both federal and state laws that govern confidentiality and release of information about clients receiving alcohol and/or drug treatment.

Wheeler and Betram (2008) note that privilege is not always recognized for *group and family counseling* because of the complexities inherent in the number and/or the relationships of the clients who are involved. It is helpful for the group leader to clearly communicate that confidentiality cannot be guaranteed by all members, although he or she will not reveal any unauthorized information, and to get group members to sign a document to honor and protect the confidences of other group members.

When working with *public offenders*, especially incarcerated clients, group leaders are bound by the same ethical requirements as they are in other settings. However, conflicts can exist between these ethical guidelines and the requirements for information sharing among correctional agencies. Offender clients should be informed from the beginning of the therapeutic relationship as to just what the parameters and needs for sharing revealed or disclosed information are, and the limits on what the counselor can keep confidential.

Confidentiality for *deceased clients* is still protected under many circumstances, and the ACA code recognizes that there may be situations where confidentiality cannot be maintained. The inability to maintain confidentiality for deceased clients may be required by law, the agency's policy, and/or state stature that permits access by the administrator or executor of the estate.

Technology and Documentation

The use of *technology* for generating and storing case notes, personal notes, session recordings, reports, and all forms of documentation is increasing at a phenomenal rate. Medical records are computerized, and other medical and insurance professionals can access electronically stored records. There may be instances when the court obtains these records, and it is only the viability of the computer system's security measures that prevents unauthorized people from access.

Group leaders should remain highly aware of the sensitivity of information in documents, and of the possibility of unauthorized access to them as well as the client's legal rights for access and for privacy. These are important concerns that should guide your record keeping and report generation, and how this information is presented and framed. Some points for guidance include the following:

1. Do not write anything that you do not want the group member to see or know.
2. Write everything as if you will have to read it out loud, and defend it in open court.
3. Be aware that the security system for electronic storage may or can be breached.
4. Don't record your speculations or the like in any form, even in your personal notes, as these are subject to subpoena.
5. Stay alert to the possibility of unauthorized access to any form of electronic documentation and record keeping.

Documentation provides evidence of what was done, and group members' progress. Bennett et al. (2006) propose adequate documentation as a means to help reduce risk and as basic in ethical practice. Examples of documentation include case notes, recordings, and mandated and optional reports to others. Standards and expectations for documentation are found in state laws and state licensing boards' standards, professional organizations' standards, and standards by insurers.

Group leaders should know the various federal, state, and institutional requirements for record keeping, including the content and laws governing privileged communications. Suggestions for personal and case notes include maintaining a focus on observable behavior, descriptions of the context for counseling and/or the group, note progress and evidence for progress, concerns that need to be addressed, and any hints of suicidal or homicidal tendencies or concerns.

Professional Boundaries

Dual relationships are to be avoided where possible and, if avoidance is not possible, care must be taken by the leader to ensure that harm to the client does not result from the dual relationship. The large numbers of dual relationship cases handled by professional regulatory boards and professional organizations concern sexual misconduct. The American Psychological Association's 2006 ethics report noted that 36% of the dual relationship cases opened were for nonsexual violations, and 64% for sexual misconduct with an adult or a minor, and sexual harassment. Other areas of sexual misconduct that merit attention by group leaders are sexual exploitation, and after-therapy sexual involvement.

Dual relationships are those where the leader and a member (or members) have a significant relationship outside the group. It need not be an intimate one, such as lovers or spouses. It can be social and involve activities such as attending parties, weddings, and the like. They may have a work relationship with regular, evaluative, or supervisory requirements. Or it may be an educational relationship such as teacher and student. A dual relationship can occur in many forms, but is recognized when the role(s) could negatively affect either the leader or member, or both. For example, if the leader is a supervisor and a member works in his or her unit, the possibility of the work-evaluative-supervisory relationship outside the group being affected is a definite possibility, either consciously or unconsciously.

It is recommended that group leaders consult with supervisors, personal therapists, or colleagues when issues or concerns about dual relationships emerge. Bennett et al. (2006)

recommend that adequate documentation be kept about the situation, to include observable behaviors, therapist's thoughts and actions, and consultation outcomes. There should be clear evidence of the ethical decision-making process revealed in the documentation.

Sexual concerns include sexual harassment, sexually provocative behavior remarks and the like, seduction, the act of sex with a client, and handling of sexual overtures by clients. In all cases, the group leader should remain aware of the vulnerability of the client, the need for safety and trust for the relationship, the ethical and legal standards and requirements, and of his or her professional responsibilities.

Faculty and supervisors also have the professional responsibility to not engage in sexually exploitive behavior with students. There is a power differential, and this with the evaluative task make these behaviors unethical. Both counselors in training and counselor educators should abide by the profession's ethical codes and stay aware of the duty to inform when violations occur.

The AGPA ethical standard directly and forcibly states that sex with a client is unethical. Other ethical codes also prohibit sex with clients. Bennett and colleagues (2006) state that "although the frequency of sexual exploitation is decreasing, it remains a major source of complaints against psychologists" (p. 87), and the same can be said for counselors. Further, there is considerable research that clearly demonstrates the harm that clients suffer as a result of being sexually exploited by their therapist.

It is extremely important for group leaders to maintain their professional boundaries, and to manage and contain their sexual feelings. These feelings can emerge during therapy or group sessions, but should be dealt with using the assistance of the supervisor or personal therapist.

Professional Practice

Screening of potential group members is of considerable help when planning the group. Ethical concerns that can be addressed fall into two categories: protection of the group member, and protection for the group. The screening process can provide information about the group member's language facility; expectations and hopes for benefits from the group experience; fears about the group and the leader; personal cultural and diversity needs; fears about emotional contagion; barriers to participation such as a disability that would prevent or hinder participation in art activities; level of commitment to personal change and growth; emotional control and regulation; and other factors that will play a role in the member's participation and potential for growth. Protection for the group is seen from information gathered during screening that may negatively impact the group or other members. The suitability of the member for the proposed group, the mix of group members, and any personal negative attitudes, prejudices, biases, or other cultural and diversity characteristics may affect acceptance by and of others, and participation.

Professional standards and qualifications may differ slightly for the various mental health professional organizations. Consult your state's professional standards for the particular mental health profession. Most professions and state licensing boards' standards of practice list specific coursework and supervised experiences required for group leaders.

The Association for Specialists in Group Work (ASGW) requires core coursework as well as observation and participation as a group member and as a group leader. Specialization training requires additional hours and coursework for that specialty in task/work group, psychoeducational groups, counseling groups, and group psychotherapy.

Use of techniques refers to the preparation of the leader to implement the technique, and the potential benefit for the client. Many techniques are relatively easy to implement, but should be used only after the leader has received sufficient instruction and supervised practice, and there is a defendable clinical rationale for its use. This training reduces the risk of improper use, and for potential harm to the client.

The most important rationale for using a technique is its purpose for helping the client, and group leaders need to carefully analyze the potential benefits and harm that might ensue before implementation. This can be especially important for nonclinical groups where leaders are not usually knowledgeable about group members' unresolved issues and concerns, current functioning levels and problems, or inner resources that can be used for growth and development. In short, leaders in these groups may not have enough information to understand the impact of a technique on members, to be ready to effectively use what emerges, or to realize the level of emotional intensity that can be aroused. Sufficient training for particular techniques can prevent these and other problems, and is strongly encouraged.

Why not use techniques that seem to work for the leader's growth, that sound feasible and potentially helpful for the group, or that were successful for other group leaders?

- There can be unanticipated and unintended negative effects.
- Members' histories may be unknown, or not fully understood to anticipate their personal reactions.
- The leader may not be experienced enough to manage and contain intense affect that can emerge.
- There is a possibility of countertransference in the selection of techniques and how these will be explored.
- The technique may promote forced disclosure.
- Group members can potentially experience loss of face, have inadequate defenses against the material or intense emotions, and so on.

Duties to Report, Warn, and Protect

Mental health professionals at every level have ethical and legal duties to report, warn, and protect for certain circumstances and conditions. There are circumstances where other urgent concerns take precedence over confidentiality. The ACA code states that counselors may have both an ethical obligation and a legal responsibility to disclose information to the proper authorities and/or to notify the potential victim, or to take other appropriate steps to protect (ACA, 2005, B.1.c).

- There is mandated reporting for child abuse or neglect in all states.
- Almost all states permit or require reporting of abuse or neglect of those who are elderly, disabled, or mentally ill.

Counselors should call or notify the applicable protective service agency for guidance when encountering suspected or revealed abuse.

Because the following situations are complex and state laws differ as to reporting responsibilities, definitive guidelines cannot be responsibly provided here. Instead, I will provide suggested contacts for answers and guidance.

Domestic violence—consult state domestic violence reporting requirements. Counselors insured by the ACA Insurance Trust can consult that group's Risk Management Helpline.

Past crimes—these do not have to be reported in many states, except when the crime involves abuse as discussed, or there is threat of harm to a third party. It would be advisable to consult with a lawyer, supervisor, or colleague.

Colleague's unprofessional conduct—use the ACA guidelines for seeking resolution. Try first to resolve it informally without violating confidentiality. Other possible actions include referral to state or national ethics committees, or to the state licensure board.

HIV/AIDS—if there is reason to believe that the infected person engages in risky sexual behavior and that others are at risk, consult with your state public health department for guidance.

Wheeler and Betram (2008) present eight clinical assessment procedures to use before breaking confidentiality to inform about the potential for harm to others.

1. Review the clinical diagnosis.
2. Consider the context and manner of the threat.
3. Assess the client's opportunities to act on the threat.
4. Review the client's history of violence.
5. Evaluate the factors contributing to the threat.
6. Evaluate the client's response to treatment.
7. Assess the relationship with the potential victim.

Threats of *suicide or self-harm* should always be taken seriously, and an assessment made of the possibility that the threat will be carried out. Is there a specific plan, how lethal is the plan, how available is the method, and are there others in proximity that could interrupt or prevent the plan from being carried out (Bauman, 2008)?

Bennett et al. (2006) suggest that mental health professionals know the procedures needed to reduce the likelihood of suicidal behavior, how these can be integrated into treatment, and the state law governing reporting responsibilities. It is helpful to learn a systematic method for assessing suicide.

Application of the In Situ Ethical Decision-Making Model

Let's return to the group situations presented earlier in the discussion and compare our answers.

1. The group leader had neither the child's nor the parent's consent to reveal his problem/issue/concern. The group leader should have introduced the new member, and invited other group members to introduce themselves, providing him with whatever

information each member wanted to disclose. It would be important and ethical to allow group members to choose the personal information for disclosure and to not instruct or direct them on what to disclose for an introduction beyond basic information. This action was unethical.

2. Enough information was provided so that the person could be identified during the discussion. It is professionally responsible and ethical to refrain from discussing clients in social settings, or in environments that are not secure. What can be discussed in these situations are general concerns that do not identify or target a specific person. The group leader could have asked for suggestions to handle resistance in general, and then the conversation would not have violated confidentiality. This was unethical.

3. The group leader did not intervene to prevent the scapegoating behavior, nor did the leader remind that group member of the consequences for leaving as is needed for informed consent. A more professionally responsible group leader response would be to block the attacks, ask other group members to try and empathize with the sullen silent member about having to attend mandated sessions, and then to ask the silent member if these were some of his feelings. Other group members may have some resentment that they had not expressed, and this would have been an opportunity to openly discuss feelings about mandated attendance, and the consequences for leaving the group before it ended.

4. The group leader had not received training in the use of this powerful technique. Although the group leader personally benefited from the demonstration, he should have more training and practice under supervision before trying to implement it. Counselors and group leaders in training are advised to be careful about using techniques that require training separate and in more depth than is usually present in a master's level counselor education program.

Future Challenges

Koocher (2007), in his presidential address to the American Psychological Association, presented three ethical challenges for the 21st century that have implications for the counseling profession: electronic delivery of services, the role of the invisible psychologist (mental health professional), and the demise of psychiatry.

Electronic delivery of treatment, assessment, and support services requires consideration of ethical concerns for contracting, competence to practice electronically, the limits of confidentiality, and control. We do not have guidelines in place yet that adequately address all of these concerns, and those that are yet to emerge.

The invisible psychologist (or other mental health professional) presents ethical challenges that also are not adequately addressed, especially those of allegiance and confidentiality. Invisible refers to services to multiple individuals that are delivered as a unit such as providing conflict resolution; providing services to someone at the behest of a known third party, such as what happens with some court-mandated treatment services; undertaking professional activities on behalf of a third party unknown by the individual, such as what happens when advising on jury selection; providing jury simulation, or profiling; and treating or studying individuals who are not aware of the identity of the researchers.

The demise of psychiatry may be an exaggeration, but this is the current situation: fewer people are entering the field; the emphasis is on psychopharmacology in training programs rather than psychotherapy; most prescribing of medication is done by family and other physicians; and psychologists with required training are obtaining prescribing authority. Koocher (2007) points out that it would be wise to learn that mental health treatment involves more than medication, and to not fall into the trap of medicating oneself, as has happened to many medical personnel who have access to prescription drugs. The ethical challenges are to learn from the past, and not repeat the mistakes for the future.

Summary

1. The importance of ethics, professional standards of practice, and legal concerns cannot be overestimated as guides for safe group leadership practice. Learning the ethics for the profession, federal and state laws governing mental health practice, and state licensing boards' standards of practice is essential for all group leaders.

2. Many ethical decision-making models exist, and all involve knowing the ethical code, identifying the problem, developing action alternatives, and evaluating these. Most models advise consulting with a peer, supervisor, or other consultant. All models seem to describe a process for decision making that has several steps outside the group, and ample time available for reflection and consultation.

3. An in situ ethical decision-making process can be used during the group session to guide the group leader's immediate response and intervention.

Chapter Activities

1. Search the state laws that relate to group counseling and report these to the class. Do the same for the state licensing board's standards of practice. Compare these to ACA's Code of Ethics and identify any potential conflicts.

2. Designate one or more students to contact the state licensing board for counselors and get a summary of the kinds of ethical violations that were reported to them in the past 5 years. This is public information available under the Freedom of Information Act. The information should be reported to the class. Institute a discussion of the findings.

3. Designate a group of students to review the ACA Ethics Committee report found in the *Journal of Counseling and Development* for each of the past 5 years, and present the information to the class for discussion.

Personal Development Exercise: Draw a timeline for your adolescence with the major events noted. You can use symbols for the events.

Chapter 5

Effective Use of Developmental Group Stages

Major Topics

1. An overview of developmental group stages.
2. How understanding group stages and development benefits the group and the leader.
3. A model for group stages, major leader tasks, and major member concerns for each stage.
4. Application of group stages for leader understanding and intervention.
5. Facilitative leader strategies for each stage.

Introduction

Important to understanding what is taking place in the group at any time is an awareness of expected events and members' behaviors during different group stages. This understanding can reduce some ambiguity and provide clues and suggestions for interventions. This chapter presents different conceptualizations of group stages that are summarized in a four-stage model from beginning to ending. Although some nonclinical groups may be too short to develop and move through all stages, all groups will have beginning and ending stages. It is just as important to understand stages for short-term groups as it is for longer term groups.

The leader's knowledge and understanding of expected events and members' behaviors are also helpful to reduce leader anxiety. Whereas all behaviors cannot be predicted, some common ones have been established through research, and these are presented along with some suggested leader interventions. Finally, facilitative strategies for each stage are presented. Initiating these strategies can help anticipate and prevent problems, help foster safety and trust, set constructive group norms, and provide structure to help reduce members' anxiety.

Research Findings

Tuckman (1965) was among the first to propose and document developmental sequences for groups, which later became known as *group stages*. These stages are not separate, distinct, or clear-cut, but almost all types of groups seem to move through some sequence of development. The literature shows several ways to categorize these stages. Tuckman categorized stages as forming, storming, norming, and performing. MacKenzie (1990) categorizes them as engagement, differentiate, individuation, intimacy, mutuality, and termination. Yalom's (1995) sequence was orientation, conflict, cohesion, stability, and termination. Rutan and Stone (2001) devised four group stages: formative, reactive, mature, and termination. Johnson and Johnson (2003) describe seven group stages as (1) defining and structuring procedures, (2) conforming to procedures and getting acquainted, (3) recognizing mutuality and building trust, (4) rebelling and differentiating, (5) committing to and taking ownership, (6) functioning maturely and productively, and (7) terminating.

Wheelan (2005) presents a review of the literature that supports a developmental sequential model for group development, with four stages and four phases within two of the stages. The stages and phases are identified by major member issues about the group.

- **Stage 1:** Inclusion, dependency, and expected behavior (Bennis & Shepard, 1956; Bion 1961; Mann, Gibbard, & Hartman, 1967; Slater, 1966; Stock & Thelen 1958)
- **Stage 2:** Counterdependency and conflict (Bennis & Shepard, 1956; Mann et al., 1967; Miles, 1971; Tuckman, 1965; Yalom, 1995)
- **Stage 3:** Cohesion and cooperation (Dunphy, 1968; Mann, 1966; Mann et al., 1967; Mills, 1964; Slater, 1966; Tuckman, 1965; Tuckman & Jensen, 1977)
  - **Phase 1:** Trust and tasks assigned and assumed (Lundgren & Knight, 1978; Mills, 1964; Slater, 1966; Wheelan, 1990)
  - **Phase 2:** Work phase (Bennis & Shepard, 1956; Slater, 1966; Tuckman, 1965)
- **Stage 4:** Fears and concerns about termination (Braaten 1974/1975; Dunphy, 1964; Gibbard & Hartman, 1973; Miles, 1971; Mills, 1964; Slater, 1966; Yalom, 1995)
  - **Phase 1:** Disruption and conflict (Farrell, 1976; Mann et al., 1967; Mills, 1964)
  - **Phase 2:** Acceptance (Lundgren & Knight, 1978; Yalom, 1995)

Rationale and Importance for Group Leaders

The different perspectives can add to the complexity of understanding what is taking place in the group at any time and over the life span of the group, identifying members' spoken and unspoken needs, planning for group sessions, and so on. The value of the group leader's knowing the group's expected sequence of development cannot be overstated. Among the benefits are reduction of ambiguity, surprises, and the like; clues for intervention; allowing for better planning; allowing the leader to anticipate some group needs; and helping support the leader's confidence in his or her efficacy.

No two groups will be exactly the same and leaders are often faced with considerable *ambiguity*, especially for nonclinical groups where screening and pregroup interviews are not usually available. So much is unknown about members that would be helpful when planning and implementing the group that group leaders are often faced with many *surprises*. Information about stages of group development, expected member behaviors, and usual issues and concerns associated with particular stages can assist in reducing ambiguity and surprises. For example, knowing that the group is likely to challenge the leader, no matter how mild the challenge may be, can permit the group leader to recognize the challenge when it is happening and not react negatively or defensively.

Clues for intervention can also be gleaned from an understanding of group stages. The usual concerns and issues for each stage can allow the group leader to have a better sense of what the group as a whole may be struggling with, and to use this information to make group process commentary. Even though members may be expressing their needs, concerns, or issues in different ways, there is a commonality among these, and a process comment can be helpful.

Effective group leaders *plan* their groups as much as possible, even when faced with little or no information about group members. Knowledge and understanding of group stages can assist in planning for appropriate activities to meet the usual needs for the particular stage. For example, no matter how it may be termed, there is always a beginning stage, and group members will experience some anxiety about what is expected of them and so on. When planning, group leaders can think about activities and information that will help reduce some of the anxiety.

Along with planning, leaders can *anticipate some group needs* and make arrangements to effectively meet and cope with them. For example, in the stage where cohesion and productivity are prevalent, the group leader can anticipate that members will likely suppress conflict in order to preserve harmony, work independently, and be very cooperative. Anticipating these behaviors lets the leader understand when it is time to let the group progress on its own as much as possible, and to remind members that conflict is more constructive when worked through than when it is suppressed.

The group leader's *confidence and self-efficacy* are supported when there is the likelihood of some events occurring that are known in advance. Understanding the sequence for group stages gives the leader some assurance that he or she will be able to handle them, and that, although there are sure to be unanticipated events, at least some are anticipated and can be planned for.

A Model for Group Stages

The literature discusses many different models of group stages, so it can be confusing to know which one to use as a guide. Proposed here is a model that incorporates much of what is presented in the literature, and that adds major leader tasks and member concerns for each stage. The discussion about each stage also includes some hidden or unexpressed member concerns that may be present. Finally, the discussion focuses on applications of group stages for different types of nonclinical groups. There are four stages in the model.

- Stage 1—meaning and purpose
- Stage 2—challenges, creativity, and options
- Stage 3—unfolding, becoming, and interdependence
- Stage 4—summarizing, evaluating, and culminating

Table 5.1 presents an overview of leader tasks and expected member behaviors for each stage.

Table 5.1
Group Stages, Member Behaviors and Major Leader Tasks

Major Theme	Expected Behaviors	Leader Tasks
Formative Stage		
Orientation	Search for similarities	Establishing trust and safety
Hesitant participation	Giving and seeking advice	Collaborative goal setting
Search for meaning	Symptom description	Structuring and directing
Dependency	Questions about value of experience	Promoting universality
Safety	Leader seen as "all knowing"	Facilitating expression of issues
	Desire for acceptance and approval, respect and domination	
	Need for an omnipotent, omniscient, all-caring parent	
Challenge Stage		
Conflict	Conflicts among members	Identifying conflicts and demonstrating a process for working through these
Dominance	Conflicts between members and leader	Blocking attacks
Rebellion	Negative comments	Reacting constructively to challenges, hostility and negative comments
	Intermember criticism	Containing intense emotions
	One-way analyses and judgments	
	"Shoulds" and "oughts"	
	Jockeying for position	
	Hostility toward the leader	
	Discounting of leader's expertise	
Working Stage		
Cohesiveness	Increased morale	Accepting members' independence
	Mutual trust	Identifying suppressed conflict
	Self-disclosure	Encouraging and supporting
	Development of intimacy	
	Suppression of negative affect	
Working through process	Subgrouping may appear	
	Conflict expressed as	
	a. mutual contempt	
	b. self contempt	

(*continued*)

Table 5.1   *Continued*

	c. transference	
	d. mirroring	
	e. projective identification	
	f. rivalry	
	Self-disclosure	
	a. appropriate	
	b. inappropriate	

Termination Stage

Termination	Ignoring the impending end of group	Keeping focus on closure
	Denying feelings around the ending of group	Highlighting accomplishments and progress
	Unresolved issues around separation	Demonstrating a constructive process for closure

Stage 1: Meaning and Purpose

This title describes the concerns that members have in varying degrees as they enter the group. It was noted earlier that members tend to perceive the group as ambiguous, with much uncertainty about what's in store for them and even confusion about what they are expected to do. No amount of preparation, description, and other information will eliminate the ambiguity and uncertainty. Clarifying the group's meaning and purpose can help reduce members' personal anxiety but not eliminate it.

The major member concerns are safety, inclusion, personal gains, and symptom relief. *Safety* concerns can be mild or extensive depending on members' past experiences. Basically, they are concerned and apprehensive about being shamed or humiliated by the leader or by other members. They may fear appearing stupid or incompetent where others ridicule, embarrass, or devalue them in some way, and this would be painful to endure. Although the leader ensures that this does not happen, the members don't know enough about him or her or other members to have confidence that this will not happen to them. No amount of reassurance can eliminate this fear, and few members are willing to openly express their fears, thus complicating the matter even more.

Members also have concerns about being *included* in the group, as they do not yet know what the overt and covert norms will be. It's impossible to know these because they emerge as the group develops; this uncertainty only fuels anxiety. Everyone carries secrets and some can be shame producing, which arouses fear of being discovered, revealed, or disclosed. If the feared action were to occur, the member's overriding concern would be that he or she is too flawed to be acceptable and thus will be excluded. Group leaders can foster and support inclusion by asking for every member's input; showing respect and tolerance for diverse views, perspectives, and values; responding directly and empathically to members; and repairing empathic failures. It can also be helpful to highlight commonalties and similarities among group members as a way of inclusion.

All members have some level of concern about what they can *gain from being in the group.* Even involuntary members who may be extremely resistant want to know what's in it for them. If members cannot see any positive benefits or outcomes for participation, they do not commit to the group, the level of investment and involvement is minimal at best, and their anxiety levels remain high. There are many reasons why it is important for members to understand what personal gains they may reap from participating in the group. Leaders can facilitate this process with collaborative goal setting. Inviting members to verbalize some personal goals and using the group to set group goals that incorporate individual member's goals can show members that their goals are important to the successful achievement of group goals.

Symptom relief is sought by some members, and this need or wish can be realistic or unrealistic. That is, the symptoms may not be addressed by this group, it may not be possible to provide the desired relief, or the focus may be on the wrong symptoms. For example, in a psychoeducational group for a chronic illness, the member may want relief for the symptoms associated with the illness. Symptom relief is beyond the scope of the group, but what can be gained is how to manage the symptoms for more relief.

These hidden or unexpressed concerns may be similar to the following:

- Will I be liked, or will I be rejected?
- Will I be hurt, insulted, or offended?
- Is the leader competent?
- How can this help me?
- Will my flaws be revealed to everyone and I am shamed?
- Will I be forced or seduced to disclose something I don't want to disclose?
- Can I let my real self be seen, or should I keep it hidden?

The major tasks for the leader focus on setting a group atmosphere where members can feel safe, promoting inclusion, and reducing fears and anxiety. Basic and fundamental leader actions to accomplish these tasks include providing information about the leader's qualifications and the intended purpose for the group; guiding members to set reasonable rules and regulations for the group; identifying possible concerns and expectations about confidentiality; soliciting input from all members; engaging in collaborative goal setting; and designing activities to help members begin to become acquainted. It is also helpful for group members to discuss any fears or apprehensions they have about the group and their participation, but to not try to either talk them out of the fear, or to overly reassure them that the fears are groundless. That does not work to reduce fears, but openly expressing them does seem to reduce the anxiety, and provides encouragement that they will be able to take care of their self.

Stage 2: Challenge, Creativity, and Options

In the second stage of group development, group members begin to assert their individuality, experiment with new or different behaviors, connect with each other through their commonalties, and start to become less reliant on the leader. Disagreements and other forms of conflict emerge, and how these are managed is a strong determiner of whether or not the cooperativeness and productiveness of stage 3 is achieved.

Stage 2 behaviors can make this an uncomfortable time for the group, and group members need reassurance that the discomfort will be manageable, temporary, and is to be expected. Reassurance is particularly helpful for members who fear conflict and have experienced only the destructive nature of conflict. Further, the leader is an authority figure, and it is scary to challenge, or see someone challenge, the authority figure. The leader's lack of defensiveness in response to these challenges is important because these responses reassure members that they will not be shamed or destroyed by them, and that it is possible to have conflicts that are constructive and positive when worked through. Members learn a constructive conflict resolution process in an atmosphere where conflict is tolerated. All of these are predicated on the leader's ability to recognize, tolerate, and constructively resolve conflict.

Hidden or unexpressed concerns can be as follows:

- Will I be liked or tolerated if I express a different opinion or perspective than other group members or the leader?
- Will the leader destroy me if I challenge him or her?
- I've only experienced fear, dread, anxiety, and destruction from conflict. Will it be the same here in the group?
- Can the leader protect me from attacks by other members?

The leader's major tasks for stage 2 are to recognize attacks and challenges, manage personal anxiety and defensiveness, block attacks on members by other members (it goes without saying that the leader will not engage in attacks on members), directly or indirectly teach conflict resolution skills, reframe disagreements and other such remarks, and highlight empathic failures and repair them. The extent of the leader's personal development and the kind of past experiences encountered will contribute to the ability to recognize conflict when it emerges in the group. Some group members openly express their disagreement or challenge, whereas others suppress, repress, and deny theirs. In addition, social convention is usually present, which contributes to an unwillingness to openly express a different opinion or perspective, or to challenge the leader. These conditions make it necessary for group leaders to be sensitive to the fears that members may have about conflict, and the indirect ways in which conflict is expressed.

Group leaders must examine their *comfort with conflict, with being attacked or challenged,* and their *characteristic way of responding to conflict.* It is easy to become defensive when attacked or challenged, or to use the leader's expertise and authority as responses. Neither of these are helpful for the group and its members. The unfairness and sometimes unexpected nature of the challenge can be disconcerting, and leaders may unconsciously use their characteristic way of responding to a challenge—withdrawing, becoming conciliatory, returning the attack, or meeting it head-on and trying to constructively resolve it. These are also members' characteristic responses to conflict. Leaders' personal development can help moderate or change the first three characteristic responses to conflict, and can enhance the fourth one. Because leaders are expected to model desired behavior in the group, it is imperative that leaders continue their personal development.

A major leader task for all group stages is to *block member-to-member attacks,* but it is especially important in stage 2, where how this is handled can significantly impact members' participation. Disagreements and challenges are not attacks, they are differences of opinion or perspective. Some members can have a "win at all cost" attitude and use attacks to try to get others to "lose" or to change and agree with them. Some forms of verbal attacking behavior include:

- Asking a barrage of questions designed to keep the receiver defending his or her position
- Using pejorative terms to describe the other person

- Making numerous value-laden comments about a person or a particular perspective, such as right or wrong
- Poking fun or making sarcastic remarks
- Using actions such as talking loudly to drown out the other person, and frequently interrupting the speaker

It is not helpful to the group and its members when these attacking behaviors are tolerated even when there seems to be considerable support for a particular perspective.

Another leader task is to *reframe disagreements* and other remarks so that the constructive or positive aspects will not be lost. Reframing does not change the essential message; it highlights something important about the message and is especially important when there is emotional intensity; when the member gets caught up in his or her own experiencing and does not attend to the impact on others of what he or she is saying; or when the message is insensitive, unempathic, and so on. Reframe for the following:

- When a comment to someone appears to be harsh and uncaring
- If a negative comment is repeated
- When emotional intensity for the speaker seems to be high
- If the receiver reacts negatively or defensively
- To soften an attack on the leader, and to not seem to be retaliating against the speaker
- If the speaker becomes isolated or excluded because of his or her perspective
- When members lack the vocabulary to adequately express their thoughts

A major leader task, one that can be the subject and purpose for the group, is to *teach conflict resolution* so that the conflict is resolved to all participants' satisfaction where possible and relationships are preserved and strengthened. Again, the most essential components for this task are the leader's personal perspective about conflict, his or her tolerance for conflict, and a desire to work through conflict. If the leader fears conflict, ignores or minimizes it, denies that it exists in the group, sets up a win–lose atmosphere, or either becomes defensive or goes on the offensive when challenged, then the group's culture will not be supportive for conflict resolution.

Leaders need to stay aware that some form of conflict is likely to emerge in the group. In addition, they must be alert to identify conflict when it does emerge, and realize that disagreements among members can be a substitute for challenges to the leader, bringing them out into the open, and that it is the leader's responsibility to teach members how to constructively work through conflicts. We will discuss specific actions for constructively working through conflicts later in this chapter.

Highlighting and repairing empathic failures is extremely helpful in building trust and safety, and in reducing the negative effects of conflicts and challenges. Members want to be heard and understood even when they are not expressing their thoughts and feelings very well or appropriately.

Stage 3: Unfolding, Becoming, and Interdependence

This is the stage where both task and relationship factors combine to foster collaborative task accomplishment. Individual members are helped to achieve their personal goals through the combined resources of the group as a whole, and other members. Members' primary concerns are maintaining harmony, providing constructive and helpful interpersonal feedback, increasing awareness of self and of others, achieving personal growth in understanding, knowledge, or skills, and so on. The distressing behaviors experienced in stage 2 disappear, members become more considerate of one another, the group norm becomes achieving the group goals and accomplishing individual tasks, and there is a sense of shared purpose for the group.

In stage 3, leaders need to understand at a deeper level that *less is more*. The less the group leader intervenes, the more group members gain independence and confidence and guide their own development. It takes faith that the group can do the work it needs to do, that members need less guidance from the leader, and patience to allow the group to find its own way. It can be difficult for some group leaders to give up their positions of authority and expertise, and let members become more independent of them. However, leaders will find that it is affirming for group members when leaders demonstrate trust in their abilities to learn, grow, and develop with a minimum of input from the leader.

Group leaders still have a lot to do in stage 3, although they may be less active in the sense that planned exercises and other stimulus activities are not needed, or are less needed, and members communicate more effectively and directly. In addition, fewer empathic failures occur and, when they do, members work to repair them rather than the leader. The desire for harmony leads to more open discussions about differences of perspectives, and members are better able to tolerate differences. And, the leader does not have to push or guide members to interact with each other. Some groups may have developed to the point where members are making process commentary, which is helpful for the group. The major group leader task is to stay out of the way.

The leader will be very helpful to the group by understanding that the good feelings generated by the harmony in the group and that the desire to maintain these can lead to suppression of conflict. Leaders can help guide members to work through rather than suppress even minor conflicts. There can be a reluctance among members to do or say anything that has the potential for discord.

Stage 4: Summarizing, Evaluating, and Culminating

However you term it, the final stage is some form of ending the experience. Members' concerns and initial feelings seem to reemerge and there is panic because there is so much that seems unfinished. The potential loss of meaningful relationships and support and other separation issues affect the group. It is important to prepare members for the group's ending, and leaders should plan in advance how this will be handled. One way is to announce the number of remaining sessions after half of the sessions are completed, and to comment on this each session thereafter.

Usual member behaviors for the ending stage can include regression to some stage 1 concerns and behaviors, suppression of sadness and potential loss, devaluing of experiences and connections, resistance to ending the group, and emergence of new material.

Some stage 2 behaviors that can reemerge in stage 4 are confusion, anxiety, uncertainty, and a return to a self-focus where, in stage 3, members were focused, confident, connecting with one another, and concerned about other members' progress. These behaviors can reemerge because members are once again facing ambiguity and uncertainty—that is, life without the group. Leaders cannot prevent the regression, but they can be aware that some regression may be likely, recognize it when it appears, and be prepared to deal with it. Leaders who are prepared will not be taken by surprise, and will be better able to manage the regression and members' feelings.

Some members will openly admit to feelings of sadness about the ending of the group and the impact of the loss on them, but many will suppress their feelings or even deny having them. Suppression of feelings may occur by members rationalizing that they will be relieved that the group is over and that it's not sadness they feel; saying that they are more focused on the future; minimizing the impact of the group's ending; and acting in other ways to avoid experiencing even mild sadness. For some groups, such as training and task groups, members will note that they will continue to see and interact with each other, so that the group ending is less relevant. This simply is not true, as this particular group experience is ending and needs formal closure. Relationships outside the group experience are different, and the particular group experience cannot be restarted or recaptured. Leaders can find it difficult to get members to express any sadness. This should be accepted, and members should not be pushed to voice sadness. It is best to just raise the possibility that some members may experience sadness at the loss of the relationships developed in the group, the encouragement and support they received, and that they will no longer have access to the resources of the group, and to allow members to voice what they wish.

Leaders need to get comfortable with hearing that they did not give group members what they wanted or needed. Some members will devalue what they did get from the group, especially when approaching the group's ending. Some will make deprecating comments or say that it wasn't enough or what was wanted. Others may try to soften their disappointment by making appreciative comments before the devaluing statement. It is important for leaders to recognize that members' devaluing comments are a way to provide distance from feeling the emotions around the loss, and to not try to moderate or change these. They can and do change during the process of ending, especially when the ending is well planned.

Members can resist ending the group in many ways: setting dates to continue meeting, arranging annual dinners or other social events, refusing to discuss ending or denying that they have feelings about the group's ending, initiating conflict in the hope that the leader will not let the group end without resolution of it, and by even asking the leader to meet for additional sessions or voting to continue the group. The group leader must understand these delay tactics and have patience to allow members to accept that the group is ending. They should not be seduced into deviating from the contract that was set in the beginning about the number of sessions. When group members mention continuing to meet on their own, or holding annual meetings, this can and should be discouraged by the leader. One way is for the leader to point out that they cannot recapture or continue the group's experiences and that the group's ending means that additional experiences would be vastly different. It is important for the leader to acknowledge his or her inability to prevent the group from reforming after the group is over, but to not condone them doing so.

One way that members resist ending the group is by bringing up new material to demonstrate that the group is needed to help members work on these important issues. On one hand, the leader is faced with the inner personal need or desire to not leave the members unfulfilled or dangling, to assist in learning or exploration of new material. On the other hand, there is also the need to honor the contract and end the group. It can be of little help to understand that the presentation of new material is a delay tactic; leaders will be conflicted at this point. However, the responsible leader acknowledges the seriousness and importance of the new material and his or her sadness, and dismay at not having sufficient time to work on it, but continues to end the group. Leaders should also check in with the members who surfaced the new material to ensure that they are able to handle the inability to address the new material.

One part of the process for ending the group, and continuing to make members aware of its ending, is an evaluation. It can be helpful to have two types of evaluation: a written evaluation such as what is described in the next chapter, and an oral evaluation in the group setting. The oral evaluation can provide an opportunity for members to reflect, summarize, and express appreciation or regrets. For example, in the final session, the leader can ask members to reflect on goal attainment, both personal and group; summarize personal gains and other benefits; comment on what is appreciated; and note any regrets about lost opportunities. This activity can set the tone for culminating because it permits group members to become aware of personal progress, and growth and development. It also offers opportunities to become aware of connections forged among members, to highlight what was valuable for them, and to think about how they contributed or did not contribute.

Actually ending a group can be emotionally intense, but group leaders should not seek to avoid this intensity as it can be a valuable learning experience for some members to learn how to say good-bye in a more satisfying way so that there is minimal or no unfinished business.

Application of Group Stages

The most important variable that determines if a particular stage will emerge for different types of nonclinical groups seems to be the time involved, or the duration of the group. Brief and short-term groups probably do not have sufficient time for each stage to be completed and another stage begun. The type of group will also have a role in stage progression. For example, a one-session career education group would have information dissemination as its main focus so that the relationship factors that produce stages 2 and 3 would not receive attention, or have sufficient time to unfold. On the other hand, a task group that had members who already worked together could very well experience stages 2 and 3 because of existing relationships established prior to the beginning of the group.

Skills training groups are generally structured to develop a set of predetermined competencies, and the group setting is intended to teach these and provide for practice and feedback. Relationships among members must receive attention if feedback is to be accepted and valued. However, unless the focus for the group was conflict resolution, there may not be sufficient time to change the focus to teaching conflict resolution skills in addition to the primary goal for the group. This is not to say that conflict would fail to occur, but it would have to be contained and managed so that valuable training time was not diverted and the main focus derailed.

Stage 3 as described is unlikely to emerge in most nonclinical groups because of time constraints (MacNair-Semands & Lese, 2000). This does not mean that individuals and some groups will not be productive, but that they will be productive in different ways than those described in the clinical literature. It takes time for relationships, trust, and safety to be developed among members so that they become more confident in disclosing, and in giving and receiving authentic feedback. This is not a focus for many nonclinical groups. So, being productive must be defined and perceived differently.

Being productive, for most nonclinical groups, means that the narrowly defined objectives or tasks are worked on and achieved. This in and of itself is sufficient and should not be underestimated. For example, I've reviewed nonclinical group plans that have broad and unrealistic goals that could not be accomplished in the time available. Goals such as improved relationships, increased self-esteem, greater self-confidence, and the like are all laudable goals. For example, conducting a group that teaches study skills should not have these goals because they are longer term goals and objectives that need a different group focus. Goals for such a group would more appropriately be related to the group's topic of study skills such as better academic performance.

All nonclinical groups, except for support groups, will have an ending stage. Support groups are usually open groups with members entering and leaving throughout the group's existence. Therefore, members may terminate, but the group continues to exist. Support group leaders should plan for continual beginnings and endings for members, and for the impact of these on the group's functioning. This planning and process is discussed in a later chapter.

Facilitative Strategies for Each Stage

There are four strategies for stage 1 that leaders will find facilitative regardless of the type of group.

- Introductions and ice breaker
- Collaborative goal setting, schedule of activities and events
- Rules and guidelines
- Task introduction

Introductions begin the group and they can be important to help reduce tension and anxiety. Leaders should start the process with a self-introduction that presents professional qualifications, but not take a lot of time or give a lot of detail. This is also the time when leaders can acknowledge any prior relationships with group members. For example, the group may include the leader's neighbor, a child's teacher, a former college roommate, and so on. This can be modeling and encouragement to group members to bring out their existing or prior relationships, such as two members who are spouses.

Members' introductions then follow. If the group is small, it's best to have members introduce themselves to the entire group. If the group is large, break it into small groups of five or six members, let the small groups do introductions within that group, and then have each group introduced collectively. Examples of introductions and ice breaker exercises are presented in Chapter 15.

There are some activities and exercises that are *not* recommended for use.

- Do not break the group into dyads or triads because doing so keeps the focus on individuals.
- Do not use any exercise that calls for the members to provide misinformation. Deception, even when used for teaching purposes such as how initial perceptions and judgments can be erroneous, do not help develop safety and trust among members.
- Do not use exercises that call for touching or movement until more is known about members' backgrounds, previous experiences, and conditions or issues.
- Do not select long or complicated exercises as they take too much time to complete and sufficiently debrief participants.

The next step would be to either *collaboratively set the goals* for the group, or to have members use their previously determined personal goals to derive group goals. This step highlights the meaning and purpose for the group, and involves group members in their education, growth, and development. This can be accomplished by asking members to present their goals, linking them to find commonalties and themes, and using this information to develop one or two group goals that would incorporate the essence of the individual goals. The leader presents these and asks members to commit to the goals.

The chapter on planning suggests some basic *rules and guidelines* that will likely be appropriate for all types of groups. Group leaders are encouraged to add to these when desired, or when they would meet the group's need. Do not have too many rules because members will not remember then. Do review rules in the first session and get members' to agree to follow them.

The final major activity in the first session is to *introduce the task* for that group. The introduction can take the form of a mini-lecture, an exercise or other activity, a discussion, and so on. It can be important for members to focus on a task to set the tone for future sessions.

Three strategies are presented for stage 2, challenge, creativity, and options: Bring the focus and attention to the group leader when there is conflict among group members, do not ignore conflicts, and pay special attention to empathic responding and empathic failure repair.

Although leaders may feel prepared for challenges and conflict, these can emerge without warning and may be disruptive to the planned session. Disagreements should be promptly and directly addressed as soon as possible. If not addressed, they can lurk and fester underground, and erode the members' participation and the group's progress.

Because it can be risky and scary to challenge the leader directly, the first discord may be among group members, but is often a disguised desire to *challenge the leader*. Bringing the focus to the leader accomplishes several objectives.

- Signaling that it is acceptable to challenge the leader
- Setting a tone or atmosphere where challenges and conflicts can be tolerated and worked through
- Illustrating possible displacement
- Protecting members from experiencing displaced negative feelings, and possibly arousing defenses
- Beginning the process for teaching conflict resolution skills

Bring the focus to the leader by saying something like, "Group members are beginning to openly disagree and challenge each other, and I wonder if there are some disagreements and challenges for me that are not being spoken." Use your words, but make it clear that you are ready to hear what members have to say.

On the other hand, a conflict may emerge among members that is open, direct, and of importance. This type of conflict needs attention, and members need to be guided through the process of conflict resolution. The intensity of emotions is a sign that the conflict needs attention, even when it appears that the intense feelings are mainly one-sided. Enlightenment is a valuable technique for conflict resolution and is presented in Chapter 13.

Although empathic responding and empathic failure repair are important for all stages, they can be particularly important for stage 2 because of the discord where members need to know that they are heard and understood. Negative feelings can escalate and intensify over misunderstandings. Leaders need to model how to respond to convey understanding of the other person's perspective, view, opinion, and so on. Leaders should also be alert for empathic failures as there will likely be many of these during this contentious stage, and leaders should intervene to repair them as quickly as possible.

Stage 3, unfolding, becoming, and interdependence, has three suggested facilitative strategies.

1. Praise, encourage, and let members alone
2. Foster therapeutic factors emergence
3. Do a goal checkup

Stage 3 needs careful leader interventions that do not interrupt the work members are doing, curb the independence of the group, and/or suggest that members are not effective or capable. Leader interventions are more helpful when they enhance the productivity and progress of the group. Bringing members' attention to their positive gains and accomplishments, their constructive use of therapeutic factors, and how members help each other can be more effective than trying to guide them to where the leader *thinks* they need to go. Stage 3 is a period of harmony, appreciation, and encouragement.

However, leaders have to be alert to members' suppression of negative feelings and conflict, and encourage members to not let their reluctance disturb the good feelings in the group prevent them from expressing feelings and working through conflicts. Leaders can simply ask if members are experiencing any negative (mild) feelings that are not being expressed, or if there are any conflicts (mild) that could be worked through. Asking may be enough to let members know that it is helpful to verbalize them instead of suppressing them.

This is also the stage where a goal checkup can be rewarding to members. Review the individual and group goals set in the beginning, and ask members about their accomplishments for individual and group goals, their satisfaction with their progress toward achieving the goals, and if any goals need adjustment or modification. This process highlights progress, especially when it has been gradual.

Stage 4, summarizing, evaluating, and culminating, has five facilitative leader strategies.

1. Introduce culmination of the group
2. Direct evaluation of the group
3. Focus on gains, progress, and development
4. Discuss appreciation and the concept of not leaving with unfinished business
5. Do an exercise for saying goodbye

It is the leader's responsibility to introduce termination; the process begins about halfway through the life span of the group. Culmination should be planned for prior to the beginning of the group and those activities implemented at appropriate times leading to the final act of closing. Mentioning the time remaining, such as the number of sessions left, introduces culmination and keeps members focused and aware of its existence. Other leader preparation actions to facilitate ending are to highlight gains and progress for members, and to encourage members to stay aware of the positive feedback and understanding they received from each other, and appreciate what was done. These steps can be encouraging, enhancing, and teach members how to end the group so that there is little unfinished business, such as leaving something important unsaid.

One strategy to highlight gains and progress is to ask members how they are different now from when the group began, to add leader observations about progress and gains, and to invite other members to express their observations about the person. This can encourage members to recognize and express appreciation, which can lead to an opening to discuss what else was received and given that was appreciated. It can also be helpful for members to acknowledge any regrets they may have about missed opportunities, things that could have been said but were not, and how their anxiety or resistance got in the way.

Nonclinical groups will not have much time to discuss termination, practice saying what needs to be said so that most unfinished business is completed, and work through how saying good-bye could be made as satisfying as possible. All of these take group time, and time for members to individually work through and be able to express and discuss. Because of these constraints, it may be constructive and helpful for the leader to use a closing exercise. Such an exercise should not focus on additional personal material, relationships outside the group, or be too long, involved, and complex. A simple exercise could focus on the following: personal gains; thoughts, ideas, and feelings about the group and its members; new realizations, awarenesses, or skills development; and repair of any empathic failures. Such an exercise will improve members' facility with saying goodbye, and possibly teach them a more satisfying way to end relationships and experiences that can carry over to their lives outside the group.

Examples of Integration and Application for Stages and Interventions

Following are examples for applying information about stage development and expected member behaviors to formulate leader interventions. All four stages are illustrated. First I will describe the group session, followed by a description of the usual process for that stage, expected member behaviors and what they can signal, and possible leader tasks or interventions. The sample interventions are not the only interventions that could be made; they are simply used as examples.

Stage 1. Example:

> **Group Session:** *This is the third meeting for the group composed of 8 college students ages 18 to 22. The group was required for all students who violated the college's policy on alcohol use. The first two meetings focused on introductions, goal setting, and getting acquainted. This session starts quietly with members reporting on their weekly activities. However, about 15 minutes into the 2-hour session, members begin to ramble on about topics that do not appear to be group related. The topics include difficulty in finding a parking space, the Survivor television show, an unfair boss at work, and nosey siblings. The leader lets the rambling proceed for a few minutes.*
>
> *(Leader understandings and possible interventions are presented later.)*

Stage 1 Analysis: The *beginning* stage could be called the sorting through and connecting process. Members are generally strangers to each other, confused and frustrated with the ambiguity and the unknowns about the group, fearful of being rejected or excluded, and concerned that their flaws, shameful secrets, and desires will become visible to all. In addition, they may be carrying considerable stress over an illness, condition, or other life situation, and have intense uncomfortable emotions they are trying to manage. Members can have questions about the efficacy of group for their personal need, and mistrust or fear about the competency and ability of the leader to take care of them. Most often, none of this is directly expressed, but emerges through metaphors. That's one of the reasons it is extremely important for leaders to pay particular attention to how members use metaphors to express needs for safety, concerns about trust, and fears of abandonment or destruction in the very first session. The importance of this session cannot be minimized, and is discussed in more detail in another chapter.

The confusion and fear members bring to the group will vary in intensity and antecedents, but it is safe to say that all members will bring some measure of these to the group, and that their participation, disclosure, and emotional expression will be affected. In addition to sorting through all these emotions, formulating goals, and deciding how much of the real self can be shown in the group, members also try to make connections to other members and to the leader. This, too, takes place in a variety of ways. It is important for leaders to try to support those attempts to connect by focusing on significant, but not visible, commonalities. It's easy to spot commonalities such as age, gender, and race/ethnicity much of the time, and revealed commonalities such as education, marital status, geographic location, careers or jobs, hobbies, and recreational pursuits. These are surface similarities that probably do not help members become connected at meaningful levels. Those connections seem to be forged around shared intense experiences that continue to carry meaning for the members, deeply held values and other principles that guide their lives, similar emotions around a common event that occurs in the group, and similar self-perceptions around similar issues or concerns. The visible and revealed similarities are those that emerge in social situations, tend to be nonthreatening to the person(s) involved, and don't have intense emotions associated with them. These could be called benign similarities, whereas meaningful connections are at a deeper level. Leaders will probably not be able to help members connect at a very deep and meaningful level, especially in the beginning stage, but can help this occur by linking the more meaningful similarities whenever they appear, even in the first session, and by having this as a priority for their work with the group. It is always helpful to keep in mind that members become cohesive around similarities, and fail to do so when differences are paramount.

Members tend to focus on differences rather than similarities, especially when they zoom in on visible and revealed differences. This is where stereotyping, bias, prejudice, and intolerance can keep members from recognizing less visible similarities. Then too, disclosures about more meaningful characteristics, experiences, values, and so forth emerge when members develop some confidence in the group and the leader, feel safe enough to reveal these, and trust that they will not be destroyed or excluded. All of these take time to develop, and for some groups and members, there is not enough time in the group. Thus, leaders will have to be patient, understand members' concerns about safety and trust, link meaningful connections when they appear, and not push members to foster connections and disclosure before they are ready. Approximately halfway through the life of the group is the time to begin the process of termination.

Expected Member Behaviors and Leader Tasks: Member behaviors in stage 1 are fueled by their anxiety and fear, and the pattern for their relating to each other and to the leader is largely determined by their family-of-origin experiences, past experiences, and unfinished business or unresolved issues. Expected member feelings can include confusion, fear or dread, irritation or anger, resentment, defiance, and shame. Members are confused about the ambiguity that surrounds the unknown experience of the group, and they can fear or dread exclusion or rejection by other members and by the leader. They can feel irritated or angry about the conditions that brought them to the group or at other external people and situations, resent being as or where they are, feel defiant of authority (as in the leader or the forces that sent them to the group), and feel shame about many aspects of self.

Expected member behaviors include:

- Expressions of discontent that are indirect and disguised
- Considerable questioning where given answers do not appear to be satisfactory and continue to be repeated in different ways
- Expressions of frustration and anger at external events, people, and the like
- Talking only to the leader, and seldom if ever to each other
- Saying and doing things to be perceived as nice and cooperative
- Frequently saying "I don't understand"

Leader tasks are to contain and manage anxiety both personal and that of members, to reduce ambiguity surrounding the group process, to forge a therapeutic relationship with members, to help set group goals and group norms, and to begin establishing trust and safety in the group. It is helpful for leaders to understand tasks such as establishing trust and safety that are less visible, take time to do, and are affected by members' personal characteristics interacting with family-of-origin experiences and other past experiences. There may be groups in which this can never be adequately accomplished. In Chapter 6, the section titled "Facilitating the All-Important First Session" gives some suggestions for how to begin to accomplish the leader tasks for stage 1. These will probably take more than one session, but leaders can accomplish more and members are better served if expectations are realistic. An understanding and intervention for the example follows.

Leader Understandings: _The members are still searching for purpose and safety, and are concerned about confidentiality and if they can be helped. There is considerable unspoken anxiety about these topics, and the verbalized topics are metaphors._

Possible Interventions: _The leader may state: "Group members are wondering how safe the group is, if their needs will be met, and if they will find meaning and purpose in the group. It can be helpful to explore these concerns in the group." Or: "Members did not choose to attend this group, and have some unspoken feelings about being mandated to attend. You may be wondering if confidentiality will be maintained, and if you can be safe in this group. Let's explore some of your feelings about the group."_

Stage 2. Let's return to the group example described for the first stage.

Group Session: It is now a later session and the members can only be described as very quiet and withdrawn. The leader wonders what happened, because the previous session seemed to go very well with all members participating, interactions among members increased, some significant self-disclosures were made, and members said they were pleased with their progress. However, this session is a complete reversal of the previous one.

The group begins in silence, and no one speaks unless addressed directly by the leader, and then the speaker is very terse without volunteering any additional information. The leader asks what has happened to change the mood from the previous session, but no one responds. The leader then produces an exercise to try to get the group motivated. Members complete it, but there is no energy around it and it does not seem to produce any insight or learning. The session ends as it began—with silence.

The next session is even more different from earlier, more productive sessions. Members are cranky and irritable, challenging and arguing with each other over almost everything said. The leader tries to intervene, but is ignored. Finally, one member says angrily and loudly that he is bored, tired of the group, and doesn't feel he is being helped. Some other members say that they feel the same way, and that the group isn't going anywhere.

Stage 2 Analysis: The very idea of conflict is disturbing to many group leaders and members. To some, it is so threatening that they work hard to keep it from appearing in the group, failing to realize or accept that conflict does not have to be destructive; it can be managed to accomplish all of the following:

- Increase understanding of self and others
- Make visible unconscious projections and transference
- Allow uncomfortable feelings to be expressed and explored as catharsis and interpersonal learning
- Teach how to contain and manage one's personal feelings, such as anger and hurt
- Show how to let go of grudges and resentments
- Strengthen relationships
- Highlight closely held perceptions of authority and sibling relationships

Conflict is an opportunity for enlightenment for all members, including the leader. Thus, leaders should strive to become more comfortable with some level of conflict, accept and understand its importance for group progress, and learn how to make constructive use of it. Members will catch the leader's attitude about conflict, put their own spin on it, and act on it in some way.

How can a leader know that conflict is being resisted by group members? Some clues can be an insistence on describing the group as cohesive in the beginning stage, making comments about how well they are getting along; a quick and unquestioning acceptance of whatever the leader and other members propose; nonverbal behavior that communicates a desire for flight or considerable discomfort in the group; provocative or teasing comments, sarcasm, or soothing and reassuring responses when a member or the leader seems annoyed; and a minimizing of differences among members and with the leader.

Among the group dynamics that leaders can observe to understand members' perceptions of conflict is how members manage conflict—member–member conflict, leader–member conflict, and personal internal conflict. The common ways are repression, denial, suppression, acting out, and constructive resolution. Leaders who are uncomfortable with conflict will fail to capitalize on these clues. These leaders can feel the underlying discomfort and, just as the members are doing, ignore or smooth it over for fear that conflict will emerge. However, if leaders can recognize the clues, this would be an opportunity to determine how members would feel if conflict were to emerge, and their characteristic ways of managing conflict. This discussion could also include statements about the inevitability of conflict in groups and that there are ways to constructively manage it. It can be a very positive learning experience when the leader identifies a member's conflict with him or her, and then demonstrates how it can be worked through and resolved. This leader–member conflict can be a mild one, such as questioning why the leader is doing something, disagreeing about what was meant and said, or disguising ways of questioning the leader's competence. How the leader handles conflicts can send a powerful message to members about the safety of allowing other conflicts to emerge.

When members experience constructive conflict resolution,

- Their fears about conflict are reduced
- Feelings are more openly expressed instead of being suppressed or denied
- Feelings of safety and trust are increased and enhanced
- Connections among members and the leader are forged and become more meaningful
- Defenses against self-exploration are ignored
- Members become more receptive to feedback, thereby increasing interpersonal learning
- Anger, fear, guilt, and shame are openly expressed when they emerge
- Members learn a conflict resolution process that can be used outside the group

These are the behaviors, thoughts, and attitudes that provide the basis for stage 3—the working and cohesive stage—to appear. Stage 2 member behaviors can include the following:

- Challenges to the leader's competence or authority
- Expressions of discontent about the course or progress of the group
- An emphasis on differences among group members
- Expressions of irritation to each other or to the leader
- More open expressions of negative responses to each other
- Efforts to exert power and control
- More visible projections and transference
- Few empathetic or understanding responses
- Open conflict with the leader or other members

Most groups will probably not have a clearly defined stage 2. What likely will happen is that some of these behaviors will surface from time to time, but entire sessions will not have all or some of these member behaviors. Most will be mild expressions, such as challenges to the leader that are expressed as what appear to be reasonable questions about what the leader is doing, or about his or her intent or motives. However they are expressed, they are a challenge.

Expected Member Behaviors and Leader Tasks: Leader tasks in stage 2 are to recognize the emergence of conflict, model and teach constructive conflict resolution, help members express negative feeling and reactions, show members how to effectively become more independent, emphasize similarities among members, and not take challenges to the leader's competency and authority personally. Leaders' extent of personal development will play a major role in how they manage stage 2. Let's review some understandings and possible leader interventions for the group described earlier.

Leader Understandings: The group is entering the second stage where members are dissatisfied with the leader, but are unable to challenge the leader directly and do so in indirect ways such as silence and irritability.

Possible Intervention: The leader might say: "It could be that your silence, irritability, and dissatisfaction is with me and not with the group and each other. You may feel that I am not meeting your needs, and I invite you to talk openly about your feelings." (Members can either speak of what they feel, or deny feeling this way. However, the group will start up again.)

Stage 3. Example:

Group Session: During a later session for the same group, the leader observes members responding directly with each other, making reflective or empathic responses, engaging in significant self-disclosures, and generally working well together. It is a very different group from when it began, and as it was just a couple of sessions ago.

Stage 3 Analysis: Leader tasks at this stage are to stay out of the way so that members can work; identify group resistance; make group process commentary to help members become more aware of what they are doing collectively; encourage and support members' self-exploration; highlight members' growth, development, and progress; and use the therapeutic factors that emerge.

The group members feel wonderful, valued, and productive at this stage. One negative point is that members can become reluctant to do or say anything that has the potential to destroy this harmony and pleasant feeling, so negative responses and feelings can be suppressed. The leader's challenge is to stay aware that this could happen, identify when it is probably happening, and encourage members to continue to openly express their immediate thoughts, feelings, and ideas.

This is also the stage where cliques can form and exert a felt negative impact. Cliques are impossible to prevent as members get to know each other and forge meaningful connections. Then too, if the members are together in a setting, such as a hospital or rehabilitation center, they can or will have considerable interactions outside the group, and this can also facilitate the emergence of cliques. Members not in the clique can feel excluded, that secrets are being shared outside the group, and that clique members have a certain bond that encourages an us-against-them attitude. The most group leaders can do to nullify these possible negative effects is to emphasize that group matters are not to be discussed outside the group, even among group members. Leaders will not be able to enforce this, but the awareness of what behavior is expected can help prevent it. Leaders can also discuss with the group the negative effects of cliques. Cliques promote secrecy and mistrust, which most group members will want to avoid.

The transition to the ending or termination stage can be easier to notice than transitions to other stages. Even when the leader does not comment on the number of sessions untill the group ends, or on the time remaining, members begin to sense the ending on some level. Their behavior begins to be more reflective of the behavior in stages 1 and 2, and the harmony and warmth that characterize stage 3 begin to disappear.

Expected Member Behaviors and Leader Tasks: Expected member behaviors in stage 3 include expressing immediate feelings and reactions directly to other members and to the leader, making personal statements, acknowledging and accepting similarities, engaging in catharsis that includes interpersonal learning, responding empathetically, and giving and receiving constructive feedback. Attitudes can include considerably less defensive behavior and resistance, increased awareness of self and others, and a sense of the group as a safe place to let the real self appear.

Major leader tasks during the stage are few because members come prepared to work, and engage in effective member behaviors. This is the stage where group process commentary is most effective as members are more open to reflecting on the commentary, and do not imme-diately reject it unexamined. Leaders have to be careful to not push members too much, to let them work through disagreements and clashes, refrain from intervening too quickly, and to give members more leeway in self-examination and self-exploration.

Leaders can observe if there are cliques, and when these are identified can then make visible the impact of their outside-the-group behavior on other group members, and on the feelings of safety and trust in the group. This is the stage where boundaries may not be as strong and inad-vertent confidential material can be revealed. Members may need to be reminded of this potential threat. Another possible threat to the group's progress can be the unwillingness to bring up neg-ative responses and reactions among group members. Leaders can ask if members are suppressing these as a way to remind them that progress can be made when members are genuine.

> *Leader Understandings: Once members know that conflict and challenges to the leader will not mean destruction for members or for the leader, and are shown how conflicts can be worked out, they become more secure and feel safer to let more of their real selves be seen. Personal connections among members are strengthened, and more trust that they will not be rejected or excluded is developed. Members are less fearful that their unpleas-ant behavior will result in destruction or exclusion.*

> *Possible Interventions: The leader can provide encouragement and support and, most important, stay out of the way and let members work.*

Stage 4

> *Group Session: Although the leader has continually reminded members that the group is scheduled to end, members have ignored it for several sessions. It is now the next-to-last session and members are still refusing to consider the group's ending. Members begin top-ics and then drop them, they interrupt each other, many empathic failures occur, and the general mood is one of irritability and somberness.*

Stage 4 Analysis: Members can have mixed feelings about ending the group. There can be a sense of relief that they survived the experience, pleasure at realizing the growth and development they made, regret for missed opportunities, sadness for loss of meaningful connections made as a result of the group experience, panic at the thought that the group will end before they are ready or have completed their work, and excitement or despair about their futures. Each member will have different sets and degrees of some or all of these feelings. The leader's task is to prepare members for closure of this experience in a way that leaves them with few or no regrets or a sense of unfinished business.

It is essential that leaders plan for termination and not just have the group stop. Members need to be prepared for the ending in sufficient time to internalize it and make their personal adjustments, and to be shown how to effectively end experiences and relationships. Leaders will find that few people know how to do this. Thus, the ending of the group is as an opportunity for further learning for members.

The final stage of the group is also where existential issues can emerge, or reemerge, and become acute, although this is likely to happen in disguised ways. Existential issues of death, loneliness, alienation, and the human conditions of pain and suffering can be a significant part of members' termination fears and process. Their physical or mental conditions that brought them to group are still of concern, and may not have improved—or may have even worsened. They begin to retreat from reaching out to others, and return to self-absorption. The loss of group support and encouragement is major and significant and should not be minimized, although some members do so as a way to cope.

Leaders can expect the group to go through some variation of the grieving process, which involves shock and numbness, denial, anger, attempts to make the group continue, and acceptance and accommodation. This is a process that may not be fully accomplished for some members, but any progress is better than none. The need for a satisfactory group termination is crucial, and leaders should begin the process approximately halfway through the life of the group. A process for termination is described more fully in Chapter 6. If the group is open-ended, members should be encouraged to notify the leader several sessions before they intend to terminate. This allows the leader to guide that member, and the members that remain in the group, through the process.

Leader Understandings: *In the termination stage, member behavior may regress to stage 1 in some ways. Expected member behaviors can include all of the following:*

- *Denial that the group is ending*
- *Increased crankiness, suppression of feelings, and withdrawal*
- *Minimizing the value of the group, the leader, or what has been gained*
- *Panic at the thought of the loss of support provided by the group*
- *Dependency on the leader reemerging*
- *Depression or despair about "getting better"*
- *Confusion about the ambiguity and ambivalent feelings about termination*
- *Feelings of abandonment*

A leader has to work hard to keep these from overwhelming members, which can lead them to prematurely cease working.

Possible Interventions: The leader could do the following:

- *Highlight members' progress and accomplishments*
- *Illustrate how goals were met*
- *Teach members satisfactory closure for the group, and for relationships*
- *Provide encouragement, support, and faith in members' abilities to continue to grow and develop*
- *Model strategies for coping with loss and grief*

It is important that closure not be minimized, truncated, or ignored. Save a social event for after the session, and do not let such activities substitute for closure. Saying goodbye is as important as saying hello.

Types of Groups and Stages

Task and psychoeducational groups are not likely to have a sufficient number of sessions to fully experience all the stages, but many stages can be experienced. Even support groups that continue for years may not experience all the stages because they are open-ended, have different purposes and goals that do not emphasize personal growth and development, and there is a lack of a definitive time frame where termination can be anticipated and planned. This is not to say that some personal growth and development cannot be achieved, because it can be. However, these are not the focus or emphasis for support groups. Therapy-related groups are usually characterized by a definite number of sessions over a specific time period that can range from a 1-hour group to a multiple-session group over several months. However, almost all groups will experience a beginning and an end. Following are some characteristics for how support and therapy-related psychoeducational groups can experience development through the stages, to give you an idea of how different types of groups may have different sets of stages, and how leaders can accommodate these differences.

Example: Support Groups

Leaders of support groups that have met for some time have to be prepared to constantly introduce and integrate new members into the group, and to help members who terminate do so satisfactorily for them and for the remaining group members. These can be challenges in many ways as leaders have to attend to both the individual and to the group. In addition, it can feel regressive when either new members arrive, or when members leave. The most important leader tasks are to contain and manage members' anxiety, recognize regression and resistance and understand it, help members verbalize concerns and fears around the entrance or exit of members, join with the members to facilitate inclusion of the new member or loss of a member, and divide attention among the new or leaving member and the remaining members.

Members can experience a reemergence of the anxiety they experienced when they first came to the group, and leaders should be prepared to manage and contain that anxiety by doing the following:

- Encouraging all members to verbalize immediate responses and feelings about the event, such as fantasies about what the group will be like with the new member
- Taking time for meaningful introductions more than name

- Accepting that there may be jealousy arising over the attention given to the new member
- Planning how to foster inclusion of the new member

If there is sufficient time before the new member attends the group, it can be helpful to brief that member on what is expected of him or her and what the group is like, and to prepare group members for the new arrival. This latter process can be similar in some ways to planning for the arrival of a sibling in a family. Careful preparation reduces ambiguity and anxiety, but does not totally eliminate it.

Termination of a member should also be planned as much as possible so that the other members have an opportunity to try and complete any unfinished business, and to explore their feelings around that member's termination and around their possible terminations and loss of support. The condition around which the support group is formed can bring premature termination stress and fears, especially when that condition could mean death. If or when a member dies, expectedly or unexpectedly, the group leader can expect to have to deal with members' termination issues and fears. The loss and grief process should be part of every support group leader's knowledge base so that whenever termination occurs, the leader can deal with it effectively.

Long-term support groups can develop some measure of cohesiveness. Members encourage and support each other, exchange information, and develop intimate and special relationships with each other. The most important negative outcome is that the members become so cohesive that a new member finds it almost impossible to join and be accepted. The cohesive group members are not aware of how they act to exclude "others," but the "other" person can be aware of feeling excluded, and like an intruder. Leaders have to work especially hard to keep this from happening, and develop a process for integrating new members into the group.

Because there can be a greater measure of shared leadership responsibilities, the challenge to the leader can be minimal. Members are more apt to engage in conflict with each other, but even that conflict can be muted. It may be that the leader recognizes the conflict stage only in retrospect. That can make it difficult to model and demonstrate constructive conflict resolution, but there will probably be numerous opportunities to teach these skills as members bring outside-the-group conflicts to the group. Teaching conflict resolution skills is helpful for members, but not working on inside-the-group conflicts can prevent cohesiveness from being formed. There will be some cohesiveness, but not the part where personal issues are freely shared and worked on.

Even though group stages are experienced somewhat differently than in therapy-related psychoeducational groups, it is still important that leaders of support groups have similar leadership training. As you can see from the discussion about stages for support groups, much can and does arise that needs the guidance of a well-prepared leader.

Example: Therapy-Related Psychoeducational Groups

The usual stages for therapy-related groups will also be modified in therapy-related psychoeducational groups because these groups have the following characteristics:

- Are formed around a common illness or other condition
- Have strong educational components that require considerable information giving

- Generally meet for a specified time that can range from a 1-hour session to usually 12 or fewer sessions
- Do not emphasize or focus on relationship building among members although that does happen
- Tend to be narrowly focused

Termination should be expected and planned for in advance for nonclinical groups. If the group meets for several sessions, some elements of stage 2 (conflict) can emerge. The group probably will not meet long enough for stage 3 to be fully developed.

Leaders should be prepared for the chaos and confusion members in nonclinical group's will bring to stage 2. Their lives have been turned upside down, and they are trying to deal with that in addition to the ambiguity of the group situation. Leaders need to expend considerable time, effort, and patience to deal with the intense emotions and confusion members bring to the group. All members will benefit if the leader does the following:

- Takes time to let members express their feelings about what brings them to the group, and their fears and perceptions about the group experience
- Demonstrates, models, and teaches them how to capitalize on the group experience
- Provides sufficient structure but realizes that members' anxiety keeps them from ever having enough structure
- Limits the amount of information to what members can absorb, and not what the leader thinks they need to know

If stage 2 is reached and there are challenges to the leader and among members, leaders can meet those challenges by demonstrating calm acceptance, and guiding members to work out the disagreements and other manifestations of conflict. Although it is unlikely that stage 3 will be experienced, some elements of it may be possible, especially if members are highly functioning. The time frame for most, if not all, therapy-related psychoeducational groups is too brief to allow events to emerge that move members to stage 3.

Leaders can expect members to arrive at the group with considerable anxiety about their condition, fear of the future and their ability to care for themselves, pain or loss of function, and either overt or repressed anger at their fate. These emotional states will vary among members, but almost all will have some version of these feelings in addition to the anxiety and apprehension about the group experience. These feelings can cause stage 1 to be prolonged as there is so much to work through and settle. Further, leaders must present a body of information, and this too takes time. The process suggested in Chapter 6 can be used with appropriate modifications to meet the needs of a particular group.

Termination can be more easily planned for therapy-related psychoeducational groups than it can be for support groups. This planning provides for a more orderly ending for the group as a whole, and can give members a sense of closure for this experience. It is important for leaders to stay in touch with members' feelings about the group experience to help in planning for successful termination. The greater the emotional investment members have in the group experience, the more keenly felt the loss may be. However members invest in the group, some measure of loss will be experienced, and planned termination can help members express these feelings, and to work through them so that they do not carry unfinished business after the group. The process described in Chapter 6 on termination can be adapted and used for various groups.

Phases of Member Development

Members can also go through phases of development that parallel the group stages in some ways. For example, the first stage of group is characterized by confusion, fear, and dread. The first phase for individual member development is characterized by shock, confusion, and denial. Proposed are four phases of member development: autistic, despair, clearing, and adjustment and new beginnings.

The *autistic* stage is so termed because the members' focus is on internal experiencing that can be difficult to express in words, and little effort is made to connect with others. There can be an inner muting or turning off of self-expression and engagement with others. Group members are tentative, cautious, concerned about inclusion and rejection, unsure of what benefits the group can provide, and have concerns about the leader's ability to protect them.

Just as with everything else, members will differ in their responses. Some become talkative, but tend to talk in circles trying to get a handle on what is happening to them. An example of considerable autism is group members who have serious medical illnesses, such as cancer. Their confusion, denial, and shock renders them incapable of absorbing information because they are focused on their internal experiencing and fears for the future. They can be acutely aware of the existential or reality-based dread of death, but can also be unaware that this is what is fueling their responses. They are in turmoil with many feelings swirling around, and nothing is making much sense at this point.

Leaders of all groups can assist members during this phase by guiding them in expressing whatever they are feeling; giving a voice to the negative thoughts, feelings, and dreads; providing sufficient information to help reduce anxiety but not overloading them at a time when they cannot absorb and use new material; and by highlighting the universality among members around significant characteristics. Understanding what members are experiencing, what they are unable to integrate or express, and facilitating connections among members is an important leader task that helps members transition from a self-absorbed, autistic focus to a more connected and collaborative focus where they are able to take a more productive role in the group. This also fosters the growth of trust and safety in the group, and encourages members to reach out to each other. Leaders find it beneficial to join with members where they are emotionally, and to not engage in overwhelming members by telling, selling, and directing. It can be more important for the leader to let his or her inner self be seen as a calming, accepting, and nurturing self, and to form a therapeutic alliance. This is the phase where task functions should be secondary to relationship functions.

Phase 2, *despair*, could be characterized as the flight phase. Members begin to emerge from the confusion and tentativeness experienced in phase 1, and try to get away from the problem or concern by blaming, displacing, and projecting, using anger to mask despair, guilt, and shame. They are cranky and irritable, unable to be satisfied with anything. If physical pain is a component of their condition or illness, there can be considerable discomfort and anger about unsuccessful treatment of the pain.

Leaders can expect members in this phase to be dissatisfied with the leader, the group, and almost everything else. Nothing is satisfactory, and attempts to reduce the discomfort and dissatisfaction will have minimal results at best. This phase can be particularly difficult for group leaders as nothing they do seems to help members out of their mixed anger and distress. Phase 2 demands that leaders understand member developmental phase behavior; have sufficient confidence in their competence so as not to get discouraged at what seems to be lack of progress; skillfully guide members to accept reality and avoid denial or suppression of feelings; demonstrate and teach adapting and coping skills; and be able to accept the negative feelings members can project onto the leader. This phase can be difficult and takes an emotional toll on leaders.

Phase 3, *clearing*, is characterized by attempts to adjust, frustration at progress, and glimmerings of hope and optimism. This is the phase where members can begin to actively participate in their own therapy by experimenting with new behavior, accepting awareness and understanding, reaching out to form new connections for new and old relationships, and learning new ways of behaving and relating. Thus, hope and optimism can be introduced and acted on to maximize the mind-body-spirit connections. Members who reach this phase of development can contribute significantly to their growth, development, healing, recovery, progress, and inoculation against relapse.

Primary leader tasks during this phase are to

- Teach, model, and demonstrate the efficacy of a fighting spirit, hope, and altruism
- Encourage members to reach out and connect to others in meaningful ways
- Support efforts to adapt and change
- Emphasize and highlight changes and progress no matter how slight
- Capitalize on receptiveness and openness to maximize teaching opportunities
- Let members do the work they need to do

It can be a delicate balancing act to both give support and show confidence in members' abilities to heal, grow, and develop. Leaders do not want to foster dependency, nor do they want to fail to give needed support, direction, and guidance. What is ideal is that leaders teach members independence, and how they can take care of themselves to the best of their ability.

Phase 4 is termed *adjustment and a new beginning*. Members need to know that whatever they get from the group is only the start of a new phase in their development. This stage is characterized by adjustment and reenergization. There can be excitement at anticipating changes, confidence in their self-efficacy, a recognition of the reality of their lives, and a desire to continue to grow and develop.

Leaders can teach members maintenance skills that will help reduce stress; keep hope as a factor; strengthen self-esteem, self-confidence, and self-efficacy; highlight the importance of meaningful and satisfying relationships as part of their quality of life; and encourage optimism and a fighting spirit. Helping members get to this phase is a goal that may not be achieved, and leaders need to be aware that much of the success or failure rests with the individual members. Leaders can present opportunities, understand the phases and course of development, and have an inner faith and conviction in the efficacy of the group experience to promote the development, and this can get communicated to members. However, each member decides how, what, and when to grow. Leaders can only present opportunities.

Teaching Group Membership Skills

Teaching membership skills has many advantages. This is one way to help reduce some of the uncertainty and ambiguity about what behavior is expected in the group, improve ways of relating and communicating, build trust and safety, and guide members in constructive self-exploration (Piper & Marrache, 1981; Piper & McCallum, 1994; Piper & Perrault, 1989; Santarsiero, Baker, & McGee, 1995). Using these behaviors and attitudes can ensure that members get the most out of the group experience. They are also useful for relationships outside the group. Many skills presented here can be used in all types of groups no matter what the duration of the group. Some skills may need a longer time to be developed, such as learning how to make your feedback constructive, but many are just good basic relating and communication skills. The following sections describe the first two skills in more detail.

- Productive group behaviors and attitudes
- Counterproductive behaviors and attitudes
- The importance of goals
- Personal statements
- Constructive conflict and conflict resolution
- Direct and effective communication
- Expression of important feelings
- Expression of thoughts and ideas
- Constructive feedback
- Why being present centered is important
- Responsibility for your progress

Productive Behaviors and Attitudes

There are behaviors and attitudes that contribute to productivity for the group as a whole and for individual members. Critical and basic expectations are that members attend all sessions, arrive on time and be prepared to work, actively participate, engage in self-exploration, and interact with other members and the leader.

Many group members report feeling confused and frustrated because the expectations and directions are not specific enough for their needs. These feelings can emerge around an ambiguous, new, and unfamiliar situation and can occur even for members who have considerable experience with group participation. Although these constructive behaviors and attitudes can help reduce anxiety, they cannot eliminate it. Only the group member himself or herself can reduce personal anxiety. This is why extensive explanations by the leader do not work to eliminate members' feelings of ambiguity, uncertainty, and anxiety. Group leaders are advised to respect and acknowledge the anxiety, ambiguity, and uncertainty about the group, provide sufficient structure and direction so that the group can begin its work, but not try to explain in such detail so that members are no longer anxious. This is futile and delays the group beginning to work.

Effective and productive members:

- Have a personal focus for the group and each session
- Are flexible and open to experiencing
- Arrive ready to work each session
- Ask for what they want or need
- Pay attention to their feelings, and are aware of the feelings of other members
- Openly express important feelings, thoughts, and ideas
- Actively participate in sessions
- Experiment with new ways of behaving
- Become and remain open to receiving feedback
- Make their nonverbal behavior consistent with their verbal behavior
- Take responsibility for how much they grow and learn
- Maintain confidentiality
- Give appropriate feedback to others
- Are willing to work to resolve conflicts
- Are willing to consider that their reaction may be transference or a projection
- Use facilitative communication skills such as active listening
- Speak directly to other group members
- Respond directly to input from other group members
- Are willing to examine their resistances
- Are tolerant of diverse points of view or values
- Are able to be present centered

Counterproductive Behaviors and Attitudes

Counterproductive behaviors and attitudes are not "wrong" or "bad," they just retard learning and growth for both the individual and the group. The attitudes are internal states that can be inferred from what someone says. For example, excuses given quite often by members who sit back and wait to become involved include "I'm shy," "I'm introverted," and "I like to sit back and observe." These verbalizations all demonstrate a reluctance to become involved. Members may find it productive to honestly admit that they do not want to be involved, *and* explore what is keeping them from participating. It could be helpful to the group for them to openly verbalize their reluctance, and to describe what it is about the group that seems to be promoting these feelings.

Many of the counterproductive behaviors and attitudes could become helpful if openly acknowledged, feelings are identified and accepted, defense mechanisms are identified, and when members engage in self-exploration around these identified behaviors and attitudes.

Counterproductive *behaviors* include:

- Giving solicited or unsolicited advice
- Interpreting or ascribing motives for other members

- Asking questions except those needed for clarification
- Getting caught up in details rather than reporting on feelings experienced
- Gossiping
- Participating in a clique
- Rushing to soothe others to keep them from experiencing uncomfortable or unpleasant feelings
- Telling stories
- Using sarcasm as input or as a response
- Indirect expressions of hostility
- Labeling others
- Disparaging input from others
- Ignoring or denying conflicts with others

Counterproductive *attitudes* include:

- Waiting to work or become involved in the group
- Suppressing important feelings
- Expecting others to take care of them
- Expecting others to change just because they want them to
- Making quick evaluations and judgments about others
- Expecting others to fully understand them
- Feeling that others must self-disclose in order for them to do so

Summary

1. The stages of group development can be used to help the group leader understand the group's needs, wishes, fears, and fantasies, which reduces some of the ambiguity and uncertainty associated with groups.
2. Research has shown that certain member behaviors are associated with each stage, and the leader's ability to recognize and identify these provides clues and strategies for effective interventions.
3. There are also stages for member development that can guide some expectations for group leaders. These are also clues to the growth, development, and learning that members are experiencing as an evaluation of their progress toward their goals.
4. It can be helpful to teach member's group membership skills, as this can help reduce some of their anxiety, encourage participation, and teach them effective and constructive ways of relating and communicating.

Chapter Activities

1. Form small groups and identify specific behaviors class members exhibited in the first few classes that were reflective of stage 1 group development.

2. Working individually, ask class members to generate a list of associations and reactions to the concept of conflict emerging in a group that they are leading. When this is complete, class members can share their lists in small groups. The final step is to have the small groups report their summaries for associations and reactions.

3. Hold class discussions on one or more of the following topics:

   - Strategies to form a therapeutic alliance with abused children
   - Strategies to form a therapeutic alliance with court-mandated adolescents on anger management
   - Strategies to form a therapeutic alliance with displaced homemakers
   - Strategies to form a therapeutic alliance with men facing prostrate cancer treatment

Personal Development Exercise: Write a poem about your creative self.

Chapter 6

General Guidelines for Planning

Major Topics

1. Components of and general guidelines for planning all types of groups.
2. Guidelines for planning groups for children.
3. Guidelines for planning groups for adolescents.
4. Guidelines for planning groups for adults.
5. The critical first session.
6. Planning termination and closure.

Introduction

Planning is critical and essential for effective groups, and is the responsibility of the group leader. It should not be overlooked or minimized because of the leader's experience and expertise. There is always something to be learned, modified, or adapted for the new group, and this should be planned in advance. The discussion on planning is divided into several categories: information gathering, structural factors, preparation, and instruction and instructional style; planning groups for children, adolescents, and adults; and assessment. Planning strategies for specific types of groups, such as psychoeducational groups, are presented in those separate chapters. This chapter also discusses the first and last group sessions and the process for saying goodbye.

Information Gathering

Information gathering includes doing a needs assessment, determining the purpose for the group, identifying the target audience, and reviewing research findings on the condition, issue, or concern that will be the focus for the group (DeLucia-Waack & Kalodner, 2005; Kalodner & Coughlin, 2004). Questions explored during the *needs assessment* focus on identifying the extent to which a group experience would be beneficial. Are there sufficient numbers of people who could or would use the services of a group formed around a particular topic?

The *purpose* for the group is derived from the needs assessment that has identified a deficiency, lack of information, needed upgrade, or area of skills development that would increase efficiency and productivity. The *target audience* is also identified during this process, and all available information is gathered, such as abilities, educational levels, and so on. Some settings, such as schools or businesses, may have considerable background information about potential group members, but this information may not be available to the group leader, nor is much of it useful in planning. Basic background information that can be helpful in planning for most nonclinical groups includes age of participants, educational level(s), gender, occupation, country of origin, and if they are voluntary or involuntary group participants. The fourth task in information gathering is reviewing research findings on the group's focus issues or concerns.

Audience Characteristics

Gather information about the characteristics of your target audience. You will need basic information about members such as age, gender, educational level, and the member's present condition. Counseling, therapy, and psychotherapy groups will need to collect a more extensive personal history from members including significant past traumas such as rape, abuse, and assault. Other information that may be helpful includes personality and intellectual assessment, family history, and a health history. This information is fundamental to your planning.

Age is important, especially when forming groups for children and adolescents, and when there may be a wide range of ages for group members. The importance of age for children and adolescents will be discussed in later sections. Adult groups can have a wide variety of member ages, and this can either be enriching or can cause difficulties. It can be especially troubling if one or more members transfer their feelings about other personal relationships on the basis of age alone, respond to bias or stereotyping, or assume they should be treated a particular way because of their ages. On the other hand, a group that has members of a variety of ages can be enriching: Members learn from each other, wisdom and lessons from experience are passed on, new perspectives are gained, and bias and stereotyping are debunked. The most important point is for the leader to be aware of the ages of target group members, and the potential for trouble or enhancement.

Gender can also be a major concern, or an enhancement. A mixture of males and females can help members gain new understandings and perspectives, but also has the potential for fulfilling stereotypes. Attitudes, biases, and misinformation can fuel discord, or can be the basis for creating new awareness as these meet with reality. Leaders also want to stay in touch with members' responses and attitudes toward any gay and lesbian members that negatively impact their inclusion and participation. Some conditions, such as breast or prostate cancer, may necessitate a same-gender group, and factors other than gender will then be more important.

Educational levels of group members can be a significant factor. In groups with members at varied levels, you need to gear your presentations to *all* members so that some don't feel you are talking down to them and others don't find the material too complex for them to grasp. The ideal situation is that members have similar educational levels, such as all high school graduates. Whether members are at similar or varied levels is important to know for selecting materials, assigning homework, determining the amount of material you present and its depth, and considering instructional methods.

A member's *present condition* or illness plays a role in educational level. Leaders should be familiar with the various effects certain conditions or illnesses can have on individuals, with particular emphasis on degree of attention span that can be expected; the extent of cognitive functioning or impairment; the effects on affective functioning and expression such as mood swings, and inappropriate expressions of feelings; the effects on relationships; and so on. Careful planning will prevent you and group members from the frustration and discouragement that results when you cannot use planned materials and activities because of these effects.

The *effects of medication(s)* are also important, especially when they may impair members' attention, participation, and learning. Sedating effects, tranquilizing effects or their lack when prescribed medication is not taken, stimulating effects that produce hyperactivity, and lack of pain reduction are some effects that can impact members and their learning. For example, a member who can ordinarily concentrate on the material presented may find that the medicating effects prevent him from doing so. Some common effects of medication are known, and knowing what medications members are taking can help you plan to work around any effects that may exist.

Some members may have more than one condition or illness, or there can be another associated illness or condition in addition to the major or presenting one. For example, depression can be a condition associated with the aftereffects of a heart attack. Medications can also cause other associated conditions, and these too can play a role in members' participation. Whereas the focus for your group may be one condition or illness, you should also be aware that there may be others that will also impact some members and the group. You can prevent yourself from becoming frustrated by understanding and gearing your planning for this potential situation.

Significant *past traumas* can be of vital importance in understanding members' reactions and participation, as the current conditions or illness can trigger old memories, projections, and transference, especially when these were not resolved earlier. You will not be able to anticipate these specific triggers, but you may get some clues from the member's reactions to the information presented, films and other media, and group exercises and other activities. Once distressing memories are triggered, it then becomes your responsibility to work with the member to reduce the distress, to consult with your supervisor or other professionals outside the session, or to refer the member.

Other background information that can be helpful for planning the group can be part of the intake session(s). This information may already be available in members' files, so it becomes important for you to review all available information. Ideally, the following information would be available: personality and intellectual assessments, family history, and health history. This background information can guide you in selecting instructional strategies; choosing information consistent with members' abilities to absorb and understand; helping anticipate some possible behavior problems; giving information and guidance that is helpful and useful; realizing members' limitations and constraints; and reducing the possibility that you will unconsciously impose your values, or expect members to share the same values as you.

Structural Factors

Structural factors include membership criteria and selection: if the group is to be open or closed; the duration, frequency, number of sessions, and length of sessions; the size of the group; whether the group is homogeneous or heterogeneous; and location concerns. *Screening and selection* of group members is desirable, but not always feasible. Shulman (1994) asserts that selection cannot be done scientifically. Most authors and researchers describe the optimum characteristics for successful membership, but these tend to focus on inner characteristics that can be difficult or impossible to assess, even with a personal interview. Riva et al. (2004) and Piper and McCallum (1994) propose that the following group member characteristics be used when selecting group members:

- A moderate ability to tolerate frustration
- Moderate social ability
- Commitment to change
- Psychological mindedness
- Expectation that the group will be beneficial.

Leaders of many nonclinical groups are not able to select group members, or to screen out people who are unsuitable. The membership may be predetermined by the organization, and participants ordered or forced to attend. However, knowing this in advance allows the group leader to become emotionally prepared to deal with possible resentment, resistance, and defiance.

The decision about whether the group is to be *open* where new members are constantly added, or *closed* where no new members are added after the group begins, is also part of planning. In many settings this decision is made by someone other than the leader, but leaders should try to influence the decision. It should be noted that support groups are usually open groups.

Central to the group's structure is setting the *day and time meetings will be held, and frequency* for meetings, the *number* of sessions to be held, and the length of each session. It can be extremely important for some members to have these set *and followed* because of chaotic or inconsistent experiences they have had throughout their lives. These members may not have been able to count on anything occurring on a regular basis, such as relationships that are reliable and dependable. Attending to such fundamental things as time boundaries can be comforting and supportive, thereby relieving some of the stress and anxiety around group participation.

Decisions need to be made and communicated about the following:

- The dates when the group is scheduled to begin and end, except for support groups
- The number of sessions and the duration of each session—that is, the number of minutes or hours for each session
- How often the group will meet—for example, once a week for 8 weeks
- The day, time, and place for group meetings

The *size* of the group should also be predetermined when possible, so that sufficient space and materials are available. The type of group often plays a major role in detemining size. For example, educational groups tend to have more members than do psychoeducational groups. The more focused the group is on dissemination of information, the more members it tends to have. Remember that the discussion and members' input can be limited when there are large numbers of participants.

Groups that focus on skills building, and those that have a significant emotional component such as psychoeducational groups, need to have fewer members so that there is sufficient time for each member to practice, or for personal exploration. These groups are recommended to have 5 to 10 members (Magen & Mangiardi, 2005; Smead, 1995). Educational, task, and support groups can be productive with more members than many other types of groups.

Decide if the group will have *homogeneous or heterogeneous membership*. Homogeneous groups generally can more easily develop safety and trust because of perceived similarities, but can get so caught up in the desire and need to maintain harmony that conflicts and the like are ignored or suppressed. Heterogeneous groups have more perceived differences among members that can contribute to their being tentative and wary in the beginning, and safety and trust take longer to develop. However, heterogeneous groups can have a richness of resources because of the diversity.

Location concerns refer to the size and comfort of the room (space) where the group meets, freedom from intrusion and disruption, and adequate equipment. Ideally, the space for the group meetings is adequate in size for all the planned activities, has comfortable seating, allows the temperature to be controlled for members' comfort, provides privacy from intrusions or outside disruptions, and has tables or other equipment readily available. In the real world, not all meeting spaces meet these criteria. Leaders should check on the location variables prior to the beginning of each group, and each session so as to make needed adjustments.

The final task under structural factors is to develop an *assessment plan*. Much valuable information can be gathered from assessment that can be used to do the following:

- Demonstrate the efficacy of the group for future funding, insurance, and for others who are in search of effective groups for particular issues, concerns, problems, or topics
- Document and highlight members' gains and progress
- Evaluate the effectiveness of instruction, exercises, and so on
- Assess group members' satisfaction with their experiences
- Determine the effectiveness of leadership
- Identify the group factors that were the most and least helpful
- Add to the body of knowledge

Preparation: Goals, Objectives, and Rules

After taking care of information gathering and structural factors, the leader's tasks are to develop preliminary goals and objectives, rules and expectations; select specific strategies and activities; plan sessions; and gather materials and supplies. The preliminary goals and objectives will give some structure to the group and help set realistic expectations for outcomes. These are termed *preliminary* because group leaders will find it beneficial to engage in collaborative goal setting with group members so that their individual goals will be incorporated. This can be done prior to the beginning of the group, or in the first session. What is important is that group members have some personal goals, and that they see how these are part of what the group will be doing.

Goals are expected or desired outcomes for participation in the group and should be defined as such, be measurable or observable, and be realistic for the expected group experience. Keep the number of goals to one or two. *Objectives* are steps or processes used to attain the goals and can focus on more specific behavior that is also measurable or observable. Objectives should be stated in terms of what members will be able to do as a result of participating in the group. Examples for objectives for a group goal of learning effective time management skills could be similar to the following:

- List personal time wasters and strategies to reduce or overcome them.
- Describe how to categorize and prioritize tasks to make the best use of time.
- Plan tasks to capitalize on personal high-energy time.
- Verbalize the value of "to do" lists and how to best use them.

Once the goals and objectives are developed and written, group leaders can better select strategies that are designed to help meet them. Determining which learning activities are likely to benefit the group becomes easier because goals and objectives consider the topic, time, and target audience.

Burlingame and colleagues (2001) propose that group leaders define the *group rules* and communicate them to members. Brown (2003b) suggests that the number of rules be kept to a minimum and focused on the behaviors necessary for keeping order in the group. Rules that may be common for all groups are:

- Attend each session on time.
- Turn off cell phones and other personal communication devices.
- No physical aggressive behavior is allowed.
- Respect, civility, and courtesy must be shown to other members and to the leader.
- No tobacco, alcohol, or illegal drug use or influence is allowed.

The type of group may determine what rules are developed for that group. For example, you may have a rule that states whether food or drink can be consumed during group meetings.

Select strategies that target desired learning. *Strategies* are defined here as instruction, exercises, media, demonstrations, and practice. The type of group is an important consideration when selecting strategies. For example, an educational group would not make best use of an exercise that is long and focused on group members' family-of-origin experiences. Another important consideration is the time available for implementing the strategy. There should be sufficient time for presentation, and for group members' responses and input. The chapter on exercises and other activities presents more information on this topic.

It is recommended that group leaders write a *session-by-session plan*. Plans are flexible and can be modified as the group unfolds, but it is helpful to start with a plan for how each session will connect to the goals and objectives, the strategies that will be used, what equipment may be needed, and the material and supplies to be used. When done in advance, the leader can be more confident that the session is relevant, there will be fewer surprises (these can never be entirely eliminated), and the leader can be free to concentrate on the process—that is, the here-and-now interactions among group members and among members and the leader.

The final task is to *gather material and supplies* for the group. There should be sufficient number and quantities for the size group that is planned. Leaders can reproduce forms or scales; gather pens, pencils, or art supplies; locate books, flyers, or other resource materials;

and gather other materials and supplies that will be needed. It is less stressful to do this in advance rather than trying to do it just before the group session begins. It also reduces the likelihood that needed materials and supplies will not be available.

Instruction

Groups that have an instructional component need to pay particular attention to planning and implementing instruction. There are a variety of ways instruction can be accomplished, differing instructional styles, and different learning styles. The field is so vast and complex that a whole discipline with theories and the like is devoted to it, and is too much to present here.

Our brief discussion begins with the five components for instruction.

- Develop the goal(s) and objectives.
- Determine the minimum amount of information that will be needed.
- Use the available time wisely and effectively.
- Select instructional strategies on the basis of members' capacities for learning.
- Choose strategies that are consistent with the other components

The *goal* for instruction is to present a body of information that group members will learn, use, and retain. With that goal in mind, the primary objectives can be developed regardless of the topic. Therefore, the first leader task is to decide the minimum that is desirable for group members to learn, that can be used, and is important to be retained. There is so much *information available* that can be important for members to know, that it can be difficult to try to ferret out only the most critical and essential information to present. Leaders must stay mindful of just how much information can or will be absorbed, especially if there is also a strong emotional component as there can be with some psycho-educational groups.

In addition to the amount of information, the *time available* is a critical component. Not just the time available for the group, but the amount of time available in each session. Most groups will have a variety of activities, and dissemination of information is only one. Further, *members' capacities for learning* may also dictate how much information is needed for instruction. For example, if the group is focused on coping skills development for a group of impaired teens, then their capacities may be diminished and more time needed for even the most basic learning.

The final consideration is to choose the means for delivering the instruction (i.e., the *instructional strategies*). There are several strategies that can be used, including the following:

- Lectures
- Discussions
- Media, such as videos and DVDs
- Demonstrations
- Instruction and practice with feedback
- Reading

Lectures have the advantage of presenting a large body of information in a short period of time. When well organized with an interesting presentation manner, lectures are a time-efficient and effective dissemination of information. However, there are disadvantages that should also be considered, such as group members' tendencies to tune out, become distracted, or resistant, and so on. What is recommended for lectures for nonclinical groups is that they be limited in number, such as not having a lecture every session; that they take 20 minutes or less; that they be focused on the most important information group members can use; that the facts are checked for accuracy; that simple words and concepts are used and the lectures are jargon free; and that ample time is available for questions and answers or for discussion to follow.

Discussions can be held without the lead-in of a lecture. For example, a group can be given a topic to discuss that is part of the information dissemination goals where members report on past experiences, current expertise, or information derived from other sources. The important structuring for discussions is that they have a specific time frame that is known in advance. For example, the leader can announce that 15 minutes are allowed for discussion; that the group has a specific focus, topic, and expected outcome, such as discussing alternatives for managing personal time with effective suggestions presented as outcomes; that the group has a discussion with a facilitator responsible for time boundaries, keeping the discussion on topic, and encouraging all members' input and participation; and that there is a summary of what transpired, which is reported after the group discussion. The summary can be especially important if a large group was broken down into several small groups for discussion. Each small group can then hear some of what transpired in the other groups.

Media, such as videos and DVDs, can be very effective ways to present information. Videos are available on a wide variety of topics, even on entire training programs. Videos are a visual way to stimulate thoughts, ideas, and even feelings, and can condense a lot of material. There are some advantages to using media, but they should not be the main focus for the group, even when the presentation is about the topic and purpose for the group, such as an educational group for parents of children with learning disabilities. Leaders should still ensure that the interactions in the group have priority. Other things to do or to avoid when using media are to make sure the equipment is in good working condition and is set up before the group begins. Don't use media just after lunch because sitting still can encourage drowsiness. Use short rather than long media presentations; don't use media every session; have a clear link to the group's topic and purpose; and have some means to involve members' input and participation at the end.

Demonstrations are valuable for showing just how something works, whether that something is a skill, a process, or a way of understanding. They are used to instruct before group members begin practicing. It is best when demonstrations are simple, focused on specifics, and can be easily followed by observers. Demonstrations that are complex; involve a number of concepts, variables, and the like; and are not easily followed by observers will not hold group members' interest, and the opportunity for learning can be compromised. When demonstrating a complex topic, either break it down into simpler components or have observers focus on the essential components.

Instruction and practice with feedback usually refers to some sort of skills training. This training does not have to be the purpose or focus for the group. For example, the leader may want to teach conflict resolution skills as part of a communications or psychoeducational group that is not specifically targeting conflict resolution. The general process is instruction first, practice second, and feedback third. If the skill is complex, several sections can be presented, each with its own sequence beginning with instruction. It is important to provide feedback on skills progress and attainment, for correction and for encouragement.

Reading, like lectures, can disseminate considerable information in a relatively short time period. Leaders can select appropriate books, articles, and other reading materials that present current and accurate information. These materials should be easily read and understood and free of jargon, include defined concepts and terms, and provide examples. It is important that reading materials not be above group members' reading levels, not be too complex, nor too long. Some members would profit from lengthy and complex reading material, but many would become discouraged, impatient, or anxious, and the value would be lost.

Planning for Specific Age Groups

Groups for Children

When planning for children's groups, critical components are age, educational level, and the purpose for the group. Group leaders should be prepared to fully describe orally and in writing what is planned for the group, and to present this to both the children and their parents. If taking place in a school setting, the leader should also be prepared to describe the plan to the administration. This is especially important for obtaining informed consent, which you must have *before* the group begins.

The critical elements noted previously are the ones that play the major roles for determining group membership. Try to limit the range of ages and educational levels. It will make it easier to plan activities that maintain interest and attention. Other organizing elements include planning for briefer sessions, selecting instructional strategies and activities that take into account members' attention spans, using more active experiences, building groups or sessions around themes, and limiting information.

Plan *briefer sessions* for children up to ages 10 or 11 than you would for older children. This age group works better with 20- to 30-minute sessions, although some may be able to tolerate 50- to 60-minute sessions. Because sessions are brief, this means that the leader must plan extensively and has to be as emotionally present as possible. This ensures that order is kept, behavior does not get out of control, inappropriate comments and behaviors are blocked, members retain their focus, and that emotional expression is fostered.

The *attention span* for all children is shorter than that of adults, and you will need to make many accommodations for keeping their attention. It is much better to plan for this than to have to adjust within a session, or after the group begins. You cannot rely on verbal input or interactions to keep their attention, or to help the session progress.

It can be helpful to use *active group experiences* that call for every member to participate. Yes, there will be times when the focus is on one or two people, but you will be better able to control sessions, promote growth and development for members, and accomplish stated goals and objectives when each and every member is actively involved. That said, it is also important to not have too many activities in order to give members some time to integrate the learning and understanding that the activity is intended to accomplish and to allow for self-reflection. It is a balancing act that is dependent on the leader's expertise.

Theme-related groups and sessions can bring needed structure, focus, and emphasis because activities, information, and even instructional strategies have a cohesive direction and purpose. Themes such as emotional expression, grief and loss, managing difficult emotions, self-perception, communication skills, relational skills, and so on are examples for an organized, theme-related structure for a group.

Limiting information applies to groups of all ages, but it is essential for children's groups. There is a temptation to try and provide as much information as possible, but what happens most often is that members cannot take all of it in, so its effectiveness is lost. Provide essential information, and do so in several forms because repetition can help with incorporation and use of the information. For example, it may not be sufficient to only lecture or orally present information. It could also be written in an outline with essential points, be the focus for an exercise or activity, and presented more than once. Children will be able to use information that is simple in its presentation, and when they are guided to understand what personal application it has for them.

Groups for Adolescents

Leaders of adolescent groups should first know and understand general growth and development issues for that age group. It is easier to understand adolescents when you know what is usual and expected so that you can more easily identify what is unusual and unexpected.

Some basic considerations for leading adolescent groups include determining the length of sessions, fostering therapeutic factors, containing and managing intense emotions, addressing the need for structure and direction, and encouraging them to seek other sources of information. Leaders also need to have and display patience and empathy because adolescents are encountering the expected tumultuousness of growth and development, in addition to their condition or disease. Building creativity and inspiration can also be of assistance.

Length of sessions can be longer for adolescents than for children, although it may still be wise to limit sessions to no more than 1 hour. Their attention spans are longer, but you run the risk of further intensifying emotions that are already intense, or leaving them with emotions they will be unable to adequately control outside the sessions. As with children, you will also want to limit the range of ages in a particular group. Girls tend to be more mature than boys of the same age, and this too may be a consideration when forming a group. It may be helpful to have an age span of 2 to 3 years only for a group. Any more than 3 years may lead to difficulty.

Fostering *therapeutic factors*, especially hope, altruism, universality, and existential issues, can be very helpful. Although these factors are helpful for everyone, they may be especially beneficial for adolescents who are searching for a self-identity, trying to gain independence while still in a very dependent state, and are trying to form meaningful connections. They need direct expressions and examples of hope, opportunities to be altruistic, the connections that are forged from commonalities, and opportunities to reduce loneliness, isolation, and alienation. Leaders may need to introduce these topics or use exercises that allow these factors to be explored.

Containing and managing *intense emotions* for almost all adolescents are leader tasks that should be expected. Adolescence is a time of fluctuating moods and emotions at the best of times. When a condition or illness is encountered in addition, it's no wonder that adolescents can be constantly in the grip of intense emotions. The leader's skill at containing and managing these provides relief for a short period so that they can explore issues and concerns in the session, teaches them that emotions can be managed, and provides modeling of how that is accomplished.

There is a considerable need for *structure and direction* to help adolescents know what the limits are, let them understand that safety is recognized as important, emphasize the group's purpose and goals, and give support for helping contain and manage anxiety. These psychoeducational groups are brief, and much needs to be done in a relatively short time. Add to this the intense anxiety of the age, and condition of members, and it is easy to understand that more will get done if there is sufficient structure and direction. It may even be advisable to have a set of procedures for each session, and to stick to this as much as possible. For example, each session would present information, such as a lecture or video; discussion; an exercise; and so on. The leader would be flexible enough to adapt to unexpected crises and other important needs, but there would be a set procedure for each session. However you choose to have structure and direction is your decision.

Encourage members to seek *other sources of information*. Sources such as books, self-help tapes and books, videos or DVDs, the Internet, and even other members who have experienced the same condition or illness can be of assistance. You cannot provide all the available information, nor can you know enough about each member prior to the group to tailor the information to meet his or her needs. When members seek other sources of information, they are active participants in their own progress and development, and this can be empowering.

Groups for Adults

Planning groups for adults is much less complicated than planning groups for children and adolescents in many ways. Their attention spans are usually longer so that you are not limited to a particular time frame. They usually have the cognitive skills and techniques to absorb a larger amount of information, and you don't need to do as much structuring and directing. There can be fewer behavior problems, members have more experiences and resources to share with each other, and they can be more self-reflective. On the other hand, adults can be more resistant to make needed changes, exhibit more hopelessness and helplessness, and some members will be resistant to the idea of needing or accepting help for fear of appearing weak or inadequate. Both positive and negative possibilities should be factors in planning adult groups. In addition to the previous general guidelines, significant factors for adult groups can be cognitive abilities and educational level, gender, past traumas, and current support system.

Adults, like children and adolescents, will have differing *cognitive abilities*. It can be helpful for leaders to know and stay aware of possible effects on members' participation, as cognitive ability can significantly impact learning, understanding, and interactions in the group. For example, the person who is taking pain medication may be influenced by the sedating effects, making it difficult for him or her to focus, take in, and process information, or to actively participate. The group member may not even be aware of his or her impairment, as it can be subtle. Persons with very limited cognitive ability may not benefit when placed in a group with higher functioning members, and vice versa.

Educational level is an important consideration for adult groups because it plays a role in the leader's decisions about what information to present, instructional strategies, and the amount of information that can be absorbed and learned. Then too, there can be member apprehension about being included or excluded because of having either little or considerable education. Mixing a wide range of educational levels can produce a rich experience, but sometimes it can make for a difficult and uncomfortable group experience because of members' fears, defensiveness, or arrogance. Your planning can help mediate these effects.

Gender is a factor that can produce considerable projection, transference, apprehension, and possible eroticism in groups. Members' previous experiences with members of the same or opposite sex, sexual orientation, impulsivity, and expectations for behaviors and attitudes are some of the aspects related to gender. You cannot prevent any of these effects, but you can anticipate them, recognize them when they appear, and understand their influences.

Past traumas play a significant role for everyone in all types of groups. If group leaders are able to screen members prior to group experience, they may be able to recognize when members' reactions, interactions, or responses are more related to past trauma than they are to current experience or their condition or illness.

Central to fostering hope and recovery is the extent of a *member's support system*. Although this factor is outside the group, it can be helpful for members to become aware of the strengths and weaknesses of their support system, to begin to develop and strengthen it, and to capitalize on this resource. Your planning can include what you can do to highlight member support systems: You can help members learn and practice behaviors to strengthen, develop, and maintain meaningful relationships both in and out of group; and show how the group can be developed to serve this function in the short term.

Assessment

This is a very brief discussion about assessment, although it is a critical element that should not be minimized or ignored. Not only do you gain information about the effectiveness of the group, its impact on members, and your leadership; you can also get suggestions and ideas for improvements when you assess the group. It is helpful to get in the habit of assessing every group you lead, and to use multiple means of gathering data. Presented here is a summary of different strategies and instruments that can be used. Almost all of them require specialized knowledge that is beyond the scope of this book, and I encouraged you to consult people and other resources for guidance, or to take courses focused on assessment, the developing and constructing of data gathering instruments, data analysis, and qualitative and quantitative research designs. Assessment is a broad and complex area that covers a vast amount of material.

What is helpful, even if you know little or nothing about assessment, is to plan to have the group assessed. This alone will lead you to select or develop instruments, schedule time so that it can be accomplished, or seek out someone who is more informed to help complete the evaluation. Assessment should not be an afterthought; it should be an integral part of the planning process completed prior to the beginning of the group.

An ideal assessment plan begins with a focus on the goals and objectives for the group, and to evaluate if and how these were accomplished or not accomplished. Therefore, it is critical that they be phrased in a way that allows for assessment—that is, stated in behavioral terms. It is still helpful to know the elements of research design so that you can remain aware of confounding variables, researcher (leader) bias, unintended effects, and other factors that influence outcomes, analyses, and interpretation of results. All these, and some other factors, can play roles in determining if the goals and objectives were met, and to what extent.

In addition to evaluating the goals and objectives, it is informative to also evaluate the strategies; materials; environmental factors; your leadership; and participants' characteristics, attitudes, and opinions about the group experience. It is also useful to have multiple measures for these and to not rely only on the self-reports of group members. For example, if you are in a setting where you can get information about members' progress in treatment, reduction or elimination of symptoms, reduced medication, and so on, this could be external validation of self-reporting. Let's take each of these factors and explore their usefulness to understanding and improving the groups you lead.

Evaluating Strategies

Every group uses several strategies, and it is helpful to gain information about their effectiveness and efficacy. Even though each group differs in its responses, you can learn how to adjust your strategies for each group, and this feedback can be of assistance. Your strategies will probably fall into three categories with some overlap—instructional, affective, and external. Instructional strategies include items such as videos, DVDs, or lectures, and guest presenters. Affective strategies include items such as exercises, role-play, and simulations. External strategies include homework, field trips, presentations, and other external resources such as the Internet.

Evaluating Materials

If you use forms, brochures, books, art supplies, and other materials, it can be informative to evaluate their contributions to the goals and objectives for the group. Members can give their opinions about the impact, readability, and general helpfulness of materials, and you can evaluate your observations of members' reactions. This information can lead to refinement of choices for materials and, in some cases, refinement of the materials.

Evaluating Environmental Factors

Be sure to evaluate environmental factors such as the physical comfort of the facilities, the privacy of the room, the extent to which disruptions were eliminated or minimized, and so on. The environment may not have been of concern to you, but some members could have been affected by something that could be fixed for the next group. You'll never know if you don't ask.

Evaluating Your Leadership

The vast majority of groups that have any assessment at all use participants' opinions to evaluate the leader. You will certainly want to gather information about any changes you could make in your functioning, coping skills, and your attitudes, in addition to members' reactions to your selection of materials, instruction, leadership, exercises, and so on.

Data Gathering Instruments

There are numerous ways to gather data for assessing members' attitudes and opinions. Presented here are brief descriptions for some of the most frequently used methods—surveys, rating scales, the semantic differential, and qualitative descriptions. You are encouraged to learn more about each of these methods.

Surveys are comprehensive and ask for responses to open-ended questions or statements. Examples of such questions or statements are:

- What group activity did you like least? Most?
- List the characteristics you most valued, liked, or appreciated about the leader.
- Describe the most important information you received from this group experience.
- What changes do you recommend for future groups?

Rating scales are lists of topics, activities, or opinions and the like to what members assign a rating, such as 5-good. These are easy to construct, administer, and score, and can yield valuable information. The results can be compiled by adding the ratings and deriving a total score, deriving a mean rating for all items, or computing a mean rating for each item. It could be particularly useful for planning purposes to look at items with ratings of 3 or less by many members, or items with mean ratings of 3 or less.

The Semantic Differential. Osgood's (1957) *semantic differential* is a particularly useful measurement tool. It consists of pairs of bipolar adjectives on a 7- or 9-point continuum that are used to describe or evaluate a concept or topic. Participants select 1 point on the continuum between bipolar adjectives; for example, good—7 ✗ 5   4   3   2   1—bad to describe their reaction to the stimulus concept or topic. The results have the robustness of integral data so that parametric statistics are appropriate for analyses. Participants can complete the rating of several concepts in a relatively short period of time, and the results are easy to compile and compute.

Qualitative Analysis. This, too, is a specialized field of study encompassing narrative analysis, conversational analysis, fieldwork, ethnography, and case studies. These tools cannot be easily described, and are much too complex to present in this book. However, if you understand qualitative research methods, such as narrative analysis, you could derive rich material from analyzing group members' responses to carefully formulated open-ended questions. Both overt and covert meanings can be derived that are good indicators of progress, learning, awareness, and emotionally laden content.

Critical Sessions: The First and the Last

All groups have a beginning and an ending, and these two sessions are of critical importance. The beginning session sets the pattern, tone, and expectations for the group and its members, but much of what is set is not on a conscious level. Group leaders can influence what is set, but must be aware of what needs to be done to influence what takes place. The pattern, tone, and expectations can be modified as the group progresses or evolves, or changes with the introduction of a new member or the termination of a member; any crises, a change in group leaders, and so on. So, although these factors are set in the first session, they can be changed, but with considerable effort.

The ending session is also critically important for group members, and leaders should plan for an orderly closure: what will be done when a member leaves the group, and how to accommodate resistance to ending. Regardless of the age of participants, the voluntary or involuntary nature of members attending the group, or the length of time, and the purpose for the group, it can be important to reflect on what was accomplished or gained, what was of value, what will be missed or lost, and how the relationships that developed in the group fostered intrapersonal learning. Even cognitively focused groups, such as meetings and other task and educational groups, will profit from planned closure.

This chapter presents some specific strategies and basic understandings the leader needs for the first and last sessions. Sessions are defined as the beginning and ending, whether the life span of the group is 1 hour or several years.

Facilitating the All-Important First Session

The pattern, tone, and expectations for the group are set in the first session, although much is not always visible or done consciously. This is why it is extremely important for the leader to do all of the following. Organize the first session so that all activities contribute to reduction of ambiguity and uncertainty. Basic tasks include:

- Calm fears
- Help members understand what behavior is helpful in the group
- Set standards and rules
- Observe interactions
- Provide for inclusion of all members
- Help develop group goals and objectives to ensure members' understanding of what can be accomplished and what cannot
- Foster an atmosphere where disclosure is encouraged

Leaders are extremely busy during the first session. However, much of what needs to be done cannot be directly addressed because it is not done consciously by members, as stated previously. In addition, members look to the leader to take care of them, but do not verbalize this desire. All this makes for considerable complexity for the first session.

The group's pattern for interacting, disclosure, relating, and acceptance is set in the first session, but it is difficult to see except in retrospect. Adaptations, adjustments, and modifications can be made and members' actions will change, but the essential nature of the group's pattern will remain throughout the life of the group.

The pattern, tone, and expectations are greatly influenced by what the leader does and says. For example, if the leader encourages members to ask questions, then much of the interaction and verbalization will be in the form of questions, not just about the cognitive material, but also when members are trying to relate to each other. Leaders have to understand that their unconscious and nonconscious behavior and attitudes are being observed and responded to more than their conscious ones. Members try to give leaders what they think the leader wants, although none of this is spoken. Other examples can include the following:

- If a leader fails to recognize emotional intensity, members can refrain from verbalizing deep and intense feelings.
- If a leader is not alert to metaphors, members can feel the leader does not or cannot understand.

- When the leader fails to make an empathetic response, members can feel devalued, minimized, or even shamed.
- If a leader assumes that he or she is the expert, members will be reluctant to contribute their knowledge and wisdom.

Organizing the session to reduce ambiguity and uncertainty includes the following:

- Formulate specific goals and objectives to include members' goals. This is a collaborative task.
- Develop a short list of rules and distribute these in writing.
- Lead a discussion on confidentiality, the requirements for reporting, and the limits imposed on the leader.
- Introduce yourself, and have members introduce themselves. This can be a planned exercise so that members know what personal information to provide.
- Initiate a discussion about expectations for participation, self-disclosure, and the like.
- Restrict questioning by the leader and limit questions from members to factual information, unless there is something urgent brought to the group.
- Openly acknowledge that the group can seem ambiguous, and that new situations arouse uncertainty.
- Allow members to express their anxiety, and make empathetic responses.

Calm Fears. Members can be fearful of the group, especially when the group is their first such experience. They can be worried about their personal safety. One leader task is to calm fears. However, the first leader task is to help members identify their fears, because every member may have a different fear.

Many members will not admit that they are fearful, or speak openly about their fears. Indeed, even mentioning the word can arouse resistance. Thus, the group leader has to listen carefully, understand metaphors, and make these fears visible. Additionally, the leader must understand that members use certain words that signal fear in a milder form. Words such as *disquiet, dread, apprehensive,* and *anxious* can be substituted for *fear,* and for some, fear may be too intense to describe what they are experiencing.

Group leaders cannot provide enough reassurance to members that they are safe and can trust other members and the leader. Leaders who try to answer each fear with logic and rationality run the risk of intensifying the fear or arousing other fears. Leaders must become comfortable with allowing members to express their fears, provide minimum reassurance when possible or necessary, respond empathetically to let members know that their fears are understood, and act to reduce the situations that could have the fears realized. It is also important that leaders do not minimize, ignore, overlook, or fail to respond to fears. Members need to feel that the leader is capable of taking care of them, and acknowledging their fears helps with this task.

Let's examine some metaphorical statements members may make and questions that may crop up that can reflect fears. Also presented are some possible leader responses that try to make the underlying concern or fear more visible.

Situation 1

Metaphorical Statement: What can this group do for me? I don't know what this group will do for me.

Possible Fears: Fear of not being helped, or of not getting better.

Leader Response: You're wondering if you can be helped to get better. You don't want to be disappointed.

Situation 2

Metaphorical Statement: Things will get too intense, and I don't like intense situations.

Possible Fears: Fear that sessions will get out of control, that they will be hurt or destroyed, or that the leader is not capable of taking care of members.

Leader Response: It can be scary when there is a lot of intensity because it's hard to predict what will happen to you. You're wondering if I will be able to manage it.

Situation 3

Metaphorical Statement: I hope we can all agree. I like harmony in groups.

Possible Fears: Fear of conflict and negative outcomes, and fear that the leader may not be able to prevent destruction of the group or its members.

Leader Response: Although conflict can be destructive at times, it can also be constructive. I will show you how to work through any conflicts that may emerge.

In situation 1, what the leader does not want to do is to provide a list of possible benefits such as learning coping skills or developing better relationships. Those benefits are probably available in writing or were presented verbally, so that's not the real question. The leader should also avoid saying anything that suggests that members will get out of the group what they put into it. That can convey blame and criticism. Recognizing the underlying fear, such as the leader's response in situation 1, is much more helpful.

In situation 2, the leader may be dealing with several fears including that member's fear of losing control, or of becoming overwhelmed or enmeshed by others' intense feelings. It's too early in the group to focus on a response for this possibility because the therapeutic relationship has not been firmly established. It is better to view these metaphorical statements as a plea for reassurance that the leader is in control and can take care of group members. A response that recognizes this and directly addresses it could be enough for the present.

In situation 3, the leader may be encountering deep-seated and long-term fears about conflict. Members may have had experiences, such as abusive situations or conflict that was hurtful and destructive, and are fearful of any hint of conflict. Leaders too may have these concerns and will work hard to keep conflict from emerging in the group. The response should clearly identify the commonality for these possible fears, even those about mild disagreements, and address the positive aspect that can result from working through and resolving them.

Member Behavior. It is helpful to describe what members are expected to do in the group because many of them will come to group not having any notion of how this group experience is different, and having some concerns about their expected behavior. They are facing an unknown situation and may be anxious because of the uncertainty. Thus, it can be calming to tell members some basic behaviors that can enrich their group experiences. It is probably best to limit these to just a few to discuss verbally, and to give them some guidance. Tell members to practice basic behaviors, such as the following, as these are likely to be nonthreatening and can be helpful.

- Speak of your thoughts, ideas, and feelings as you experience them in the session.
- Respond directly to other members.
- Ask for what you want or need instead of expecting others to read your mind.
- Take responsibility for your feelings and don't blame others for "making" you feel as you do.
- Speak for yourself, and make personal, not group or global statements.
- Realize that you determine the amount and extent of your self-disclosure; you will not be pushed or forced.

Standards and Rules. Having group standards and rules may seem self-evident, but needs to be verbalized or even provided in writing. This, too, can reduce ambiguity and uncertainty and, if written, can help ensure that members don't have to rely on their memories, which could be affected by anxiety. These standards and rules may be part of the organization's expectations as well as those you may want for your group.

Group leaders will find it helpful to have standards and rules about attendance, missed sessions, arriving on time and staying the entire session, notification of emergencies and crisis, allowing or not allowing food and drink in the session, policy on coming to sessions under the influence of alcohol or illegal drugs, aggressive behavior, contact or socializing outside the group, electronic devices, and so on. These can be constructed to meet your group's needs.

Facilitating the Critical Session

Observe interactions among members and with you, as this provides considerable information about members' characteristic ways of interacting and relating. What members do in the group reflects what they do outside the group in other relationships. Some behaviors to note follow. Don't comment on these, or highlight them in group, because it is too soon in the relationship to have them received positively.

- Members' tendencies to interrupt others (note who interrupts and who is interrupted)
- Storytelling and monopolizing, especially when considerable details are presented and members keep it going with questions
- Thoughts expressed as feelings
- Ignoring or minimizing someone's disclosure or feelings
- Members excluding other members, (never ask to give an opinion or feeling, and so on)
- Facial expressions when looking at other members
- Eye contact or lack of eye contact when speaking with others (be sure to remember the cultural component when observing this)
- Projections and possible transference
- Lack of effort to connect or relate

The patterns for interacting and relating that you see in the first session are likely to continue in some way. You can help modify these by teaching more effective ways to interact, communicate, and relate, but you need to know members' needs in these areas to focus your teaching.

One leader task is to *foster inclusion of all members*. Inclusion is not the same as helping them feel comfortable in the group; it carries a deeper significance. Don't try to act as host or social director because this group situation is different. Members who are included feel respected, valued, cared for, and connected at a significant level. Past experiences with relationships and family-of-origin experiences have formed members' attitudes and behaviors that determine how accepting or resistant they will be to the group experience, and how easy or difficult it will be to help them feel included. Their feelings of safety and trust play major roles in developing feelings of inclusion, and given some people's life experiences, they may not be able to feel safe or to trust.

The leader's inner self as genuine, accepting, and caring is the major asset for helping members feel included. Behaviors that can help are empathetic listening and responding, soliciting members' feelings and other reactions, having patience with resistance and defensiveness and not trying to battle them into agreement or submission, and providing encouragement and support. Members will feel included by who you are more than by what you do.

Reviewing or Establishing Group Goals

Group goals and objectives should be reviewed or developed. If you were able to screen members, then you had an opportunity to discuss individuals' goals and objectives and to begin to formulate the group's goals to incorporate them. This was also the time to help members develop realistic and attainable goals. If you were not able to have an individual meeting with members, then it becomes necessary to use part of the first session to survey members about their goals, objectives, and expectations, and to combine and integrate them into realistic, attainable, and agreed-on group goals.

If you have time, you can repeat this process to develop objectives—that is, short steps to meet the goals. The leader may want to take on this task and bring them back to the group. Keep the final goals to bring back to the group for review and evaluation approximately halfway through the life of the group, and at the end of the group. This will help keep members focused on the primary expectations for the group experience.

Being Receptive to Members' Self-Disclosure

It can be crucial that an atmosphere receptive to appropriate disclosure be established in the first session. Once again, this is something that depends on the leader's inner self and on his or her actions. Notice that the term *receptive* is used; the first session may be too soon for members to be ready to disclose much of what concerns them. If they are to do so later in the life of the group, what you do or say during the first session will play a major role in their decision to disclose or not, the level and extent of the disclosure, and in how other members receive it.

Leader actions that facilitate developing an atmosphere receptive to disclosure include the following:

- Nonverbal attending to the speaker
- Active listening or empathetic responses
- Responding directly to each speaker

- Repair of any empathetic failures that occur
- Recognizing significant disclosures that are masked, hidden, or expressed as metaphors
- Blocking verbal attacks, put-downs, and sarcastic remarks or responses
- Rephrasing member comments to highlight feelings
- Linking members' comments to show commonalities or similarities

There are also some actions that leaders refrain from doing.

- Ignoring, overlooking, or minimizing a disclosure
- Suggesting that a disclosure is trivial or meaningless
- Failing to respond, or to respond directly
- Pushing or demanding that a member disclose
- Allowing personal values of the leader to impact responses to members' disclosures
- Ignoring empathetic failures
- Not intervening in attacks and the like
- Indicating verbally or nonverbally that a member is wrong in his or her expression, thought, feeling, or response

Using basic attending skills, having inner resources that are genuine and that promote empathetic responses, and staying in touch with the impact of the group on members are the basics for facilitating disclosure. The first session is extremely important in direct and indirect ways, and requires a lot of attention and leader expertise.

Sample Outline for a First Session

Following is a sample outline for the first session.

- Welcome members to the group.
- Introduce the leader and members.
- Establish limits and the extent of confidentiality.
- Do a get-acquainted exercise that is short, firm, and nonthreatening
- Review collaboratively set goals and objectives.
- Present an overview of the group, the proposed schedule, and the rules (you many want to have a handout for this part).
- Discuss members' expectations, feelings, and so on.
- Summarize session.

The Importance of Planned Group Closure

Closure is the term used, instead of *termination* because it denotes a process, whereas *termination* denotes an end to something. The group leader should have a deep understanding of the need for a process to end the group rather than abruptly ending, or worse, no definitive ending of the group. Leaders should make closure a part of the planning process and use the expected member behaviors, feelings, and attitudes described in stage 4 as a guide for what to expect. The leader's own experiences with loss, saying goodbye, and unfinished business can have an unconscious impact on the extent to which he or she approaches planned closure for groups.

The benefits or value of planned closure include:

- A boundary is established, agreed to, and understood by all members at both the cognitive and affective levels.
- Time is allocated for the completion of unfinished business.
- Members are taught a process for saying goodbye.
- Focus is on essentials of the experience and the relationships.
- The leader demonstrates how to work through loss and grief.
- There is validation and legitimization of sadness.

The Time Boundary

Many types of groups have a specific *time frame* for existence, but others such as support and some psychotherapy groups do not have a specific time for ending. Members of these groups terminate on an individual basis throughout the life of the group. A process for individual termination is described in a later section. This section focuses on closure for time-bound or time-limited groups where all members are terminating.

Even when there is a specific time frame for the group, some members may not consciously accept that the group will end. This can be especially troublesome for members who are profiting from the experience, value the learning and relationships established, and who don't want the good feelings of stage 3 to disappear. These are the members who will deny to themselves that the group is ending. Other members may not consciously realize the value and importance of the group for them until the very end, and they too can be oblivious to the ending of the group. Other life experiences, such as chaotic family of origin, can lead members to not be consciously aware of an impending end for the group, as their experiences did not always have clear time boundaries.

It can be helpful for group leaders to begin the closure process about halfway through the group by stating how many sessions are left. It isn't necessary to do this every remaining session, but it should be done often enough so that members don't lose sight of it. Too many announcements can arouse fear and panic for some members, and they can begin to pull away from the group and severely limit their emotional investment in the group and in their learning. The issues to be addressed for closure include decreasing unfinished business, working through grief and loss, reflection on gain and progress, and expression of feelings about the experience.

Unfinished Business

Almost everyone has some unfinished business where they did not say or do some things, the relationship stopped or ended, and they are left with regrets, yearnings, or wishes about the person or the relationship. The group is an opportunity to prevent this from happening once again, to demonstrate the value of completing and communicating feelings and thoughts to each other, and to experience the feelings of a satisfactory ending to relationships.

Closure is the time when members can say those things they want the others to know, usually positive. What many people regret is that they did not tell someone that he or she was liked, appreciated, respected, admired for a trait or action, and so on. Although there can be unfinished business about negative or uncomplimentary things, most would satisfy a revenge need, such as a pay-back for real or imagined offenses. These, too, can carry regrets, but not as much as failure to say positive things.

A Process for Saying Goodbye

There are reasons for members to stay in touch with the real impending closure of the group, and to use a process for saying goodbye that includes speaking their thoughts, feelings, and so on in the group. That way they will not be left with much or any unfinished business relative to the group. Members may have to be taught how to phrase comments they think have the potential for negative reception. Both leaders and members may need to say things that are uncomplimentary, such as telling someone that they have a habit of interrupting others. The basic guidelines for phrasing what may be a negative comment are as follows:

- Doing so to help the other person become aware of the impact of the particular behavior on oneself—not on others
- Having motives for telling this that do not include revenge or superiority
- Phrasing it carefully with sensitivity to the impact the words have on the receiver
- Limiting it to a particular action, behavior, or situation
- Focusing on something that can be changed, not something that is fixed
- Not using words such as *always, never, good, bad, right,* or *wrong*

It is possible to tell someone how you feel about him or her, or the behavior that may be negative, without blaming or criticizing. In fact, you really want the person to receive and accept the information in a positive, nondefensive way. Members can be made aware that this group process is an opportunity to leave a relationship or experience without carrying unfinished business.

One strategy leaders can use to help members understand and accept the importance of satisfactory closure is to ask members how they usually say goodbye. Ask them to reflect on the experiences and relationships in their past, and how they ended them. You will likely have several members who do not say goodbye at all, who find ways to avoid saying it. They just leave, don't show up or call on the last day, or substitute a social or other activity so that they become too busy to say goodbye. It is unusual to find that most members are satisfied with how they have said goodbye.

The leader can describe the advantages for a thoughtful goodbye process by asking members if they have residual feelings of regret for how they said goodbye in one or more previous relationships. Most members will admit to having regrets. This presents the leader with an opportunity to point out that it is common for it to be difficult to look at someone, and know that you likely will never see him or her again. You may feel sad about the loss of the connections, but still have the courage to tell that person how much you have appreciated him or her and valued the relationship, and let the person know that you are experiencing sadness at saying goodbye. This process doesn't have to produce depression, or stay mired in the uncomfortable feelings, but it benefits both of you to have at least said something about the relationship and its ending.

Tell group members that it is important to say goodbye in some way, and explore with them the possible means of doing so. It is important to do this because saying goodbye is a necessary part of letting go.

Focusing on Essentials

Having to say goodbye and letting go can assist members in focusing on the essentials of the experience and of the relationships with other members and the leader; it is not sufficient to just focus on the group as a whole. Members may want to reflect on questions such as:

- What actions, attitudes, responses, and so on were helpful during group sessions?
- Whom did I have strong reactions to (both positive and negative) and what produced these?
- How did my perceptions, reactions, and the like of group members or the leader change over the course of the group?
- What do I want to make sure is said before the group ends?
- What do I value about the group, the members, and the leader?
- What am I taking away as a result of this group experience?

Working Through Grief and Loss

It would be unusual to have a group where members had not experienced grief and loss in their lives. Indeed, some members experience these as a result of their illness or condition, giving the leader a great opportunity to demonstrate a process for working through them. In addition, closure can also bring up unresolved grief and loss, and generate its own sense of grief and loss around the ending of the group. Brammer and MacDonald (2003) describe normal grief consisting of most or all of the following:

- Physical reactions such as sleeplessness and loss of appetite
- Feelings of emptiness and alienation from other people
- Occasional observing about thought and images of the deceased
- Guilt over real or imagined actions, failings, and the like
- Usual pattern of behavior changes, lack of direction, energy, or focus

When grief becomes prolonged, intense, or complicated, the normal grief behaviors are increased and other troubling behaviors and attitudes are added. This state requires specialized treatment, and it is mentioned here because group leaders may encounter this with some unresolved grief issues members may have.

Leaders can adapt the following process for demonstrating how to work through grief and loss.

1. Accept the end or loss.
2. Express feelings about loss.
3. Deal with the memories.
4. Readjust to changes.
5. Build new relationships (Brammer & MacDonald, 2003).

Validation of Sadness

Sadness is an uncomfortable emotion, both to the person experiencing it and to the people around him or her. Because of the discomfort, many people do whatever they can to try and not feel it, or have someone else feel it. This happens throughout one's life, and many times the grieving process is truncated whether it is a child whose pet fish died, or an adult whose long-term spouse died. The failure to experience or validate the sadness around a loss can have long-term effects on the person.

One leader task is to validate the sadness experienced by members around closure. Although the experience and relationships developed may not be either long term or deep, connections were made that are now being severed. In fact, the possibly mild sadness is an opportunity to help members realize and accept that sadness can be expected and worked through; that you don't have to become mired in sadness, either personal or for someone else; that you are not responsible to make someone, or yourself, feel better; and that sadness can be enriching, showing you how to better appreciate someone, or a relationship, while it is still available.

Validation of sadness means that

- Expressions of loss and sadness are recognized even when expressed as metaphors
- Empathetic responses are made
- Other group members are invited to give their reactions to the expression of sadness
- The validity of the ending of the group is affirmed
- Members are asked for suggestions about a satisfactory ending for each of them

Dealing with Difficult Closures

It is much easier to plan closure for the group as a whole than it is for an individual member, such as what occurs in support groups, where members can terminate at any time. There are other situations that can also present difficult closure—the death of a member, relapse or another illness, moving away, military service, a member decides to leave or stop attending without notice, family crises that affect attendance, the breakup of a romantic relationship established between two group members, reduced income, and so on. What all or most of these situations have in common is that they tend to be unexpected. This is why leaders should plan in advance for possible premature termination, as it has a definite impact on the group and its members.

Members of support groups can have notification of intent to terminate as one of their expectations. That can mean that members who desire or intend to leave the group are expected to notify the leader as far in advance as possible. This notification gives the leader an opportunity to prepare that member and the group for the departure. Leaders can assist the member in deciding on how much information to communicate to the group about the reason or circumstances for leaving, and then telling the group. The leader can then facilitate members saying goodbye, and empathetically responding to the loss of that member.

Much more difficult to handle will be the unexpected circumstance, such as death or no information about why the member leaves. These unexpected terminations can arouse deep feelings about abandonment, personal failings, and other such emotions that arise from the various members' family-of-origin and other past experiences. It is not unusual for some members and some leaders to feel that they did something to "cause" that member to leave. Adding to the complexity is that some members experience these emotions, but do not openly verbalize them. Leaders may not be aware of the possibility of these emotions and do not do anything that could help these members work through them.

Care should be taken to not minimize or overlook the impact the unexpected leaving can have on members. This is a case where something urgent and important occurs for the group, and that takes priority over whatever was planned. Leaders can be most helpful in leading members to become aware of and work through their feelings about the particular member, the unexpected termination, and residual feelings about other unsatisfactory terminations they may have experienced.

Leaders should also stay in touch with what they are feeling and use this inner experiencing as a way to help group members express what they may be feeling. It is not appropriate for leaders to work on the issues that cause their feelings in the group setting, but it is appropriate for them to report their feelings to the group. For example, if the unexpected termination brings up feelings of fear around abandonment for the leader, he or she could say something like, "I'm upset about _____'s unexpected termination and fear that others will abandon the group." Or, "Leaving is bringing up some old feelings of anger and sadness around the loss of a relationship." Leaders would resist members' attempts to get them to "tell the story" and would ask members to report on what feelings emerged for them around the unexpected termination. This permits the leader to teach members how to address losses from the past, in the present, and for the future.

Closure is as important and difficult as is the successful beginning of the group, and needs careful attention and consideration by the leader. This is another instance where the extent of the leader's personal development can be helpful in providing inner guidance about what to say and do to assist group members. Leaders are encouraged to think, reflect, and plan for closure of all types.

Summary

1. Planning is an important and critical task for the group leader. Components for planning include information gathering, structural factors, preparation, instruction and instructional styles, and assessment.

2. Groups that have a major cognitive component also need to plan the instruction to facilitate the needed learning. This planning includes session plans, learning goals and objectives, mode of instruction, and needs of the target audience.

3. Planning groups for children involves consideration of their level and stage of development, the topic or focus for the group, age levels, and intellectual abilities.

4. Planning groups for adolescents involves an understanding of their developmental needs, major issues for their stage of development, and the focus for the group.

5. Planning groups for adults involves information about background factors to better target needs, strategies for information dissemination, and varying abilities that may be present in the group.

6. Assessment of group is advised and encouraged to provide evidence of its effectiveness and impact on members. Several modes for gathering data are described.

7. The importance of the first session is critical to developing the therapeutic alliance and establishing trust and safety. The termination of the group with proper closure is also vital. Suggestions for how to deal effectively with both are described.

Chapter Activities

Plan two group sessions for one of the following topics: one session for a children's group, or one session for either an adolescent or an adult group.

1. Personal anger management

2. Loss of a friend to illness or death

3. Unfair treatment, or bullying

4. Building trust in a relationship

Personal Development Exercise: Construct a collage of your spiritual self.

Chapter 7

Group Facilitation Skills

Major Topics

1. The therapeutic alliance factors and procedures.
2. Empathy and empathic attunement
3. Process and process commentary.

Introduction

There are relationship attributes and other therapeutic competencies that apply in both individual and group therapy, and are recognized as important across theories. For example, empathy and empathic responding are accepted as important for individual and group by theories such as client-centered (Rogers, 1970), self-psychology (Kohut, 1975), cognitive (Beck, 2000), interpersonal (Yalom, 1995), psychodynamic (Rutan, 1993), and psychoanalytic (Aron, 1996). However, these relationship attributes and therapeutic competencies are manifested in different ways when used in groups because of the number of individuals involved, members' various stages of development, their presenting problems that appear similar on the surface but are not, and the need to build relationships between and among members, not just between you and the client. In addition, the process is more complex because it occurs between you and individual members, among individual members, and there is also group level process that merits attention.

This chapter focuses on basic relational attributes that enhance group leadership, advance group facilitation competencies, the importance of empathy and empathic attunement, and the identification of group process and making group process commentary. Specific knowledge, strategies, and techniques are presented and emphasized to aid the group leader to do the following:

- Effectively use group-level process commentary
- Foster emergence of therapeutic factors

- Understand the importance of his or her emotional presence in the group and use the here-and-now experience
- Capitalize on the resources of the group to help individual members
- Increase use of his or her inner experiencing to monitor countertransference and better understand what group members need and want
- Recognize the barriers and constraints for group members

Following is a brief discussion of the basic attitudes that, when developed, form a foundation for more advanced skills. Also presented is a rationale for their usefulness to the group leader. Most of the described skills will be used throughout all group stages but are especially helpful in stage 1. These are divided in two categories: therapeutic relationship attitudes, and verbal and nonverbal communication skills.

The Therapeutic Relationship

It is vital that the leader establish a therapeutic relationship with group members (Aron 1996; Jordan, 1991; Rogers, 1970; Rutan, 1993. This can be more difficult to do with a group than with an individual because group members are also likely to be

- trying to establish relationships with one another
- wondering if it is safe for them in the group
- fearful of being rejected by members and the leader
- apprehensive about their role in the group
- unsure that the group's goals are consistent with their personal goals
- tentative about participating
- defensive about their reason for being in the group or feeling shamed about their problem or issue
- nervous about the ambiguity and uncertainty
- trying to manage their anxiety

Many members will not have any experience as a group member, whereas others may have had an unpleasant group experience. These are but a few of the reasons why establishing a therapeutic relationship may be more difficult. However, that does not lessen the importance of making it a priority.

Establishing the therapeutic relationship demands certain attitudes and development of the self, and are not specific skills that can be taught and learned. Polster and Polster (1973), Scharff (1992), and Rutan (1993) all emphasize the use of the self as a significant part of the therapeutic process, and that the most important components in relationships with clients rely more on who you are than on what you do.

Fundamental Relationship Attributes

The basic relationship attributes needed for a group leader are essentially the same as those needed for individual therapy, but may need to be used in a different way. For example, attending is used in both individual and group therapy. In group, the leader needs to attend to all members in the group and stay in touch with the group as a whole, not just the person who is talking. Fundamental relationship attitudes are genuineness, caring, positive regard, respect, and acceptance.

Being authentic or *genuine* is essential when establishing the therapeutic relationship. It is infinitely more difficult to mask or fake attitudes in a group, especially because members are paying very close attention to you. Being real and authentic in your attitudes and behaviors is important to build trust between you and members and to encourage disclosures about shameful and painful personal information. Can you fool someone into believing you are genuine when you are not? Yes, you can. But, on some level, the other person knows you are faking. You do not want to pretend to have an attitude you do not have if you expect group members to trust you enough to reveal secrets they may never have talked about to anyone before. Deceit does not build trust in a relationship.

The leader can promote feelings of trust and safety by making members feel *cared for* and that they are held in *positive regard*. Group members must develop feelings of safety and trust in the leader and group before they can conquer their fears enough to allow themselves to talk about sensitive issues and concerns. Many members enter group feeling guilty, ashamed, and afraid that they will be perceived by the leader and other group members as bad and fatally flawed. Many fear rejection and destruction if their "real self" were to be revealed. However, letting the real self be known is helpful if healing is to take place, if behaviors or attitudes are to change, or if growth and development are to occur. On the one hand, members must reveal their shamed "self"; on the other hand, revealing it is feared to have dire consequences. What a leader does and says is critical to providing a group atmosphere to encourage self-disclosure and overcome fears.

Positive regard and *respect* for others are intertwined. Positive regard is more a part of who you are and your basic view of human nature. Respect is also internal to some extent but has external manifestations that convey to the other person that you do, or do not, respect him or her. You have to be able to regard others as worthwhile unique individuals in order to respect them. They are separate, different, and no less worthy than anyone else. They have positive characteristics, flaws, failings, and potentials; and you remain aware that each person has something to contribute.

Respect, caring, and positive regard all contribute to being able to *accept* group members *as they are*. Yes, they have issues, problems, and concerns; and yes, they are there to get help and change. But before any of this can take place, members have to feel that they are accepted. This acceptance builds trust for the leader and the group.

Accepting group members as they are can also contribute to the therapeutic group factor of hopefulness. When the leader is aware of group members' problems and does not dismiss or write them off as hopeless, members "catch" the leader's hopeful attitude that they can and will resolve their problems, overcome their concerns, and work through their issues. Do not underestimate the importance of this factor or the contribution acceptance can make to the group and to individual group members. Eye contact can be used to show interest in the other person and this can make the member feel accepted. However, if the interest is not genuine, your eye contact can become glazed and, on some level, the person knows that you are not interested.

Responding or Communication Competencies

Responding or communication competencies are divided into two categories: basic and fundamental skills used in individual and group counseling, and skills that have a particular application to group leadership. Although the therapeutic relationship is important, it is not sufficient to promote work in the group. The leader also has to be competent and use responding skills that promote the development of safety and trust, encourage members to self-disclose, promote interaction among members, model more effective communications and recognition of emotional investment for members, and that direct a focus to important content and feelings for both individual members and for the group as a whole.

Basic competencies include active listening and responding, appropriate questioning, using directness, and reframing and redirecting.

Listening and Responding. It is essential that group leaders hone their listening skills because the ability to hear what is said, what is meant, and to understand the underlying feelings is crucial to helping group members. Listening in a group setting is considerably more difficult than in an individual session as the interactions are faster and more complex. Listening is basic to empathizing, confronting, and redirecting. Content may be important; however, the feelings carry the most important part of the message. Hearing the content allows you to make hypotheses about the feeling the person may not be expressing (Rutan, 1993). Listening and responding are discussed more fully with examples and strategies later in the chapter.

Questioning. Knowing when to probe and how to probe so as not to make the receiver feel attacked or become defensive is a skill that can be learned. The most important aspect of this skill is learning when *not* to ask questions. That is, there are situations where it is more helpful to make statements rather than to ask questions, and becoming aware of your habit or tendency to ask questions is a major step in learning. Brown (1998b) lists three basic uses for questioning: to obtain data and information, to clarify misunderstandings, and to pinpoint something in order to take immediate action (pp. 52–53).

The group leader should be careful not to ask numerous questions as guides or stimuli and to refrain from pelting an individual member with questions. Even if what that person is talking about needs considerable clarification, many people feel as if they are being attacked when they are asked several questions, regardless of the manner or tone of voice used by the questioner. These people do not view questioning as a display of interest but as a hostile interrogation. Further, much information sought by asking questions is not necessary or relevant to either accomplishing the task or developing relationships in the group. Trotzer (1989) notes that most questions are statements that signal what the speaker wants, especially questions that are used as probes to guide the receiver to areas the speaker feels are important.

Some types of questions are less useful and should either not be used, or be used sparingly Brown (1998b):

- Limiting questions
- Hot-seat questions

- Hypothetical questions
- Disguised demands
- Masked needs
- Rhetorical questions

Limiting and hypothetical questions may have some small value. For example, limiting questions force members to make a choice from a few options. There may be instances when the group seems bogged down and needs to make a decision. The leader can present the options in question form (e.g., "Do you want option A or option B?"). Hypothetical questions could allow for some creative brainstorming to take place by posing a "what-if" scenario. However, it is most helpful to the group if the leader announces why the hypothetical question is used rather than just throwing it out to the group.

Some questions are *disguised demands*. Instead of directly asking for what is wanted, the person tries to manipulate the other person by asking a question. A simple example of a disguised demand is when someone asks, "Would you do me a favor?" What they are really asking is, "I would appreciate it if you could do me a favor."

Another way that questions are not direct communication is when they are used to *mask needs*. The person wants or needs something but, instead of saying what he or she wants or needs, a question is substituted. Asking a question puts the burden on the receiver to do some mind reading about what is wanted or needed.

Rhetorical questions are questions to which there are no answers, or to which the answers are already known. Neither is useful to facilitate communication, understanding, or the relationship.

There are some instances where questions can be helpful and, if you use the following as a guide, your questions can be constructive.

- Reserve your questions for gathering facts and initiating clarifications.
- Limit the number of questions asked even if you feel you want or need to know more.
- Stay aware of the impact of your questioning on the receiver and on other group members and stop when the receiver appears uncomfortable.
- Do not use questions to indirectly criticize or blame.
- Block questioning by group members when they become focused on one member and are asking many questions. This behavior can have the effect of making the person being questioned feel like a target.

Some questions are useful and necessary, but many are neither useful nor necessary.

Using Directness. If the leader models speaking and responding directly to group members, then members most likely will follow that example. Part of being direct is attending to the person with whom you are talking. That is, orient your body to the person and maintain eye contact. Another part of being direct is to not go off on a tangent but to make sure you first respond to what the person said in some way. This could be via paraphrasing, reflecting, saying you agree or disagree, acknowledging the person's perspective, and so on. This is valuable in communicating even when your next statement shows that you disagree or have a different viewpoint.

People feel respected and valued when you are direct in your communications. Refusing to maintain eye contact, shifting around in the chair, fiddling with possessions, changing the topic or going off on a tangent, presenting your view without first acknowledging that you heard what they said are all ways that your communication is not direct.

Other ways that you can be direct are to openly express important feelings as you experience them in the interactions, give constructive feedback, not suppress important feelings for fear of alienating someone, and be patient when members are talking and not interrupt. Directness begins with the nonverbal attending behaviors. Always orient your body toward the person, become present, centered, and maintain eye contact. Try not to be distracted, and be willing to express your important feelings, when appropriate. It may not always be appropriate to openly express your feelings; you need to learn to judge when you should and when it will be best for all concerned if you do not. For example, it is probably not wise to express your anger openly and directly in the beginning stages of group.

Practice paraphrasing and reflecting so that they become an integral part of your communication style. It may seem somewhat artificial and redundant when you first begin to use these skills, but you will reduce misunderstandings and miscommunications and, most importantly, you will make the receiver feel valued and respected. Group members find this an invaluable skill that has implications for their relationships outside the group.

Reframing and Redirecting. Reframing and redirecting are also termed relabeling by Waltzlawick, Weakland, and Risch (1974); positive connotation by Selvini-Palazzoli (1974), and noted as a positive group leadership skill by Malekoff (1997) and Agazarian (1997). Reframing occurs when you repeat to the group member what he or she said, giving it another perspective. The change is a different way to say whatever was said. For example, if the member noted that conflict was upsetting and she could never be comfortable with it, a reframe could be noting that she prefers that her relationships be harmonious.

Reframing is most useful when the speaker's statements are focused on deficiencies, weaknesses, or mistakes, whether personal or directed at other members; a member fails to perceive positive aspects of the situation or of his or her effectiveness; when a member cannot see personal strengths; or when the speaker has a negative perspective, such as hopelessness, and another perspective could provide hope. The important thing to remember about reframing is that you do not change the content, as that could distort the original meaning. The reframe points out current experiencing, how it could be viewed differently, and opens the door for consideration that there are other possibilities.

Redirecting is similar to reframing except that in this case, you are actively asking the person to go in another direction. You, as the leader, have noted something you consider important that is being missed, ignored, overlooked, or minimized by the speaker or the group. Reframing is generally used with individual group members, whereas redirecting can be used with both individuals and the group as a whole. It is particularly effective when used at the group level.

Group-Level Skills

The next set of skills discussed is those that expand and enhance growth and development for the group. These are group leader behaviors that are not usually inherent but must be learned. Some are fairly easy to learn, such as giving encouragement and support, but most are more difficult, such as linking and blocking. Linking and blocking are more difficult because the leader has to first develop the other characteristics and skills listed under relationships and communication before the group leadership skills can effectively be used. The group-level skills take time and effort to develop, and you will probably feel somewhat uncomfortable when you begin to use them because they are unfamiliar. The more you use them the more positive results you will see, which then reinforces your desire to continue to practice. The skills discussed in this section are blocking, linking, encouraging, and supporting.

Blocking. This is a skill used to protect group members, either from attacks or from proceeding in the wrong direction. It could be called redirecting, but the usual term used is *blocking*. Blocking is usually indicated when emotional intensity is high or is displaced on other members. For example, when a member feel attacked or fears being attacked he or she can displace this fear on others to prevent being the target. The group leader has to intervene to protect both members.

There are times when members will ramble or tell stories instead of being focused or getting to the point. Blocking is also indicated in these situations. The leader may also need to block a member's intensifying of emotions. For example, if a member appears to become angrier as he or she talks, to prevent the anger from becoming fury or rage, the leader may need to intervene.

Blocking has to be done very carefully. Although the intent is to keep something that is destructive or potentially destructive from escalating, how you do it is also important. It is relatively easy to block something from happening because you can always use your authority as the group leader to insist that it be halted. However, the consequences for this approach are not generally positive. The member being blocked is likely to feel attacked or criticized. Other members who observe the action may end up fearful that they, too, will be attacked or chastised in some way. The leader is then faced with restoration of trust and safety.

To effectively use blocking the leader should do all of the following:

- Listen carefully to discern the level and intensity of emotional involvement for the member.
- Gauge the strength of the leader's relationship with that member.
- Attend to the level of emotional involvement and status for other members in the group.
- Carefully select the words that will be used.
- Approach blocking in a somewhat tentative manner.

When members are in the throes of *intense emotions* they are very touchy or sensitive, leading to misperceptions of your intent. They may become unexpectedly enraged, leaving you floundering and wondering what to do next. This is one reason why the leader needs to stay aware of what members are experiencing and become adept at gauging the level of emotional intensity.

The *strength of the relationship* with that member and other group members is very important. The group should be at a point where the members have developed some trust and safety among themselves and with the leader. Unless the situation is destructive, or potentially destructive, the leader should refrain from blocking too soon in the group's development.

Awareness of the *emotional status for other group members* is also important; whatever you do with one member also impacts other members. You can never be sure what will be an emotional trigger for members. This is another reason why it is important to observe the impact of your blocking on members.

Selection of words can be somewhat tricky. Words that have one meaning for one person can have a very different meaning for another person. Further, you want to use words that do not carry an implied criticism or threat. Remember, the member you will be blocking is likely to have some emotional investment in what he or she is saying and because of this may be more sensitive to your words than usual.

Be somewhat *tentative* when you use blocking. This will allow you to be able to back off quickly if necessary, to select different words if necessary, and to stay in touch with the impact on other group members to intervene with them when needed. When you block, you may even want to preface your remarks with a statement of your intention and the reason. Doing this can convey to the person that you are not devaluing what he or she is saying; you just feel a need to redirect the comments. For example, if someone is storytelling you could say something like, "Jane, I want to interrupt you at this point because I think your point about _____ is getting lost in details." You are clearly communicating your intent to block, and saying it this way provides the member with an acceptable reason for your intervention.

Linking. There are times when the discussion appears to be disjointed, fragmented, and chaotic. Of course, the perception may be correct and this is indeed what is happening. However, on a deeper level the group is most likely talking about something taking place in the group or is indirectly discussing something that the group does not feel comfortable tackling directly. This is where linking is a critical skill for making group-level process commentary.

Linking refers to bringing together underlying ideas, themes, concepts, understandings, and so on whose associations are not apparent on the surface. That is, there is a commonality that is not readily discernable. The leader is usually the person who is detached enough and experienced enough to perceive these commonalties.

The commonalties do not always have to occur in the immediate or same session. They can be exhibited over time, which is another reason why the group leader has to pay close attention. You may want to try writing a journal or minutes for sessions to help discern links.

To link, the leader must pay close attention to what happens in the group, remember most of what was said and by whom, reflect internally on what commonalties are being expressed directly or indirectly, and express the commonalties to the group with specific examples of what was done or said that illustrates the associations. Linking is discussed further in the section titled "Process Commentary Skills."

Encouraging and Supporting. Group leaders can be very helpful to the group and in accomplishing the task when they provide encouragement and support. This is especially crucial in the beginning stages of group as group members are anxious and may be floundering because of unavoidable ambiguity.

Being too supportive is counterproductive and promotes dependency. Also, group leaders must take care not to be supportive to meet their personal needs by giving encouragement and support. For example, if a group leader has a need to suppress, repress, or deny personal anger, he or she may be very supportive of group members to make sure they do not openly express anger even when members' nonverbal behavior is screaming that they are very upset and angry. This kind of support is meeting the leader's needs and not the needs of the members or the group as a whole.

Giving encouragement and support is somewhat difficult for beginning group leaders because they are struggling with their own insecurities about the group and competencies as leader. It is understandable that their attention is given to personal needs and to the task rather than being aware of members who could benefit from encouragement and support.

In the beginning stage of group, it can be helpful to think of the group as being in a child-like stage of development. Group members have considerable undeveloped or underdeveloped resources, are capable of being spontaneous and creative, and are timid and tentative in this new situation. The leader is the coach that coaxes them into trying new activities, the teacher that helps them see new ways to learn and gives them new knowledge, and the counselor that helps them develop their perception and awareness skills. To accomplish all this, members must be coaxed and led, not left to their own devices or given orders. Even small steps members make toward gaining confidence should be reinforced.

Leaders can use the following strategies to give encouragement and support:

- Focus on how members have made positive movements and developments on their problems, concerns, and issues.
- Become aware of changes and shifts members make—especially positive ones.
- Demonstrate your faith in their abilities and competencies by your words and deeds.
- Block negative statements or attacks by other members.
- Solicit and consider members' input.
- Do not discourage off-beat ideas.
- Try to use some part of everyone's input.
- Act pleased about the group's progress.

The overview of basic attitudes and skills presented thus far has focused on attitudes and skills that are fundamental for group leaders. These must be brought to the leader's awareness, practiced, and internalized if the more advanced group leadership practices are to be effective.

The Importance of Empathy

Empathy has the same importance in the group as it does in individual therapy. Its use is similar in most respects, but there is a significant difference. In individual therapy, empathy is a major responsibility or necessary condition for the therapist. He or she is expected to be empathic with the client. The client, of course, does not have a reciprocal responsibility toward the therapist, although there may be some clients who are empathic with their therapist. However, in group sessions the leader and members share this responsibility, and this can be a rich resource for the group. Therefore, one of the primary tasks for a group leader is to model empathy and encourage members to be empathic with one another. This contributes to the process of developing a cohesive and productive group by building trust and safety, forging connections among members, making members feel included, helping set group norms, encouraging emotional expression, and promoting a willingness to engage in self-exploration. These states and conditions are extremely important to the functioning and success of the group.

The impact of empathy on individual group members is also considerable and important. Members come to the group confused, frustrated, and anxious about their various concerns and problems. They have additional concerns about being "lost in the crowd." Experiencing empathy can help reduce this fear and address the concern about being included, which is always present in the group. Empathy can help members feel valued, understood, cared for, respected, and connected. Empathy can reduce feelings of alienation and loneliness that, in turn, promote hope. Members receive some glimmer of hope that they will not have to stay mired in their misery. Empathy can be one of the most significant contributors to therapy.

Empathy Defined and Described

Many people consider *empathy* and *sympathy* as being synonymous. They are not, although both can be of value in therapy and in everyday life.

Empathy is commonly defined as "sensing the inner world of the other and sharing their feelings" (Rogers, 1951). This experience necessitates that the empathizer be able to enter another person's world with sufficient ego strength and strong psychological boundaries so that his or her sense of self is not lost, enmeshed, or overwhelmed by the other's emotions. Individuals who do not have considerable ego strength or strong psychological boundaries are at risk of being overwhelmed with the intensity of the other person's emotions, *or* of becoming enmeshed and taking into self those emotions that are the other person's. Yes, they are feeling what the other person is feeling, but they are not able to adequately separate which feelings are theirs and which are the other person's.

Empathic Failures

In addition to being empathic, group leaders also have the task and responsibility to reduce empathic failures—both their empathic failures, and those by members. Not providing some measure of empathy when needed can be wounding. It is also wounding to do or say things that demonstrate lack of empathy. Empathic failures result when no one provides empathy, and when something is said that is unempathic.

The discussion in this chapter focuses on reducing empathic failures as a means of increasing empathy. The emphasis is given to personal growth, rather than skills development. That is, the focus is on learning how to be empathic, not just giving responses that reflect the speaker's feelings.

Empathic Behaviors and Attitudes

Following are some behaviors and attitudes that indicate, or contribute to your ability to be empathic. It is not realistic to expect you, or anyone, to be empathic all the time and with everyone, but there are some behaviors and attitudes that should become an integral part of who you are and how you relate to and communicate with others, especially in the therapeutic setting. Consider the behaviors and attitudes listed as guides and not as absolutes.

- Attend to the speaker by orienting your body toward him or her, and stop talking.
- Listen carefully for underlying meanings and feelings.

- Block out distractions, mind-wandering, and preparations for your response.
- Reserve judgment about the goodness, badness, rightness, or wrongness of what the person is saying.
- Do not become defensive or resistant.
- Notice what you are feeling as the person speaks.
- Do not interrupt or finish thoughts for the speaker.
- Respect the speaker's right to his or her feelings, opinions, values, and so on.
- Stay in emotional connection with the speaker.
- Do not disconnect, minimize, or ignore the emotionally laden content of the speaker.
- Do not change the subject, tell your story, or go off on a tangent.

Increasing and Enhancing Empathic Responses

Notice that the emphasis is on behavior. Empathy is an internal state of being and a product of the extent to which you have developed healthy adult narcissism. This development is personal and unique to the individual and continues to be a lifelong process. This discussion is about the external manifestation of empathy: empathic responding is a lower level of empathy that recognizes what the speaker is experiencing, but you do not experience those feelings. You remain somewhat detached from the other person's feelings. It helps if you are responding from a genuine inner state that shares the feeling, but it can also be helpful to have or give a response that reflects a lower level of empathy but which is empathic in nature.

Levels of empathy range from moderate to complete. Anything below moderate is termed sympathy or lack of empathy. The terms used here are moderate empathy, connected empathy, and complete empathy.

When you experience *moderate empathy*, the duration is short, but during that period you know you are in tune with the other person. You come away with a strong sense of what the other person is feeling. Although you did not stay with the person or the feeling, and you quickly pulled back, enough residual feeling remains so that you can use the information to make an empathic response. Why you retreated is less important at this point, but could be a fruitful area for you to explore.

Connected empathy occurs when you forge a strong bond with the person and sense his or her inner world for a longer period than you would with moderate empathy. Connected does not occur in a flash or instant, but happens to the extent that you "catch" some of the intensity the other person is feeling. You feel and understand the breath and depth of the emotional experience, plus you do not immediately retreat from it. You may not remain connected much longer than the previous level, but you do stay long enough so that you are much more in tune with what the other person is feeling.

Complete empathy is rare. Some parents can be totally empathic with their child most all of the time, but the majority of us are rarely that connected with anyone for long periods. Complete empathy implies that you are able to put aside defenses, lower boundaries, retain enough ego boundaries and ego strength so as not to be overwhelmed or become enmeshed, and fully enter the other person's world and sense all that he or she is experiencing. In other words, you feel the person's full range of emotions. Gifted therapists are able to experience complete empathy on a regular basis. Most other people can do it on occasion.

Moderate empathy is sufficient to convey to group members that they are heard and understood. You may want to stay at this level until you have a better understanding of your psychological boundary strength to prevent your becoming overwhelmed or enmeshed with others' feelings. You will also want to work to become empathic, and not just give empathic responses. Building therapeutic alliances and helping members get better, solve problems, improve relationships, and change behavior demands a higher level of empathy. Think of this as a building process, not an all-or-nothing act.

Becoming and Being Empathic

On your journey to becoming empathic you can increase your ability to make empathic responses. Practice the following to become more emotionally present; to be with the other person; to hear what is said, meant, and felt; and to remain with that person instead of attending to your concerns, such as "Am I doing right?"

- Orient your body to the person.
- Become still and relax.
- Focus your thoughts on the person and really listen to what he or she is saying.
- Let go of your self-absorption.
- Allow the person's emotions to become focal for you.
- Use your self-reflection.
- Identify the person's emotion with an emphasis on the most intense emotion.
- Try to feel the message.
- Speak to him or her of what you sense and feel.

Orienting your body means to try to obtain and maintain eye contact and become aware of your facial expression. This stance conveys attentiveness and that you are interested in the person. Do not analyze, judge, evaluate, or bring your cognitive side into play. Focus your energy on the person. *Be still and relaxed* and *focus your thoughts*—empty your mind.

It is important that you become *less self-absorbed*. Thinking about how you can help, if you are "doing it right," making a mistake, appearing incompetent or stupid, floundering, or wondering "what should I do?" are examples of being self-absorbed. Whereas all of these are valid concerns, the task at hand is hearing and understanding the other person—not if you are competent or right.

As you *focus on the other person*, hear his or her words but also try to sense any feelings about the topic. Many times group members do not openly express their feelings, attempt to hide feelings, minimize the intensity of the feeling, or mask what they are feeling. What are you sensing and personally experiencing as the member speaks? This is *self-reflection*; and what you sense or feel may be a reflection of what is felt by the speaker.

Often the person will speak of, or otherwise exhibit, many emotions. Some may even be conflicting emotions, such as shame and self-satisfaction. Gauge the intensity of the person's various feeling, and *identify* the most intensive feeling, as this is what carries the real message. When you are empathic, you not only can identify the feeling, you also experience it and can better understand what the real message is that the person is trying to express.

The final step is to express the real message that the person's feelings are conveying that he or she is not expressing. With empathy, you are right there with the person and can name or label the feelings, summarize the complexity and ambivalence he or she is experiencing, describe the effect on you, say what action you would like to take, such as, "I want to protect you." There are numerous ways to make an empathic response, but you have to put the feelings into words. Simply looking concerned about the person is not empathic; sympathy is not the same as empathy. Nonverbal resonating is not empathic, unless you also verbalize it.

It is not reasonable to expect that you will be empathic with everyone all the time. Nor should you expect that you would be empathic throughout all sessions. However, what is reasonable and realistic is to make empathic responses much of the time, to realize when empathic failures occur, and to repair empathic failures you and other group members make.

Developing a Personal Empathic Self

The Johari window (Luft, 1969) illustrated the self as having four components or levels. The most visible part of the self is perceived and known both by the person and by others. Another part is perceived and known only to the person and is hidden from others. Another part is perceived and known to others but hidden from both the person and others. That is a concise and simple way to describe the "hidden self" that must be explored by the leader in training for himself or herself to better understand the hidden self of group members.

The hidden self is composed of two parts—the part that you can see, but others do not, and the part that remains hidden to you and to others. When you increase your awareness of your projections and transference, resistance and defense mechanisms can reveal and help you understand not only part of your unexplored self, but also how these mechanisms are being used to defend against your knowing about yourself when the hidden parts are no longer invisible to you, and are less threatening if seen by others. This development allows you to better empathize with others because you better understand yourself.

The model of the hidden self described here uses levels that can overlap, are dynamic, incorporate the role of defense mechanisms and resistance, account for feelings such as shame and guilt, and provide for a use of transference and projections to understand them. Accessing and understanding your hidden self is an unfolding process that takes considerable time and effort.

The more you can employ empathy with group members, the more they will feel understood, cared for, valued, respected, safe, trusting and, willing to work. The same is true for making empathic responses. Group members tend to feel more deeply and respond more intensely when you are empathic than when you just make a reflective response.

Because making empathic responses is helpful, you should work to increase your ability to do so. But first, you must be willing to engage in self-examination and accept that you have areas that need work. Basically, you need to do the following:

- Be willing to critically examine your behaviors and attitudes, and not evaluate them as good or bad.
- Be accepting of yourself as you are.

- Develop a commitment to changing, identify what changes you want to make, be realistic about changes, and try not to make too many changes at once.
- Be patient with yourself, celebrate or be happy about your progress, and accept that this is a long-term undertaking.

Chapters 8 and 9 on the leader's personal growth provide more information and strategies for personal development.

Being Empathic in the Group Setting

It is much easier to try to be empathic with one person than it is in a group because you have to attend to all members, not just the one speaking. The speaker may have and need most of your attention, but what this person is saying can also trigger significant associations and feelings for other members, and leaders need to stay aware of this possibility. To increase your ability to be empathic in the group you must be present centered, sense the inner world of members, use active listening, tune in to your inner experiencing, and speak of your feelings because these can be an accurate representation of what one or more members are feeling.

The first step is to stay present centered. Bring all of your attention to what is currently taking place in the group and with members. Try to limit your thoughts about the past or the future—even those that relate to members, although you occasionally will need to link to past events and make associations to the present. Try not to anticipate what you will need or want to say. Carefully consider what you say, but try to make your response a result of the present.

Associated with being present centered are staying focused on the group and its concerns, and being emotionally present. Use your inner experiencing to better understand what is happening in the group. Being with the group, its members, and their concerns promotes your ability to make empathic responses.

Next, consciously try to "sense" the inner world of members. Do not jump from one member to another, but stay focused on the person who is speaking, or the member who is most focal for you. It may be the member who is quiet, the distracted member, or the one who is fidgeting. Try doing this throughout the session, not necessarily with the same person each time. The more you practice this, the more proficient you will become in listening to the content and tuning in to the emotional piece of the message.

A skill that will be helpful in increasing empathic responses is active listening. Members are telling you what they are feeling all the time, but they do not always use words. You have to learn how to identify their feelings whether or not they are spoken. This is not an easy thing to do, and must be constantly practiced.

While all the external events are happening, you also need to tune in to what you are experiencing as your feelings may very well reflect what the other person is feeling. Even if you are not empathic in what you feel, your inner experiencing has valuable information for you. What you are feeling could be a reflection of what is happening in the group, or a barometer for your countertransference, and so on. Either way, it is important to identify what you are feeling and mentally explore it for clues.

Members cannot be sure that you are empathic or understand what they are feeling if you do not openly express it. When you judiciously choose to express your feelings, you will find that what you are feeling and expressing is empathic for the person, other members, or for the group as a whole. If what you are feeling is related to your countertransference, you are better off exploring that for yourself, with your therapist, or with your supervisor. You need to practice verbalizing your feelings and, above all, being genuine in what you express.

Restrict questions because, when you are trying to sense another person's world, you have to be emotionally present and limit your present centeredness. Questions require that you be cognitive, and you are trying to be affective at this point. If you want to be empathic you need to use your energies to try and tune in to both their experiencing, and your inner experiencing. Don't forget that some part of you also needs to be attending to other group members. When all that is happening, if you divert some attention and energy to asking questions, that is counterproductive to being empathic.

There may be times when you want to make an empathic response, but you need something clarified to make sure you understand what the person means. These are legitimate questions and appropriate for the situation. The person may be sending conflicting signals, be contradicting himself or herself, or you may have some doubts or ambivalence about what you are sensing. Under these conditions it may be wise to ask for clarification.

However, when you are trying to be empathic or make an empathic response, you would not ask rhetorical questions, questions designed to elicit a specific response, ask a question instead of expressing feelings, or as a way of showing interest. Practice making statements about what you are identifying, thinking, or feeling instead of asking questions.

It can be hard to sit patiently and allow the other person to organize his or her thoughts, decide what to say, fumble for words, and speak slowly. However, it is not empathic to interrupt the speaker, finish his or her sentences, or tell the member what he or she is thinking.

You display empathy when you allow others to express their thoughts, and you use the time to try and tune in to their feelings. When you interrupt or finish their thoughts you run the risk of being wrong which, in turn, destroys any chance of the connection needed for empathy. You have not "sensed their world," you have imposed one on them. It also indicates that you are more focused on content than feelings. Some members, who are less confident, may agree with what you say even though you are wrong. The same may be true for members who are seeking your approval and want you to like them so they accept your interpretation. Others may be in awe of you so they accept what you say instead of trusting their inner experiencing. There are many reasons why you may be leading them in the wrong direction.

There are also times when you may be right on target. You are empathizing with the speaker and really understand what he or she means or wants to say. It is safer to resist the temptation to interrupt or finish the thought for the other person rather than run the risk of being wrong. Further, some people find it irritating and disrespectful when others do this, even when they are correct and empathizing. These risks are threats to the relationship.

Resist giving your answers. They are not likely to fit the other person or the situation. You are not making empathic responses when you introduce your material. Being empathic and making empathic responses means staying with the person, where he or she is at that moment. Avoid doing any of the following:

- Thinking of the future or the past
- Mentally solving a problem
- Proposing solutions or alternatives
- Making decisions

- Obtaining information
- Guiding or directing

You are simply in the present, with the speaker, feeling their presence and understanding what they are feeling. Save these actions for the next step. The first step is to be empathic.

Becoming More Comfortable. Increasing your empathy and empathic responses is a process. You can develop some skills as described in this chapter. You can grow in underdeveloped aspects of self, or you can cultivate an attitude and adopt certain behaviors that will assist you. Following are some suggestions. It would be helpful for you to become more tolerant of silence and more accepting of the limits of your responsibility, to allow others to assume personal responsibility and control, and to tolerate a higher level of conflict, intense emotions, and ambiguity.

Practice just being there with someone. Relax, open yourself to experiencing, tune in to your feelings while still reaching out to try and feel the other person's presence, be patient, and note what emerges. You could even tentatively tell the other person what emerged for you, and ask if he or she had a similar experience. Like almost everything else, you can improve with practice. Be patient with yourself; it takes time to develop the capacity to be empathic. Be encouraged by the small successes.

Avoiding an Unproductive Attitude. It is not uncommon for people to say or think that they cannot empathize with someone because they have not experienced what that person has. For example, some people feel that they must experience marriage, divorce, death, substance abuse, and so on to empathize with someone who has experienced it. As the group leader you must ensure that you do not have this unproductive attitude. You do not have to experience something to empathize with the feelings someone has about it. It is true that you would lack information about the context, but this information is not needed in order to empathize. In fact, sharing similar experiences can trigger old feelings in you and create confusion about whether they are your own feelings or those of the other person.

If you have this attitude or feel that what the other person is experiencing is so foreign to you that you do not have a basis for empathizing, you are most likely doing some or all of the following:

- Focusing on content instead of feelings
- Fleeing from the person's emotional intensity
- Refusing to validate his or her feelings
- Making value judgments
- Protecting yourself

Whatever your reasons, you are empathically failing that member at that time.

It is sobering and humbling to realize how you may be empathically failing others, especially if you consider yourself to be an empathic person. However empathic you consider yourself to be, it is possible to become more empathic, or at least make more empathic responses. You can also reduce the number of empathic failures and, in the group, repair empathic failures.

Repairing Empathic Failures

There are three simple steps to identifying empathic failures—reflect, identify, and act or repair. If you are currently leading a group, you still have an opportunity to repair some empathic failures, either yours or those of other group members. If you are not leading a group at this time, you can recall a past group or group session and use that for the exercise.

The first step is to *reflect* on the events of a group session, or a series of sessions. You may want to try it with the latest session first because you are probably able to still get in touch with some residual feelings you experienced during the session. If you have a recording of the session, you may also want to review that. Review the session by sitting quietly and allowing images of the session to emerge, but do not try to order or evaluate the images in any way.

As you reflect on the events of the session, *identify* possible empathic failures. These can be identified by noting when the following occurred. As you become more adept at identification, you will be able to do this immediately when it happens.

- No responses were given to what a member said.
- The topic was changed.
- You became bored.
- You thought about there-and-then concerns.
- Content was the focus for responses from you or from other members.
- You thought something said was trivial or unimportant, or that was how another member termed it.
- You were not emotionally present.
- Emotionally laden content was ignored.

You may recall when a member's nonverbal behavior was incongruent with his or her verbal behavior and you either ignored, overlooked, or did not realize at the time how intensely he or she was feeling. Now you realize that you missed something important.

Acting, or *repairing,* is the final step. After identifying what you consider to be an empathic failure, in the next group session you can say something like:

"In the last session you said (or did) _____ and I feel I empathically failed you because I [pick one of the following]:

- *did not respond directly to you."*
- *did not pick up on your emotional intensity."*
- *allowed the subject to be changed."*
- *did not fully hear or understand what you said."*

"What you were sharing was important to you and I regret that I missed that importance. I want you to know that I do realize it—albeit delayed."

The results for trying to repair an empathic failure will vary. Some members will deny that they felt empathically failed. Others will respond that because they were empathically failed, they assumed it wasn't important. There may be attempts to minimize their concerns saying that what they were talking about was trivial. Some may even not remember what you are talking about. However, there are members for whom it will be a huge relief to finally know they were heard. Group members may act puzzled, and challenge you when you say that there was an empathic failure. Your task, as the leader, then becomes one of pointing out that it was important to not do whatever it was that produced the empathic failure, such as not directly responding to the person. It is also important to emphasize that empathic failures are not always dramatic or about something major, but that all such failures act to prevent members from feeling included, understood, safe, valued, respected, cared for, and so on. The person may be able to shrug it off, but the empathic failure still affects the relationship.

When you act to repair an empathic failure it also gives you an opportunity to show members how to become more sensitive to one another's needs and their own personal needs, and model for other group members how to repair empathic failures, teach what behaviors and attitudes constitute empathic failure, increase members' awareness of when they have empathically failed others, and help members better understand when they empathically fail others, and the value of empathy for relationships.

Once you start focusing on empathic failures, even in retrospect, you also increase your sensitivity to possible empathic failures in the present. You will become better at identifying these during the group session which gives you an opportunity to immediately repair them. Another benefit is that members also become more sensitive to empathic failures, both when they commit them and when they are empathically failed. Depending on group norms, members may also then be more willing to speak up when they feel failed and openly ask for feedback, input, and opinions. All those things than enhance communications and help build relationships.

Process and Process Illumination

Process refers to the relationship being expressed in the here and now. The relationship may be between individuals, between subgroups, or between the group and the leader. Although reasons for expression may have antecedents from past relationships, such as parental, or from past experiences, the focus for using process relies on here-and-now expressing.

Process illumination, or *highlighting*, tends to promote understanding for both personal individual issues and group issues. Chapman (1971) proposes that a person's personality can be understood in the context of interpersonal relationships. Observing interpersonal relationships in the group provides a mechanism for some understanding of what life experiences have formed the individual. We can only speculate about the nature and quality of the person's early relationships, as we only have the present interpersonal relationships with which to work, and the person's recollections and feelings about early relationships, which are generally flawed.

Process commentary can focus on what is happening between group members, or in the group as a whole. Some unconscious, nonconscious, and unspoken relationships between members that can form the basis for process commentary include:

- Members seeking to connect
- Attempts to dominate or control
- Solicitation of support or approval
- Rejection

- A need to take care of others
- Avoiding intimacy
- Yearning for fusion

Some unspoken needs or desires for the group as a whole are safety, trust, resistance, aggression, fear of engulfment, fear of exclusion, depression, clarification of norms, feelings of helplessness, or fear of destruction. Once you identify what the needs are, this forms the basis for your process commentary.

Because it is considerably more difficult to make whole-group process commentary, this discussion presents information to guide you in understanding when process is important to illuminate, how to tune in to process, and guidelines for making commentary. The most important points to remember are that the primary responsibility for making process commentary lies with the group leader, and that process commentary is effective when an issue critical to the existence or functioning of the entire group takes precedence over individual issues. It is also helpful to remember that what is taking place in the group is also reflective of what is taking place for members, although their experiencing may be different.

Indices of Process

How does the leader identify process for the group as a whole? What are some indicators? These questions, and others, are difficult to answer in definitive terms because process is ever present, changing, and about as substantial as fog. The group leader is busy tuning in to the dynamics in the group, the needs of individual group members, the objectives for the sessions and goals for the group, as well as the leader's personal experiencing on both the cognitive and affective levels. Further, identification of process is very complex and a group leader develops confidence in his or her ability to tune in to process over time. Whereas it can be helpful to observe a group leader making process commentary and receiving explanations of the basis for the comments, the only way to learn is to practice identifying process and making commentary.

It is difficult at first to focus on the group. Most leaders first develop their skills with individuals and tend to want to focus exclusively on individuals in the group. Focusing on and intervening with individuals is productive, but until group members learn how to coat-tail—that is, use what the leader is doing with one individual to work on their personal issues—the leader is not doing group therapy or group counseling but rather individual therapy in a group setting. Group therapy and group counseling that use the resources of the group to help individuals is very effective and allows all members to work at the same time. Making group-level process commentary allows the leader to work with all group members.

Some specific indices that indicate that there may be a need for group process commentary are the following:

- Behaviors of the group—what the group is doing or is not doing
- Feelings generated in the leader
- Similar feelings noted in members from their nonverbal behavior, but not verbalized by them
- The negative impact of some behavior on members
- Links between members' issues, concerns, and feelings

- Themes that emerge in group
- When the group becomes mired or stuck

Assumptions

Four assumptions guide this discussion on process and process commentary.

1. There are numerous effective ways to respond or intervene; some are more effective than others.
2. An important source of information about the group and what is happening are your reactions and feelings. Learning to access these and use the information takes a high degree of self-awareness, self-knowledge, and a willingness to confront your countertransference.
3. Some responses or interventions are made at the group level, others to individuals. Both are important and crucial.
4. To know what is going on in the group you have to observe the dynamics. Developing the expertise to tune in and identify important dynamics at the moment takes time and effort. Practice, with feedback, aids in developing expertise.

Leader Tasks

Because the primary responsibility for process commentary lies with the leader, there are certain tasks and skills that the leader must develop and use. These tasks and skills include:

- Assuming a present-centered focus
- Containing the group's anxiety, fears, rage, and other emotions without becoming overwhelmed
- Understanding group dynamics
- Using the expected behaviors for the stage of group as a guide for understanding what the group is experiencing when using process commentary
- Teaching members to assume a process orientation by learning to accept process illumination remarks
- Providing constructive feedback
- Being judicious in the use of process commentary

Present-Centered Focus. The skill of immediacy will be of great help in the ability to have a present-centered focus when making process commentary. It is easier to reflect on what is taking place and think about what to do; you do not have the time to come back the next session, or even later in this session, to decide to make the commentary. To be effective, process commentary must occur as close to the time when the behaviors were observed as possible.

A major premise for group-level process commentary is that whatever the group is doing or discussing is a reflection of what is taking place in the group. Another premise is that the behavior of any group member at any time must reflect both his or her personal needs, history, and behavior patterns *and* those of the group. Focusing on the present and making it visible helps both the group and individual members.

Observe what is being done and what is being avoided or resisted, and what behaviors are expected for the particular stage of group development. This forms a basis for your commentary. In addition it is helpful to use the present tense when phrasing process commentary. It is more difficult for group members to deny observable behavior that takes place in the here and now, and to resist. Process commentary is more likely to be accepted when you do this because there has not been an intervening period when events could be forgotten or distorted. Resistance is also lessened because the leader does not make inferences about motivation, but only highlights what is taking place at that time. Although members are free to accept or reject the process commentary, they are more likely to accept it and work with it because of the immediacy.

The Leader as a Container. The leader who uses process must be aware of his or her ability to function as the container for the group's most uncomfortable feelings, such as fear or rage. This is one reason why it is crucial for the leader to be able to tune in to his or her current experiencing as this experiencing most often provides clues or data about what the group is experiencing. For example, if you as leader find yourself experiencing fear or dread and the group continues to discuss outside concerns, it is likely that you are containing the group's fear of establishing relationships, intimacy, and so on, although you identify your feeling as dread.

Group members use the leader and the group to contain primitive affects, such as rage and fear, and to defend against experiencing anxiety, shame, and guilt. Most often, the leader has to be the container for the group so that feelings of safety and trust can be established, members do not feel overwhelmed by affect, control of intense affect can be maintained, and modeling of effective ways of dealing with intense emotions can occur.

Group Dynamics. The ability to identify group dynamics aids in understanding process and making process commentary. Group dynamics define the process taking place and provide the mechanics or structure for identifying and understanding process. Basic dynamics are levels of participation, communication patterns, resistances, nonverbal communication, and feelings aroused and expressed or not expressed.

The leader uses current experiencing and observation of group dynamics in focusing on process: What are members doing or not doing, saying or avoiding? How are feelings being expressed or suppressed? What do nonverbal behaviors signal? Changes in levels of participation? Changes in communication patterns are dynamics that can be observed and used. The leader can use the dynamics for the group as a whole to better understand both what the group is experiencing and what individual members are experiencing.

Stages of Group. Groups go through stages of development, although the stage of development the group is currently in is sometimes hard to determine. Transition points are not definitive. Further, if the group is an open group and new members are added at any time, the group regresses in some ways and stages become even more difficult to distinguish. Most groups, both open and closed, do move through stages. Review the material in Chapter 5 for more suggestions on how to use this information.

Teaching Members. A continuing task for group leaders is to teach members to accept process commentary. Members have to learn how to assume a process orientation—that is, tune in to the process as well as their personal thoughts and feelings. This is not an easy task and a group leader needs to realize and accept that it will take time before members are comfortable with process commentary.

It may be helpful to explain to members that you will make group-as-a-whole comments, especially when linking members' concerns or issues, addressing an impasse, when the discussion becomes stuck or circular, and when the group appears to be resisting. There will also be times when you will make process commentary about what seems to be happening between individual members or between you and the group. Assure members that they do not have to agree with your comments but, if they do take exception to them, to say so directly and be willing to work on any differences in perception with you in the group. No outside meetings should be used for this.

The most helpful characteristic for a group leader to possess when teaching members to accept process commentary is patience. Do not expect members to be comfortable at first with either your comments on process, or when they openly disagree with you. After all, in the beginning stages of group the leader is expected to be all-knowing and all-powerful and members are reluctant to openly disagree.

Constructive Feedback. Leaders generally consider all their feedback to be constructive. However, when feedback is interpretative it tends to be perceived as threatening by members instead of constructive. Members tend to hear old parental messages of blame and criticism, awakening shame and guilt when interpretations are made. These perceptions and reactions are the main reasons why process commentary should limit interpretation and be given in a way that reduces defensiveness and resistance. It should be presented so that it increases willingness to accept the comment. Process commentary is not helpful if you then have to work through defensiveness and resistance. Group leaders who use constructive feedback take into account the emotional needs of members, limit feedback to that which is of most importance for the functioning of the group, link together commonalities of group members, tie it to observable behavior(s), and do not couch the feedback in terms that place blame or criticism.

Judicious Use of Process Commentary. Even when members become accepting of process commentary, a group leader should not overuse it. Group-level interventions are very helpful and seem to address individual members' concerns as well as the group-as-a-whole-issues. Members learn how they contribute to conditions such as group resistance and how to accept responsibility for the group's condition, such as suppression of anger, leading to self-exploration of how this behavior in group reflects their behavior outside of group.

Process commentary can arouse intense feelings, trigger old parental messages, tap into shame and guilt feelings, and strengthen defensiveness and resistance. These are reasons why the group leader should reserve process commentary for those times when highlighting and emphasizing process would promote understanding, resolve an impasse, or highlight progress.

Process Commentary Skills

There are characteristics and skills needed to be an effective group leader and many of these also apply to making process commentary. Characteristics such as warmth, caring, positive regard, acceptance, and genuineness all contribute to establishing trust and safety in the group as well as confidence in the group leader. These characteristics are fundamental in helping group members accept process commentary.

Skills such as immediacy, concreteness, reflection, active listening and responding, and linking can be refined to provide effective process commentary. Other skills, such as timing, are developed as a result of experience and cannot be taught or adequately defined to provide specific guidelines or steps.

Immediacy, as a skill, refers to the here-and-now part of the commentary. This means that the group leader phrases the comment to focus on what is taking place in the present. The present may be defined as the entire session, a portion of the session, or even an event that is currently taking place. Although there may be other related events in the past that can be tied to current experiencing, the most effective process commentary uses current events. Further, resistance is much less when the comment focuses on observable behavior—that is, when it can stand up to consensual validation by group members.

Concreteness is helpful because it does not infer motives or make judgments. Again, observable behavior is the focus: what group members are doing or saying, not what someone infers. It is helpful when leaders can describe specific behaviors or label their personal feelings. For example, if there are several behaviors—such as several members using the same word, term, or phrase—that is behavior that can be highlighted as part of the description, and is specific about what was said or done. If leaders are using their personal feelings as clues to group process, then label these feelings and accept responsibility for them. Say very clearly that these are your feelings about what is taking place. Give members some wiggle room just in case accepting the process commentary is too threatening at the present moment.

Reflection is probably the most useful skill of all because it holds up a mirror to a member or the group without blaming, criticizing, or judging. Simple reflective statements can be very powerful in encouraging or forcing members to examine what they are saying, doing, and feeling. Whereas the leader may understand why they are acting this way, or certain feelings were triggered, there is no need to report that information at this time. It is much more effective to simply reflect and allow members to self-examine and come to these understandings on their own. By doing so, defensiveness and resistance are reduced or more easily worked through.

Active listening and responding relates to the hidden messages that the feelings are communicating. These useful skills highlight expressed and unexpressed feelings in the group. Highlighting feelings aids group members in coming to grips with their emotions. They may be unfamiliar with awareness of current feelings, openly expressing them, methods used to block feelings of self and others, or of soothing behavior. Process commentary points out what they are doing and the impact of the behavior.

Linking is a valuable group leadership skill. Tying together feelings and behavior, commonalties among members, and current and past experiences or events are ways by which members gain awareness and understanding of their issues and how the group begins to become cohesive. Linking is also the way in which a leader can know the emerging, or emerged, group theme that is defining underlying issues being worked on in the group. These underlying issues may be very different from presenting problems or expressed objectives. Making them known or visible promotes progress for the group and members.

There are several ways to link, and a group leader may use any or all of them. One way is to use the feeling words expressed by members and tie them together. For example, if group members express irritation or feelings of being devalued or criticized, even though they are using outside events as the vehicle for these feelings the leader can link them to highlight members' feelings about the group.

Another way is for the leader to use free association. This calls for a high degree of self-awareness on the part of the leader as well as the ability to think fast. To free associate, you allow thoughts and feelings about what is happening to emerge until you can discern a pattern that leads to some understanding of the process to the point where you can feel comfortable making a process commentary.

Sometimes when the leader is functioning as a container for the more uncomfortable feelings for the group, you can sort through those feelings and link them to events in the group. You then are expressing the unexpressed feelings as well as helping members understand how they are avoiding, suppressing, or projecting feelings in the group that, in turn, can be linked to characteristic behaviors outside the group.

Metaphors

Learning to identify and use metaphors as process illumination is an advanced skill. Issues and concerns for the group often appear as metaphors, and thus are abstract and ambiguous. Basically, the metaphor is expressing the issue and relationships in the group whether it is being discussed or avoided. Members find it easier to express these topics by using metaphors because of the following:

1. The real topic is too sensitive to talk about directly, so it remains on a nonconscious or unconscious level.
2. The topic is both urgent and important.
3. Whatever the real issue is, it is being expressed in the present.
4. It is related to the group, its members, and its functioning.
5. It is couched in vague, abstract terms that tend to use or evoke vivid imagery or feeling; or it is characterized by an absence of significant affect.
6. It is related to the group's developmental stage.
7. Generally, one member brings it to the group, most often in the form of a story about a live event or as a dream.
8. Its expression speaks both for the individual and for the group.

Metaphors emerge because the group is struggling, is at an impasse, is resisting awareness of significant material, is fearful of overwhelming affect, is unaware of real issues, and so on and needs a metaphor to understand what is happening in and to the group.

Analyses of Metaphors. Following are three steps to use in analyzing metaphors.

1. Listen carefully to the content and feelings expressed in the group by one or more members.
2. Associate the basic issue with the group, the relationships between members, group resistances, and so forth.
3. Decide which associations are most important or focal, and focus on them.

The following three examples illustrate how to do the associations.

Clinical Vignette: Analyzing a Metaphor

A member tells of a fight or disagreement where the response was to soothe and hold back expressing negative feelings to preserve the relationship, leaving the person with residual feelings of resentment and being treated unfairly. Group members seem uncomfortable, and do not respond.

Basic Issues: Conflict, suppression of negative affect expression, smoldering resentment.

Group Associations: Ineffective conflict resolution or suppression of conflict in the group is resulting in suppression of negative affect and resentment.

Clinical Vignette: Metaphor—Intimacy Dangers

A member tells of receiving a rejection letter from a boyfriend with whom she is living. Members express some reassurance, but say very little.

Group Associations: Developing intimacy only leads to disappointment, betrayal, rejection, and feelings of anger, sadness, and shame; loss of self-esteem for not being "good enough"; loneliness, detachment, and fear.

Clinical Vignette: Metaphor—Change

A member tells of receiving a suggestion to dye her hair when she wonders out loud if she will face rejection in job searches because of her age. Other members start to tell their stories of discrimination, but reassure the member that she does not need to dye her hair.

Group Associations: Apprehension about changes, fear of the future, helplessness over physical characteristics or the image one projects; acceptance depends on having others judge them fairly or unfairly.

Developing Process Commentary

As you can see from the previous examples, several associations can be made. It is seldom that there is only one association, although there may be one that is focal or is so evident that it assumes prominence. What follows is a process for deciding what to focus on and how to make process commentary.

1. After making associations with what is happening in the group, select what appears to be the most important association for you, especially if it is very apparent at the current time. If something emerges for you but there is nothing happening at the present, wait until you can tie it to a specific behavior for the group.
2. State to the group that the story or comment reflects what is taking place in the group.
3. Identify basic elements of the "story" or link comments. For example, in the second vignette you could use the issues of rejection and betrayal of a significant or

meaningful relationship and the feelings associated, such as anger, sadness.

4. Report on how you, the leader, have noticed this being reflected and played out in the group; previous events, other stories, *or* how the group is avoiding the same circumstance or issue; for example, how the group is avoiding establishing intimacy for fear of loss, betrayal, or being found to be "flawed" or inadequate.

Vignette: Suppressing Negative Feelings

Group association is suppression of negative affect. Process commentary could be, "Much soothing behavior has occurred in the group, conflict is ignored or suppressed. This happened when [give specific instances and behavior]. The group seems to want to keep any hint of negative feelings from emerging."

Vignette: Fear of Intimacy

Group associations are fear and detachment. Process commentary could be, "Members have not developed strong connections and attempts to do so are met with intellectualizations, deflections, empathic failures, and so on [give specific examples of observable behavior].

Vignette: Lack of Genuineness

Group association is fear of rejection. Process commentary could be, "Maybe expressing how members fear rejections if the real 'self' is known has led to use of masks in the group."

5. Bring the attention to the here-and-now behavior in the group and how the story or comment is similar to other behaviors in the group with specific examples. This provides an opportunity for members to discuss their relationships, concerns, fears, and issues in the group as being similar to those they have outside the group, and/or to notice if there is something taking place in the group that is hindering progress.

Building a group culture where members are able to accept open, honest, and direct communication and process commentary is critical to the group's movement through stages of development as well as fostering the psychological growth and development for members.

Summary

1. There are fundamental group leader relationship attributes and communication competencies that help establish the therapeutic relationship. These are developed as part of the therapeutic self of the group leader. Examples include positive regard, warmth, caring, and empathy.

2. Group-level leader skills include blocking, linking, and encouraging and supporting. The group leader must develop the facility to respond in a manner that takes into consideration the needs and the impact on all group members.

3. The importance of being empathic and not just giving reflective responses is emphasized. Actions by the group leader that are empathic failures are not constructive for the group, or for individual members.

4. Group process is defined as the here-and-now relationships among members and with the leader. The group is always acting on its needs which can be masked, hidden, or expressed in indirect ways.

5. The responsibility for process illumination rests with the group leader, and this is a skill that uses considerable knowledge and understanding of the group and its members. Process commentary uses attention to whole-group factors, and leader expertise in conveying this in a manner that members can accept and use.

6. The group may use metaphors to communicate its needs, wishes, desires, fantasies, and so on, and a process for analyzing metaphors is described.

Chapter Activities

1. Individually, list all the events, thoughts, and feelings that you noticed or experienced during this class session. Share these in triads, and then try to discern metaphors for what you listed.

2. Write a brief description of the relationships in the class as you perceive them, especially during the class session. What hidden, masked, or unspoken needs may be in this process?

3. List two or more additional behaviors for each relational attribute that would convey the attribute to group members. Share these in a small group, and then have the entire class report on the lists.

Personal Development Exercise: Construct a collage of your greatest disappointment and one for your most notable accomplishments.

Chapter 8

The Group Leader's Personal Development

Major Topics

1. A rationale for continual personal development and how it benefits the group leader's efficacy.

2. How the developed inner self of the group leader produces personal characteristics that are facilitative to the group and its members.

3. Suggestions for beginning your personal development.

Introduction

The art of group leadership—which focuses on a leader's personal qualities, attitudes, and inner experience—is difficult to describe, as many of the concepts are abstract and complex, interwoven, and difficult to discuss individually. However, these components can enrich the group and its members, contribute to the efficacy of the group, and enhance the knowledge and skills of the group leader. The art component emerges from the level and extent of the leader's personal development, where his or her personal issues and unfinished business are addressed. A deeper understanding of his or her needs, wishes, and desires can emerge, and the leader's self and its boundaries can be strengthened. This personal development is instrumental in enriching an understanding of members and how their personal issues and unfinished business impact them, building trust and safety in the group, establishing the therapeutic alliance, and reducing the negative effects of the leader's possible countertransference.

The art component for group leadership is concerned with intangibles and unseen forces that impact the leader, members, and the group as a whole. Intangibles may include family-of-origin and other past experiences that shaped the leader and members; personality characteristics; beliefs and values; inner resources such as hardiness and resilience; unmet needs; cultural and diversity factors; and the extent of self-esteem, self-confidence, and self-efficacy. These cannot be measured or even described very well, but still continue to exert considerable influence. Some examples of their influences are presented later in the chapter. Leaders' extent of personal development plays a major role in understanding the intangibles and unseen forces for self and for others, recognizing their influences when they appear, identifying appropriate interventions, and in helping generate the therapeutic or change factors.

Leaders must be able to identify and use these intangible forces in a constructive way to promote the growth, development, and healing for all members. This ability is not a result of skills training; rather, it involves considerable personal development on the part of the group leader, a critical need recognized and supported by leading experts in the field such as Yalom (1995, 2005), Corey (2004), Gladding (2004), Postuma (2002), Brabender (2002), and Rutan and Stone (2001).

A Rationale for Personal Development

It can be overwhelming and intimidating to consider all that has to be learned to be an effective group leader. The notion that you must learn how to sort through behaviors, possibilities, personal experiencing, personal issues, and various events occurring all at the same time, and decide what to do, can feel overwhelming. Because of this complexity and dynamism, you may be tempted, as many are, to focus only on concrete information. At least the structured part of group leadership can be articulated, described, and observed.

However, in the long run it will be more profitable for you to give much of your energy to the art component of group leadership. The personal work you do can help expand your knowledge and understanding of members' needs and concerns, which, in turn, aids in their resolution of problems and self-understanding. You can be significantly more effective when you truly understand what members are experiencing, confident that your perceptions and reactions are not countertransference, and that your inner self is accurately portrayed to members so that they see you as caring, concerned, and genuine.

It can be extremely beneficial to group members to feel heard, understood, and valued. The art of group leadership expands that understanding to be more comprehensive than an empathic attunement, although that is extremely important. This expanded understanding recognizes the continuing impact and influence of members' family-of-origin experiences, unfinished business, and their relationships over their life span. Leaders can then convey this understanding to members through their responses and actions.

The leader also needs to have examined his or her personal issues and unfinished business to reduce and eliminate the possibility that current perceptions and reactions to group members are not unduly and unconsciously affected by the leader's past relationships and experiences (countertransference). Although unconscious associations cannot be ruled out entirely, awareness and resolution of personal issues arising from family-of-origin and other past experiences can help reduce the possibility of unconscious associations.

Why this focus on personal development? How you appear to group members is a function of who you are, and this plays a significant role in their responses to you. Members arrive at group in turmoil, pain, confusion, and frustration, feeling hopeless and despairing, or fearful. You, as the leader, want them to trust you to take care of them, to reveal their shameful secrets. You want them to trust that you will protect them from attack and rejection, that you understand their needs, and that you can and will provide what they need—not necessarily what they want. You expect members to open up and let you see their "real selves," even when they have only known scorn, betrayal, put-downs, failure, and other negative reactions and life experiences. You have your job cut out for you, and your inner self that is revealed to members is a critical part of establishing the therapeutic relationship. There are other practical reasons for the emphasis on personal development: It helps you decide what to focus on in session; how and when to intervene; to better understand what members are indirectly expressing; and to know what the group as a whole needs. In addition, you can contribute guidance and modeling.

There is so much going on during a session that demands the leader's attention that it can be difficult to decide what is of most importance and should be the focus at that time. What you elect to do, not do, and select as focal makes an enormous difference to the success of the group and outcomes for individual members. And, your decisions are significantly determined or influenced by your personality—past issues; conscious, nonconscious, and unconscious emotions; and your ability to use both internal and external experiencing at the same time. It is important to use your observations, knowledge, and your experiencing to make wise decisions.

It is also important that you learn to make your decisions about interventions immediately—that is, in the here and now—because you do not have the option of consulting someone else, doing reading on the topic, or analyzing the situation. You must sort through the details and make choices, responses, or interventions in the moment—or in that session—for maximum effect. This is why you have to be able to trust what emerges for you to guide your decision and to be confident that your countertransference is not leading you to make an inappropriate intervention. Let's take a look at just how complex even a simple-appearing and common event can be for deciding on an intervention.

Clinical Vignette: What Do I Do Now?

Your group of adults in their 20s and 30s is meeting for the first time. It is composed of three White males, three White females, one African American male, and one Asian female. They are seated as you enter the room and all eyes focus on you. You introduce yourself and ask each member to intro-duce himself or herself. Once that is complete, silence falls and everyone looks at you.

There are numerous options for intervention that are available. You could do any of the following:

- Say or do nothing and allow the silence to continue.
- Ask members what they want to do.
- Comment that the group seems to expect you to tell them what to do.
- Tell members it is their group and they have the responsibility for its functioning.
- Disclose what you are feeling at that moment.
- Start an exercise or activity.
- Ask members about their problems that brought them to group.
- Comment about the usual tension, conclusion, and fears members can experience in a new and ambiguous situation.
- Ask members what they are feeling.
- Tell members that nothing will happen if they do not talk.

These are only some of the possible responses. Whereas an appropriate response is given based on the group and its needs, some of the listed possibilities would be better than others. Which possibility are you drawn to? Whatever selection you made, do you know why you chose the one you did? Consider how much more anxiety you would feel sitting in the group with everyone looking at you and expecting you to provide direction and guidance. Would you be able to relax enough to tune in to the feelings tone in the group as well as your personal feelings, and provide the appropriate response for a particular group?

Example of Applications

Applications that illustrate the need for the leader's personal development include:

- Establishing the therapeutic alliance
- Fostering safety
- Promoting trust development among members and with the leader

Developing the Therapeutic Alliance. The therapeutic alliance leaders establish with members relies on the group leader's essential self being seen as trustworthy, and as competent to care for the members. Members must feel protected, cared for, valued, understood, accepted, and perceived as worthwhile before they feel comfortable enough to disclose painful material. This feeling of being safe is a process that unfolds, and it is unlikely that members begin the group willing and able to trust.

You can reassure members as much as you want, but that will not convince them they are safe. You need to be genuinely warm, caring, accepting, and act in accordance with who you are, and not just use a set of techniques. There are some nonverbal behaviors, such as maintaining eye contact and orienting your body to the speaker, and techniques that can help convey these qualities to members, and you are encouraged to develop and use these.

What you may not realize is that, although you may physically engage in these nonverbal behaviors, if you are not "real" or authentic, there are group members who will pick up on the falseness conveyed by your nonverbal behavior. They will, in turn, feel the falseness and be wary. Thus, it will be difficult or almost impossible to build sufficient trust and safety in the group.

You need to develop your skills to the point where they are a part of you—not just something you use in a therapy session. This incorporation and integration of skills with your inner self are what allows you to react without having to always consciously analyze before deciding what to do. Your interventions are not impulsive, they are spontaneous.

Establishing Safety. Psychological safety is individualistic, and not easy to define for that reason. Group members, no matter their ages, come to group with varying degrees of intimacy tolerance, fears of being destroyed or abandoned, having experienced events that have left them cautious, and with painful associations as well as the presenting problems. Members may not have a good understanding of what their psychological safety needs are, much less be willing to openly express them. If you rush to give members what you need to feel psychologically safe, you may be fueling even more uncertainty for them.

For example, suppose you feel safer when you are verbally reassured you are doing it right, and begin to respond to each member with the kind of verbal reassurance you would want. What can happen is that some members will feel less safe. These reassurances will resonate with members who have needs similar to yours, but not all members have those needs. Your reassurances may appear off-target, patronizing, and unresponsive to any member who has different needs. This is why group leaders need sufficient personal development—so that they know what their own needs are, and that they are responding to members' needs and not satisfying their personal needs.

Promoting Trust. Members also arrive at group with varying levels of trust for others. The group leader has the task of building trust, not only in himself or herself as leader, but also among group members. What you generally get is a collection of people who do not trust you or other members, and in some cases, who do not trust themselves.

Before the group can become a place where members will risk revealing secrets, innermost thoughts and feelings, deep fears, or recall of painful events, they must have sufficient trust. Trust means they have come to believe that they will not be rejected, unfairly evaluated, destroyed, abandoned, ridiculed, or perceived as weak or inadequate by the leader or other members. This is a crucial task for the group leader because the work stays on the surface if members do not disclose important material.

Regardless of how trustworthy you consider yourself to be, you cannot expect members to trust you just because you want them to trust you, or because you reassure them that you are trustworthy. You can expect that it will take time to develop trust.

Trust will be even more difficult to develop when members are involuntary, had abusive experiences, fear that what they say can and will be used against them, have suffered numerous betrayals, or when they perceive other members as projecting aggression, and sadism. The leader who has done prescreening and preassessment may know some of their social history, but other events may not be mentioned or be buried so deeply that even that member remains unaware of their existence. These issues may be especially important in determining their ability to trust.

These, and other circumstances, can contribute to difficulty in establishing trust. From the very moment you meet a client, he or she is assessing your trustworthiness and, as the vast majority of communication is nonverbal behavior, much of the assessment and judgment is based on what and who you appear to be. Your understanding and acceptance that trust takes time to develop, your willingness to accept members as they present themselves, and your ability to convey caring and positive regard and faith in the group process and empathic responding can be facilitative. These are the inner self characteristics that contribute to building trust.

Personal Issues for Leader Development

Group leaders can benefit from counseling, therapy, and personal growth group experiences in many ways. Leaders learn what effort it takes to be effective members and how difficult it can be to share painful material and shameful events. They become aware of the power of appropriate self-disclosure; the value of being understood and supported in constructive conflict that can strengthen relationships; their perception of and relation to authority figures; and the anxiety of uncovering unrealized issues and unfinished business.

What are some of the attitudes, behaviors, and personal issues that you can address that are particularly useful for your group leadership? Following are some examples.

- Managing personal anxiety
- Tolerating ambiguity

- Identifying personal defenses
- Addressing competitiveness, dependency needs, and unresolved family-of-origin issues that could contribute to transference and countertransference

Managing Personal Anxiety. Managing your personal anxiety is crucial for the effective functioning of the group. Group members can catch your anxiety, just as you can catch theirs. In addition, the leader is a model and your behavior teaches group members. So, if leaders have difficulty managing their anxiety, or are not aware of or deny being anxious, then group members become even more anxious and concerned about safety in the group. It is extremely important that group leaders be aware of acknowledge, and manage their personal anxiety to reassure members that the leader will take care of them, and to model containing and managing anxiety. Your personal development will guide you in learning how to do this.

Tolerating Ambiguity. Group leaders must have a high tolerance for ambiguity because groups are not predictable, individual members bring hidden and unconscious material to the groups, and life circumstances can cause crises to arise. Whereas research has shown that some things about groups are consistent, such as moving through stages of development, we still don't have enough information about what to expect, when to expect it, and in what form it will appear. Further, each group is different; what works or doesn't work for one group may not be true for another group. Groups tend to define their needs as they work, and this contributes to ambiguity.

Leaders in training will want to examine their reactions to ambiguity and uncertainty to determine if they are able to contain and manage their anxiety so that they do not become paralyzed, overreact, or transmit that anxiety to group members. Leaders' tasks are to model anxiety containment, guide members to feel safe and secure, assure members of the leader's competence to take care of them, and demonstrate how to use that anxiety in a constructive way for self-understanding and self-development. Building tolerance for ambiguity calls for self-reflection about the causes of the fears about ambiguity and uncertainty because these fears can be debilitating and negatively impact the group.

Identifying Personal Defenses. It can be helpful to think about and get feedback on which defenses you seem to use most often, and in what circumstances. This can help you more easily identify when others are using them, and what they may be possibly defending against. Defense mechanisms are used to prevent conscious awareness of unacceptable and threatening material because this awareness produces anxiety and psychic pain, some of which can be intolerable. Use of defenses distracts us from this awareness. Defenses are used when the self feels that there is danger of the material emerging into awareness, thus leading to pain and anxiety. Prevention is a main function of the defense.

Each person uses a variety of defenses in unique ways, and it is not readily apparent what is being defended by a particular defense. For example, repression is not used by everyone to keep memories of physical abuse out of the conscious mind, because not everyone experiences physical abuse. Repression is used by everyone, but for different reasons. The unconscious material is complex; this is why therapy can be helpful in guiding awareness and understanding.

Following are some common defenses that you may be using. The ones presented here can be more easily recognized than those, such as repression, that protect very threatening material from becoming conscious. Further, the defenses described here are less threatening to most people when they are recognized by themselves or by others.

- *Intellectualization*—introducing cognitive material to prevent or minimize intense emotions.
- *Rationalization*—dismissing or minimizing the importance of an unacceptable thought, action, or feeling through the use of excuses, alternative explanations, and the like.
- *Suppression*—an attempt to reduce or dismiss uncomfortable, intense, or unacceptable thoughts and feelings. The real thought or feeling is felt to be too dangerous to think or feel.
- *Displacement*—a substitute target for anger, aggression, and so on. The real target cannot be challenged and the energy is then directed to the substitute, such as what can happen when you are angry with a parent, and express that anger by starting a fight with a sibling.
- *Projection*—unacceptable faults, flaws, inadequacies, shame, and so on are unconsciously put on another person (projected) and the other person reacts as if he or she possesses the unacceptable characteristic or feeling.

Becoming aware of your defenses is not only helpful to you, it can also increase your awareness of group members' individual and collective defenses. When they use defenses, you as the group leader can reflect on what triggered them. For example, if several group members started intellectualizing after another members' emotional disclosure, the defense could be protecting against their becoming enmeshed, overwhelmed, or of having their memories triggered.

Addressing Competitiveness and Dependency Needs. Competition in the group setting is to be expected, but many people find that their competitiveness is a personally unacceptable characteristic and deny having any competitive needs. However, unconscious competitiveness can exist that has negative or positive influences on behavior. Group leaders will want to be aware of their own competitiveness both inside and outside the group to better recognize and understand group members' competitiveness.

The level and extent of competitiveness are most likely to be an interaction of personality, development, and family-of-origin experiences. Personality characteristics, such as aggression and the need for dominance, seem to be present at birth and are enhanced and modified by the environment. Development refers to undeveloped narcissistic behaviors and attitudes, such as the need for attention, admiration, and an entitlement attitude. Family of origin experiences with parents and siblings can have lasting influences on competitiveness. Everyone may have some measure of competitiveness, but it can be displayed in various ways.

What might be some indicators for competitiveness?

- Playing one-upmanship
- Discounting or disparaging comments
- Minimizing someone's accomplishments
- Seeking to form special alliances, relationships, or cliques
- Having a superior attitude or frequently pointing out others' inadequacies, mistakes, and so on
- Displaying attention-seeking behaviors such as being silent, being loud, or monopolizing

- Displaying admiration-seeking behaviors such as fishing for compliments or constantly flattering others
- Displaying approval-seeking behaviors such as always agreeing or hiding real opinions
- Tattling
- Having a need-to-win attitude, and that others must lose

Family of Orgin Issues. It is not uncommon for group leaders to have unresolved issues that have their roots in early family of origin experiences (countertransference), just as group members have these (transference). The importance of working on these issues is crucial so that group leaders do not let them unconsciously negatively impact the therapeutic reloationship. These are very powerful forces that may not be fully understood by the leader and may remain below the level of awareness, but can still emerge unexpectedly in responce to one or more group members. Working to resolve these issues can reduce the likelihood of negative countertransference.

Family of origin issues are those that relate to the parent-child relationship, sibling relationship, events and situations occurring that impacted the child's development and functioning, and the extent to which the child received appropriate nurturing and empathic responding. While it is difficult work to uncover and resolve these issues, some of which may have happened during the preverbal period, it is still very important personal work that needs to be done in order to increase the effectiveness of the group leader.

Developing the Therapeutic Inner Self

The therapeutic inner self is developed through addressing and resolving personal issues—building healthy adult narcissism characteristics of empathy, wisdom, creativity, and meaning and purpose for one's life; and developing an ability to initiate and maintain satisfying and enduring relationships. These form the basis for the core therapeutic personal characteristics identified by Rogers as warmth, caring, genuineness, acceptance, and respect (Rogers, 1951). The core characteristics apply in all settings, but the additional ones described here are especially helpful in groups.

Core Characteristics

Basic group facilitative characteristics include the following:

- Willingness to take risks (Brabender, 2002)
- Openness to and awareness of experiencing (Rutan & Stone, 2001)
- A range and depth of emotional experiencing
- Clear and firm boundaries (Kline, 2003)
- Faith in the group and its members (Yalom, 2005)
- Toleration of ambiguity (Brown, 2003b)

These are some of the characteristics that emerge from the level and extent of your personal development. Let's examine what these characteristics contribute to the functioning of the group.

Risk Taking. Group leaders must be willing to take risks if the group is to be effective. Taking risks means the leader can and will do the following when appropriate.

- Be willing to be wrong or make errors and not always play it safe
- Respond even when he or she fears being wrong
- Play hunches
- Take a chance that conflicts with the leader will emerge
- Accept that members will resist, challenge, or attack the leader
- Manage the fear of being perceived as fallible by members

It is difficult for some people to accept that they make errors or can be wrong in any way. They seem to believe that they must be perfect, and are devastated and ashamed when they make mistakes. Leaders who have this attitude can be detrimental to the group's progress because they will be so tentative that members will become anxious. These leaders will tend to stick to what has always worked for them, fail to tap into the resources of the group, and model this attitude for group members. None of these are helpful for group members.

Creative group leaders act on their hunches. They trust their inner experiencing and find it a rich resource for understanding what is taking place in the group, and to help understand what group members are experiencing. You do risk being wrong when you act on your hunches, but you may also make an intuitive leap that can be very helpful to the group and its members.

When you become more familiar with group stages, you will be aware that conflict with the leader is likely to emerge, but can be constructive and beneficial for the group. Effective group leaders do not avoid, minimize, or ignore conflict or challenges to their leadership; they use it to model conflict resolution, how to manage personal anxiety, and demonstrate how to not take these personally.

Resistance and direct or indirect attacks on the leader are common and expected events in the group. It is not a personal failing on the leader's part when members resist, and leaders need to become comfortable with allowing the resistance to occur until the members are ready to deal with it. Much constructive work can be done without trying to break down resistance.

Leaders who have a personal need to remain infallible are being more self-absorbed than they are being self-reflective. No one can be right all of the time, and leaders who can teach members how to accept their errors, mistakes, and other flaws are teaching invaluable lessons.

Openness to and Awareness of Experiencing. Effective group leaders must remain open and aware of what they are experiencing both internally, such as their thoughts and feelings, and externally, such as their observations of group dynamics. It is not easy to develop and maintain this state because there is always considerable activity within and among members, as well as a dynamic internal state.

Knowing yourself is an important part of being open and aware. You need to stay in touch with what you are experiencing in the present, be aware of how and when your past experiences may still have an influence on your current experiencing, and not rely on thoughts or cognition as the sole source of information. In other words, you need to use your feelings as well as your thoughts. To use your feelings you must be able to trust the information they are providing. However, you cannot trust the accuracy of your feelings until you are also willing to consider that they can be, and are, influenced by unconscious defenses, past issues, and so on. The potential for countertransference is great and must be recognized.

While all this internal work is going on, the group leader is also expected to remain open and aware of what is taking place in the group *and* what is happening for individual members. Tuning in to group dynamics is critical and is a skill that must be developed. The group as a whole is important because what the group is doing, feeling, or not doing is generally reflective of what individual members are doing, feeling, or not doing. For example, if the group is ignoring conflict, it is likely that members are ignoring conflict in other relationships. That, in turn, is contributing to what brought them to group in the first place.

Modeling of Emotional Experiencing. Many group members will be emotionally constricted. They will defend against experiencing intense emotions, especially unpleasant ones such as anger and shame. Others will be aware only of intense emotions and will not realize milder emotions. For example, members can realize when they are angry and express it, but not be aware of feeling annoyed or irritated. They seem to skip straight to anger. Still others do not allow themselves to feel more positive emotions such as pleasure, happiness, or joy.

These are some examples to illustrate the need for a group leader to have, express, and model a wide range and depth of emotional expression. Your personal development can expand and enhance your ability to do the following:

- Learn the levels and graduations of your emotions.
- Be willing to openly express your emotions in appropriate ways, and at appropriate times.
- Have an awareness of your current or immediate emotions.
- Realize and accept when you are blocking or resisting, and have a willingness to explore these.
- Develop an extensive feeling vocabulary.

Clear and Firm Boundaries. It is essential that group leaders have a strong and definitive sense of their boundaries—that is, where their "self" ends and where others begin. Leaders who do not understand this, or who do not have strong resilient boundaries, can become enmeshed or overwhelmed by group members' strong or intense emotions. To be an effective group leader you must understand the importance of clear and firm boundaries. An example may help clarify what is meant.

One ethical concern that exemplifies boundary issues is dual relationships where personal and professional relationships clash. All mental health professional ethical guidelines have specific prohibitions against having dual relationships with clients. One of the major reasons for disciplinary actions by licensing boards is the failure of counselors to adequately monitor and control their dual relationships, such as treating friends, or developing an intimate relationship with a client. Now, it may seem simple to avoid dual relationships but, like many other concepts, it is considerably more complex than it appears. There are numerous ways to enter into a dual relationship without being aware that you are doing so, especially when you do not fully understand your boundaries.

Boundaries are very important in therapy because the counselor–client relationship is an intimate one with powerful feelings on both sides. The client is there to work on unfinished business and unresolved issues, and the task is known to both the client and the counselor. The particulars may need to be specified, but both know the general task. The therapist also has unfinished business and unresolved issues. We all do, but personal issues are not brought into the therapeutic relationship by the counselor, except through the unconscious level over which he or she has no control. If a counselor has significant unresolved issues, or is unaware of these issues, the potential for these issues to influence the counselor is great and can easily lead to entering a dual relationship without conscious awareness of it.

For example, the intimacy and affection that can grow in a therapeutic relationship leads some counselors into sexual affairs with clients, in part because the counselor has unresolved issues that led to his or her having weak and fluid boundaries. These counselors did not fully understand that they were violating boundaries because they had not fully developed a sense of where they end and others begin. Engaging in personal development can build boundary strength and provide a clearer understanding of being separate and distinct from others.

Tolerance of Ambiguity. It is essential that group leaders have a high tolerance for ambiguity. The nature of groups is ambiguous at best, and added to this are the unknown needs and expectations of group members, their varying personalities and how these will interact, the unintentional and unexpected uncovering of sensitive material that could not be planned for, and other such situations that occur in groups. Things don't always go as planned, there can be unwelcome glitches and other distruption, members can act inconsistently without explanation, and so on. Group leaders have to be emotionally prepared for surprises.

Reflect on your need for structure, knowing what to expect, reactions to surprises and unanticipated events, and how ambiguity feels to you. You cannot eliminate ambiguity from your life, or from your groups, but you can learn to increase your tolerance for it so that you are not unduly affected. Further, you will serve as a model for your group members, and help them learn how to stay centered and grounded even when everything seems murky and uncertain.

Faith in the Group and Its Members. Group leaders must model faith in the group process, especially in the beginning stages of group. They must understand that there is considerable anxiety, frustration, and fear in the beginning stage, and that conflict must be allowed to emerge and be constructively resolved in stage 2 in order for stage 3, the cohesive working stage, to emerge. It is not always easy for leaders to contain and manage their personal anxiety in the face of members who need and want reassurance and nurturing, who become frightened at conflict, who use conflict to avoid intimacy or being known by others, and so on. A tendency of many leaders is to work to soothe, reassure, promote harmony, suppress conflict, protect members from intense or uncomfortable emotions, and make members feel good or happy. These are all worthwhile actions and are needed at times during the group. However, leaders must ensure that they are not engaging in these actions because of their own personal needs. For example, leaders who suppress conflict because they are not comfortable with conflict are attending to personal needs, not group needs.

Experience with observing group stages, seeing the progress of the group and members, and using the resources of the group to help individual members get better promote faith in group process. Leaders become more skillful at knowing when to intervene and understanding when the group is working on its own and does not need an active intervention. Knowing when to leave it alone is an important leadership skill and task. Having faith in the group's ability to manage itself develops over time with experience. The best that beginning group leaders can expect is to be able to suspend disbelief for a time and trust that they are not being misled when told to have faith, and that the group will do the work it needs to do.

A Focus for Personal Development

There was some discussion earlier about the importance of art components for effective group leadership. Chief among these are the inner characteristics and resources of the group leader. These are not skills that can be taught; they are what make up the self of the group leader. The self contains inner characteristics and resources that contribute to forming the therapeutic alliance; the emotional presence the leader brings to the group sessions; the understanding and empathy at a deep level; the trust that the leader's experiencing is free from personal issues and is a valid representation of what is taking place in the group or with members; and the modeling of desired behaviors and attitudes. The self is a significant part of the leader's proficiency for containing and managing his or her personal anxiety. These are intangibles that have significant impact on the quality of the group experience for both the leader and the members. They also provide a rationale for the group leader's need for continual personal development.

This personal development should focus on the following at a minimum.

- Family of origin experiences and their continuing positive and negative effects on functioning, relationships, and the quality of life
- Past experiences that carry unfinished business and unresolved issues that may continue to unconsciously impact perceptions and relationships
- Positive and negative aspects of one's personality characteristics
- The extent of undeveloped narcissism
- Cognitive functioning
- Spirit factors

Family of Origin Experiences. You may wonder how family-of-origin factors relate to your expertise as a group leader. The clinical vignette illustrates possible connections.

Clinical Vignette: The Leader's Family of Origin Issues

Bob, the group leader, grew up in a home where there was considerable conflict, particularly noisy fights between his parents almost every day. One or both parents would displace their anger and dissatisfaction on the children. Bob's brother and sister reacted by rebelling; Bob became the "good" child who tried very hard to please his parents. As an adult, Bob valued harmony among people in his world, and would go to great lengths to achieve it.

Bob is the leader of a group of young adults who were court-referred for Driving While Under the Influence (DUI). He was uncomfortable from day one with the group because the three males in the group would verbally snipe at each other. When this happened, he would try to reframe the remark or redirect the topic. The group has met for six sessions, and on this night one of the women joins the males in sniping at other members. Bob tries to stop it but that only results in all the group members getting angry or annoyed with him. Both Bob and the members leave the group upset.

Analysis: Bob's need for harmony fueled his interventions and made him prone to jump in to try to defuse the situation rather than modeling how to constructively work through conflicts, and helping members learn how to express their thoughts and feelings. He seemed to take any hints of conflict personally, as if they were directed at him or that he was supposed to do something about it. When a female group member joined in the sniping, old fears from his childhood when his parents fought emerged and his reaction was predictable. He was more interested in meeting his own needs (stopping the fight) than he was in meeting the group's needs. If he had been more confident, self-knowledgeable, and understanding of the group's needs that session, he would have redirected the conflict among members to their real concern, such as dissatisfaction with the leader. He would have expected the attack because the group was in stage 2, and could have used it to show members that it was possible to express negative feelings and have positive results. Neither the group leader nor members would be destroyed, and negative comments could be accepted without retaliation. Members could express negative feelings and have them accepted and carefully considered. Personal associations could be explored, and members could learn how to constructively work through conflicts and understand how it is possible to not personalize negative comments and thereby become narcissistically wounded.

Some Important Experiences. These family of origin experiences are probably the most significant experiences that shaped your development and are significant contributors to your values, perceptions of self and of others, and other factors that have influences on the self that the leader brings to the group. Parental conscious and unconscious messages, sibling relationships, traumatic events, and so on can continue to influence self-perceptions and relations with others and provide material for countertransference in the group. Parental messages were received, incorporated into the developing self, acted on unconsciously, and are likely to continue to be major influences throughout life without your conscious awareness. For example, your parental messages may still be affecting you. Read these and reflect on how you are still relating to and acting on these open and hidden messages.

- Your value and worth as a person
- Your looks, intellectual abilities, talents, and the like
- The extent to which you were loved and cherished
- Your parent's pleasure and admiration for you or the lack
- How you were (are) to behave and relate to others
- Unspoken expectations

There are other messages through which you learned early interpersonal relations, became acculturated to the family and to the community, and developed your self-perceptions. The responses, reactions, tolerance, acceptance, caring, and concern you convey to group members are greatly influenced by these old parental messages.

Another important family-of-origin experience is the sibling relationship(s). Transference is also not only from parents, it also can be from siblings and other significant early relationships. Kohut (1977), Mahler (1975), Klein (1952), and other object-relations and self-psychology theorists feel that these early parent and sibling relationships are critical to the developing self, and are major determinants in the quality and kind of subsequent interpersonal relationships a person has throughout life. Review the previous parental messages with your sibling(s) as the focus. Add to those the extent of competition among siblings for the attention, approval, and admiration from your parents and others; the extent to which you and your siblings were compared among yourselves and with others; any unresolved issues and feelings that persist to the present; and their characteristics you especially liked or disliked. These too can be conscious or unconscious, but still provide material for transference.

Past Experiences and Unfinished Business. To illustrate the power of past experiences, let's do an exercise. You will need several sheets of paper and a pen or pencil.

1. Begin by sitting in silence with your eyes closed and reflect on the course of your life from your earliest memory to the present. As you reflect, note any relationships, people, and events that emerge. Do not edit or evaluate these, just allow them to emerge.

2. Open your eyes when you are done reflecting, and make a list of the relationships, people, and events that emerged. Try to have some from your childhood and teen years, as well as from your adult years. You don't have to list these in chronological order; they can be ordered later.

3. Beside each listing, write your approximate age when it occurred. Reorder your list so that all childhood events are together, the teen material is together, and do the same for the adult time frame.

4. On the other sheet of paper, write one item from your childhood years and try to recall the feelings you had then. List these under a heading "Then." Rate the intensity of each feeling as 1 (scant or no intensity) to 5 (extremely intense). Now list the feelings you experienced about this item as you recalled and reflected on it under a heading titled "Now." Also rate the intensity of these feelings.

5. Repeat step 4 for a teen item.

6. Repeat step 4 for an adult item.

7. Review your "Then" and "Now" feelings to determine if the intensity has reduced over the years, and if the perspective has changed. If the intensity is still rated 3 or higher, this indicates that there is still likely to be some unfinished business.

8. Repeat steps 4–7 for the remaining items on your original list.

Positive and Negative Aspects of Personality Characteristics. Personality characteristics are neither positive nor negative, they just are. However, each characteristic can have positive and negative aspects, and it can be helpful to understand how the positive aspects can be increased and the negative aspects reduced. The value judgments of positive or negative are subjective and individualistic, and may even differ depending on the situation.

There are many approaches to describing personality characteristics, and you are encouraged to read the research to gain a deeper and better understanding both for yourself, and as a way to better understand your group members. The important piece is that you learn about yourself, increase your awareness of your self, gain an appreciation for others whose personality is different from yours, and learn to understand yourself at a deeper level. This can contribute to a better and deeper understanding of your group members.

Undeveloped Narcissism. A difficulty with undeveloped narcissism is that you cannot see that part of your self. It is a part of you that is difficult to access, and you can have powerful defense mechanisms that you use to restrict your access and awareness. However, this critical development needs to be pursued and grown. Some of the work can be done on your own, but some of the work may need the guidance of a mental health professional for optimal results.

Why focus on undeveloped narcissism? What does this have to do with being a group leader? How or does this affect the group and its members? The leader's self is the single most important element for the success of the group, and the extent to which that self is adequately developed is critical and essential. The self that the leader brings to the group affects all of the following to a significant degree.

- Emotional presence that is focused on the group, and on individual members
- The extent to which the leader is genuine and authentic
- The capacity to be empathic, not just reflective of feelings
- Creativity, spontaneity, and flexibility to meet the demands and ever-changing dynamics in the group
- Wisdom from a variety of sources that allows acceptance of the unknown and unexpected
- A centered and grounded perspective
- The ability to focus on and meet group needs, and not the leader's personal ones
- Reduction of the possibility of countertransference
- Capacity to be aware of feelings in the moment, and to manage and contain these
- Understanding of the difference between thoughts and feelings, and when thoughts can be cognitive distortions

Cognitive Functioning. Thoughts, ideas, fantasies, imagination, and other mind activities are included under cognitive functioning. It can be helpful to become aware of how personal cognitive functioning operates and affects perceptions and relationships, and where these may be cognitive distortions, faulty beliefs, or the use of defenses such as intellectualization to protect the self from real or imagined threats. Four examples of faulty beliefs and cognitive distortions are presented, with possible effects on the group and its members: overresponsibility, perfectionism, personalization, and excessive external validation needs.

Overresponsibility is demonstrated through thinking that you are responsible for others' feelings, that you "should" never say or do anything that would be upsetting to others, and that you must do everything possible to ensure the comfort of others. This sort of thinking can be detrimental to the group because the group leader is so intent on keeping the climate hospitable, harmonious, and comfortable that group members become reluctant to express negative emotions or create any sort of disagreement. The results are that stage 2 of group development may never appear, the leader is certainly not attacked, members stay on "safe" topics, and the therapeutic work is compromised.

Perfectionism is the thought that you must always be perfect and not make mistakes, that mistakes are wrong and shameful, or that others must or should meet these high standards. Just good enough is not an option, and considerable time and effort is wasted in self-blame, hiding shame for not being perfect, or finding reasons and excuses. When the leader cannot be content with less than perfection, group members stay constantly on edge trying to please the leader, and become profoundly disappointed when their efforts fail. Opportunities to capitalize on what exists are missed in the search for perfection. The leader models lack of self-acceptance for personal flaws and shortcomings, and is less focused on strength building.

Personalization or overpersonalization is the tendency to see everything that happens as related to yourself, usually as detrimental to yourself. Comments and remarks are perceived as focused on flaws, shortcomings, shame, and the like, and the responses reflect this perspective. Leaders who personalize can be easily hurt at any hint of perceived criticism or blame, and the response can be to attack or withdraw. Both responses are intended to protect the self from further injury.

Group members can be very adept at picking up on the tendency to personalize, and will moderate their behavior to prevent injury and the possible response to that. They can become tentative and circumspect in what they say, and constantly monitor their thoughts and feelings rather than expressing them. They can be cautious about what they disclose—particularly family of origin issues that made them feel responsible for parents' feelings or welfare instead of the parent being responsible for theirs.

Excessive need for external validation occurs when conscious and unconscious thoughts and feelings are focused on obtaining approval and liking from almost everyone, including group members. This need is a deep one that has its roots in family of origin experiences. The self is fearful of becoming destroyed or abandoned if it does not obtain everyone's liking and approval. This need may lead the group leader to do and say things that are less than wise or therapeutic in order to obtain members' approval and liking. The leader is not fully genuine and is more focused on getting his or her needs met than on the needs of the group members.

The possible effects on the group and its members are that the leader is more open to manipulation by the members and can fail to encourage members in self-exploration for fear of their disapproval. This leader also seeks harmony and is uncomfortable with disagreements, and thus does not demonstrate or teach members how to constructively deal with them. He or she can become injured when the group attacks, and can miss an opportunity to demonstrate confidence and absence of defensiveness, and many other opportunities that would foster growth and development for group members.

Spirit Factors. *Spirit factors* and their importance are often overlooked. Leaders' development of their spirit factors provides a source of encouragement and support for group members. Yes, these are thoughts, ideas, beliefs, and attitudes that are personally rewarding, but are also significant factors for the group and its members. Leaders have to model and demonstrate the efficacy and promise for spirit factors, not just talk about them. There is also evidence that can be provided, but the leader's self is much more powerful as group members can sense and see how these have enriched the leader's self.

The spirit factors referred to here include the following:

- Faith, especially faith in the group process
- Hope that is realistic and logical
- Altruism and reaching out to help and support others freely without personal gain or payback
- Resilience that keeps despair at bay, and supports one's self-help and self-efficacy
- Optimism that it is possible to face adversity without becoming defeated or overwhelmed
- Courage to risk making mistakes, being seen as wrong or as inadequate, to be genuine
- Creativity in thought and action

- Inspirational connections to self, to others, and to the universe
- Meaning and purpose for one's life
- An openness to wonder and beauty in everyday life
- Living in accord with one's principles, values, morals, and ethics

Positive psychology emphasizes and researches the roles and influences of spirit factors. The results show that people who have traits similar to those listed are better able to constructively handle and cope with life's adversity. These spirit factors are empowering, enriching, and help provide a strong and cohesive self.

Other Helpful Personal Explorations

The remainder of the chapter focuses on some other personal explorations that can be helpful as a group leader: resistance, emotional regulation and control, emotional expressiveness, psychological boundary strength, and seductive behavior. Learning more about these can assist you to model desired behavior for group members, be more empathic and responsive, and prevent becoming enmeshed or overwhelmed by members' emotional intensity and unconscious seductive or manipulative behavior.

Some of these factors are at the unconscious level; your challenge is to bring them to your awareness. Some may be too threatening to the self to allow this awareness, some are buried deeply and not easily accessible, and some may never be known to you. The real uncovering can be facilitated by work with a competent mental health professional. What is presented here is only intended to get you thinking about your self.

Resistance

Some resistance is easy to identify: You are aware of what you are doing, and some of the reasons for doing it. However, other times you are not aware of the resistance nor the reasons for it. In both instances, the resistance occurs for a valid reason, which is to protect the self. What is proposed here is an examination of your resistance in order to better understand it. Leave the resistance in place until you feel safe enough to lessen or eliminate it.

Some indications of resistance include these events that occur in interactions with others.

- Reluctance or unwillingness to give an opinion even when invited
- Refusal to directly express negative feelings or perceptions, or to only a few select people
- Unwillingness to deal with conflict or acknowledge that there is conflict
- Deflection of the topic or attention away from you
- Attacking and aggressive behavior
- Withdrawal and passive behavior
- Keeping the focus on safe topics
- Avoidance of disclosing personal information, feelings, concerns, and so on

These are but a few of the behaviors that indicate personal resistance and usual resistance for group members.

What are some possible reasons for this resistance? Past experiences such as rejection and betrayal, family-of-origin experiences such as criticism and blame, fears, and unknown or unacknowledged self factors that produce guilt or shame are some possible reasons. Resistance, like defenses, is individualistic and each person can be resisting something different. Here are examples of what could be resisted.

- Intimacy—fear of becoming too close
- Manipulation by the other person
- Fear of being controlled
- Revealing of the person's real and possibly shameful self
- A defense against rejection
- Fear of becoming enmeshed in others' emotions
- Fear of becoming overwhelmed by self or others' emotions
- A defense against being attacked

One process for analyzing your resistance begins with a personal acknowledgment of the resistance. Accompany this awareness with an affirmation of the validity of the resistance as protection for the self. The next step would be to identify a possible threat in the environment that triggered the resistance. Use the previous list to check on possible threats such as, "Could I be resisting because I fear I will not be liked or approved of if I give my real opinion?"—which is really a resistance based on fear of rejection. Remember that all possible reasons for resistance are not in this list. Once you identify a possible threat, you can then assess the validity of the threat, and evaluate the positive and negative consequences for reducing or eliminating your resistance. This is the point where you can decide to take action, or not.

Emotional Regulation and Control

Containing and managing personal emotions are very important tasks for group leaders because they must model and teach them to group members. In addition, as discussed earlier, leaders may have to act as the container for members' emotions or for the group as a whole so that the intense emotions the leader carries for them do not get in the way of the group's work. The leader must be able to let go of the contained emotions, and not let them become a part of himself or herself. A brief example illustrates this complex concept and process.

Clinical Vignette: The Leader as the Container

The group is meeting for the first time. All are strangers to each other, and are attending the group developed for adolescent (14–16 years old) alcohol abusers. They are required to participate in the group in order to be reinstated in school. Although only two have admitted to their parents that they are angry and ashamed for being in the situation, other members are also feeling guilty, angry, fearful, shamed, and some are defiant. The group sits in silence waiting for the session to begin.

The leader enters the room, smiles at everyone, and greets the group. As the leader looks around at the members, he becomes aware that his stomach is tense, he wants to move his feet, he cannot seem to get comfortable in the chair, and he is blinking his eyes. He comments that he is somewhat anxious during the first session of group. In contrast, group members seem to be less tense than they were just a few minutes ago, and are even making funny comments as part of their introductions. (The leader and members' experiences are the container part.)

Later in the session, the leader asks group members to describe the feelings they are experiencing as they sit in the group. Members report on how they are feeling at the moment in contrast to how they felt waiting for the group to begin, and in the first part of the session. (This is the returning emotions part.)

Modeling containing and managing includes awareness of the particular feeling, acknowledging its existence and effects, but not allowing it to overwhelm, mire, or paralyze the person. Managing emotions also includes an appropriate exploration or expression of the feeling, and of the effect(s). A lot of detail does not have to be provided, nor does the exploration always have to be verbal. But part of managing seems to be facilitated when that person understands what it is in the environment that triggered the emotion(s), and what past experiences, unresolved issues, and the like may be the root cause(s) for the particular response.

Emotional Expressiveness

There are times in the group when it can be helpful for the leader to disclose his or her feelings. There may be members who have difficulty or are unable to express their emotions, or there may be members who do not know appropriate ways to express their emotions. These are some major reasons why it is important that group leaders become aware of the extent of their emotional expressiveness, and build these abilities and capacities.

One step in developing emotional expressiveness is the ability to distinguish between thoughts and feelings. This can be important because when you think about a feeling, that act can prevent you from fully expressing the feeling. It can promote intellectualization, reduce intensity, and allow you to keep important information submerged. Feelings begin with a sensation that the person can name or label. The sensation can be mild or intense and is experienced, embraced, pushed aside, or rejected. When pushed aside or rejected, it can become a thought about a feeling that then lessens its potential threat. You may want to become more aware of when you express thoughts instead of feelings.

You may want to also increase your awareness of when you are suppressing or repressing important feelings. Some indices of suppression and repression are when you feel

- bored
- tired
- numb, blank, or nothing
- rebellious and defiant
- wishing to attack another person
- resigned
- turned off

You may rationalize not expressing your feelings with thoughts and concerns similar to these:

- I don't want to offend.
- The group won't like me; I'll be rejected.
- The other person may feel rejected.
- It may provoke conflict.

Rationalization is a defense and it would be constructive for you to become reflective about what you are defending yourself against. Although you may think that you are being considerate of others, what you are really doing is protecting yourself against personal issues, concerns, or feelings.

The fear of being rejected is more apparent, but it is still disguised because it is really a fantasy or a projection. You would probably say and feel that you are accepting of group members and would not reject them. However, you are not so sure they could be accepting of you when you use this rationalization.

The fear of provoking conflict is also a projection. Some degree of conflict is already present in the group, and what you are doing will keep it hidden instead of allowing it to emerge before it intensifies. If allowed to emerge, conflict has the potential to be constructively resolved and to strengthen relationships. If you fear conflict, this would be a fruitful topic for you to explore in the group, as your perceptions and feelings about conflict will significantly impact what you will do as a group leader.

One step you can take is to become more aware of what you are feeling at all times. This awareness is a foundation for making empathic responses, becoming aware of empathic failures, tuning in to group process, and for making group-level process commentary.

Awareness is only the first step. You must become more willing to openly and directly express what you are feeling in appropriate ways. Following are some suggestions.

- Choose words that accurately express the feeling you are experiencing.
- Be aware of the impact your words have on others.
- Allow your nonverbal communication to reflect your feeling.
- Make "I" statements instead of "You are" statements or inferences.
- Take responsibility for your feelings.

Word choice is important because it allows for graduated expression of feelings. For example, *disquieted, apprehensive, alarmed, fearful, scared, terrorized, paralyzed,* and *panicky* are words that express different levels of emotions. You would understand what you or someone else was feeling when any one of these words was used. You may not understand what caused the feeling, just what was felt. If the words were accompanied with nonverbal behavior that reflected the nuance of the feeling, the expression would be more direct.

Psychological Boundary Strength

Your psychological boundary is where you end and others begin. Awareness of this boundary is an outcome of successfully developing separation and individuation. Some people fail to adequately develop this awareness and remain, on an unconscious level, in the less developed state that perceives others as extensions of their selves, subject to their manipulation and control. Leaders who have not developed their psychological boundaries

- Push members for deeper disclosures before they are ready
- Insist that members do what the leader tells them to do
- Become enraged when attacked, criticized, or charged with an error
- Do things that are intrusive to members, such as forcing disclosure or shameful secrets
- Engage in questionable behaviors, such as hugging or other touching without the person's permission

Boundary strength incorporates an awareness of self and others, although this awareness may not be complete, and also includes the firmness and control to remain separate and distinct regardless of outside forces, such as projections. Boundary strength can be categorized as insufficient, rigid, uncontrollably permeable, and flexible. Read the following descriptions and examples to decide which best fits you.

Insufficient boundary strength describes people who are easily enmeshed or overwhelmed by others' feelings, find that they are constantly seduced into doing things they do not want to do, often feel manipulated, and may easily "catch" others' feelings and not be able to let go of them. Their boundaries are breeched by others' needs, wants, demands, feelings, and so on, to the extent where some people can be very anxious and unable to relax.

Rigid boundary strength is just what it sounds like. There is a strong barrier to keep others from the self, and to prevent the self from becoming seduced, controlled, manipulated, or rejected. The boundary can be so strong that intimacy or meaningful connections cannot be achieved.

Uncontrollably permeable boundary strength describes the psychological boundary that has some rigidity, but also has some spaces where the self can become connected to others; others' projections, feelings, and the like can enter the self; and where the self can reach out and feel what others are experiencing, such as what happens with empathy. However, this category of boundary strength has a weakness in that the permeability is uncontrolled, which can be inappropriately rigid, can allow "catching" others' feelings, and can cause an openness to projective identifications.

Flexible boundary strength is similar to what would be called controlled permeability. That is, persons can decide what to let in, and what to keep out. They can be empathic, but can decide when being so is warranted or not. They seldom catch others' projections, but when they do, they are aware of what is theirs and what is the other person's. They can tolerate others' intense emotions without becoming enmeshed or overwhelmed. Flexible boundary strength is an asset for the leader, and by extension, for the group members. However, it is not something persons want to do, or will do voluntarily, and can even be against their best interests or violate their values and principles.

Seductive Behavior

Seduction is a misuse of the relationship. Following are some examples of seductive behavior.

- Telling "white lies" that do not express your real feelings or thoughts
- Giving extensive or excessive flattery, compliments, and the like

- Tending to rescue, protect, and do other such actions that are not requested and may not be needed; this encourages dependency
- Withholding needed information or resources in the attempt to make others come to you
- Pushing for disclosures
- Coaxing or bullying
- Dropping hints or teasers
- Doing and saying things to arouse guilt or shame for not agreeing with you

Seduction is not authentic or genuine. It is a form of manipulation to get the other person to do something that you want them to do to meet your needs. This something is usually a form of betrayal, and can be detrimental to the best interests of group members. Group leaders who are seductive or use seduction rationalize that they are doing what is best for group members; in reality, they are meeting their own personal needs.

Becoming genuine and authentic and not using manipulation is hard work because much of social convention works against this. For example, social convention says that it is wrong or unacceptable to say something that may upset the other person even if that something may be true. There are ways that truthful thoughts, feelings, and ideas can be expressed without offending or insulting the other person. Group leaders will be much more effective if group members can trust them to be authentic and genuine.

The group leader's impact and influence on the group and its members are significant, and these can be both positive and negative. The challenge is to understand how to increase positive impact and influences and, at the same time, reduce or eliminate negative ones. Complicating matters is that the leader's inner self and other intangibles are difficult to describe, research, and associate with specifics. This chapter presented some suggestions for leaders' personal development, but there are other developmental needs, and this seems to be a continual process. Learning new techniques and skills can be of assistance and increase effectiveness, but the most significant way to increase effectiveness comes with building the leader's inner self.

Summary

1. The single most important contributor to the group is the leader's self. The leader's self must continue to grow and develop to reduce the potential for negative countertransference, which can be detrimental to the group and its members, and to develop those characteristics and qualities that are facilitative.

2. Personal issues that are the focus for this development include family-of-origin factors; other past experiences, especially those that carry unfinished business; positive and negative aspects of personality characteristics, undeveloped narcissism, cognitive functioning, and spirit factors.

3. The therapeutic inner self is developed so that the group leader can exhibit group facilitative characteristics of risk taking, openness and awareness of current experiencing, a range and depth of emotional experiencing, clear and firm boundaries, faith in the group process, and toleration of ambiguity.

4. It is extremely helpful for the group leader to be aware of personal qualities, reactions, and feelings such as resistance, emotional regulation and control, emotional expressiveness, psychological boundary strength, and other such inner qualities.

Chapter Activities

1. Brainstorm a list of the leader's inner characteristics that seem important for developing a therapeutic relationship with each of the following target audiences.

   - Children of divorce
   - Adolescents in a group home for juvenile offenders
   - Depressed and displaced middle-age homemakers with a diagnosed mental disturbance
   - City council members
   - Bus drivers

2. List the assumptions made about each of the groups in item 1, based on the leader characteristics that emerged from the brainstorming.

Personal Development Exercise: Write a poem about the major events during a significant period in your life that may influence you as a group leader.

Chapter 9

Building a Therapeutic Self

Major Topics

1. The importance of the group leader's developed self in the growth, development, and healing for group members, and in reducing negative countertransference.
2. The role of the leader's undeveloped and destructive narcissism and its impact on group members.
3. Personal development strategies to develop healthy adult narcissism.
4. A model to help build psychological boundary strength.
5. Strategies for the constructive use of the therapeutic self.

Introduction

The previous chapter discussed personal development for group leaders, and presented examples to illustrate how lack of leader personal development can impact and influence the group and its members. We now move to a discussion on building a therapeutic self, one that is not focused on the techniques and skills needed to be a group leader. Although this extent of personal development is usually expected and fostered for clinical group leaders, it can be just as important for leaders of many nonclinical groups to enrich the members' experiences, cope with what can unexpectedly emerge during group sessions, and prevent difficulties such as collusion and scapegoating among group members. In addition, it can help leaders constructively use group process, recognize and repair empathic failures, identify unseen and intangible negative and positive forces, and encourage and support members to change and adapt. Perhaps the most important outcome for building the therapeutic self is to reduce the possibility of harmful countertransference (Alonso & Rutan, 1996; Brown, 2003b; Cohen, 2000; Gans & Alonso, 1998; Horwitz, 2000; Livingston & Livingston, 1998; Schermer, 2000; Wright, 2000; Yalom, 2005).

Uses for the Therapeutic Self

The therapeutic self of the group leader brings all of the following to the group.

- A primary focus on the group and its members that does not include elements of undeveloped or destructive narcissism
- An openness to here-and-now experiencing as a means to understand group and members' needs
- Ability to remain present—centered and not anticipate or expect what needs to come next
- Ability to respond with genuineness and empathy
- Ability to use and respond to both group and individual levels of process
- Encouragement and support that is respectful of individual strengths and weaknesses and environmental constraints, and that lack value-laden judgment
- An authentic liking, caring, and concern for group members
- The firm belief in the efficacy of the group to manage its own concerns

One chapter is insufficient to address all the needed topics that relate to building the therapeutic self. This discussion will be limited to five topics: undeveloped and destructive narcissism, adequate boundary strength, increased empathy, reduced countertransference, and the reflective stance.

Undeveloped and Destructive Narcissism

Undeveloped and destructive narcissism are unconscious or nonconscious leader attitudes and behaviors that can be detrimental and even harmful to group members. When you stop and realize that some group members may be emotionally fragile—some have insufficient psychological boundary strength and are unable to repel projections or keep from catching other people's feelings; some dependent and scared, seeking sure answers; and some have low self-esteem, and other such conditions—it is understandable that the leader's attitudes and behavior can be significantly influential. Another key understanding is that the leader is unaware of his or her personal undeveloped narcissism, and of the impact it may be having on one or even all group members. There is usually no conscious intent to harm, but that does not lessen the negative effects.

But, before going any further, let's define some terms. Think of narcissism as a human characteristic that is capable of being developed so that it is helpful rather than harmful, and that it is developed along a continuum reflective of age and stage of development. References that can be helpful and provide more information include Kohut's *The Restoration of the Self* (1977), Brown's *The Destructive Narcissistic Pattern* (1998a), Horwitz's "The Group Leader's Narcissism" (2000), and Kernberg's *Borderline and narcissistic personality disorders* (1990).

Age-appropriate narcissism refers to expected levels of attitudes and behaviors based on chronological ages and stages of development. For example, infants and children are expected to have considerable self-absorbed behaviors and attitudes, and adults should have few or none.

Destructive narcissism in adults occurs when the person has numerous behaviors and attitudes reflective of those expected at an earlier stage of chronological development. For instance, an adult may have numerous behaviors and attitudes expected of children, and these are reflected in his or her troubled relationships.

Narcissistic personality disorder or pathological narcissism behaviors and attitudes are described in the *Diagnostic and Statistical Manual of Mental Disorders* (*DSM-IV-TR;* 2000) for adults. This description includes characteristics such as lack of empathy and an entitlement attitude.

Undeveloped narcissism refers to having some behaviors and attitudes reflective of an earlier stage of expected development, but not as many nor as intense or less developed as those for the destructive narcissistic pattern. Many adults can have some undeveloped narcissism, and although not categorized as destructive, some of their behaviors and attitudes can have a negative impact on their relationships.

Narcissistic Behaviors and Attitudes

Let's list a few of the behaviors and attitudes that can be undeveloped, or are part of a destructive narcissistic pattern. These are presented in three categories: the inflated self, indifference to others, and troubling to relationships (Brown, 2006a).

The Inflated Self

Grandiosity—an excessive valuation of one's self, such as trying to be a superman or superwoman. The person does not recognize his or her personal limitations.

Attention seeking—doing and saying things to remain the center of attention or in the spotlight. Talking loudly, bragging, making noisy entrances and exits, frequently interrupting others, and wearing clothing that is intended to gain attention are some examples of attention-seeking behavior.

Admiration seeking—actively and frequently recruiting admiration from others. Examples include boasting, complaining, self-nominations, and looking for flattery and compliments.

Indifference to Others

Extensions of self—assuming that others are not separate and distinct from one's self; that they do not have the right to be different; that others are under the person's control. Violations of psychological and physical boundaries are examples for this inner state that is not sufficiently separated and individuated. Other examples include giving orders and expecting to be obeyed; demanding mind reading; and entering others' space, such as an office, without knocking or waiting for an invitation.

Exploitation—manipulating others for personal gain. Expecting favors, but not returning them, and failure to recognize others' contributions are examples.

Lack of empathy—cannot feel what others are feeling. May have the words, but not the real feelings. Examples include failing to recognize empathic failures, making insensitive comments and questions, ignoring emotionally laden disclosures and the like, and abruptly changing topics.

Troubling States

Entitlement—unconscious assumption of being superior, deserving of preferential treatment, expecting deference, and the like. Examples include not waiting one's turn, trying to get more than one's fair share, expecting others to rearrange their schedules to meet one's needs, expecting to be treated as if one is unique and special by almost everyone, and frequently demanding special recognition.

Shallow emotions—the inability to feel and express a wide range and variety of emotions. For example, anger can be experienced and expressed, but not annoyance and irritation

Superiority, arrogance and contempt—the assumption that others are inferior, less worthy, and less deserving. Examples include sarcasm, put-downs, demeaning and disparaging remarks, blaming, criticism, and so on.

Possible Effects on the Group and Members

This is a very brief presentation about the possible effects of the group leader's undeveloped or destructive narcissism on the group and its members. Each characteristic is presented with one example for an effect.

Grandiosity—members are pushed to take dangerous psychological risks that are detrimental to their well-being.

Attention seeking—sessions become more about the leader than about the group and its members. Members' distress is overlooked or ignored.

Admiration seeking—members become more focused on ingratiation than on their concerns.

Extensions of self—members can feel violated and intruded on, and that there is a lack of respect for them as individuals.

Exploitation—members come to feel manipulated, taken advantage of, and not respected.

Lack of empathy—members can feel diminished, devalued, or discounted and unworthy when their feelings are ignored, overlooked, or passed over.

Entitlement—more time and effort is spent on getting the leader's needs met than on members' concerns. The group becomes too structured and directed.

Shallow emotions—members do not receive modeling or guidance for expressing difficult or intense emotions.

Superiority—members and the group as a whole can feel shamed, guilty, and inadequate.

Building Healthy Adult Narcissism

Much of the literature is focused on identifying and treating the more pathological forms of narcissism, with very little about developing healthy adult narcissism with a self-acceptance and self-care focus that is not excessive. Because it can be difficult or impossible to describe or operationalize the term *excessive* for behaviors and attitudes, this lack of guidance is understandable. What is available and could be helpful are some of the strategies and techniques used in treatment. Brown (2009) devotes most of this book to suggestions for how to build the self. Working on unresolved issues from the family of origin or unfinished business from past experiences is basic for building the self. As noted previously, this work is best done with the help of a competent mental health professional.

Given the complexity and ambiguity of trying to reduce and eliminate undeveloped and destructive narcissism, and to build healthy adult narcissism, what strategies can group leaders take to begin and facilitate this process?

1. Assume that you have some undeveloped narcissism. You are unaware of these self-absorbed behaviors and attitudes. Some can be seen by others, but most are unconscious.

2. Increase your awareness of possible self-absorption by critically examining what you think and do, reassessing past behaviors for hints, and listening objectively when you are chastised or criticized by others.

3. Examine the quality, meaningfulness, and satisfaction with your current relationships. Reflect on the same for past relationships, and engage in some reflection about the number of these.

4. Identify some possible behaviors and attitudes that could reflect undeveloped narcissism, and make a conscious effort to stop these.

5. Decide how you can think and act that would reflect healthy narcissistic behaviors and attitudes, such as increasing the ability to be empathic.

6. Build your psychological boundary strength so that it can be appropriately flexible. This is discussed later in this chapter.

7. Accept that some of your reactions may be transference (countertransference when you are leading a group), or projections, and stay aware of these possibilities when you are interacting with others.

8. Analyze your resistance, and become more aware of your defense mechanisms. Learn to quickly assess the here-and-now danger to the self to better judge if the resistance is needed.

9. Examine your beliefs about yourself, and assess their validity. For example, is it necessary or realistic to expect that you (or anyone else) need to be perfect all of the time? Can some mistakes, errors, or less-than-perfect behavior be tolerated without feeling anxious, guilty, or shamed?

10. Take active steps to build your creativity, inspiration, and appreciation of beauty and wonder. Develop hope, altruism, and a genuine appreciation for the uniqueness of others.

11. Increase the range and variety of emotions you experience and express. Learn to recognize milder versions of emotions, such as apprehension.

Building Your Creativity

Let's take one characteristic of healthy adult narcissism and discuss some possible building strategies. Creativity is generally thought by many to require special talents, such as art and music. However, that perception is too narrow and restrictive for what is meant by creativity for healthy adult narcissism. The definition and perspective is broader and more encompassing to include new and novel products, discoveries and processes for all parts of life. You do not have to possess specialized talent to be creative; it is possible to be creative in any part of your life.

How can you become more creative, or begin to build your creativity? Here are 10 suggestions to get you started thinking about what fits you, and is satisfying. Try one or more of these.

1. Capitalize on an existing talent, use it more often, and find ways to develop it.
2. Take a class to learn a new craft, extend knowledge of an old one, or to get a fresh perspective.
3. Examine how other people in your world are creative, how they discover, develop, or make something new and novel. These are models to be emulated.
4. Create a new twist for something ordinary or usual, such as creating a new sandwich or redecorating a room. Possibilities exist all around you.
5. Write a cinquain and embellish the paper around it. A cinquain has five lines.

   Line 1—A one-word title, usually a noun

   Line 2—A two-word phrase that is related to the title

   Line 3—Three descriptive adjectives

   Line 4—A four-word phrase related to the subject

   Line 5—A one-word synonym

6. Buy a craft magazine and try one project, changing something such as color, size, or a material used for the project.
7. Get a notebook of any size and write essays or poems.
8. Select an everyday object—such as a paper clip, a pencil, or a paper cup—and list 100 possible uses for it.
9. Make a collage of found materials from your purse, pocket, or junk drawer.
10. Teach a child a craft or how to fix something, or just watch how the child uses materials.

Opportunities to become more creative are all around you, if you take the time to look for them.

Psychological Boundary Strength

Rate yourself using the following scale to see where you may want to start working on your psychological boundary strength. As you read each item, think of situations where you are with someone you care about, not just strangers or acquaintances. Rate each item as 5—always or almost always; 4—frequently; 3—sometimes; 2—seldom; or 1—never or almost never.

Scale
1. I can easily feel what the other person is feeling, but find it hard to let go of that feeling.
2. I find it difficult to say no and stick to it.
3. I can be persuaded to do things I don't really want to do.

4. I keep people at a distance, and try not to get too involved with their concerns.

5. I tend to keep my thoughts and feelings to myself.

6. I am a very private person.

7. My guilt is easily triggered, and I end up doing things that may not be in my best interest.

8. I do not take adequate steps to prevent others from taking advantage of me.

9. There are many times when I want to say no, but feel that if I do I am not living up to others' expectations, or that I am being selfish.

Scoring is done in two steps. First, derive a total score for the nine items. Then, add the ratings for items 1–3 and get an average; do the same for items 4–6 and 7–9.

Your total score indicate:

36–45: Insufficient boundary strength

26–35: Adequate boundary strength at times, but there are some weaknesses

16–25: Sufficient boundary strength in many situations

9–15: Strong boundaries

The average ratings for the designated items indicate:

Items	Average	Boundary Weakness
1–3	4–5	Your emotional susceptibility
4–6	4–5	Capacity for trust and intimacy
7–9	4–5	Awareness of when and where the boundary is not sufficient

Average ratings for each set that are greater than 2 are areas that can use some attention and development. Items 1–3 describe soft boundaries, 4–6 describe rigid boundaries, and 7–9 describe permeable boundaries.

Suggestions for building sufficient boundary strength are derived from a think, analyze, and affirm model, in which actions are used before acting and feeling. The basis for the model comes from concepts in rational-emotive behavioral therapy, cognitive and cognitive-behavioral therapy, and behavioral therapy. These concepts, when put in habitual practice, can allow people to make more reasonable, logical, and rational choices for their behavior; to choose what and what not to do; and to become less vulnerable to manipulation, enmeshment, or becoming overwhelmed by others.

Think means that you consciously decide to think in situations rather than being rushed into acting or feeling. Thinking functions collect information about you, others, and the situation, and then use that information to formulate hypotheses and alternatives for what may be happening, and can generate strategies and options for action. You think it through. Thinking can occur at a much faster rate than speaking or acting.

Analyze refers to the process used to try and understand what is taking place both within you and within the situation. Analyzing can reveal what the possible impact will be on you or the relationship when or if each alternative is implemented, and what personal issues, values, concerns, defenses, vulnerabilities, and the like may be influencing you at this point.

Affirm means that you consciously use your personal affirmations to encourage and support decisions and actions that are in your best interests even when others may disapprove or be disappointed. These affirmations are self-reminders about your worth, value, rights, and accurate beliefs about your self.

Building Boundary Strength

Some suggestions for building boundary strength are presented, along with one or more strategies for each.

- Identify the inaccurate beliefs you carry about your self that may have been internalized from family of origin and other past experiences.
- Generate a list of possible actions you can take to moderate the impact of these inaccurate beliefs.
- Identify the type of boundary strength you most likely have, and relate this to your inaccurate beliefs.
- Create a list of self-affirmations.

Identify Inaccurate Beliefs. Everyone has beliefs about their self that help form their self-perceptions, self confidence, self-efficacy, and self-esteem. The family of origin is where we learn what is acceptable and unacceptable, what is expected that we be and do, and when unconscious parental messages are incorporated and internalized to become a part of us. Sometimes those messages and other family experiences can lead to developing inaccurate beliefs about the self, such as the following:

- It is critical that everyone, or almost everyone, like and approve of you.
- You are responsible for the comfort and welfare of almost everyone including people who are capable, and don't need the help.
- You must see to it that everything is always perfect, and mistakes, errors, and the like are shameful.
- When others are displeased or disappointed, it is your responsibility to remedy the matter.
- Everything and everyone is all good, or all bad; all right or all wrong.
- Anyone you let get close to you will hurt, reject, or betray you because of your inadequacies.
- You exaggerate your imperfections and minimize your achievements to avoid being perceived as conceited.

These are only some of the possible inaccurate beliefs that people can hold; you can think of many more. Challenge the personal ones you identify by asking yourself how reasonable, rational, or accurate is it for you to believe and act on this. For example, if one of your inaccurate beliefs is about always being perfect, or making sure that everything is perfect, the challenge statement would have you think about the validity of the belief.

Moderate Actions. It is not sufficient to just list your inaccurate beliefs about your self—although this awareness is a critical step. It is much more helpful to also generate some possible actions you can take that would moderate or even eliminate their impact on you. These would be the building blocks for more positive self-esteem, greater self-confidence, and increased self-efficacy.

1. Begin by examining your list of inaccurate beliefs and think about how each is reflected in your conscious thoughts, behaviors, and feelings.
2. Take each inaccurate belief separately and list the negative impacts they are having on you, your self-efficacy, and so on.
3. List some events and situations where you knew, or you now see, the negative influence or impact of the inaccurate self-belief.
4. Because some or all of these events and situations are likely to recur, try to think of alternative ways you could respond or behave that would not reflect the inaccurate self-belief.

Let's give an example of an inaccurate self-belief and generate some possible actions. Assume that you must be perfect at all times, and that mistakes, errors, and such cannot be tolerated.

1. The examination step generates the following for how the inaccurate self-belief may be reflected in thoughts, behaviors, and feelings.
   a. I am constantly on edge fearing that I will make a mistake.
   b. I check and recheck everything almost or to the point of compulsive behavior.
   c. No one does things to my satisfaction, and some people get irritated when I point out mistakes, or try to correct them.
   d. When I make an error, it greatly upsets me for a long time.

Identify Types of Boundary Strength. The scale at the beginning of this section can provide some information about your type of boundary strength. Although you will want to use more than the three examples given to illustrate the various types, they can help begin the process for understanding where and how your psychological boundaries have insufficient strength.

If you have *soft* boundaries you are most often captivated by others' feelings, projections, and so on, which you then incorporate, identify with, and may even act on. This is emotional susceptibility, which makes it difficult for you to refuse requests or demands, stick to your principles and values, or to put your self-care needs ahead of others' needs. Yon may also be unable to avoid caring for others, at great cost to your well-being, just because they want you to, and you may unconsciously be constantly seeking out what others need or desire. Associating this with some inaccurate beliefs about your self can help begin the process for change that can lead to stronger boundaries.

If you have rigid boundaries you can remain unmoved by others' feelings, needs, desires, demands, and so on. Your detachment and disassociation keep your self safe, but do not allow others to connect with you, nor you with others. The fear of being hurt, rejected, or betrayed was learned through experience and cannot be easily overcome. Every negative relationship experience is reinforcing and you stay constantly on edge fearing the worst. Associating these reactions with inaccurate beliefs about your self, and recalling the positive experiences you did have without forgetting the negative ones, can provide encouragement, support, and reaffirmation of your core worth and value that can help reduce some of the fear and dread.

If your boundary is *permeable* you are frequently surprised at your inability to consciously screen out unwanted thoughts, feelings, projections from others, and so on. There are times when you do screen out unwanted material, can connect with others and let them connect with you, and protect yourself from undesired intrusions, but not as often as you wish. You may even work to stay conscious of what you are letting in, and what you are keeping out, but are frequently disappointed with the results. Associating these with inaccurate beliefs about your self can assist you in strengthening the weak spaces in your boundary strength, becoming more conscious of when your boundary may be under assault, and being less disappointed with your lapses and failures.

Create a Self-Affirmation List. Many people have the tendency to focus on their faults and imperfections, and may even minimize their positive characteristics and their unique and special attributes. Whereas this culture and others do promote the concept of modesty, and we are cautioned against boasting, bragging, and self-aggrandizement, that does not mean that one should ignore or forget his or her more positive side. This suggestion to create self-affirmations tries to address this tendency by providing a means for a more positive self-perspective that reaffirms, encourages, and supports the self, but not to the point where characteristics that are in need of continuing development are ignored or denied. Think of self-affirmations as falling between an inflated, excessive, and grandiose self-perspective, and the impoverished, unacceptable, flawed, and shameful self-perspective. A focus on some self-affirmations can provide a more balanced, realistic, and centered self-perspective. The following exercise can be one process for developing self-affirmations.

(**Exercise 9.1**)

Self-Affirmations

Materials. A quiet place to think and write, a couple of sheets of paper, a pen or a pencil, and a 3-by-5-inch index card

1. Sit quietly and think about your hopes, aspirations, and dreams for the future; the person you are at the present time; and what is pleasing you about your self at the present. If thoughts about what is not pleasing about yourself emerge, don't try to dismiss, edit, or change these at this point.

2. Make a list of the pleasing points about your current self, and if something about any of the following was not noted, try to think and list something now.

    Sensitivity and thoughtfulness

    Creativity

    Actions that provide personal meaning and purpose for your life

    Hope and optimism

    Actions in accord with personal principles and values

    Determination and persistence

Physical health habits

Emotional expressions, management, and control

Quality of close relationships

Ability to learn, grow, and develop

3. Review your expanded list and reflect on how these positives in your life are fulfilling, satisfying, and enriching. It may be that they could use more developing, but at this moment they are pleasing.

4. The final step is to select the five that most appeal to you and list them on the index card as endings to "I am," or "I can" stems. For example, "I am practicing good nutrition habits." Do not write what you are *not* doing, such as "I am not eating sweets." Make all statements positive. Keep the card with you, and review your self-affirmations once a week or more often. Then, in a month, add to them or change them.

Increased Empathy

Empathy is central and of importance in several theories such as client-centered (Rogers, 1951), self-psychology (Kohut, 1977), relational (Jordan, 1991), psychodynamic (Rutan & Stone, 2001), and analytic (Alonso & Rutan, 1996). Empathy by itself is not enough to effect change, but it allows clients to feel accepted and understood sufficiently to reduce defenses. The result is that the exploration of painful topics and affect is not as feared, and it also provides encouragement and support.

The literature uses different terms for empathy. Kohut (1984) defined empathy as the capacity to think and feel the inner life of the other. Alonso and Rutan (1996) describe it as the partial and temporary merger with another person's internal experiencing and the ability to disengage from the merger. Fossage (1995) sees it as listening and understanding from the other person's perspective. Stolorow (1993) refers to empathy as empathic resonance. Finally, Livingston (1999) refers to empathic immersion. Although empathy is not a central concept for cognitive therapy, Beck (2005) writes that the therapist "acknowledges and empathizes with how the patient feels" (p. 94).

All definitions seem to have the same elements as did Rogers's original one in 1951: to enter the world of another person, feel what that person is feeling and experiencing, and to not lose your sense of being separate and distinct from him or her. The latter is very important because the experience of empathy does not mean that you become overwhelmed or enmeshed by the other person's feelings or experiencing. Empathy is the ability to open your self, allow it to enter into another's inner experiencing at that moment, to be able to leave when desired, and to never lose your core self as being separate.

Empathy is a characteristic of healthy adult narcissism, as described by Kohut (1977). Alonso and Rutan (1996) write, "Empathy is not possible for the individual who has not arrived at an adequate stage of separation and individuation" (p. 158). Thus, it is a developed and aware group leader who can become empathic which, in turn, can lead to the vulnerable moments described by Livingston (1999) as opportunities for enhancing intensity and intimacy, and for deepening the curative process. Becoming vulnerable in a safe place where one is supported by being deeply understood is what the group and the sensitive group leader can provide. Empathy opens the door to a deeper, richer, and more rewarding experience.

Kohut (1977) also refers to empathic failures as a continuing source for narcissistic injuries, and says that these failures begin at birth. He also stated that a major task for therapists was to repair empathic failures that occurred in therapy. Stone (1992) defined empathic failures as "over-or-under responsiveness by the selfobject" (one of the roles for the group leader) (p. 336), and that empathic failures can produce narcissistic injuries that are experienced from a mild state to an intense one where the person experiences the self as falling apart or disintegrating. Hahn (1994) notes that shame in later life is related to "empathic failures of early object-relations" (p. 453). These early failures were experienced as a defect of the self and shameful.

Group leaders should not have the unrealistic expectation that they should be empathic with everyone all of the time, or that it is possible to fully prevent empathic failures. Although these empathic failures are regrettable, Rutan and Stone (2001) assert that they are not ultimately harmful, but that the group leader's lack of effort to be empathic produces the most harm. Shapiro (1978) proposes that safety in the group is established and enhanced when the leader empathically understands members' vulnerability and their personal meanings, and when empathic failures are recognized and repaired. Livingston (1999) writes, "When the leader succeeds in repeatedly repairing breaks in empathy and returning to an empathic stance, patients often have an experience of being deeply understood" (p. 27). There are many positive outcomes when the leader is empathic and attends to the repair of empathic failures.

Being Empathic

The capacity to be empathic requires:

- An openness to experiencing
- An awareness of here-and-now feelings
- Emotional regulation and control
- Permeable psychological boundary strength at the very least
- The facility to accurately express what you are experiencing and feeling
- Trust that what the self is experiencing is not related to personal issues, such as what happens with projection, transference, and projective identifications
- An ability to recognize empathic failures and repair them

Openness to experiencing means an absence of defenses and resistance, a willingness to enter the world of the other person, and an absence of fear that you will become enmeshed or overwhelmed. Your nonverbal postures and gestures, such as body orientation to the other person and eye contact, convey this openness.

Awareness of here-and-now feelings is very important for empathy, and refers to being able to focus on the other person and on your present feelings at the same time. You are not thinking about responses or other matters, distracted, trying to get away, or other concerns that would prevent you from being aware of your bodily sensations and the accompanying feelings.

Emotional regulation and control means that you are able to contain and manage your feelings without becoming mired or denying them. In addition, you do not become enmeshed or overwhelmed by others' emotions.

Adequate psychological boundary strength allows you to be confident enough in your ability to not lose your sense of self as separate and distinct from the other person when you enter his or her world to experience his or her feelings. You are able to choose when and if you are empathic, and do not let your self be taken over or swamped involuntarily by others' feelings.

Accurate expression of feelings calls for an expanded vocabulary to take into consideration variations and levels of feelings to more precisely describe what you sense the other person is feeling. You have many feeling words, not just a few.

Trust that your experiencing is an accurate reflection, uncontaminated by your counter-transference, of what the other person is feeling, and is not an unconscious triggering of your unresolved issues and/or unfinished business, calls for an extensive self-examination and continual self-development to address unresolved issues and unfinished business. These unresolved issues and unfinished business could mislead you to believe that you were correct about the other person's experiencing when, in fact, you are reflecting your personal world.

Empathic failure recognition and empathic failure repair are critical capacities for group leaders. Many problems can be prevented and group process enhanced when members feel heard and understood. It may not be possible to prevent all empathic failures, but the sensitivity to recognize and repair them can be increased.

Skills to Practice

Your personal development is the key to being empathic, but there are some skills you can practice that will help increase your facility to respond empathically even when you have not entered the world of the other person and feeling what he or she is experiencing. Your responding can be developed and will be facilitative to relationships, especially those in the group. There are three components: attending, listening, and responding.

Attending is primarily nonverbal behavior and includes the intent and decision to listen, orientation of the body and mind to the speaker, and a focus on the speaker, screening out other distractions. Some specific strategies and attitudes include:

- Stop talking and listen. You cannot listen and really hear the other person when you are talking or thinking about what you want to say.
- Look at the speaker. Try to maintain eye contact, but not to the point where the other person becomes uncomfortable.
- Orient your body to the speaker. Turn all of your body to squarely face the other person whenever possible. For example, if seated, turn in your seat so that the top of your body faces the other person, and turn your legs and feet in that direction.
- Empty your mind as much as possible. Stop thinking about other things, or letting other sounds and thoughts distract you.
- Stop talking.

Listening includes hearing the words and understanding the content, not interrupting, asking questions only for clarification, and hearing the feelings the person seems to be experiencing. Although the content of the message or communication may not be the most important part, it still has much valuable information to contribute to an empathic response. Hear the words and make sure that what you heard was what was said or meant.

Don't interpret for the person, as that is what contributes to misunderstandings, and could be your projection.

Let the speaker finish what he or she wants to say without interrupting or trying to anticipate what you think he or she wants to say. Do not change the subject, bring something else into the interaction at this point, or distract the speaker in any way. This includes refraining from asking questions except if you think you did not hear or understand something clearly or accurately. Do not ask for details that you think are needed for your interest; let the person tell you what he or she thinks is important. Try to restrict questions to the bare minimum.

The most important part of listening is to hear the spoken and unspoken feelings part of the message, because this is the real message—how the person feels about what he or she is communicating. Attending and listening help keep a clear focus so that you can use the speaker's content, nonverbal behavior, and what you are sensing to accurately discern the feelings.

Responding is critical and it is recommended that this be done openly, directly, and verbally. Do not rely on nonverbal communication; a response can be missed, overlooked, or ignored by the other person who is intensely involved with his or her own message. Nonverbal responding can be effective at times, but empathic responding uses verbal responses.

An effective empathic response reflects the content and feelings of the speaker without additions, subtractions, interpretations, or elaborations. Some alterations can be appropriate *after* the empathic response is made, but should be limited when used, and not used as a substitute for the basic reflective empathic response.

- Do not parrot the speaker.
- Use different words and descriptors.
- Identify one or more unspoken feelings.
- Identify spoken conflicting feelings or thoughts.
- Wait for confirmation of the accuracy of your response.

Reduce Negative Countertransference

Yalom and Leszcz (2005) describe countertransference as the group leader's reactions to group members. They further divide it into objective and subjective countertransference. Objective countertransference is though to be the reactions aroused by group members, but these are not just aroused in the leader; they are also aroused in other group members giving the reactions more objectivity because they are shared. Subjective counter transference stems from the group leader's past, and influences his or her current relationships and interactions. Subjective counter transference can thus be both positive and negative. What the group leader has to do is to understand his or her own past experiences and relationships well enough to be able to identify whether the reaction is a result of the past and has negative associations, as this fuels negative counter transference, which can have harmful effects on, the group member(s).

Some reactions that suggest that possible countertransference is present include:

- Having a strong liking or disliking for one or more group members
- Ignoring or minimizing conflict

- Experiencing leader empathic failures
- Becoming deeply wounded or angry at perceived member criticism
- Being disappointed with group members or with the group as a whole
- Telling, demanding, or thinking how a member, or members, should or ought to think, behave, or feel
- Becoming exasperated, irritated, annoyed, or angry with a member or members

These are only a few of the numerous reactions that may indicate the presence of countertransference. Other than working to resolve family-of-origin issues and to satisfactorily complete unfinished business, there are six actions you can take to help reduce the possibility that some of your reactions are countertransference. Although there can be other reasons for some of your responses, such as undeveloped narcissism, the possibility of countertransference is always present.

- Stay aware of your reactions, and their possible association with your family-of-origin issues and unfinished business.
- Review your conscious old parental messages for their continuing impact and unconscious influences on your reactions and responses.
- Examine your reactions to group members for possible countertransference, especially reactions that are strong and intense.
- Reflect on your possible suppression, ignoring, or minimizing of conflict, and become more comfortable with tolerating a higher level.
- Be willing to do some self-exploration of the antecedents of your feelings and reactions to group members, but do not do so in the group setting.
- Try hard to see others as they really are, and not through the lens of past experiences or other people.

The Self-Reflective Stance

It is important to adopt a self-reflective stance as a group leader to gain a greater understanding for group members and their issues, and a deeper understanding of group process. When the leader is able to tune in to his or her personal experiencing in the session and understand it, it increases his or her ability to gauge when and how to intervene and how to use the resources of the group to help individuals, and his or her ability to make group-level process commentary.

A self-reflective stance can be enhanced through personal growth experiences. This is one way of building your self-understanding and, as a consequence, your inner resources. But, it is also a valuable tool for understanding what is of importance or even crucial for the group and its members. Knowing what the group needs, and what to do or how to intervene becomes easier with a self-reflective stance.

None of the following are conducive to self-reflection.

- Meeting the leader's personal needs at the expense of members' needs
- Being self-absorbed

- The leader distancing or disassociating himself or herself from the group
- The leader retreating or allowing members to retreat from conflict or intense feelings
- Minimizing members' concerns
- Withdrawing support
- Failing to be empathic, or appropriately intervene

Guidelines for becoming more self-reflective are presented later in the chapter.

Benefits and Outcomes for Self-Reflection

Self-reflection can be of enormous benefit when leading a group. You need to develop your own style and expertise to both tune in to your inner experiencing and to what the group and its members are doing and saying. This is not easy to do. You may get lost in your own thoughts, or be consumed by what members are doing and saying. As noted before, when you can trust what emerges for you personally, you know better what will be effective responses and interventions.

Group leaders, who want to use the resources of the group to help individual members, make constructive use of group-level process commentary. Being able to trust your inner experiencing provides vital clues to what is taking place in the group that provides the commentary. Group process can also provide information about the relationship between the leader and a member. Other uses for group process commentary include the following:

- When there is an impasse and discussions become circular
- When there is a continuing conflict, or the reemergence of a conflict that was thought to be resolved
- If nothing seems to be taking place in the group
- When prolonged silence produces considerable discomfort

The ability to tap into the leader's personal experiencing can help clarify what is wanted, needed, and desired on a much deeper level that just using content.

This use of self-reflection is immediate, quick, capable of mirroring, and uses both thoughts and feelings, but it is also prone to being influenced by your unfinished business, transference, acculturation, values, old parental messages, and so on. However, when you act on what you gain from self-reflection inside the group, you may also be tapping into your inner wisdom.

When and How Self-Reflection Benefits

Self-reflection is helpful to the group in the following circumstances. It can identify the concern and allow the leader to make a process comment.

- Members seem distracted and unable to stay focused.
- There is considerable chit-chat among members.
- Members insist on focusing on there-and-then topics.
- Expression of intense affect is ignored.

Self-reflection is helpful when a member exhibits dependence on the leader, challenges him or her, engages in problem behaviors such as monopolizing, tries to express experiencing but cannot verbalize it, or when a member is hostile, aggressive, or competitive.

Leaders do not have time to engage in considerable or considered self-reflection. There is a time, place, and need for that, of course, but not during the session. The use of self-reflection as described here demands that leaders remain emotionally present in the session while also engaging in self-reflection. Thus, leaders must be aware of and not ignore the feelings that emerge for them. They must have confidence that these feelings are not reflective of unresolved issues, biases, transference, and so on, but are an accurate reflection of what is taking place in the group, or with a member.

The leader should respond immediately, and not wait until later in the session before deciding what to say or do. Sometimes the leader may do nothing because that is the best response. However, it is preferable that the leader does some responding rather than doing none because he or she is paralyzed, or completely ignorant of what to do. And responding later in the session is better than not responding at all. However, learning to quickly engage in self-reflection and make appropriate responses at the optimum time is a skill to be learned and practiced.

Mirroring allows you to know when you are the container for the group's feelings. When the leader becomes aware of what feelings are clearly personal, or when projective identification occurs, or when the leader is acting as the container for the group's feelings, then he or she can mirror the particular feeling for the person or the group. This can be useful when the leader is the container for the group's feeling. For example, when all, or most, group members are anxious and fearful but refuse to accept their feelings, if you try to suppress or deny them, you will find yourself becoming increasingly anxious; you could be the "container" for the group's feelings. They are projecting their feelings, if you you are incorporating them, then they do not have to experience them. You are containing and managing their unpleasant feelings. If you can realize what is happening, mirror this to the group, and get members to accept and acknowledge their feelings, then you can cease being the container.

It is helpful to be able to use both thoughts and feelings during self-reflection. Your thoughts will help you analyze and stay connected to objective reality and your feelings will provide valuable and probably accurate information for you to use. You will not want to rely solely on either one as being truthful, real, accurate, or better. It's best to use both.

A good question is, how is self-reflection different from self-absorption? That is discussed in the next section.

Self-Reflection Versus Self-Absorption

There is considerable difference between being self-absorbed and being self-reflective. Leaders who possess either of these traits greatly impact the emphasis and focus for the session, choice of intervention, the extent to which members' growth and development is fostered, the group's willingness to explore personal issues, and the quality of the therapeutic alliance (Brown, 2006b; Gans & Alonso, 1998; Horwitz, 2000).

The self-absorbed leader will internally explore questions and statements similar to the following:

"Do they like me?"

"They won't like me if I _____."

"Am I doing it right?"

"They are being so stubborn [unfair, defensive, etc.]."

"Why aren't they cooperating?"

"I'm doing the best I can."

"I want them to think I'm good [competent, likeable, etc.]."

"What can I do that will please them?"

"They should _____."

"They ought to _____."

"They are so unappreciative."

"I want to do or say something that will make them appreciative [awed, sit up and take notice, etc.]."

All of these statements and questions are concerned with personal effectiveness and illustrate a leader's need for attention and admiration, a need to be considered unique and special, and most importantly, a lack of empathy. Self-absorption is more concerned with protecting the self from experiencing potential inadequacy, incompetence, and a realization of flaws. For example, the question "Do they like me?" and the self-statement "They won't like me if I _____" are both concerned with the underlying need and assumption that the leader has to be liked by members. This need and assumption satisfies the leader's need for approval and acceptance, and is not focused on group members' needs, which illustrates the need for personal development on the part of the leader. The same focus is also seen in the questions and statements that appear, on the surface, to be concerned with group members. They are deceiving, however; the real concern is once more on the needs of the leader. For example, the question about resistance, and the "should" and "ought" statements are really concerned about the leader's feelings about self-efficacy.

Self-reflection is considerably different from self-absorption. Self-reflectiveness is characterized by the following:

1. There is an inner experiencing that asks questions, or makes statements about personal feelings in the here and now, which is an attempt to understand the group and individual members.

2. There is not an attempt to deny, suppress, or ignore the feeling. The leader allows herself to experience whatever emerges.

3. The feeling is not evaluated or judged; it is accepted as a valid experience. Neither is there an attempt to impose "should" or "ought" on the feeling (e.g., "I should feel _____" or "I ought not to have this feeling.") Acceptance of what emerges is perceived to be valuable information, and is not perceived as a personal flaw.

4. The feeling is silently and internally analyzed to consider if there is a root basis of transference, countertransference, or projection. The possibilities of unresolved issues, family-of-origin concerns, as well as underdeveloped narcissism are not avoided but are carefully considered.

5. Even when the feeling is associated with personal concerns, the analysis continues to try and determine what about the group, the event, the interaction, and so on, triggered the feeling. This, too, can be valuable information the group leader can use for the benefit of the group.

6. The self-reflective leader will consider the possibility that he or she is acting as a container for the unspoken feelings present in the group, when the possibility of transference and so on can be ruled out, or is only a faint possibility. The triggered feelings in the leader, in this instance, reflect feelings that are not accepted, spoken, or realized by one or more group members. The leader is responding to these feelings on a nonconscious level by unconsciously allowing his or her feelings to be triggered. This understanding of acting as a container can be invaluable to a group leader.

Guidelines for Developing Self-Reflection

Statements and questions associated with self-reflection are similar to the following:

"What am I feeling, or aware of right now?"

"I am feeling _____."

"What happened that seemed to trigger this response or feeling?"

"Did the exchange, event, interaction, and so forth hold the potential for my personal projections and so on?"

"Could it be that what I am experiencing is countertransference?"

"What are my personal associations for the triggering event?"

"To this point I don't think what I am experiencing is due to my personal issues. What other possibilities are there?"

"Would it be helpful to the group to openly speak of my experiencing, relate my feelings, and so on?"

"Is it possible that I am containing some unspoken feelings for the group?"

Suppose the last question is the one that seems most focal for the leader, and she or he is the repository for unspoken feelings in the group. Suppose the feelings the leader is experiencing are anger and dread. As the container for members' feelings, the leader then knows that one or more group members are experiencing some form of the same feelings, but are either suppressing or not openly acknowledging their feelings. This is information that can be used to intervene, and can lead to some effective leader interventions. Some possible interventions include:

- The leader could report on his or her feelings, and ask if there are group members experiencing similar feelings.
- The leader could ask members to label or otherwise identify what they are aware of or feeling in the here and now.
- The leader could make statements or do other actions designed to address the fear or anger.
- The leader could take steps to ensure that anger and fear are not improperly displaced on other members, and that they are expressed directly to the leader.
- A discussion could be initiated about the suppression of these feelings and the impact on members and the group.
- A discussion of the reasons for suppressing these feelings or the unwillingness or inability to openly verbalize them could be helpful.

In other words, the leader does not have to search for effective interventions; he or she has only to choose from several options. Further, the members are not being blamed or criticized for failing to meet the leader's needs or expectations. The group and its members benefit and progress continues.

Reduce Self-Absorption. Use instances where you are self-absorbed to consciously become more self-reflective. Do not blame, criticize, or chide yourself for having self-absorbed thoughts or feelings. These are yours, and they emerged for a reason. Being self-absorbed is "all about you," and as a group leader you need to be "all about the group and its members" for that period of time. When you find that you are thinking and feeling about yourself, note what you are thinking and feeling to explore later. At this moment, turn your conscious thoughts to the group and open yourself to what the members are saying, doing, and feeling. Turn your attention and emotional investment to the group.

The thoughts and feelings that you put aside for further exploration could fall into one or more categories (e.g., underdeveloped narcissism, countertransference, projection, or projective identification). All these are indicative of personal issues that have the potential to negatively impact the group when you function in your role as group leader. Let's examine some of the items in the self-absorbed thoughts and attitudes list at the beginning of this discussion to illustrate how the leader's personal issues are embedded.

Understand How Personal Issues Influence Thoughts and Feelings. "Do they like me?" is just another way to express a deep need for liking and approval. An individual who has such a need can be deeply hurt if someone does or says anything that hints of dislike or disapproval. He or she will do anything to gain others' liking and approval, even to the point of not behaving wisely. It is desirable, but not essential, that the group leader be liked by group members. What is essential is that the group leader be trusted and respected, and that is unlikely to occur if members feel that you can be manipulated to gain their liking and approval. Members will like you if you "are" the kind of person who is caring, and can attend to their safety needs.

"Am I doing it right?" also speaks of the need for approval, but could reflect a mind-set such as "If I do this, then that will occur." If-then thinking is not yet applicable to group counseling because the dynamics of the group and its members are unique for each group. It is not possible to accurately predict what will happen for anything you do or say. The need to "do it right" assumes that there is a "right" way and that you are inadequate or flawed if you don't do what is right. Again, the focus is on you rather than the group and its members.

"Why are they resisting?" is a thought that carries an implication that members should not have resistance. It also implies that you think that you should do something or that you did something to cause the resistance. It's all about you, not about group members. It is much more constructive to note where there is resistance, what seemed to trigger it, and what defense mechanism is used. You do not have to "do" anything. In fact, it's best if you do not do anything. If the group as a whole is resisting, you would be more constructive if you would turn your thinking to analyzing what the group is trying to tell you by the resistance. The group may be saying:

"This doesn't address our need."

"It doesn't feel safe."

"This is too scary [sensitive, etc.]."

"We are afraid of being hurt."

"You are meeting your need—not ours."

At some point the group will mount an attack on the group leader. The attack may be mild, indirect, or open and direct. This is an expected behavior in stage 2, and is perceived as a positive event for group progress. The group leader who fears attacks and works to keep the group from attacking him or her is not helping members learn how to manage, contain, and appropriately express aggressive, hostile, and destructive feelings. The leader who has a strong need for liking and approval can be hurt when the attack occurs, and not react in a constructive way. This leader can think, "Why are they [the group members] so stubborn [unfair, defensive]?" or "Why aren't they cooperating?" or "I'm doing the best I can." These are not constructive thoughts, as they are all focused on the leader and his or her thoughts and feelings. The leader is more concerned about personal feelings and is blaming and criticizing members for arousing the feelings instead of focusing on the group, its needs, and what members are trying to communicate via the attack. It is much more helpful for the group leader to use the personal feeling aroused as a guide to understanding what members are feeling and trying to communicate.

For example, suppose you are the group leader, and members have been cooperative and participating for the first four sessions. You are expecting the same behavior for the fifth session, and have planned what to do and say to move the group toward a goal. However, shortly after the session begins, members begin making comments, and asking questions that arouse irritation and mild resentment in you. One member in particular continues to press you for answers you feel you have already provided. Another member interrupts you to ask what are they supposed to be doing, and how this is supposed to help. You begin to wonder what is happening, and your feelings of irritation and resentment are joined by feelings of inadequacy, incompetence, and uncertainty.

A constructive use of these feelings would be to focus on the group and its message. The underlying message could be that members are getting in touch with their personal feelings of being flawed, and are irritated at you for putting them in a position where they cannot escape experiencing them, and are expected to examine these uncomfortable feelings. They are uncomfortable, and are blaming you for their discomfort. Once you reach this point in your understanding of what the group may be experiencing, your response could be to acknowledge their feelings with something like, "It's not easy to do this work and experience the uncomfortable feelings that are aroused." Another response could be an acknowledgment of their irritation with you (e.g., "You are irritated that I am doing and saying things that trigger uncomfortable feelings for you, and you wonder how that is supposed to help you"). It is not constructive to say things like:

"The group seems really hostile today."

"Let's work on your goals."

"We're here to work on your problems and I'm trying to help you."

"What happened to make you so cranky today?"

"What do you want to talk about?"

"I've tried to answer your questions but nothing seems to satisfy you."

The key to becoming more self-reflective is to reduce your self-absorption by working on your lingering aspects of underdeveloped narcissism, resolving family-of-origin issues, completing unfinished business, and building your self. You become more self-accepting and self-confident when you do these things. As a result, in turn you gain greater acceptance, understanding, and respect for others. You can begin to make more effective interventions that are based on the other person's needs, rather than interventions that address your personal needs. That stance is the basis for being an effective group leader.

A self-reflective stance has both a personal growth outcome, and is a group leader skill and technique. This is one way of building your self-understanding and your inner self. But it is also a valuable tool for understanding what is taking place in the group, what is important for the group, what is crucial for the group, and what is a concern for its members. Knowing what the group needs and what to do or how to intervene becomes easier with a self-reflective stance.

However, you must take care that your self-reflection does not result in destructive forces for the group or its members. Destructive forces include countertransference, meeting your personal needs, self-absorption, distancing yourself from the group, retreating from conflict or intense feelings, minimizing members' concerns, withdrawing of support, or failure to be empathic or appropriately intervene. You may wonder how any of these relate to your expertise as a group leader. The clinical vignette about Bob presented in chapter 8, on page 185 is an example of what is meant.

It is highly possible that Bob had participated in counseling or therapy, but had not completely worked through some personal family-of-origin issues. Thus, when faced with a situation that tapped into his personal issues, he reacted on the basis of his personal needs. It is much more beneficial for the leader to explore and work on personal issues outside the group. Working with a therapist is the most effective way to become aware of personal issues, especially family-of-origin issues. However, personal growth can take place in other ways, and can enhance therapy.

Summary

1. The therapeutic self has many aspects, and one that is important for the group leader's focus is the extent of undeveloped or destructive narcissism. These undeveloped and unconscious attitudes and behaviors can be troubling to relationships of all kinds, but have the potential for exerting extremely negative effects on group members.

2. Group leaders will want to explore their behaviors and attitudes that can be reflective of an inflated self (examples are grandiosity and entitlement); indifference to others (examples are lack of empathy and exploitation of others); and troubling states (examples are shallow emotions and attention seeking).

3. In addition to becoming aware of personal undeveloped narcissism, group leaders will want to build healthy adult narcissism with characteristics of empathy, inspiration, creativity, an appropriate sense of humor, wisdom, and a sense of responsibility.

4. Group leaders are encouraged to become self-reflective and to reduce or eliminate self-absorption. Self-reflection demands that one is aware of current experiencing, and can consider personal responses to determine if they are projections, conuntertransference, or associated with personal issues and concerns rather than those of group members.

Chapter Activities

1. List five to six personal characteristics you have that you think would be strengths for building a therapeutic relationship with group members. Share these in small groups.

2. List five to six personal characteristics, behaviors, or attitudes that you have or that others say you have, that are not constructive for building a therapeutic relationship, and which need further developing. Share these in small groups.

3. Identify the subject, condition, issue, or target audience that seems likely to trigger your countertransference, and write a few sentences about it.

Personal Development Exercise: Construct a collage that depicts your disappointments and regrets.

Chapter 10

Educational and Skills Training Groups

Major Topics

1. Categories of educational groups: learning, prevention, guidance or developmental, and related.
2. General characteristics of educational groups.
3. Descriptions and illustrations for groups in each category.
4. The educational component for these groups.
5. Theories and research findings on skills training effectiveness.
6. Descriptions for four types of training groups.
7. General guidelines for planning skills training groups.
8. Planning for deficits skills training.
9. Planning for managing skills training.
10. Planning for expansion skills training.
11. Planning for enhancement skills training.

Introduction

The primary focus for educational groups is on teaching and learning a body of knowledge. The cognitive component is the most important with the affective component included, but is not emphasized or explored in detail. Emotions are not ignored, but they are not used as much for personal learning, such as what happens in psychoeducational and therapy groups. There are several categories for educational groups: learning, prevention, guidance or developmental, and related.

- Learning groups can be used in all types of settings, but are usually found in organizations, such as schools and industry. These groups are also called cooperative or collaborative learning groups (Johnson & Johnson, 2006).

- Prevention groups generally have the goals of providing information to keep people from self-destructive acts; harmful behavior; disease and other conditions that can impair the quality of life, or their growth and development; and negative impacts on relationships (Coyne, 2004).

- Guidance or developmental groups are focused on providing knowledge about expected life tasks and transitions. These groups can reduce some of the ambiguity and complexity members face with unknown and unfamiliar life tasks and transitions.

- One category for educational groups is termed "related groups" because the educational experience is for the families and caretakers of someone who has an emotional disturbance, medical illness, or other condition. The affected person needs help to cope physically and or emotionally, and educating families and/or caretakers fulfills this need. Groups for the affected person are presented in the chapter on psychoeducational groups. Related groups for families and caretakers will be discussed later in this chapter.

Characteristics of Educational Groups

Educational groups have some characteristics in common: size, composition, limitations, and an emphasis on cognitive material. These groups can be relatively large in the number of participants compared to clinical groups. For example, some guidance or developmental groups are routinely conducted in classrooms where there are 20 to 35 students, whereas clinical groups are usually limited to 8 to 10 members. It would not be unusual for a group leader to have either a small number of participants, or a large group.

The *composition* of these groups can be homogeneous, such as in the case of guidance groups in the classroom, or heterogeneous, such as a range of ages and educational levels for parent education groups. Many groups will have a homogeneous membership because of the topic, but leaders should expect that some groups will have a heterogeneous membership and be prepared for the variations that may be present.

Limitations refers to the narrow topics that will be addressed, the time constraints, and the lack of prior knowledge about participants for some groups. Topics for the group's focus and/or for each session are narrowly focused to concentrate on basic or critical information. Although there can be digressions, deviations, and expansion of material, they should be minimal because these groups tend to stay on topic.

The reason for a narrow focus is time constraint. Some educational groups may meet as little as one time, or in the case of some guidance groups, meet only one class period of 50 minutes. Some groups may meet several sessions, but the time available is still limited. There is usually not sufficient time for stage and member development, the emergence of many therapeutic factors, or for the extensive exploration of personal issues and concerns.

An important defining characteristic for educational groups is the emphasis on *cognitive material*, even when other topics, such as emotions, are presented. For example, if emotions were the topic, the information presented would be about feelings without the expectation or stimulus for expressing these feelings in the group. The value of the cognitive approach for this topic would be a lessening of intensity, a thinking versus feeling or action perspective, reduction of the possibility for uncontrolled expression, and a safety containing and managing function.

An emphasis on cognitive material allows the leader to guide members to new information and personal applications, describe alternative processes and procedures, demonstrate and model thinking through and problem solving, and illustrate their value. Feelings are not ignored or discounted; they are encouraged and are a vital part of the learning process for many topics. However, feelings and catharsis are not the first priority; cognitive material holds that position. Let's move to a broader description and illustration for each type of educational group.

Learning Groups

Cooperative and collaborative learning groups have substantial evidence of their effectiveness. Johnson and Johnson (1989) conducted a meta-analysis of these groups, which were primarily held in school settings. Their analysis revealed that outcomes for these groups showed the following:

- Significantly higher achievement and retention
- Higher-level reasoning, critical thought
- Gains in generating new ideas, strategies, and solutions
- Transfer of learning
- Positive attitudes toward the subject
- Increased time on task
- Social support

These positive outcomes can be helpful for learning groups in other settings such as colleges and universities, businesses, community organizations, industries, and other such organizations where learning new material is important.

Cooperative and collaborative learning groups are usually formed from large groups, such as a class, with the teacher, trainer, or counselor as the large-group leader. These large groups are reformed into small groups with a leader for each. The small-group leaders are very important, although most will likely not be trained leaders or even know much about group issues, such as group dynamics. These leaders will need some orientation to the tasks of coaching, supervising, and monitoring. This is the responsibility of the trained large-group leader.

Basic Guidelines. Basic guidelines for learning groups include:

- Large groups, such as a class, should be divided into smaller groups of five to eight members. Each small group should have a designated, elected, or selected group leader or facilitator.
- It is helpful if another member takes minutes of group meetings; this task may be rotated among members.
- The task, purpose, or objectives should be clearly defined, narrow in scope, and easily assessed.
- If the small groups are to hold separate meetings, these should be regularly scheduled, the large-group leader notified of the meetings in advance, and held at a time when all group members can attend.
- Conflicts among members and with the small-group leader are to be expected, and a resolution process taught and implemented.

- Arrangements should be made to have both individual accountability and group account-ability, and a reward system in place.

Many of these groups tend to meet over several months, such as a school semester or quarter. They can meet one or more times per week, and have numerous opportunities to interact and work. However, they should not be left entirely on their own for meetings. It is best if some rules are in place such as meeting days and times when all members can meet; no subgroup or impromptu meeting should take place because this is how cliques form and members are excluded. There should also be a record of attendance, actions, and decisions kept for each meeting and submitted to the large-group leader. The designated leader or facilitator will receive guidance and direction from the large-group leader (Brown, 2000). Other rules and guidelines should include how conflicts are to be handled; what to do when problems arise; the necessity for all members to contribute; if electronic meetings can be held; and basic expectations for members' behavior, such as civility, tolerance of diverse viewpoints, and respect.

Leader Tasks. There are several tasks for large-group leaders when creating and facilitating a learning group.

- Planning the focus, rules, and rewards in advance
- Forming, structuring, and monitoring the small groups
- Preparing and supporting the small-group leaders
- Providing feedback to the small groups that are meeting separately
- Fostering the development of a group identity

Planning is critical and should include a well-defined focus and goal. From these follow the material that must be gathered and learned, the sequence or process for learning to occur, the product or desired outcome to be accomplished, the evaluation and assessment plan that encom-passes both individual and group performance, guidelines and rules for how the groups will be facilitated and are expected to operate, and the strategies that will be used (Brown, 2000).

There are several ways in which the *small groups* can be formed from the large group. The list of participants could be reviewed in advance, and divided to form smaller groups of five to eight members each. Or, at the first large-group meeting, participants could count off so that those having the same number would form a group. For example, all number ones would form a group, and so on. The large-group leader needs to predetermine the number of groups that can be formed if the latter procedure is used. Another possibility is to let the participants self-select the group to join. There are advantages and disadvantages for each of these methods, and there are also other variations.

Structuring the small groups is also done in advance by developing the rules and guide-lines. Once the groups are formed, the leader should orient the groups for how they are to function, and other expectations. It is vital that group members understand the task, the process or procedure, and expected or desired outcomes. Selection of group leaders occurs at this point. The large-group leader could designate leaders that rotate, where each member gets a turn to be the facilitator. Or the leader can allow the small groups to select their leaders. The small groups should be monitored on a regular basis. The minutes or reports for group meetings is one avenue, but the large-group leader needs to have other methods for monitoring to keep the group on task, provide for members' safety, and for problem prevention.

As stated, it is unlikely that the small-group leaders will have training in leadership, so it becomes important to prepare them for this essential task, and to *provide guidance and support* over the life span of the collaborative group experience. Preparation and support includes meeting with the small-group leaders separately to structure their group facilitation, monitor progress and prevent problems, and to help give them confidence that they are on the right track. Advance preparation topics for small-group leaders include the following:

- Hold meetings only when all members can attend.
- Begin and end meetings at the designated time.
- Solicit input from all members, not just a few.
- Describe the task(s) and make sure all members understand what needs to be done.
- Respond in some way to every member's input no matter how silly, off topic, or different it may be.
- Try to keep meetings focused and on task.
- Refrain from criticizing, blaming, or other devaluing actions.

Monitoring and continued support efforts include requiring the small groups to submit regular reports or updates on progress, problems, or barriers to task accomplishment, and other such information. The large-group leader can then make suggestions for how they are to proceed, approve actions taken or proposed, and note the positive aspects and progress the group has made.

A *system for feedback* to groups that are meeting separately, such as a meeting outside of class time, is helpful to group members. This system can be written, electronic, via a visit from the large-group leader, or a combination of these. If there are several small groups, the large-group leader should visit each small group one or more times to provide consultation and encouragement. Groups that are having problems, such as conflict among members, may need more visits.

Developing a *group identity* has many positive outcomes and takes time to develop, but there can be the risk that it encourages competition between groups. The positive outcomes include members' self-identifying with the group and having a stronger commitment to the group and its task, encouraging the development of universality and cohesion, helping foster inclusion, and providing enrichment and excitement. All of these are positive, but take time to develop. The large-group leader can facilitate this development by planning exercises and other activities that are designed to give a group identity, and by recognizing the groups in some way. Here are some suggestions.

- Have small groups create a group name as part of an ice breaker exercise.
- Provide the materials for groups to create group logos. They can use the logos on their reports or other communication.
- Take a picture of each group and post these in a display.
- Make some time for each small group to report to the large group.
- Recognize groups' progress rather than always focusing on individuals' progress.

Collaborative or cooperative group experiences can be productive and enriching when properly planned and facilitated.

Prevention Groups

Prevention groups are educational groups that provide information as an intervention to prevent physical, psychological, or emotional distress that interferes with growth and development, the quality of life, and development of meaningful and satisfying relationships. They also take steps that can forestall an illness, disease, and psychological or emotional problems. There is evidence that prevention works (Coyne & Horne, 2001; Durlak & Wells, 1997; Price, Cowen, Lorion, & Ramos-McKay, 1988; Romano & Hage, 2000).

Some examples include the following:

- Substance abuse prevention for adolescents (Botvin, Schinke, & Orlandi, 1995)
- Sexual aggression at work (Kagan, Kagan, & Watson, 1995)
- Eating disorders (Mussell, Binford, & Fulkerson, 2000)
- Youth suicide (Toumbourou & Gregg, 2002)

A wide range and variety of prevention groups is currently used, and studies indicate that they have desired outcomes, such as abstinence.

Basic Guidelines. The primary guiding principle for prevention groups is that information can guide and direct decisions, choices, attitudes, and so on that in turn affect behavior in a positive way. There are other outcomes that are also positive, such as reducing alienation, increasing a sense of universality or similarities with others, providing social support, infusing hope, promoting interpersonal learning, and empowering. There are numerous benefits for prevention groups.

Basic planning for prevention groups include:

- Consulting with the target audience
- Ensuring that group members are relatively healthy or at risk, but are not involved in what is sought to be prevented
- Describing what is to be prevented precisely and in observable behavior terms
- Ensuring that outcomes can be assessed—that is, what was being addressed, prevented, modified, delayed, and so on can be evaluated

Coyne (2004) lists the following steps for planning.

1. Ecological assessment to identify target audience and their needs
2. Collaboration with representatives of the target audience
3. Identification of current knowledge
4. Goal setting
5. Creation of a session-by-session plan

Ecological assessment refers to gathering information from and about the target audience's needs and the various information-gathering devices and procedures. Information can be obtained through interviews, focus groups, surveys, and other such devices. This step is essential because it is difficult for an outsider, or even someone who is involved, to have a thorough and comprehensive perspective of what the target audience's needs may be. Basic information includes:

- Problem identification—what needs to be prevented
- Risk factor determination and what would happen if not prevented
- The impact on the quality of life for failure to prevent
- Barriers and constraints to prevention
- Motivation and encouragement factors and strategies

Let's see how data gathering might work for group of girls aged 13 to 15 who were sexually harassed by their peers. This plan is designed to prevent them from becoming sexual harassers in turn (Wexel & Brown, 2000).

> *Problem Identification. A national study conducted by the American Association of University Women's Educational Foundation (1993) found that 81% of all students reported being sexually harassed by their peers, with approximately 86% of females and about 70% of males reporting these actions. The study also found that peer sexual harassers were themselves sexually harassed (Wexel & Brown, 2000).*
>
> *Risk Factors. Very high.*
>
> *Lack of Prevention. Failure to prevent peer sexual harassment increases the likelihood of the cycle of harassment continuing, with many negative impacts on the person.*
>
> *Impact of the Quality of Life. Eitel (1996) reviewed the literature and concluded that there were significant negative impacts for peer sexual harassment on the victims. They were found to suffer from psychoemotional, psychosocial, academic, behavioral, and even physical negative outcomes. School attendance and achievement were negatively affected; there was an erosion of self-confidence during the critical formative years; depression or acting-out behaviors were other consequences.*
>
> *Barriers and Constraints. School personnel fail to take peer sexual harassment seriously, as do many parents, and do not intervene; an atmosphere is formed in schools that minimizes the seriousness of the harassment; the students do not know how to respond; they can develop feelings of isolation and of being different; and they do not want to be excluded or derided so harassment is underreported.*

Although this is an example where the target audience was not directly consulted, they could be in the planning process. Interacting with those who experienced the condition, issue, disease, and so on or those at risk can provide much valuable information.

Try to get one or more representatives of the target audience and cultural consultants to help plan the prevention group. These representatives can assist in selecting the needed information, identifying any cultural or diversity concerns, and in understanding what activities may be effective, or what should be avoided.

The review of literature is a critical step, as new knowledge and information is emerging every day. But, don't restrict your identification of current knowledge to the literature. Use professionals and experts in the field, reputable Internet sources, and other valid resources.

Using the gathered information from assessment, consultation, and other sources, the next step is to formulate the goals. These should be few, realistic, and achievable. The desire is to prevent something from happening, or to lessen its impact, but the goals for the group must focus on what is doable or achievable. Therefore, goals should refer to the body of knowledge presented, action plans developed, and the like. For example, in the previous example about peer sexual harassment, it would be unrealistic to have a goal that the group experiences would prevent the girls from becoming sexual harassers. That's the hope. It would be more realistic to have goals like the following:

- Increase awareness of the acts that constitute sexual harassment and its negative impact.
- Understand actions the harassed person can take to moderate the negative impact of peer sexual harassment.
- Develop a plan for a peer sexual harassment free school setting.

The final step is to create a session-by-session plan as described previously in the chapter on planning.

Guidance or Developmental Groups

These educational groups are designed to give participants information about expected and usual developmental and life issues and concerns. They are usually focused on children, adolescents, and young adults. They occur in school and university settings and are not intended to solve or prevent problems—although those may emerge during the life of the group. The intent is to help participants to be prepared to cope with life's changes, their personal expectations, and needs. Guidance or developmental groups may focus on topics such as:

- Career exploration in an elementary school setting
- Orientation to high school
- Choosing a major in college
- Physical changes and what they mean to middle school students
- Friendship development for high school transfer students
- Job search skills

Basic Guidelines.   Basic guidelines require the leader to attend to obtaining parental or guardian permission, determining the setting, reviewing the professional literature about the subject for the group, selecting the topic, and ensuring the information is accurate.

Most participants for these groups are not of legal age and *parental or guardian permission* must be obtained in advance. Therefore, it is essential that the group leader develop the plan for the group far enough in advance so that a description of activities can be created to send to parents or guardians to obtain consent. It takes time to distribute these and for their return. The description should state the major goal for the group—when, where, and how often the group will meet; the assessment procedures with a copy of the data-gathering instrument(s); a brief description of activities; and a statement of consent for participation for the parent or guardian to sign.

Most groups are conducted in a school *setting*. The leader may need to adjust the group activities to better fit the setting because many schools make multiple uses of the facilities. Some groups, such as career education, lend themselves to a classroom setting, but there are other groups that need more privacy. Group leaders must do the best that they can to secure appropriate settings, but also must be flexible and adaptable to make the best use of the available facilities. For example, if a group must be held in the cafeteria where group members may be overheard and there is distracting noise, the group leader could adapt the material to minimize the need for personal expression or exploration, and notify the participants about the possibility of being overheard and that noise may be encountered.

The *professional literature* is a rich resource for material for guidance or developmental groups, and there are commercial programs that can be purchased for use. It is likely that other groups have been formed around a particular topic and group leaders can capitalize on these experiences. It becomes essential to consult the literature when planning.

Assumptions to guide planning and facilitating these groups are that the topic is shared or universal; that accurate information can guide, direct, and support; that participants are in or about the same stage of development; and that participants can learn from the material and other experiences. These assumptions have some constraints and limitations, and some may not be valid for certain groups, but they form working hypotheses.

Topics for guidance or developmental groups are usually selected because the target audience is at a particular stage of development where the information could be of assistance, or is part of a longer-term developmental process. For example, choosing a career is a long-term process that has many variables that also need to be part of the choice, such as knowing about the different kinds of work that people do, or learning what education and training is needed for various careers and jobs. However, children, adolescents, and young adults are expected at some point to obtain employment, or to have a career, and information is valuable to help make informed choices and decisions that give them the fundamentals for making career or job choices.

Accurate information can be invaluable because it reduces ambiguity and uncertainty, increases self-confidence, and can provide guidance for how to proceed. This can be especially important for development because the child, adolescent, or young adult lacks experience for the developmental task that must be accomplished. The new and unknown can be anxiety producing, and anxiety can prevent him or her from making good and informed choices, or from becoming paralyzed and unable to choose, or withdrawing and refusing to choose. Providing accurate information at the right time can be empowering.

Forming the Group. When forming guidance or developmental groups, the information and plan are predicated on an assumption that all participants are at about the same stage of development. Although participants are usually around the same age, their stage of development may vary widely. Individuals develop at different rates, and there are numerous variables that contribute to their rate of development such as genetics, environment, personality, experiences, and so on. The group leader can plan based on the assumption, but the reality can be very different. It can be helpful and enriching to have participants who are at differing stages of development, as long as there is not too much variation. The enrichment can be twofold: Members who are at a higher level of development can serve as models, and provide hope and encouragement so that others too can be successful. Members who are not yet fully developed can learn about the practice and benefits of altruism from the more developed members, and may be more inclined to listen and follow their peers. Both can learn from each other. The leader can capitalize on the differences in developmental levels, but can also plan as if there would be few if any differences, and for some groups there may not be any differences.

The final assumption is that participants can learn from the materials and experiences, and leaders certainly hope that this assumption is valid. The challenge is to accurately select materials, exercises, and other activities that foster this learning. Learning can be enhanced when planning and selection of materials are based on knowledge and understanding of the target audience. The ecological assessment described for prevention groups can also be of assistance for guidance or developmental groups.

Related Groups

All of the other categories for educational groups provide direct services to the client. Related groups provide indirect services because the target audiences are the families, caretakers, and others who interact with the affected client on a regular basis, but not the affected individual or at-risk person. Some examples follow, and other examples are discussed in the chapter on psychoeducational groups.

- Empowerment-based parent education program on the reduction of youth suicide risk factors (Toumbourou & Gregg, 2002)
- Suicide and violence prevention—parent education in the emergency department (Kruesi et al., 1999)
- Group-based parent education for behavior problems (Barlow & Stewart-Brown, 2000)
- Group-based education program for families on addictions (Little, 2005)
- Focus groups for research in alcohol and drug education (Sharma, 2004)

The literature shows that all of these studies had positive outcomes for the population indirectly addressed.

Several premises form the basis for this type of educational group.

1. The client is not the only person who is affected by the condition, topic, disease, and so on. Parents, siblings, spouses, and caretakers also experience some impact.
2. Support and understanding from others in the environment are encouraging and meaningful when they show some knowledge of what the person is experiencing.
3. Families and other caregivers can better cope when they have some knowledge of what can be done, what is not helpful, and what are some expected reactions and outcomes.

Most related groups are focused on a condition, illness, disease, and the like, and there can be considerable anxiety for both the person experiencing them, and for those who live with or care for him or her. When the condition is not well understood, neither side can cope very well, and relationships, quality of life, self-esteem, self-confidence, and even social lives for both the affected person and the caregiver can be negatively affected. Their ability to understand the situation is an important component for both the client and for themselves in reducing anxiety and increasing hope and motivation, and can be empowering. So, it is helpful for both to receive education.

What should education for related group members address? Suggested areas of information include the following:

- A description of the condition, disease, illness, and so on
- Treatment options
- Expected outcomes
- Precipitating factors when these are important to know to prevent relapse, or becoming chronic
- Suggested helping strategies

Group leaders should expect that members of these groups will likely be very anxious, may be fearful, some will engage in self-blame or in blaming others such as the affected person; they may want to be reassured that the outcome will be positive; and some will be depressed. These states are not the optimum for learning, but are not unusual and should not be ignored, minimized, or overlooked in the planning process. Much of the emotional content will be addressed in the chapter on psychoeducational groups, but if your group has primarily an educational focus, you will not spend as much time on this. Using exercises and other activities that allow expression of feelings, asking about current feelings, and acknowledging the validity of expressed feelings but not exploring them, may be sufficient.

The Educational Component

The educational component is the major component for all types of educational groups, and is mainly focused on teaching and learning. Considerable research has been done on both, and there is no one method, style, or approach that addresses everything. Group leaders need to know about the theories, research, and current practices for teaching and for learning for various audiences and content material, and should also be aware of their preferences for both teaching and learning. The primary intention remains that of presenting information that participants can internalize and apply to their personal situations. The four important questions for group leaders to answer and prepare for are: What information does the target audience need? What information should I present? How should I present it? How and when will I get feedback on its efficacy? Let's explore these four questions in the example group previously used about peer sexual harassment. Assume that the group will meet for eight 1-hour sessions.

What Information Does the Target Audience Need? Although you did not consult representatives of the target audience for this example, you can make some educated guesses. The audience probably needs information about these topics:

- The extent of the problem—peer sexual harassment
- Definition and descriptions of harassing behavior
- The short-term and long-term effects on the victims

- Strategies to prevent and reduce these behaviors
- How the victims can emotionally, psychologically, and physically protect themselves
- The roles of parents and school personnel in prevention and elimination

What Information Should I Present? The challenge is to present needed information without overwhelming the audience. There is a wealth of information about sexual harassment, statistics about its prevalence and its impact on victims, legislation and policies, the chilling atmosphere produced when officials do not intervene to prevent or address it, as well as strategies that are found to be effective. The age and stage of development for the example target audience members suggest that they would not be able to absorb and apply information that does not directly affect or apply to them, such as the penalties for sexual harassment in the workplace, or legislation. This is useful and valuable information, but these adolescents would probably benefit more from learning about what directly affects them where they are at this time. The purpose for the group is to intervene to prevent the cycle of sexual harassment from continuing. Further, there are only eight 1-hour sessions, so time is limited.

Given these conditions and constraints, all of the information that they need can be presented if modified and selected carefully. In addition, how to present some of the information may help with the decision about what to present. Let's assume that the decision is to present something about all of the points. The group leader can prioritize these so that the most essential ones get the most coverage.

How Should I Present the Information? There are numerous modes and methods for presenting, and the selection of which to use depends on the leader's assessment of the target audience, the leader's style and preferences for presenting information, the time available, and other environmental concerns. Use these questions as a guide.

- What method is most likely to engage the group?
- What information is relevant to members' current situations?
- Is there sufficient time for all group members to become involved if an exercise or activity is used?
- Are the materials or other resources available, and in sufficient quantity?
- Will the activities or mode of presentation arouse intense and uncomfortable feelings, and am I prepared to manage these if, or when, they do emerge?

Methods The choice of methods can vary depending on the topic and expertise of the leader. For example, I might tend to use an exercise as a lead-in to the presentation on the impact of peer sexual harassment on the victim. Two exercises come to mind, and either could be used.

1. Ask group members to brainstorm about possible effects, or about their experiences. Write these on posted newsprint or a chalkboard or whiteboard, and then discuss each.
2. Prepare a form in advance that has a list of possible effects, and ask participants to check all that they experienced. (A previous mini-lecture or discussion described sexually harassing behaviors.) The group can then have a discussion about the negative impact, and begin to increase awareness of why it should be stopped.

Almost any topic can make use of either mini-lectures, exercises, or demonstrations. Some may lend themselves to presentations by media, homework, bibliotherapy, and expressive techniques, such as imagery and art.

The example group needs information relevant to their current circumstances, and some information will be eliminated. The members may not be interested in information that relates primarily to adults in the workplace such as court cases, legislation, employment policies, and so on. If the history and development of laws and policies were to be presented, the information would be very brief, just enough to let members become aware of its existence. The topics listed in the section "What Information Does the Target Audience Need?" would be the information selected for the example group.

The number of members and the time available would determine what could be presented—in what form, how to allow for all members' participation, and how to debrief the exercises. Mini-lectures can present the most information in the shortest period of time, but these would be limited to no more than one every other session, and then limited to 15 to 20 minutes at most to allow time for discussion. Only short exercises of about the same number of minutes would be used to allow time for debriefing. If media, such as a film, were selected, only part of it would be shown, again limited to 15 to 20 minutes.

It is helpful and efficient to gather all the materials needed for all the sessions before the first session. That way, the leader will not have to be concerned each session about locating materials, or having sufficient materials for the group. All forms, art and drawing materials, newsprint for a brainstorming exercise, printed materials for outside the group reading, and so on would be gathered and stored in a safe place.

Because the topic of sexual harassment is very personal, the emergence of intense and uncomfortable emotions is expected, especially if members start to reexperience the emotions they had when they were harassed. Shame, guilt, anger, and so on could emerge around the incident(s), or when the reactions and inactions of adults are recalled. These uncomfortable emotions could also emerge when participants become aware that some of their actions could be sexual harassment. These feelings would not be explored in depth in this group, but would be acknowledged as valid responses, and suggestions provided for how these uncomfortable feelings could be reduced. For example, realizing that they did not cause the harassment could relieve shame and guilt. Developing an action plan for a peer sexual harassment free school environment could relieve anger. All of these are part of the original plan for the group.

Group leaders can get some immediate feedback on the efficacy of the material although its major impact may take some time to develop because this occurs after the group is over. However, some feedback is possible in the present before the group is over by using one or more of the following procedures:

- Ask group members about their immediate thought, feelings, and ideas about the material, and their personal applications during the closing session(s).
- Insert questions on the assessment form that ask for members' reactions to the material.
- Guide members to develop a personal action plan based on the material and how they see its influence on them.
- Observe if and how members' behavior changes over the duration of the group.

Getting feedback involves planning, so as to have some process or means in place.

Skills Training Groups

Introduction

Skills training groups focus on providing participants with skills to increase functioning in social environments, such as home and work (Wheelan, 1994). These groups are not always problem or deficit focused; some are enhancing, even within a category. For example, social skills training groups can be problem or deficit focused as with disaffected and difficult children (Howatson, 2005); or enhancing as with friendship building for first graders (Lavallee, Bierman, & Nix, 2005). Skills training can be focused on academics, such as test taking and study skills; or even as part of professional training programs, such as those for mental health professionals. Components that all skills training groups have in common are the theoretical basis that is drawn from one or more behavioral theories, the use of modeling and practice with feedback, and the demonstration of personal connections for group members to make the material personally relevant. This chapter presents a brief overview of some theoretical principles and research findings about efficacy; four types of skills training groups with examples; developing plans for groups around deficits, management, expansion, and enhancing; the use of demonstration and role-play; and practice with feedback.

Theoretical Principles

Behavioral theories begin with the principle that all behavior is learned behavior, but the theories differ among themselves about the process and methods for learning. For example, Skinner (1968) emphasizes types and schedules for reinforcement, Bandura (1977) emphasizes imitation, and Thibaut and Kelley (1959) focus on balance of rewards and costs, interdependence, and social exchange. However, for all such theories the focus is on observable behavior that is systematically established, modified, or extinguished.

Research findings over the years since classical conditioning was established (Pavlov, 1927) support the validity and efficacy of different behavioral techniques for specific target behaviors. These theories do not attend to issues such as family-of-origin experiences; they are intently focused on current behavior that can be changed. This narrow focus, and the use of systematic behavioral interventions that can be replicated by others trained to use them, has resulted in considerable empirical evidence about their applicability and effectiveness. This discussion is only a brief one to introduce you to some concepts and techniques that are used in nonclinical groups. You are encouraged to read the literature for more information and to receive specialized training in their techniques. Some behavioral techniques that can be helpful to use with nonclinical groups include:

- *Relaxation* techniques are used to reduce body tension and to promote receptivity. When someone is tense and anxious, that person can be fearful for a variety of reasons, and this state interferes with the ability to absorb and use information. The technique can be used in a variety of ways—contracting or tensing sets of muscles as directed, and then consciously letting go of the tension; meditating; listening to soft and calming music; and so on.

- *Systematic desensitisation* (Wolpe, 1958) uses the principles of reciprocal inhibition to reduce anxiety, and institute an exposure to progressively larger amounts of the anxiety-inducing stimulus in a step-by-step progression.

- *Shaping* teaches new learning by reinforcing responses that are successive approximations to what is to be learned.

- *Assertiveness training* teaches people to respond in a manner that is neither submissive nor aggressive.

- *Modeling* allows learning of new behavior from observing other people's behavior and its consequences.

Cognitive-behavioral therapy (CBT) uses a combination of cognitive and behavior theoretical principles (Beck, 2000; Meichenbaum, 1977). Cognitive therapy focuses on changes to the client's perceptual system that has negative beliefs, thoughts, and attitudes about himself or herself, and his or her relation to the world. Techniques from cognitive therapy used in conjunction with behavioral theory principles and techniques include the following:

- Socratic questioning to determine the accuracy and utility of the person's ideas

- Activity scheduling where the person plans weekly for pleasurable activities, tasks, socializing, exercise, or previously avoided activities

- Behavioral experiments to directly test the validity of someone's thoughts, assumptions, and the like

- Role-playing, taking several forms—reexperiencing or reenacting an event or situation, taking another perspective, uncovering automatic thoughts, developing rational responses, or modifying core beliefs

Research Findings

A survey of the literature for studies, reviews, and meta-analyses produced numerous studies and considerable evidence for the efficacy of skills training groups. The PubMed database (created by the National Center for Biotechnology Information) alone identified 3,629 citations for such publications. Here are some examples.

- Reduction of disruptive behaviors for boys (Ison, 2003)
- Adult psychiatric populations—a meta-analysis (Corrigan, 1991)
- Severe mental illness (Dilk & Bond, 1996)
- Persistent schizophrenia (Liberman, Wallace, Blackwell, Eckman, et al., 1998)
- Adolescents and young adults with diabetes (Boland et al., 2001)
- Chronic pain (Keefe, Beaupre, & Gil, 2002)
- Reduction of aggression in adults with brain injuries (O'Leary, 2000)
- Cancer patients (Cunningham & Tocco, 1989)
- School adjustment (Ousdigian, 2001)
- Adolescents at risk for depression (Phillips, 2005)

The outcomes generally reported from research are positive. Participants, observers, and other measures show an increase in functioning, attitude changes in a positive direction, reduction of negative thoughts and behaviors, and increased self-efficacy.

Four Types of Training Groups

It may be helpful to try and categorize the wide variety of skills training groups for ease of discussion. There are differences in the target audiences, how and what to plan, and expected outcomes that are easier to present and understand if the groups are categorized. Proposed are four types: deficits, managing, expansion, and enhancing.

Deficits Skills Training Groups. *Deficits* skills training groups focus on providing participants knowledge and facility to navigate better in social situations, such as schools and the workplace. One premise behind this type of group is that although these skills were not taught and learned as the person grew and developed, many other people did learn these skills, and repairing the deficit can lead to improvement in other aspects of members' lives. For example, Conway (2005) evaluated social skills training for children and adolescents with learning disabilities and found that the participants' social skills increased significantly as measured by the parent, dorm parent, advisor, and self-report. In addition, total problem behaviors decreased over time. Weitlauf, Smith, and Cervone (2000) found that self-defense training to help women experience less fear in everyday situations led to improvements in their perception of self-efficacy, decreases in hostility and aggression, and other self-reported personality changes. The final example is Corrigan's (1991) meta-analysis of 73 studies about social skills training for four adult psychiatric populations—developmentally disabled, psychotic, nonpsychotic, and legal offenders. Participants increased their social skills, had reduced psychiatric symptoms related to social dysfunction, and these outcomes persisted for several months after treatment.

The most frequently cited group training in this category is social skills training. Also included in this category are groups focused on problem solving, decision making, test taking, time management, and study skills. The emphasis for these skills training groups is on teaching for development of something thought to be missing.

Managing Skills Training Groups. The *managing* category refers to teaching and learning skills to cope with a condition, illness, or disturbance that can be new, chronic, or acute. Knowledge about the situation, research findings on what the person can do or not do that would be helpful, and strategies to reduce anxiety and stress are central to this type of group. Examples include the following:

- Coping skills training for cancer patients reported greater improvements in depression and anxiety than the discussion group only treatment (Cunningham & Tocco, 1989).
- Managing Type 1 diabetes training for youths 8 to 12 years of age with the disease resulted in less anxiety and stress for the participants, higher measured self-efficacy, and better metabolic control (Grey et al., 2003).
- Treatment for cocaine abuse with coping skills training reduced cocaine abuse during a 3-month follow-up (Rohsenow et al., 2001).

- Pain coping skills for children with sickle-cell disease were successful in reducing pain and negative thinking (Grus, 2001).

Expansion Skill Training Groups. *Expansion* skills training refers to training programs that involve skills development focused on professional interactions. These are usually associated with careers and jobs where abilities are already present for the participants, and skills training enhances these. Examples for this category include:

- Retail alcohol bar and restaurant workers' training program on responsible service practices (Gehan, Toomey, & Jones-Webb, 1999)
- Management of violent situations (Jauregui, 2004)
- Here-and-now training groups for prospective counselors (Bernstein, 1999)
- Intercultural training (Fowler, 2006)
- Teacher training in life skills training (Schechtman, Levy, & Leichtentritt, 2005)
- Critical appraisal skills for clinicians (Taylor, Reeves, et al., 2000)

Enhancing Skill Training Groups. The *enhancing* skills development category is similar in some ways to the expansion category, but is more focused on remediation in addition to building on strengths. The skills in this category are establishing and maintaining satisfying relationships, and developing effective communication skills. Examples include the following:

- Communication skills training for alcoholics and their families (Monti et al., 1990)
- Communication skills training in oncology (Baile et al., 1998)
- Conflict resolution skills for persons who are mentally ill (Douglas & Mueser, 1990)
- Nonassertive undergraduates and conflict resolution skills (McFall & Lillesand, 1997)
- Friendship development for first graders (Lavallee et al., 2005)
- Reducing shyness (Booth, 1990)
- Communication and relationship skills training for group counselors (Toth, Stockton, & Erwin, 1998)

General Guidelines for Skills Training Groups

The next discussion presents general guidelines for planning and facilitating these skills development groups. The framework used is derived from behavioral and cognitive-behavioral theories. The behavioral modeling process (Bednar, Corey, Evans, Gazda, 1987; Trimble, Nathan, & Decker, 1990) that calls for (1) theoretical instruction, (2) leader modeling, (3) demonstration using simulation, (4) personally relevant interactions, and (5) transfer of training also plays a part in what is presented. Embedded in these are spacing of practice (Holladay & Quinones, 2003) and use of incorrect and correct models (Balwin, 1997). Fundamental to any approach used is establishing the therapeutic or working relationship.

Planning for Deficits Groups. Planning groups that fall in the *deficits* category follow the general guidelines for planning presented in Chapter 6, with a few additions.

- Groups should be homogeneous around the topic or condition.
- Deficits should be similar in nature, but because modeling or imitative behavior is an important component, some variation is permissible.
- Leaders must be extra careful to not appear blaming or critical.
- Leaders need to select the most important skills to develop, and keep them few in number and as simple as possible. Complex skills take more time to develop.
- Exercises and other activities must emphasize universality while, at the same time, demonstrate individual personal connections to the material.
- Behavioral indicators must be used for assessment of progress and achievement of skills.

Whatever the focus for the group, the membership should have the same condition. It is too complex an undertaking to try to remediate or develop several different sets of skills, and the group members can become bored or impatient when they do not perceive the information and other activities as relevant to their situation.

All group members need not have exactly the same deficit, but it is easier for the group leader to manage the skills training if the deficits are in the same category. For example, in a group of underachieving adolescent males, all need not be unmotivated. Some could have poor attention skills, some poor note-taking skills, and others poor time management skills. All of these deficits contribute to underachieving, but are not the same. This situation would be an opportunity to capitalize on members' strengths while working to increase their academic performance. For example, those members who do not have poor attention skills could describe how they stay focused, and what they do to interrupt mind-wandering. This could be modeling for the members who do find it difficult to stay focused and pay attention. The leader would then have introduced the therapeutic factors of altruism, hope, and imitative behavior.

It is extremely important that group leaders not do or say anything that blames members for having the deficiency, or that is critical of their efforts to develop the skills. Doing so can increase defensiveness and resistance, and allow guilt and shame to emerge. All of these feelings can be difficult to overcome. A better approach is to be accepting of members as they are, demonstrate confidence that they can learn and change, encourage and support even the smallest attempt and gain, and build a relationship with group members that can be a motivating factor for working to develop the skills. This does not mean that the group leader should overcompliment or flatter members. Rather, the leader needs to be genuine in encouragement and support, recognize efforts expended by group members, point out progress that maybe they don't see, understand what difficulties or constraints they may encounter, and empathize with them.

The leader's expertise is critical in selecting skills to develop, as it can be easy and tempting to be too global or complex. Select the most needed skills as a focus, keep the number of skills to a minimum, and keep the skills simple. For example, in a group of young adults in a college setting who self-identify as shy, the group leader might be tempted to have members make contact with someone outside the group, speak to a stranger, or start a conversation with an instructor. These are all worthwhile activities, but may be too complex or overwhelming for a shy person. It would be more helpful to begin the skills development in the group, explore reactions that members have experienced in social situations, model and teach members the elements of establishing contact, have demonstrations and behavioral rehearsals for desired experimental behaviors, and so on before encouraging members to try the behaviors outside the groups. After all, the group is the safest and easiest place members could begin to address their shyness and gain confidence. Skills training for this group could begin with nonverbal attending behaviors, such as making eye contact and orienting the body to the speaker, and with communication, such as speaking directly to one another.

Group members will need to feel that they have a personal connection to the material presented in the group. If they don't have this personal connection, then they are apt to tune out and resist in other ways. This is only one reason why it is important to have collaborative goal setting, to help members set personal goals, and to carefully select information, exercises, and other activities. Group leaders can help members recognize their personal connections by linking current and previous self-disclosures, pointing out universality, and by directly asking members to explore what personal connections they may have.

Progress and assessment of progress and gains can be facilitated when behavioral indicators are established during planning. These should be connected to the objectives, and should be observable or measurable. Some example objectives for the shyness group are listed, along with the behavioral indicators.

Objective	Behavioral Indicator
Maintain eye contact	Increased sustained eye contact when talking to the group leader and group members
Initiate verbal contact	Entering the room and greeting each person by name
Increase verbal responsiveness	Increased number of direct responses to the leader, or other members without prompting

Behavioral indicators can demonstrate progress and gains that provide encouragement and are motivators, especially when these changes receive positive reactions and feedback.

Planning for Managing Groups. Self-managing or coping skills training groups are intended to teach participants strategies that will assist them in adapting to a significant change in their lives, such as an illness, condition, or disease. The professional literature has many studies on the efficacy of teaching how to manage symptoms; prevent relapse or an escalation of the disease, illness, or condition; and other such ways by which the person can help himself or herself.

Examples topics in the literature include the following:

- Brain injury (O'Leary, 2000; Singer, Glang, & Nixon, 1994)
- Chronic pain (Keefe et al., 2002; Snijiders et al., 1999)
- Children's aggression (Prinz, Blechman, & Dumas, 1994)
- Stress (Pincus & Friedman, 2004)
- Cancer (Cunningham & Tocco, 1989)
- Cocaine abuse (Rohsenow et al., 2001)

- Diabetes (Grey, Bolard, Davidson, & Tamborlane, 1999; Skilling et. al., 2003)
- Chronic illness adjustment (Bombardier, D'Amico, & Jordan, 1990)
- Methadone patients (Avants, Margolin, Kosten, Rounsaville, & Schottenfeld, 1998)
- Obesity (Grey et al., 2003)
- Adolescents (Boland & Davidson, 2001; Frydenberg et al., 2004; McGillicuddy, Rychtarik, Duquette, & Morsheimer, 2001)
- Alcoholism (Tapert, Ozyurt, Myers, & Brown, 2004; Monti & Rohsenow, 1999); spouses (Hansson, Zetterlind, Aberg-Orbeck, & Berglund, 2004; Rychtarik & McGillicuddy, 2005; Zetterlind, Hansson, Aberg-Orbeck, & Berglund, 2001)
- Sickle-cell disease (Gill et al., 2000; Grus, 2001)
- Physician stress (Scott, 1989)

Some managing skills groups can also be found in the chapter on psychoeducational groups. Some overlap can occur for these two types of groups, but this discussion will focus on the education for managing a disease, illness, or condition.

Group leaders can expect homogeneous membership around the topic, and in some cases there can be age and gender homogeneity. These groups can be very brief, 1 to 2 hours, or longer over several weeks. Group members may be depressed, despairing, in shock, angry, or experiencing other intense negative emotions. Thus, group leaders need to be emotionally prepared to encounter resistance, defiance, and displacement of anxiety and anger, which is usually displaced on the leader. Although the group's main purpose is not focused on emotions, it would be very unusual to have a managing group whose members did not have some intense emotions.

Planning for these groups involves a lot of consultation and research because many group leaders will not have experienced the illness, condition, or disease. Further, cultural differences can play an important role in planning for what information to present. The leader must recognize that the Western medical model is not the only model and that some group members may have a different model or perspective. Accurate information and an openness to understanding alternative perspectives are critical.

Central to the goal(s) for these groups is selecting useful and valid information that can be absorbed and understood in the time available for the group. There is always more information that could be helpful, but group leaders need to pare it down to the minimum, and to take into account group members' emotional states that may constrain how much can be absorbed and understood. This is where consulting with an expert and the professional literature is helpful. The following reflective questions can be guides for selecting information.

- What basic, fundamental, or essential information do group members need to know?
- What coping or self-management strategies have been found to be helpful for this condition, illness, or disease, or for the target audience?
- How can other perspectives be incorporated if they emerge?
- How can group members be empowered to self-manage?
- What techniques would be most useful?
- How can the group leader be prepared to manage intense and negative emotions without losing the educational focus?

Let's apply these questions to an example group of adults recently diagnosed with hypertension. The group is primarily male, from all socioeconomic levels; age levels vary from young adult to middle age; and members are from three ethnic/racial groups.

1. Basic information includes genetic, personal, and environmental factors that lead to hypertension; the long-term effects such as cardiac and vascular disease; medication, side effects, and possible interactions with other medications and food; the roles of nutrition and exercise in moderating hypertension; and needed lifestyle changes.

2. Coping and self-management strategies found to be effective include daily medication; medical monitoring; reduction of fat and calories; increased consumption of fruits and vegetables and decreased consumption of fats and meats; reduction of stress-related activities and increased relaxation; weight reduction; and regular exercise. All of these strategies require individual initiatives.

3. Incorporation of other perspectives, such as the condition being "fate," would necessitate open discussion that accepted the perspective as valid for the person, but also presented alternatives, such as steps the person could take to moderate what cannot be eliminated. Yes, fate may have predisposed developing hypertension—for example, genetics—and that has to be accepted, but the person can take action that will arrest future negative effects.

4. Empowering group members to engage in self-management strategies could involve asking members to commit to one or two lifestyle changes. An exercise could be conducted similar to this one.

   • Participants are presented with a list of change strategies to rate from 1—not at all doable, to 10—very doable.

   • The ratings are discussed in the debriefing period.

   • Group members report how they might or could change.

   • Members are asked to commit to one to two changes that are of high priority for them.

   • Weekly reports are made to the group on progress, constraints, and so on.

   Another strategy could be to have members prioritize changes, such as medication as number 1, exercise as number 2, and so on. Discussion of the various members' priorities would follow using that information to develop individual action plans.

5. Techniques that may be useful for this group include teaching relaxation techniques; developing cognitive self-affirmations as encouragement and support; using members' positive experiences with change as models; and role-playing getting started on lifestyle changes. Developing specific and individual action plans that prioritize actions, identify constraints and barriers, and that have behavioral indicators for progress would also be helpful.

6. Dealing with the possible triggered emotions would include:

   • Recognition that some members will have negative or intense feelings about developing hypertension, and focusing their existence from the beginning of the group, but not exploring these in depth.

   • Teaching stress reduction by helping members realize that they choose their feelings, and that these are not caused by others' actions or attitudes.

- Helping members learn how to take responsibility for their personal feelings and psychological well-being.

Planning for Expansion Groups. These skills training groups are usually focused on expanding a set of already existing skills in an effort to refine and enrich these. Members may already have some skills, but there is always room for improvement and increased awareness. Groups are likely to be homogeneous around the topic, but may be heterogeneous in other ways, such as gender and ethnic/racial group. These expansion groups tend to have fewer members than some other skills training groups, although some groups may have 15 to 20 participants. Some expansion groups are also likely to be longer term than other nonclinical groups, which will provide more time for practice of skills with feedback. Also, it can be feasible to have practice and other activities outside the group that provide additional opportunities for skills development. Examples of some expansion groups were provided earlier in the chapter.

Planning for most expansion groups is complex, but principles used for other skills groups also apply—for example, identifying essential skills for the focus and goal. Building on existing skills and competencies can be complicated when the level is not known before the group begins, and they are likely to vary among group members. Group leaders must thoroughly understand what skills need to be developed to plan the sequence of steps and actions needed to achieve competency, to be able to describe how competency is recognized or assessed, and to be flexible and adjust to the various needs and levels of skills development among group members. A high level of competency is recommended for the group leader who will be the primary model by which group members learn. A sample process follows.

1. Reflect on possible preexisting skills members may possess, and consult with professionals who have experience with the topic and other such resources.

2. Consult the professional literature for teaching models, research on skills development relevant for the topic, and efficacy or outcomes.

3. Secure a book, program, or other such source that can be used as a guide for sequencing information dissemination, skills training, and assessment. All of these can be guides that are modified to meet the group's needs.

4. Develop preliminary goals and objectives. These, too, can be modified if needed.

5. Decide on a sequence for skills development, one that builds on preceding knowledge and expertise. Tentatively decide on the amount of time needed for each skill, and for each step leading to the skill.

6. Specify how progress and skills development will be assessed.

7. Select techniques. Expansion skills development can make considerable use of demonstrations, simulations, and role-play.

8. Provide safeguards for participants that do not require personal disclosures other than reporting on their here-and-now experiencing. The safeguards can be in the form of a general statement about expectations for disclosures, such as telling participants that they are in charge of decisions about what and how to disclose, but that they are expected to be able to report on current experiencing. Other safeguards can be the choices for demonstrations, exercises, and other activities that do not require extensive personal disclosures.

9. Develop a logical rationale for skills development such as to prevent problems, to increase sensitivity and understanding, to provide better services, and the like. These are general guidelines that can be adapted for the topic, target audience, and available time. Each group will have different needs, and those should be considered.

Here is a suggested general procedure for expansion groups.

- Introduce and overview the topic and activities.
- Specify goals and objectives, inviting additions, alternatives, thoughts, and ideas.
- Describe the theoretical background and rationale for skills training. This will answer the questions about the need for training, expected personal and career gains, and why the particular techniques are being used.
- Show or give examples that illustrate lack of skills. A film or video can be used.
- List the steps in the process for skills development and how progress can be assessed. Describe the techniques to be used, ask for responses, and make a statement about personal disclosure.
- Introduce the first skill or set of skills by fully describing what is to be done, how it can be observed, and what feedback is helpful.
- Demonstrate the skill that is being developed through a demonstration, simulation, or exercise
- Set up practice sessions that can be observed, and where each member has an opportunity to try the skill. If other group members are the observers, give them a form that lists the behaviors, a procedure for describing their observations, and space for other written comments. The group leader should rotate among the groups observing the sessions.
- Tape practice sessions for later playback for personal observation, and for feedback from other group members and the leader. If practice outside the group is part of the plan, it should be described, and reported on in the next group session.
- Once the initial set of skills, or the target skill, is mastered, introduce the next set or the next skill and follow the same procedure as outlined.
- If the members are experiencing difficulty in mastering the skill, the leader needs to examine the process or procedure. It may be too complex, or advanced. Modifications are needed at this point.

Feedback is extremely important, and the group leader has to manage this carefully to avoid appearing critical or blaming. Many people have negative reactions when told that they are doing something wrong, or that their performance is inadequate. These people do not hear feedback as an observation, they hear it as an attack on the self, can become hurt at the thought of being wrong or inadequate, become defensive or defiant, and not participate as willingly or fully. An additional concern can emerge if group members are also giving feedback because they may not know how to make their feedback constructive. The following steps for providing constructive feedback can be used, and could be taught to group members.

1. Begin with a positive comment about the member's performance. This can be an observed strength, an overlooked or minimized action, and so on.

2. Focus first on what was done well in terms of the skills development practice. This focus can help other members see a model for the desired skill.

3. Identify behaviors and how these can be modified or changed. Say something like, "It can be more effective to do _____," or "You may find it helpful to _____."

4. Do not use language that says or suggests fixed traits, something the person cannot change. Refrain from words that suggest right, wrong, good, or bad. Use words such as *better, more effective*, and so on.

5. Check to see if the feedback was understood as it was intended. It can be easy for a receiver to misunderstand or distort a message, especially if the receiver fears shame, blame, or guilt for not being "right" or for making an error.

6. Stay in touch with the impact of the feedback on the receiver, and stop if you observe withdrawal, increased emotional intensity, defensiveness, and so on. Effective feedback has to be received, and these states work against accurate reception.

7. Give suggestions for modifications, different approaches, other techniques, and the like that could improve skills.

It can also be helpful to have a process in place, such as the following, that the leader can use when a group member falters, goes in the wrong direction, becomes paralyzed, withdraws, or uses inappropriate disclosure or behavior. Begin by asking the group member what he or she was experiencing at the point where he or she faltered, and so on. Try to get the person to express the thoughts, feelings, and ideas at that particular time. The answers often provide clues to what triggered the off response. Examples of such triggers include the following:

- An inappropriate self-absorbed focus with too much concern about not making a mistake and the like
- Fear of offending or injuring another person, or of making a situation worse
- Lack of knowledge
- Anticipating the future instead of staying in the present
- Jumping to conclusions before having enough information
- Mind-wandering, zoning out, and other lack of attention behavior

Once the leader has some notion of what was taking place for the person at that time, it becomes easier for him or her to avoid these actions in the future.

Planning for Enhancement Groups. Personal and professional growth and development demand relationship and communication skills. Everyone grows up relating and communicating, but some people's skills are ineffective, whereas others need to learn professional and job-related skills. For example, mental health professionals need to learn how to establish a therapeutic relationship, which differs from the usual social relationship. Although many of the topics and skills for this category overlap with the social skills training in the deficit category, they can be developed and applied differently than for remediating deficits. Examples for this category include medical personnel enhancing their skills at delivering bad news, mental health professionals developing therapeutic relationships and other clinical skills, teachers delivering life skills training, and undertakers dealing with people who are grieving. Skills in everyday relationships and interactions are applied differently in the workplace.

Enhancement groups are likely to have several characteristics.

- Members are likely to be young adults or adults, and are usually verbally fluent.
- Groups will be homogeneous around the training program or career.
- Modeling can be more easily facilitated by the leader, and by some group members.
- Personal self-disclosure is not a requirement.
- Homework or outside practice can be used
- Resistance is usually reduced, but not eliminated.

Planning for enhancement skills groups is similar to that for most other skills training groups, but these groups tend to be more like a class than other groups. Leaders can present more material, use outside readings and homework, and have more formal evaluation procedures. Remember that the learned skills are to be used for the benefit of the general population, and not for the individual attending the group. This is an important difference.

Additional complications for skills training groups come with the unknown future group members that the present group members will face. The present skills training group leader needs to make them aware that these future group members will have numerous concerns in addition to the expected ones. This skills training should prepare them to expect and manage members who have the following characteristics:

- Intense and maybe overwhelming emotions and anxiety
- Considerable involvement with family members external to the group who have multiple relationships and complex dynamics
- Immediate and acute needs
- Apprehension, fear, and concern about other group members who are strangers

The group leaders' challenge is to prepare their group members to effectively manage and cope with their group members.

The group leader should model the relationship attributes and communication skills that are being taught as part of enhancement skills groups. Modeling demands that the leader have relational attributes such as genuineness, warmth, and acceptance; and communication skills such as attending, listening, and responding directly as part of their developed self. It is important that group members observe these and their effectiveness as an integral part of the group leader, and not as a set of behaviors adopted just for the group sessions.

Planning enhancement groups is almost like planning a class. The steps are similar to those for expansion groups, but can cover more material. It is also important to know how much time is available, the educational levels for participants, the number of participants, and expected outcomes for the training. These factors all guide the planning process for a particular group. An example follows for a group of 20- to 25-year-old undergraduate human services majors at a university. The group will hold 2-hour sessions twice a week for 8 weeks, and is a requirement for the program.

1. **Set assumptions and preconditions.**   As human services majors at a university, members can be expected to be motivated, verbally fluent, have some level of personal development, and have a moderate social support system at a minimum.

2. **Determine goals and objectives.**   The primary goal for the group is to build therapeutic relating skills, with objectives that focus on specific competencies such as:

   - Attending behaviors
   - Development of personal qualities that promote a therapeutic relationship, and how these are conveyed to others
   - Emotional presence and its importance
   - Environment of safety and trust
   - Awareness of transference (countertransference) and projections
   - Barriers and constraints to developing relationships
   - Cultural and diversity concerns
   - Reduction of self-absorption

3. **Select strategies and techniques.**   There will be three primary strategies; lecture and discussion, exercise-demonstration, and homework-reporting. The lectures will present basic information about the topic to include theory, research findings, and examples for incorrect and correct skills. Exercises and demonstrations will focus on increasing awareness of behavior and feelings that emerge in response to the behavior, and on more effective ways of relating. Homework-reporting will provide additional opportunities for practice and reflection.

4. **Plan the sessions.**   Decide the sequence for presenting the topics, locate materials, and prepare the syllabus and other materials.

An example application for the described group follows, beginning with the syllabus.

Syllabus.   This is an outline for the information and skills to be learned, the required activities such as readings, the techniques and strategies to be used, a schedule for readings and other assignments, expectations of students, and assessment. A sample syllabus is at the end of the chapter.

Instructional Plan.   Develop a session-by-session instructional plan that includes all activities for that session with expected time needed for each activity. The first session for the sample group is illustrated.

Greetings, introductions, overview of group	15 minutes
Collaborative goal-setting activity: Each member writes 2–3 goals on a 3 × 5-inch card.	20 minutes
These are reported in the group and written on posted newsprint. The leader identifies similarities among members' goals, leads a discussion on the purpose and goals for the group, and the leader and members identify the major goals that incorporate most individual goals.	

Mini-lecture. The importance of establishing the therapeutic   20 minutes
relationship, and the components. Includes discussion, questions,
and comments.

Exercise. Self-ratings of relationships and relationship skills.   45 minutes
Includes debriefing and discussion.

Summary and Homework Assignment. The homework is an essay   20 minutes
description of members' different personal relationships, such as
parental, sibling, extended family, friend, lover, workplace peer,
supervisor, and so on.

The other 17 sessions are planned along the lines of the first session.

Practice and Feedback.   Videotaping facilities and equipment are available. Group
members are divided into groups of three members—a client, an interviewer, and an
observer. They tape three practice sessions each group meeting, switching roles so that each
group member plays each role. They each make a 15-minute tape focusing on a specific
relationship skill, or a group of skills. Portions of tapes are played in the large group where
observers, the leader, and other group members will provide feedback. There are a
minimum of eight practice sessions.

Other Exercises.   The other sessions have significant components for personal
development. Exercises, homework, and other activities focus on elements of relationship
building that members need to strengthen.

Assessment.   Evaluation of progress by reviewing the first, fourth, and eighth tapes
provides information about improvement and gains. Self-reports by group members are
also used.

Summary

1. Educational groups have a strong cognitive thrust, and attention to the level of learning
   for participants is critical. Information dissemination must be geared to the target
   audience's abilities, but this important information may not be known in advance of
   planning the group.

2. Group leaders must select the kind and amount of information that participants can use,
   not the kind and amount the leader thinks they should know. It is also helpful for the
   leader to use a variety of instructional modes to convey information.

3. Educational groups are categorized as learning groups, prevention groups, guidance or
   developmental groups, and related groups.

4. Skills training groups generally use a format that incorporates presentation or
   demonstration of the skill to be learned, practice with feedback, and evaluation.

5. Categories for skills training groups are deficits, managing, expansion, and enhancing.
   The target audience's level of skills development can play a major role in deciding the
   category for a particular group.

Chapter Activity

1. Prepare a plan for an educational or skills training group for adults on the topic of your choice. The plan must include the following elements:

   - Description and literature review of the proposed topic (your choice of topic)
   - Identification and description of the proposed target audience
   - Goals and objectives
   - An outline of each session to include goals and objectives of the session, proposed strategies, and schedule for activities
   - One or more mini-lectures
   - A copy of all proposed forms, scales, tests, and the like
   - A full description of all activities, such as exercises, to include expansion questions
   - An assessment plan

Enhancement Group Sample Syllabus

Relationship Building

This group will meet for 2 hours each week for the next 5 weeks.

Goal: Build therapeutic relating attributes

Objectives

1. To understand the value and importance of therapeutic relational attributes
2. Become aware of the personal level of development that is influential in building relational attributes needed for therapeutic purposes
3. Identify personal sources of transference and projections
4. Increase awareness and understanding of self-absorbed behaviors and attitudes.

Techniques and Strategies

A variety of techniques and strategies will be used: assigned readings, homework, group activities and exercises, and mini-lectures and discussion. Your personal reactions are an integral part of these sessions, and you are encouraged to openly express your thoughts, ideas, and feelings. However, you are in charge of your self-disclosure and can choose when, how, or if to disclose. Group members are asked to keep confidential all personal material disclosed during sessions.

Participant Tasks

1. Attend each session on time
2. Complete assigned readings according to the schedule

3. Participate in group activities

4. Write personal reactions to exercises and other activities, and submit these to the group leader each week

Session Reading Schedule

1. Read the assignment prior to the designated session. No reading for sessions 1 and 10.

2. The importance of interpersonal skills

3. Developing trust

4. Communication skills

5. Express feelings verbally

6. Nonverbal communication

7. Listening and responding

8. Managing difficult feelings

9. Cultural differences

10. Ethics

Chapter 11

Psychoeducational and Task Groups

Major Topics

1. Definition and descriptions for various types of psychoeducational groups.
2. The importance of therapeutic factors and leader strategies to foster these.
3. Descriptions, examples, and specific strategies for primary leader tasks.
4. Descriptions for task groups—teams, work groups, committees, and task forces.
5. Definitions for effective teams and teamwork, constructive and counterproductive leader attitudes and behavior, and effective and counterproductive teams.
6. Team-building strategies.
7. Definitions for work groups, committees, and task forces.
8. Facilitating productive meetings.

Introduction

Psychoeducational groups are a blend of educational and counseling groups that combine cognitive and affective materials and foci. Elliott, Rivera, and Tucker (2004) note that these groups "address psychological content" (p. 342), and that group leaders need to be sensitive to the impact of this content on group members. Psychoeducational groups are conducted for all age groups, in a variety of settings, and address a wide range of topics.

Categories of Psychoeducational Groups

Brown (2005) proposes a classification for psychoeducational groups that has four categories, with two or three subcategories for each. The primary categories are as follows:

- Personal development—prevention, development, improving interpersonal relating and communications, and remediation

- Support and therapy-related—medical illness and disease, psychological/emotional distur-bances, and recovery
- Life transitions—general and specific
- Families and caretakers—medical illness and disease; psychiatric, psychological and emotional disturbances, and recovery

Examples of subcategory groups are:

- Prevention—violence (Fleckenstein & Horne, 2004)
- Development—self-esteem (Klose & Tinius, 1992)
- Improving interpersonal relating and communication (Cornish & Benton, 2001)
- Remediation (Browne, 1993)
- Medical illness and disease (Devine, 1996; Taylor etal., 2003)
- Psychiatric, psychological, and emotional disturbances (Honey, Bennett, & Morgan, 2002; Pekkala & Merinder, 2002)
- Recovery (Sandahl & Ronnbers, 1990)
- General life transitions—academic success (Halstead, 1998)
- Specific life transitions—grief (Piper, McCallum, Joyce, Rosie, Ogrodniczuk, 2001)
- Families and caretakers (Brown, 2005)
- Recovery (McFarlane, Lukens, et. al., 1995)

Advantages

There are many advantages of psychoeducational groups including specific time boundaries, a safe environment, dissemination of information, promotion of connectedness, alleviation of blame or stigma, correction of misinformation, strategies to better cope and manage, discus-sion of difficult topics, and so on. The expansion of the number and kind of psychoeduca-tional groups in the past few years supports the perception of their efficacy.

There are usually specific *time boundaries* ranging from a 1-hour one-session group, to groups with multiple sessions over a several-month period. However, these groups do have a specific beginning and ending date, and are usually brief.

Psychoeducational groups provide a *safe environment* where uncomfortable and distress-ing feelings can be expressed openly. Some group members may not want to express these with family for fear of causing them more distress, and others need coaching to express themselves. The group becomes a safe place for talking about feelings, thoughts, and ideas that cannot be expressed in other settings.

Dissemination of information is important for psychoeducational groups as it is for other nonclinical groups, and the value of accurate and relevant information should not be underes-timated. Because many of these groups are formed around specific conditions, illnesses, and disturbances where the leader may not have sufficient knowledge and expertise, it can be help-ful to bring in outside experts who do have the knowledge and expertise.

Reduction of feelings of isolation or alienation can be important for the physical and psy-chological well-being of group members, and these groups can help *promote feelings of connectedness.*

Caring, concern, genuineness, and warmth are core conditions that promote feelings of acceptance, positive regard, and respect. These states can be very supportive to members who are experiencing trying times and situations.

An important psychological component for these groups and their members is *alleviation of blame or stigma*. Members can blame themselves or others for what happened to them, and have considerable shame, anger, resentment, and other such distressing emotions because of personal failings such as smoking, fate, the unfairness of the universe or a deity, failure to get an accurate diagnosis or correct treatment, and because of other people's actions such as causing an accident. In addition, some illnesses, diseases, and conditions are perceived as stigmatizing and can cause shame. There can also be deep denial because of the stigma and shame. Group leaders must stay aware of the possibilities of blame and stigma, and be prepared to deal with them as they arise in the group.

In spite of the large number of resources, written information, and experts available, group members may come to group with misinformation. The group can be an excellent setting for *correcting this misinformation* and ignorance about policies, procedures, medication, the antecedents for the condition, expected outcomes, processes, and other associated states. Interactions within the group can bring out some of these misconceptions as members think about their personal situations. Some may be known in advance so that the group leader can plan to address them as part of the dissemination of information.

The group is a place where members can be taught and can learn *coping strategies* to better manage their condition or other states such as relationship problems, increase the quality of their lives, and feel less victimized because of the empowering nature of coping. The chapter on skills development presents information that can be helpful for teaching coping strategies.

Some members may not have anywhere outside of the group where *difficult topics* can be openly discussed. Topics such as the terminal outlook for the condition or other states; anger at self and others; resentment, envy, and jealousy that others are not also suffering; fear of the uncertain and the unknown; and other such distressing topics can be discussed, and feelings expressed and shared in the group. They can be carefully and respectfully considered, acknowledged, and accepted as valid concerns, their universality revealed, and catharsis promoted.

Disadvantages

There are also some disadvantages of psychoeducational groups. However, the advantages outweigh the disadvantages. Examples of disadvantages include the following:

- Time constraints do not permit exploration of many relevant and important topics.
- The root causes for some conditions, disturbances, or illnesses cannot be discovered, such as family-of-origin issues.
- The leader can lack in-depth knowledge about the group's primary concern, such as a chronic illness.
- Members can be so caught up in their individual misery that connections and cohesion do not have time to develop or emerge.
- The lack or inability to screen group members can lead to inappropriate placement of some members.

Personal Development Groups

Personal development groups are not usually formed to address a crisis, either individually or as a group. Whereas group members can have a common concern, there is not usually an identifiable problem to be solved. Members can be at risk, show signs that point to a possible deficit, seem to need improvement, or have other such concerns. These groups help members develop inner resources to better cope with life and possible adversity.

Personal development groups can take many forms and have a variety of foci, but they usually emphasize members' inner resources, such as resilience, hardiness, and strength building. Information is provided about the topic, so that group members have the awareness and understanding needed to cope with situations that can and do arise. Typically members are not in crisis, or even in a problem-producing situation, but some of these can be anticipated at some point in their lives based on past events. Coyne and Horne (2001) report that there is documentation of the effectiveness of personal development groups for the following conditions and audiences:

- Psychological conditions such as stress
- Interpersonal relationships
- Social and occupational roles such as parenting
- Physical disorders and illnesses, such as cardiovascular disease
- Children, adolescents, and adults

Developmental groups are defined as focusing on inner strength building and development of the self. They deal with abstract concepts that are universal—concepts that positively affect the physical, psychological, and spiritual well-being of all people. Through strength building these competencies and abilities can be enhanced and enriched. Examples include developing social competence, self-identity, sexual identity, and self and emotional regulation; achieving independence and autonomy; and developing self-esteem, self-confidence, and self-efficacy.

The *improving interpersonal relating and effectiveness* subcategory is similar to the groups discussed in the chapter on skills development. These groups differ in two primary ways: There is less emphasis on practicing skills, and there is a stronger self-understanding component. The latter addresses the emotions and barriers to self-awareness and self-understanding, and tries to build a foundation for continued personal growth and development.

Personal development *remediation* groups address a wide variety of topics and conditions. The premises behind these groups are that the participants did not receive the knowledge, awareness, understanding, and skills needed for constructive and appropriate behavior, relationship building, and maintenance, or sufficient self-regulation. They committed acts that are unacceptable, illegal, and self-defeating. Examples of personal development groups are anger management, spouse or child abuse, addictions or substance abuse, and sexually violent acts such as assault and rape.

Support and Therapy-Related Psychoeducational Groups

Brown (2005) presents an overview of the multiplicity of support and therapy groups divided into three categories: medical illness; psychiatric, psychological, and emotional disturbances; and recovery. These are termed support and therapy related because they are defined as such in the literature. These groups are usually defined as a major part of treatment for a condition, disease, illness, disturbance, and so on, but there are other parts or phases in the treatment plans.

Whatever the topic for the particular support or therapy group is, the group leader can expect to encounter strong emotional reactions that may be open, hidden or suppressed, or denied. The emotional component becomes prominent, and there is the possibility that the cognitive component will become minimized. That should be avoided because a major goal is to educate group members about the condition, illness, and so forth.

Some topics that can be expected and helpful for these groups include self-management of symptoms; adapting to changes in functioning, lifestyle, and relationships; possible impairment of physical, psychological, and mental well-being; forestalling the deterioration of the quality of life, acquiring adequate insurance and personal funds; and moderating the effects of medications. Empowering and encouraging members to be as proactive as possible can assist in recovery and healing.

Leaders can expect existential factors to also be an important part of support and therapy-related psychoeducational groups. They should be prepared to lead discussions on topics such as death, and the unfairness and indifference of the universe to their pain and suffering, and to deal with these as they emerge in the group. These factors are the "elephant under the rug in the middle of the room," especially if the members do not mention them. There can be considerable unspoken fear shared in common by group members around existential factors.

Group members usually have

- A common condition, illness, and so on
- Intense and uncomfortable affect
- The strong desire to "fix it," make it go away, and a denial of its severity
- Fears about the group, the condition, and the future
- Anger about the circumstances that brought them to the group, self, others, and fate
- Shame at not being able to prevent or "fix it," or not being good enough
- Resignation, depression, or despair

In addition, some members will be in physical pain.

Life Transitions Groups

The two categories for life transitions groups are *general*, where the topics refer to expected life situations and events that can have a significant emotional component associated with them, and *specific*, where the situations or events are not universal, but have become rather common in today's society. These can also have strong emotional content. These groups usually have the following purposes and goals:

- Reduce uncertainty and ambiguity about the transition
- Provide a venue for exploring experiences and expression of feelings
- Reduce feelings of alienation and isolation
- Introduce logical and rational thinking instead of concentrating mainly on feelings
- Eliminate blame and criticism of self and of others

- Suggest and implement coping strategies
- Provide accurate and valid information

General life transitions groups include groups formed around expected developmental issues, such as forming intimate relationships and dealing with grief and loss, aging parents, employment and unemployment, retirement, adolescent physical and emotional changes, and other such issues and concerns. The emotional component can be very intense, such as what happens with the topic of unemployment. But many will be more cognitively focused than most other psychoeducational groups.

Specific life transition groups are focused around a particular life transition that is expected, but does not occur for everyone, or for most people. Topics addressed include divorce and children of divorce, and deal with abusive partners, displaced homemakers, racial and cultural identity, independence for people with disabilities, and aging. The members are usually experiencing the effects of the condition and so on, and there can be considerable affect experienced and expressed in these groups. The life transitions can bring back unresolved issues around family-of-origin and other past experiences, unfinished business, and other developmental issues. A challenge can be to keep these groups as psychoeducational, and not let them become counseling or therapy groups because this does not fit with the original goals, and because of time constraints.

Families and Caretakers Groups

Some conditions, illnesses, diseases, and disturbances have shown improvement for their possessors when psychoeducational groups are conducted for their families or caretakers. The affected person does not attend group, but seems to gain from others who do attend. Topics Include:

- Cancer (Bultz, Speca, Brasher, Geggie, & Page, 2000; Landry-Dattee, Gauvain-Piquard, & Cosset-Delaigue, 2000)
- Altzheimer's/disease or dementia (Herbert et.al. 2003; McFarland & Sanders, 2000)
- Eating disorders (Uehaqra, Kawashima, Goto, Tasaki, & Someya, 2001)
- Schizophrenia (Dyck, Hendryx, Short, Voss, & McFarlane, 2002; Vallina-Fernandez, Lemos-Giraldez, Roder, & Gutierrez-Perez, 2001)
- Psychiatric disorders (Cuijpers & Stam, 2000)

In the literature, families and caretakers reported less stress and burnout, and the patients had better compliance with medication and following treatment plans, less relapse, and for some, fewer and shorter hospitalizations.

McFarlane (2002), in his book *Multifamily Group Treatment in Schizophrenia*, describes the effective groups as "those that can make the transitions from biological/pharmacological to psychological and social levels" (p. 117) It's most effective when the group process can assist in changing attitudes, produce a climate and social environment for recovery, instill motivation and hope, and encourage the development of a social network. This applies to other groups for families and caretakers as well.

The cognitive material focuses on helping families and caretakers understand subtle and overt symptoms; the effects of medications; usual ways that families and others are affected; how stress affects the patient and others in his or her world, and also impacts healing or recovery; coping and management strategies; and the prognosis. This understanding is critical to gaining a sense of mastery and empowerment, expectancy, and renewed commitment.

The Importance of Therapeutic Factors

More therapeutic factors have roles in psychoeducational groups than in some other nonclinical groups, and the leader should give some thought and planning as to how they can be fostered and encouraged. In addition, it could be helpful to group members to experience these in a deliberate and constructive way, and not conduct the group with a hope that they would appear. Some specific foci for the therapeutic factors follow.

- Universality—similarities in values, experiences, wishes, and the like
- Hope—realistic expectations, resilience, hardiness, and the role for faith
- Altruism—actions within and outside the group
- Interpersonal learning—report on here-and-now experiencing of thoughts and ideas
- Imitative behavior—appreciation of one another's coping and adapting skills, attempts, and strategies
- Guidance—homework with specific information exchange among members
- Socialization—developing a social support network among group members and with others outside the group
- Catharsis—emotional venting with new personal learning
- Corrective emotional experience—after emotional expression, the leader's responses are reflective, accepting, and empathic
- Existential factors—direct discussions that are leader initiated; acknowledgment of their importance at the present time for members
- Cohesion—this may not have sufficient time to fully develop, but the leader can stay aware of the progress made toward cohesion

The group leader should try to get members to verbalize and become aware of similarities among them around characteristics other than the common condition, issue, disease, disturbance, or concern. There can be a tendency to emphasize this very visible similarity, but members will benefit from discovering other similarities. Leaders may see these not-so-visible similarities before members do and can speak of them to the group. Another strategy is to ask if other members share something that another member speaks about. But, it is important that the leader purposefully seeks out similarities, such as values, experiences, feelings, thoughts, and ideas.

The value of hope cannot be overestimated. Numerous studies have demonstrated that it has a critical role in healing, recovery, and development (Hafen et al., 1996). Members may arrive at the group in a state of shock, unbelieving about the condition or its severity, with the fantasy that it will be "fixed" or will just go away; despairing or depressed, and in a high state of anxiety or denial. The leader's challenge is to help hope emerge that is realistic and inspiring. Keeping the focus on what and how members can help themselves, recognizing when depression needs additional treatment, and informing members of how hope plays an important role in the mind-body-spirit connection can assist hope to emerge.

There are also studies that speak to the value of altruistic acts for increasing the quality of life and promoting a sense of well-being, and as inspiration for the person who takes an altruistic action. Leaders can stay aware of altruistic acts that occur within the group among group members, and comment when they occur. Members also can be encouraged to be altruistic outside the group. Please do not confuse altruism with advice giving, as is done in some professional literature, such as Schwartz and Waldo (1999, p. 581). There is considerable difference between speaking of one's personal experiences or providing suggestions and giving advice that tells the person what he or she must, should, or ought to do.

Considerable interpersonal learning can result when group members are able to verbalize their here-and-now experiencing of one another, and when this is done in a constructive way. This feedback provides the receiver with external validation, enlightenment, new information, and so on, that helps him or her integrate other self-perceptions. Leaders may need to teach some members how to make their feedback specific, nonjudgmental or nonevaluative, focused on behavior that can be changed, and done in a way that gives the receiver the discretion of accepting or not accepting the feedback.

Imitative behavior that is positive, helpful, and inspiring can be therapeutic. The leader is a powerful model, but other members can also model desired behavior. Leaders should recognize these behaviors, and make sure that other members become aware of them.

Although dissemination of information is a major focus for psychoeducational groups, the therapeutic factor can be facilitated in many ways. Members' anxiety, despondency, or even panic can be barriers or constraints to sharing information. Leaders can facilitate member participation by directly asking for input, frequently checking about what information they found to be helpful, and by saying that sharing of information is encouraged. The leader must monitor the information from members to ensure validity and accuracy, and must also be sure to show appreciation for their sharing.

Socialization can be facilitated among members, and for some groups, some socialization skills can be taught in addition to the main purpose for the group. The group setting can be an opportunity to reduce loneliness, alienation, and even isolation through interactions with others who are having similar experiences. The similarity provides a connection at the beginning, but the leader should encourage members to also discover other ways by which members can connect.

Catharsis is much more than simple emotional venting. To truly be of benefit, emotional expression should result in interpersonal insight, awareness, or learning. Because members may arrive at the group carrying intense and uncomfortable feelings, leaders must be prepared to facilitate expression and catharsis. Strategies are to ask other members if they share the feeling, understand what that member is experiencing, report on the leader's experiencing as he or she listens to that member, respond empathically, and help the member explore and understand the multiple emotions that can be experienced, and some not expressed.

Recapitulation of family-of-origin issues and the corrective emotional experience is expected in counseling and therapy groups, but can appear in psychoeducational groups. For example, because transference appears in settings other than counseling or therapy it is almost certain to appear in psychoeducational groups. However, leaders of these groups are not expected to analyze or explore this as would leaders of some clinical groups. What can be helpful is that leaders understand family-of-origin issues, especially how these are manifested in behavior, verbalizations, and attitudes, so that constructive responses are made even when these issues are not analyzed or explored. The leader does not have to do anything to expand on the information, but should be savvy enough to respond appropriately and with sensitivity.

Existential factors around death, freedom, and the indifference of the universe to members' pain, suffering, and existence are an integral part of some psychoeducational groups, and should be anticipated by the leader. For example, a group focusing on a cardiac disease is likely to have several members whose thoughts and feelings trigger existential factors. These concerns should not be ignored or minimized, but should be openly acknowledged as valid, part of the human condition, never sufficiently or completely resolved, expected to reemerge throughout life, and can be valuable to increase personal awareness of one's life.

Leaders need to be especially alert to how religion and religious values are introduced into discussions about existential factors to ensure that their personal values are not imposed on the group, members, and to provide a climate where religious diversity and tolerance are accepted. It is also important that leaders be very clear that existential factors are not religion, although religion and other beliefs can be a part of these factors.

The therapeutic factor of cohesion may not have sufficient time to fully develop where members become more independent and do considerable personal work with one another. However, some level of cohesion is possible where members connect, care, and interact, and therapeutic work is accomplished. Group leaders can capitalize on the cohesion that does exist.

Leader Tasks

Psychoeducational group facilitation requires the same level of planning and other structural concerns as do other nonclinical groups. The difference in leader tasks for these groups is that maintenance and process functions more directly and often address the personal experiencing of group members and their relationships, particularly within the group. They do not have the intensity, depth, or exploration that would be found in counseling and therapy groups, but may have more than in some other nonclinical groups.

Primary leader maintenance and process tasks include the following:

- Reduction of anxiety
- Expressions of emotions
- Relationship building
- Empowerment of members
- Collaborative action planning
- Stress reduction

Reduction of Anxiety

As noted previously, members of many groups categorized as psychoeducational can arrive with considerable anxiety, and group leaders must address this from the very beginning of the group if members are to be in a state where they are able to take in the needed information and to apply this to their personal situations. Leaders can acknowledge that anxiety is likely to be experienced, and ask group members to openly speak about the feelings that they bring to the group, and those that they are experiencing as they sit in the session. An icebreaker exercise can also be helpful, especially a nonthreatening one that focuses on something personally relevant, and not on the reason for attending the group.

Specific Strategies

a. At the first session ask group members to name, label, or otherwise identify the feelings they are bringing to the group; to rate their level of anxiety at the moment; and to determine if other members share the same feelings or level of anxiety. Nothing more needs to be done at the first session.

b. When anxiety is expressed, either verbally or nonverbally, ask the member to focus on it, describe the bodily sensations, what action(s) he or she wants to take, and how hard it is to have to sit with the anxiety. Ask these one at a time, listen to the answer(s), and reflect before moving to the next question.

Expression of Emotions

Expression of emotions can be helpful to group members because the group setting may be the only place where some members find it safe and acceptable to do so. Others may not know how to express their emotions and first need instruction, guidance, and encouragement. Because of the probability of members experiencing intense emotions, the leader must be ready to help with expressions, and to show members how to manage and contain the more unpleasant and intense emotions.

Specific Strategies

a. Exercises can be helpful, such as the following. Give all members one 5×8-inch unlined index card. Tell them to select one color from one or more sets of crayons, felt markers, or colored pencils, and draw a symbol for a particular feeling. Each should choose a feeling that is important for him or her such as anger or fear. Discuss the symbols, colors chosen, and meanings for the group members.

b. If a member is having difficulty expressing a feeling, ask other group members to report on what they are feeling in the moment. Then ask that member if any of the other feelings seem to be similar to his or hers.

Relationship Building

Relationship building in the group can be important for two reasons: to develop an atmosphere of trust and safety, and to encourage members to use a social support system. Some strategies that can foster relationships among members include focusing on similarities; encouraging genuine expressions of thoughts, ideas, feelings, and reactions; directing members to talk directly to one another and give constructive feedback; and acknowledging appreciation, guidance, and altruism among members.

Specific Strategies

a. Continually survey members about similar or shared experiences, feelings, and wishes. Encourage voluntary reporting when something is similar or the same as what another member is reporting or experiencing.

b. Ask members to talk directly to one another, and remind them to do so frequently, especially when one member says something. Tell them that it is helpful when other members respond directly with their thoughts, feelings, and ideas, but not with questions.

Empowerment of Members

It is especially important that members receive empowerment by which they feel that they are not at the mercy or under the control of unseen forces or other people. Some members may feel helpless, hopeless, despairing, and powerless. The group leader's challenge is to reduce these negative feelings because they have been shown to be counterproductive to healing, recovery, and the quality of life. Gently guiding and teaching members to plan, solve problems, gather and use relevant information, ask questions, and participate in personally relevant decision making are some ways to empower group members. Assertiveness training is another option, as is providing encouragement and support for trying new behavior outside the group.

Specific Strategies

a. Role-play assertive versus passive or aggressive behavior for a past or future situation.

b. Ask members to make a list of steps or actions they can take that would be helpful in their situations. Rate each as feasible (5), or unlikely (1), and read them aloud. Then have members select the most feasible step or action to try to implement before the next group meeting, and to report back on the results. Reading these aloud allows members to share ideas.

Collaborative Action Planning

Action planning is carried out much like consensus decision making: The process enhances commitment and compliance because it is a joint effort. The ambiguity, uncertainty, anxiety, and confusion around members' situations, such as an illness, can be barriers to their being able to plan and execute actions. The group becomes a safe place to sort through these feelings and obtain the guidance and information needed to plan. These plans should have attainable and reasonable goals and objectives, logical and rational strategies, and a suggested timetable for implementation.

Specific Strategies

a. Provide a form for action planning that has the following sections: proposed action(s); personal strengths and other attributes that could contribute to success; barriers and constraints that would get in the way of success or of carrying out the action; specific steps to be taken; and a timetable. Have members fill out the form for each proposed action, read these aloud, and discuss how logical and reasonable the proposed action may be. Modify the actions if needed. After the discussion, complete the other portions of the form and read them aloud. Get a commitment to carry out one or more proposed actions.

Stress Reduction

Reducing or eliminating some stress can be an immense help for almost everyone, and group leaders are encouraged to learn a variety of stress reduction techniques. Activities such as meditation, yoga, exercise, progressive relaxation, and imagery are examples of stress-reducing techniques. There is evidence that these and other techniques can assist in reducing pain, controlling intense or overwhelming emotions, calming agitation, promoting sleep, and that they even can play roles in healing and recovery and contribute to positive effects on the quality of one's life.

Specific Strategies

a. Begin the group sessions with 5 to 10 minutes of meditation, breathing exercise, or silence. This allows members to more fully bring themselves into the session, it can be relaxing, or it can help them focus on the tension in their bodies to better relax.

b. Develop a form for members to list their highest stressors in the following categories: physical, relationship, spiritual, financial, work, family, and social. They can have several stressors in the same category. After compiling their lists, they can rate these as 1—not very stressful, to 10—extremely stressful. Next, have members list actions they could take to lessen each listed stressor, and/or note where the stressor is not under their control. These stressors, ratings, and actions can be shared in the group, suggestions from others incorporated, or the extent of the stressor validated. Members can become aware of overlooked solutions, or assistance that would help reduce the particular stressor, or can begin to accept that they are worrying over something they cannot control.

Task Groups, Teams, and Meetings

Introduction

Task groups are found in the workplace or other organizations. Task groups are called teams, work groups, task forces, boards, and the like. They are formed to accomplish a specific task, produce goods and services, improve processes, create ideas, and solve problems. Larson and LaFasto (1989) define task groups or teams (the terms are sometimes used interchangeably) as having two or more members, specific objectives, a recognizable goal or goals, and requiring coordination among members to attain the goal. Sundstrom, DeMeuse, and Futrell (1990) define work teams as small groups composed of interdependent members who have shared responsibilities for organizational outcomes. These and other definitions are used as the basis for this discussion about task groups.

Organizational theory and organizational development research have gathered considerable evidence about forming and working in task groups, and form a separate discipline. The literature is too voluminous and complex to try to include even a brief summary here, but some findings are used throughout the chapter. For ease of presentation and discussion, the following sequence will be used. The first discussion will be about teams, followed by work groups and committees. Teams are discussed separately from work groups because of some special characteristics, and the discussion about committees will incorporate task forces, staffing, and other such specialized small task groups.

Teams

Team is the term used to describe a collection of people working in synchronicity toward achieving a common goal. Team members are expected to work cooperatively to accomplish a mutual goal. Wheelan (2005a) presents the following summary description of effective teams developed from the literature.

- The goal is clear and worth the required effort.
- Collaboration is an integral part of the working climate.
- There is an emphasis and focus on results.
- There are known standards of excellence.
- Team members are competent and have the needed expertise for their jobs.
- There exists external support and recognition.
- The team has a unified commitment.
- The leader is principled.

Effective group work of all kinds demands that there be *clear and specific* goals that members work toward, and that the goals be personally relevant in some way. Goals for teams are usually focused on accomplishing an organization's goal, but that goal should be worth the effort team members are investing.

The team's climate or atmosphere should be one of *collaboration* from its inception. It is much more difficult to institute such a climate after the team has been working for some time because change can be difficult and must be managed well if it is to be effective. There must be room for independence, diverse perspectives, and the like, but individual preferences should be incorporated so that there is collaboration, not competition, among team members.

All task groups, and especially teams, are *results driven.* They are expected to accomplish the task and achieve the goal whether that goal be production of goods and services, improved processes, the creation of new ideas, or problem solving. The goals are specific, reasonable, observable, and measurable.

Standards of excellence refer to the expectations and organizing principles of the institution, business, corporation, or other body where the team works. Teams are expected to accomplish their goals within these standards, which are clearly stated and communicated. The actions of teams and individual members reflect on the organization.

It may seem obvious, but all team members should be *competent* and have the needed *expertise* for their expected contributions. When a team has to carry one or more members who do not have the needed skills, expertise, competence, or motivation, that team cannot be effective, nor can the needed collaboration and atmosphere be developed.

External support and resources are also critical components. Teams are part of the larger organization and must be recognized as forwarding the major purpose and goals of the organization and as being an important and integral part of it. Therefore, the organization should provide needed resources to get the job done, and team members should share in a system of rewards and recognitions for their accomplishments. Teams cannot be effective when needed resources are unavailable and when they lack management support.

A *unified commitment* is another characteristic of effective teams. All team members are dedicated to accomplishing the goals, which stay prominent in their discussions. This is why it is important to have and communicate worthy and specific goals, and for team members to understand their roles in accomplishing them. Clear goals, objectives, and strategies are helpful in developing a unified commitment.

The group *leader* needs a strong set of *principles* by which he or she lives and guides the work of the group. Ethical and moral issues are just as important for task groups as for other nonclinical and clinical groups. The group leader is a model for desired behavior, and team members will be influenced more by the leader's inner self than by what he or she says.

Teamwork.   *Teamwork* is a frequently used term to describe how teams function. Simms, Salas, and Burke (2005) define teamwork as "a blend of organized thoughts, feelings and attitudes that facilitate coordinated adaptive performance and task work objectives" (p. 408). They present a teamwork model with these elements defined:

- Think—members have the same mental model of what is to be done, how, and why.
- Feel—trust exists among members.
- Do—assistance is extended when needed, and mutual performance monitoring is done without blaming or judging.
- Coordination—the group leader directs, allocates tasks, provides motivation, plans, and organizes.
- Adaptive performance—members react positively to the dynamics of the work or task environment, multilevel influences, and contextual constraints.

As you can see from this brief definition, teamwork is complex and not at all easy to describe. However, teams are expected to function well, collaboratively, and effectively, and considerable responsibility rests on the leader. This discussion continues with a focus on helpful leader attitudes and behaviors, counterproductive leader attitudes and behaviors, effective team factors, ineffective team factors, and team-building strategies.

Helpful Leader Attitudes and Behaviors.   Leader attitudes and behaviors are significant influences on the team and impact the performance. This cannot be overemphasized. Helpful attitudes and behaviors fall into two categories—relational and communication. The relational attitudes and behaviors, communication, and facilitation skills are similar in some ways to those for other nonclinical groups, but also differ in significant ways.

Relational attitudes of acceptance, tolerance, and respect are critical elements, as each team member must feel included, valued, as having something worthwhile to contribute, and that he or she will be listened to and heard. How the leader conveys these attitudes will impact team members' commitment and dedication, and influence their behavior with one another, (Edmondson, 1999; Edmondson, Bohmer, & Pisano, 2001).

Some *relational leader behaviors* that can be helpful include:

- Making specific statements that are genuine about valuing members and their input
- Asking team members for input
- Seeking consensus whenever possible and feasible
- Highlighting and emphasizing strengths each member brings to the task
- Using reflective listening and responding

Communication is more effective if it is two-way, and both listening and responding are crucial as described in Chapter 7. Communication by the leader has another component: information giving. Because of the factors previously mentioned, such as the dynamic environment and multilevel influences, communication for teams is much more complex and information driven than for other nonclinical groups.

Studies support the value of timely and accurate information for teams. Leaders should pay particular attention to disseminating information about

- Goals, objectives, and performance expectations
- Rules for participation and behavior
- Performance evaluation for individuals and for the group
- The need and process for information exchange among group members
- Access to needed resources
- Problems, constraints, and other barriers

Helpful leader *communication behaviors* are to plan in advance for the needed information, have at least two methods for communicating this information, observe group dynamics and appropriately intervene, and be open to members' needs.

Most of the information previously listed can be developed or gathered during the planning process. Anticipating information needs and having the answers does much to reduce team members' anxiety and calm any fears around personal adequacy. The encouragement and support can be valuable in building the team's culture. But, because teams generally work in a dynamic and fluid environment, and there can be considerable significant outside influences, it becomes important for the team leader to constantly be alert to these and provide team members with needed updates when they would affect the work of the team.

It could be helpful to use two methods for communication, such as oral and written. For example, the goals and rules would be discussed in the group, but could also be written for future review. Or, they could be discussed and posted via transparencies or PowerPoint for each group meeting. Periodic review is recommended, especially if changes or corrections emerge or are needed.

Observation of group dynamics can provide clues for when information is needed. Listening to members' discussions and interactions can let the group leader know when to intervene with information, notification of changes, and so on. The group members let the leader know their needs, although they may be expressing them in indirect ways. The clues to problems, constraints, and barriers may appear through observation before members are aware of them, and can directly express them.

Openness to members' needs promotes safety and trust and contributes to commitment. The group leader has to listen, have a deep understanding of the covert and hidden messages in members' verbalizations and actions, and have a willingness to meet reasonable needs.

Counterproductive Leader Attitudes and Behaviors. Teams will function less effectively when the leader displays the following attitudes and behaviors:

- Self-absorption
- Indecisiveness
- Arrogance
- Vindictiveness
- Micromanaging
- Failure to adequately plan
- Secretiveness and/or deceptiveness
- Favoritism
- Failure to keep promises, follow through, and so on

Self-absorbed leader attitudes and behaviors can have a negative effect on the group (Brown, 2006; Gans & Alonso, 1998; Horwitz, 2000). These include being more focused on personal concerns than on the group and its members, engaging in behaviors that are designed to produce feelings of inadequacy and shame for members, being unable to admit mistakes, and so on. Self-absorption is discussed in more detail in Chapter 9.

Indecisive group leaders produce considerable anxiety for group members. There are times when it is more helpful to delay a decision—for example, when there is insufficient information to make an informed decision. But these situations are usually obvious. Group members need the security that a careful, decisive leader brings.

Arrogance, cockiness, and overconfidence are detrimental to the group, especially when the leader displays them. These attitudes convey feelings of superiority, can lead to inappropriate risk taking where group members may be harmed, and are more focused on the group leader's needs than on the group's and the group members'. Arrogance can convey that the leader has an inflated sense of self, and overconfidence can convey an unrealistic appraisal of personal abilities and limitations. Group members may model or imitate these attitudes, and that can be detrimental to them.

Vindictiveness, the act of taking revenge, is not a positive characteristic for anyone, and a group leader who has this characteristic is definitely counterproductive. Group members will fear the leader, distrust the leader and other members, become defensive in an effort to self-protect, reflect that leader's attitude and actions, and the team will be less effective or even ineffective.

Micromanaging happens when the leader is very anxious, is not confident that the team has the needed expertise and competencies, may not believe or accept team members' commitment, and keeps group members on edge not knowing what is expected of them. Insecure group leaders may not realize that they are micromanaging, nor be aware of the negative effects of this behavior on the team. Much of the creativity, trust, and cohesion can be lost when the leader micromanages.

The consequences for *failure to adequately plan* are negative for the team and the goals. The necessary team climate and atmosphere will not be developed; team members can flounder because expectations for them are unclear; the coordination needed among members is not developed; extra time is needed to correct errors or obtain resources, leading to the team not being able to meet goals and deadlines; and trust, safety, and group cohesion are compromised.

Secretiveness and/or deceptiveness are detrimental to all relationships including those in the workplace. Trust cannot be built or established when there are secrets and deception. Group leaders need to pay attention to their actions that can be perceived as secret or deceptive. Examples include the following:

- Meeting with individual team members without bringing the discussed material
- Keeping information from them that is relative to the group, its members, and the job
- Not giving correct or full answers
- Wanting to be a part of external management and not sharing information with the team to be perceived as "in the know," or "in the loop"

Showing *favoritism* to one or more team members can arouse defensiveness, hostility, and anger. These are intense emotions that may not be openly expressed, but are indirectly reflected in team members' relationships, verbalizations, and actions. Trust, commitment, and cohesion are all negatively affected when the group leader shows or is perceived as showing favoritism.

It is critical that group leaders model trustworthiness, and when they *fail to follow through,* keep promises, and the like, team members can be profoundly disappointed and question whether the leader can be trusted. Leaders should be careful to not make promises they cannot keep, or to fail to follow through when that is an agreed-upon expectation.

Effective Team Factors. Effective team factors are behaviors and attitudes among members and with the leader that contribute to a healthy group atmosphere, a dedicated work environment, and cordial relationships. Discussed here are member interactions and relationships, personal characteristics, and the leader behaviors that facilitate the group.

Interaction and relationship factors include meaningful similarities among members; mutual acceptance, tolerance and respect; and information exchange. Personal characteristics include hopes for making meaningful contributions, for having constructive and productive outcomes, and for achieving personal gain; an appreciation of one another's contributions, recognition of efforts expended by members, and a willingness to extend oneself to be helpful; and an ability to transcend the personal to attain the goal. The helpful leader facilitative factors include a focus on members' strengths, fairness and equal treatment for all group members, and modeling purpose and meaning.

The interaction and relationship factors were discussed previously, especially in Chapter 7. The three factors mentioned here are those that can be of particular importance for team meetings, and for encouraging commitment to the team and its work. Leaders should pay particular attention to encouraging and fostering the emergence of these factors.

Personal characteristics of team members are also important factors, and the group leader can emphasize these. How the leader presents the task, facilitates the group, and attends to group members can do much to help instill hope for members that they are making meaningful contributions that are valued, that their efforts and commitment to the task will result in positive and constructive outcomes, and that they, as individuals, can expect to achieve some personal gains. It is also important that the group leader sets the tone and expectations that members will display an appreciation for one another's efforts and recognize that each member has something positive and of value to contribute. The leader must be willing to assist where needed if asked or when the need for assistance is perceived as helpful, and have an ability and willingness to transcend personal concerns and ambitions to achieve the goals. The latter can be particularly important for teamwork, but members also need to feel that their individual efforts will be recognized and rewarded.

Leaders have many *facilitative tasks* and some of the most significant ones for building the team's trust, safety, and cohesion will be for the leader to emphasize strengths that members bring to the team, and not be critical and blaming for deficiencies, weaknesses, or mistakes. It is critical for leaders to behave in a fair and equitable manner because group members can be alert to anything that even suggests unfairness or inequality. This is true even when there are obvious differences among team members, such as educational level or salary. They want fair and equitable treatment by the leader within the group. The leader's belief in the worthiness of the task goals, in the group and its process, and in the abilities of group members models purpose and meaning for team members, and this belief needs to be genuine. Team members will take their cues from the leader's attitudes and not from his or her verbalizations.

Counterproductive Team Factors. There are three member factors that are counterproductive, six leader factors, and one that applies to both members and the leader. Whereas there are numerous external factors that can be counterproductive to the team, the factors here are those that are internal to the group, and will negatively impact its functioning and productivity. Counterproductive member factors include the following:

- Selfishness and self-absorption
- A lack of trust
- The inability to work collaboratively

Counterproductive leader factors include:

- Inconsistent direction or the lack of structure
- An insecure or inadequately prepared leader
- An ineffective decision-making process within the group
- Ignoring significant problem behavior
- Blaming, criticizing, and focusing on weakness, errors, and the like
- Ignoring members' feelings

A counterproductive leader and member factor is an atmosphere of intra- or intergroup competition.

Members who are *selfish or self-absorbed* can have a significant negative impact on the group, cohesion will not be developed, and the commitment to the group and its goals will be eroded. To be selfish and self-absorbed is to have an excessive focus on self-gains and self-needs such as those for admiration and attention, and an inability to understand that others are deserving and worthwhile. These members will do whatever it takes for them to succeed as individuals, and have little or no concern for other members.

There are many reasons for *lack of trust* for group members, including family-of-origin and other past experiences where there was betrayal and disappointment, an ingrained tendency to be skeptical and to withhold the self from relationships, previous experience with one or more group members who demonstrated untrustworthy behavior, and when the leader does not model or act to build trust among group members. Whatever the reason for a lack of trust, its absence is a negative one for promoting safety and building cohesion.

Both of the previous factors can contribute to the *inability* of team members *to work collaboratively.* Collaboration involves sharing of information freely, listening with respect for diverse perspectives, incorporating others' ideas and suggestions, and a willingness to seek consensus and compromises that further task achievement. Team members may have different assignments, but the task or project will usually demand that these assignments are interrelated, and collaboration facilitates completion of these and of the overall task. Team members who do not collaborate can cause delays or incomplete tasks, may allow others to make mistakes, and can negatively affect productivity.

The leader counterproductive factors have far-reaching negative effects. Leaders who give *inconsistent direction or structure* keep team members in a constant state of anxiety, not ever knowing what to expect. These leaders change assignments, objectives, and expectations seemingly on a whim, and the atmosphere is one of uncertainty and ambiguity. In some ways, it can be worse to have inconsistent direction or structure than it is to have none at all. When left on their own, team members may choose a leader, or a natural leader may emerge. The group can manage itself under these circumstances. Either way, this is a leader counterproductive factor.

An *insecure or inadequately prepared team leader* can do or fail to do things that are facilitative for building the team and fostering teamwork. Insecure leaders can micromanage in the effort to exercise control and to not make mistakes, be inconsistent in communication or relationships, overly on a few favored team members thus producing a clique, allow problems and conflicts to fester and escalate, and have a faulty decision-making process.

Decisions are a critical task, and when the *decision-making process* is faulty, that can set the tone and atmosphere where other problems emerge. It can be counterproductive when all or most decisions are made by authority, such as when a leader makes the decisions and tells the group what they are; or by an expert; or by members voting, which sets up a win–lose situation; or by any method that does not involve group discussion. Team members can feel discounted, devalued, and alienated when the decision-making process is poor.

Problem behaviors in team meetings or team activities are counterproductive. These include:

- Failing to attend team meetings
- Frequently arriving late to meetings or leaving early
- Interrupting when others are talking
- Making disparaging remarks about others or their input
- Making personally demeaning comments or remarks about others
- Refusing to participate
- Using prolonged and frequent silence to withdraw

- Displaying verbal or physical aggression
- Monopolizing, storytelling, and the like
- Lying, distorting, cheating, and misleading
- Taking unearned credit

These are some examples of behaviors that undermine the effectiveness of the team; leaders are advised to openly deal with them and to not ignore them.

It is counterproductive when a group leader engages in deliberate behavior that is intended to *produce guilt, shame, and feelings of inadequacy* for group members, or even when the intent is unconscious on the leader's part. In the latter situation the leader may not be aware of the unconscious intent, but the effects are the same. Blame and criticism do not help the group's atmosphere or members' relationships or commitment, nor do they help solve whatever problem, barrier, or constraint may be present. It is much more helpful and constructive to focus on prevention or fixing the problem than it is to focus on chastising someone.

Although task groups are more cognitively and action focused than they are affectively focused, it is counterproductive to *ignore members' feelings*. These are spoken, nonverbal, direct, or indirect expressions of the real messages, and merit attention. The group's work is facilitated when group leaders pay appropriate attention to members' feelings as part of the group's process.

Competition is often perceived as a struggle to gain an advantage, to be more successful, to obtain rewards, and to be perceived as superior. These can be counterproductive to the team's functioning, especially when they are present in the group. Intragroup competition works against collaboration and building trust and cohesion. These are sufficient reasons to monitor the competitiveness of individuals and of the group. Johnson and Johnson (2006) propose that competition can be constructively used when the following five conditions are in effect for the group: positive interdependence, face-to-face interaction, individual accountability, interpersonal and small-group skills, and group processing.

Team-Forming Strategies. Forming a team begins in the planning process, and a number of factors should be carefully considered: size, quality of expertise and skill possessed by members, potential for learning new skills, and available resources. Katzenbach and Smith (1993) surveyed effective teams and concluded that team size is best when it is small, such as having 10 or fewer members. Larger groups have more built-in constraints, such as meeting dates and times when all can attend, finding physical space sufficient to hold meetings, and building cohesion.

It may be tempting to *select team members* based on their positions or personality, but a better selection process considers the expertise and skills already achieved by members. Try to get the mix of skills and expertise the task demands, but also remember that you may not know what mix of these you need in advance. Connected to present skills and expertise is the *openness to learning new skills* that members may need. These new skills are not always task related; some may be relationship related, such as learning constructive conflict management skills. The final preparation for forming a team is to locate and have in place all of the *needed resources* including supplies and materials, equipment, access to support personnel, and so on.

Team-Building Strategies. The following team-building strategies are part of planning.

- Hold frequent and regular face-to-face meetings.
- Develop methods to observe progress and reward accomplishments.
- Determine training needs.
- Plan team celebrations and reward members.
- Hold team processing sessions.

Teams seem to be more productive and efficient when they have *regular face-to-face meetings* where progress or the lack of it is addressed and problems are identified and solutions are proposed; where the team can be part of the decisions made on its behalf; where relation building strategies are used; and where communication is facilitated. Leaders should have a schedule of meetings to disseminate at or before the first meeting.

Specific observable indicators of progress are helpful to group members rather than relying on personal subjective judgment. These indicators are also helpful in anticipating barriers, constraints, and other possible problems.

Training may be needed and should be anticipated and planned for as much as possible so that valuable time is not lost. Topics for training range from specific project-related skills such as using new software, to team functioning and related skills such as conflict resolution and problem-solving skills.

Teams need *tangible signs of appreciation* and, in some cases, a reduction of tension. Leaders should plan for celebrations and rewards for team members. Celebrations can be social events for team members, special lunches, special focus or mention in corporate newsletters, addition of the member's picture to a display for merit, and so on. Rewards are usually tangible indicators of merit and appreciation, such as money, gifts, and certificates that can be redeemed for merchandise or services.

Probably one of the most helpful team-building strategies is the *team processing* session where the leader and members focus on what is taking place in the group, among members, and with the leader. Feelings can be expressed and explored, empathic failures repaired, conflicts identified and worked through, and stronger relationship bonds forged. The emphases for these sessions, or parts of sessions, are on the here-and-now experiencing for members and the leader, and on relationship factors.

Here are some specific activities that can help build a team atmosphere.

- Develop a team logo, name, or other identifiers, and use these in reports and other communication.
- Use some time in meetings for members to report their life's special or significant events to the group, such as births, graduations, family illnesses or deaths, and so on.
- Take pictures of group members and post them with their names.
- Use exercises, role-play, and simulations to teach problem-solving strategies, diagnose productivity barriers, and so on.
- Have group brainstorming exercises to create new ideas and processes.
- Ask members to describe or bring examples of their hobbies and other such interests to the group.

- Form a sports team such as softball or bowling. Compete with other teams if this option is available.

Open and Closed Teams. Ideally, the team should be formed, no new members added, and the group should remain intact with no members leaving. However, the reality is most likely to be that the team will be an open group with the addition and subtraction of members. Team leaders should prepare for this situation and have a plan for how new members will be incorporated and assimilated, and how there can be closure for the group and the departing members. Both can have a significant impact on the group's progress and process.

Adding a new member changes the group, much like the birth of a baby changes the family. Relationships, interactions, dynamics, and communication are affected, and the team may regress to an earlier stage of group development. The introduction of a new member can allow concerns about safety, trust, and uncertainty to reemerge. Leaders must be prepared to understand and cope with these old feelings, and to realize that it will take time and positive experiences to fully incorporate the new member. Where possible, the leader can conduct pregroup preparation for the new member on the following topics:

- Description of the goals for the team, and an explanation of how individual performance is related to achieving the goal
- Specifying what contributions and other expectations the new member can provide and meet
- The rules accepted by team members
- The need for the new member's commitment to the team and its goal
- How problems are to be handled, both relationship and task related
- Evaluation and assessment procedures and how they impact the new member

Inserting a new member into the group requires some thought and planning. These steps may be useful.

1. Notify team members in advance that the team will get a new member, and provide the rationale for the addition.
2. Describe the role, assignment, or expertise that person provides the group with an emphasis on how he or she will enrich the work.
3. Solicit members' feelings about an addition to the team, and their thoughts about how the team will be different or changed. Do not skip this step even if you are apprehensive about members having intense or negative feelings about the addition. Do not minimize the apprehension, dread, or anger, or seek to dismiss these as groundless.
4. Once feelings are explored, initiate a discussion on how the new person can be introduced, assimilated, and become a contributing member.

   (Steps 1–4 are used before the new member arrives. Step 5 begins the process for what takes place in the first session with the new member.)
5. Welcome the new member and ask team members to introduce themselves and to add a piece of information—personal thoughts, feelings, and so forth. This can set the stage for how the new member introduces himself or herself.

6. Inform the group about the information provided to the new member in the pregroup preparation, and ask team members to provide other information they think would be helpful to get the new person started.

7. Ask the new member if there are questions or concerns he or she has at this point, and provide reassurance that other questions will be answered as they emerge for him or her. The usual work of the session can begin at this point.

Departing Team Members. Bringing closure for the departing member and for the team also requires preplanning, and the leader's emotional readiness to handle the situation. There are two departures, and each demands a slightly different process. One departure is abrupt and unexpected, and the other is expected. An example for the latter is when it is known earlier that a team member will be leaving and when. He or she may be moved to a new position or new location and cannot remain with the team. Although disruptive, this departure is much less disruptive and upsetting than is one that is abrupt and unexpected.

Let's discuss facilitating the group when the departure is abrupt and unexpected. The departure could be initiated by the member himself or herself, by the group leader or by outside forces, and there may be several reasons for the departure. Whatever the reason, there will be group and individual reactions that must be dealt with openly and directly because premature termination threatens the cohesion of the group (Rice, 1996). An unplanned termination of the group produces many conflicting and upsetting feelings as described for stage 4 of group development earlier in this book.

When there is an abrupt and unexpected departure, the leader should try to meet with the departing member to discuss his or her feelings about departing, the team experience, and to set the stage for that member's last session. If the departure takes place at the group session with no prior notice, the leader can encourage the departing member to speak of his or her experiences in the group, ask other group members to tell the departing member how they are reacting to and experiencing the departure, and their perceptions of him or her as a person. The leader may need to keep the perceptions focused on strengths, as there can be a lot of anger about being abandoned.

Planned departures give group members some time to become accustomed to the looming event, but there can be considerable denial of its happening, and of their feelings about the departure. Just as with the group's termination, the leader can remind members that the event is coming, and solicit suggestions about satisfactory ways of saying goodbye so that there is little or no unfinished business.

Work Groups, Committees, and Task Forces

These groups are discussed separately from teams because they differ in significant ways, and leaders of these groups must stay aware of these differences. Work group, committee, and task force members have significant outside-the-group functions and performance expectations; the group and its members function more independently than do teams, and members are less dependent on one another for achieving goals or productivity. Examples for work groups include academic departments, work-or function-related units or departments, and entire organizations such as schools. Work group members function together and separately over a period of time that can vary from brief, such as a week, to many years. Committees and task forces usually have a defined time boundary, and at some point cease to exist or are reconfigured.

The leader's planning role in these groups is similar to that for teams, but many of the functions are different.

- There is more emphasis on task than on relationship factors.
- The leader has less authority because members' primary responsibilities are other assignments.
- Performance, either individual or group, most likely will not be assessed, or be part of members' evaluations.
- Members are not necessarily selected to complement one another's expertise and skills.
- Building a group (team) identity is less important.

Relationships within the work group, committee, or task force are still important, but can be less so than in teams or other task groups. Leaders of these task groups should attend to the group relationship factors, and seek to build working professional relationships so that meetings can function well and be productive.

Leaders of these groups are likely to have *authority* only in that particular setting, and not affect members' work or professional lives in any other way. Members are more likely to be volunteers, even within a work setting, and this also affects the leader's authority. Leaders are more facilitators, unlike what is usually needed for teams.

Assessment and evaluation play minor roles, or no roles at all for these task groups. Members' individual performances will not affect much about their personal or work lives, and leaders do not usually have a responsibility for assessment or evaluation. Members' personal commitment, choices, and core values play the important roles for their performance.

Membership is determined by a number of factors that differ for each group that is formed. For example, each committee formed has a different set of factors that determines its membership, and the process for forming each is also different. Hence, members are not usually or necessarily selected on the basis of their expertise or skills, although some members may be chosen for these reasons. Leaders can sometimes find this to be a challenge.

Less important for these task groups than for teams is building *a group or team identity.* Members may be pleased at others identifying them with the group, but it is not as important for the group's functioning, cohesion, and so on that a group identity be formed.

Leader Tasks. All of the tasks for planning and pregroup preparation discussed for teams apply to these other task groups. The leader usually has more responsibility for organizing the work for the group, but less responsibility for participating in developing the goals and objectives. However, the leader can do much to help the group and facilitate the process by making sure that these goals and objectives are clear and reasonable, and that the needed resources are available.

An important leader task is facilitating meetings, as that is where ideas are generated, solutions to problems proposed, and the objectives and goals worked on. Actions are carried on outside the group when this becomes necessary, such as obtaining needed information, checking on possibilities, and so on. Thus, the leader's skill at involving members, soliciting input, and attending to relationship factors is vital to the productivity of the group, and most of this takes place in meetings. Effective meeting facilitation is discussed in a later section in this chapter.

The leader must help the group maintain its focus and not become distracted or sidetracked. It is important that the group not extend the scope of its work, go outside the needs of the particular goals or task, or to flounder because of ambiguous goals. The leader is the essential person who helps the group maintain its purpose and goals.

Because many of these groups are composed of volunteers, or of members whose participation is not evaluated, a major leader task is to foster commitment and dedication to achieving the goal. Factors that can be helpful in promoting these are respecting each member's input, listening carefully and responding appropriately, appreciating each person's uniqueness, encouraging participation, soliciting ideas, incorporating members' suggestions, refusing to have favorites or show favoritism, and blocking inappropriate behavior by other members.

Productive Meetings. Members appreciate productive meetings, and the structuring, directing, and facilitating of these are major responsibilities for the group leader. Planning meetings contributes to structuring and directing, and the leader's personal inner development and learned group facilitation skills are significant contributors to facilitation of meetings. The implementation of these factors can be different for these task groups because of the variation of other factors around particular groups. For example, some committees, task forces, and work groups meet around a meal, such as lunch, where there can be more of a social atmosphere, and intrusions from servers. The group leader must take all variations into account to best manage the group and achieve the goals. What follows is intended to be a guide, subject to modifications and adaptations to suit the particular circumstances. Discussed are basic guidelines for planning, structuring, directing, and facilitating, and for the critically important first meeting.

It is important that the group leader *plan* meetings. These should be scheduled in advance, and not set up at each meeting. Group members should be consulted about best days and times, and a schedule set when all can attend. (As a side note, do not change the schedule if at all possible, even if you cannot attend. In the event of your absence, designate a temporary leader and hold the meetings. Members will appreciate the consistency.)

Another part of planning is the *agenda*. Always have an agenda of discussion and action items that is written and distributed in advance of the meeting. Agendas can be changed, but members need that information in advance. Also, be sure to attach any documents that are to be discussed or other actions taken. Remind members of the date, time, and place for the meeting along with the agenda.

Have specific *times* for meetings to begin and end. Do not have open-ended meeting times. No one can plan to spend an undesignated amount of time at a meeting; not having specified time boundaries may result in some members not attending, or leaving before the meeting is complete. Designate time boundaries and abide by them. It can be tempting sometimes to extend meetings, and if the need should arise, either resist the temptation or extend it by no more than 10 minutes.

Gather all *needed material* before the meeting, and have sufficient quantities so that each member has personal copies. Make sure copies are clear and readable, and bring any resources, such as policy manuals that may be needed for consultation but cannot be reproduced, to the meeting.

Check with members and subcommittees who have *assignments*, and ask them to make progress reports, or to bring items for review and action by the group to the meeting. They, too, should collect or prepare needed materials and documents in advance of the meeting when possible. Their materials should also be distributed with the agenda.

Directing and structuring are accomplished partially with the agenda, gathering materials and checking in with subcommittees and so on. The other parts occur within the meeting, and require the leader to do the following:

- Maintain the focus
- Hear all perspectives
- Deal with all or most agenda items
- Solve problems
- Engage in decision making

The leader has the major responsibility for all of these tasks and should be the person who talks the least, summarizes, hears and makes visible hidden or indirectly expressed concerns, sticks to the agenda and does not let the group become distracted from the goal, links similarities such as opinions, blocks inappropriate comments and behavior, and makes sure that all members have input and that their input is respectfully and carefully considered.

The Critical First Meeting. The critical first meeting can set the pattern for subsequent meetings, and attention to some factors can assist in setting the desired culture and norms. It also can prevent conflict and other such problems, reduce ambiguity and uncertainty, and demonstrate how the work can be accomplished. Let's assume that the needed planning, attention to environmental concerns, gathering of materials, and dissemination of an agenda were accomplished. Planning and facilitating the first meeting is now the leader's task, and there are two categories for these tasks—process and functioning.

Process Tasks
- Reduce anxiety and encourage attention and acceptance
- Promote inclusion, respect, and tolerance of diverse perspectives
- Foster member-to-member interactions and connections
- Invite participation

Functioning Tasks
- Structure the group's tasks, goals and objectives, strategies, and timelines
- Manage concerns such as schedule of meetings, rules, and communications such as minutes

The process tasks are accomplished through the leader's inner characteristics such as warmth and genuineness, and skills such as listening and direct responding, and through group facilitation skills such as linking and process observation. The functioning tasks are accomplished by addressing them during the session, paying attention to details, and recognizing their importance. A sample leader's agenda for the first meeting follows.

Leader's Agenda

Welcome and introduction of the leader

Group member introductions

Overview of task, goals, and the like (keep this short, have a written summary, and disseminate some of this information in advance)

Invite questions, comments, suggestions, and so on from members

Ask for volunteers for needed assignments, actions, and so forth

Open a discussion on how the group can best function, and present the rules

Summarize the activities of the meeting and actions for the future, and announce the next meeting

Adjourn

It is important that someone takes minutes; if there is not a designated secretary or minutes taker, the leader can do the task. Minutes should include this information:

- Meeting date, time, and place
- List of attending group members, and absent members
- Actions taken, decisions made
- Assignments, the persons responsible, and the timelines for completion or reporting
- Brief summaries of each topic discussed
- Adjournment time

It is not necessary to list group members' names for topics, questions, comments, and the like.

Summary

1. Psychoeducational groups blend cognitive and affective foci, and a group leader must be able to help members cope with the intense feelings that can arise. These groups require that the leader balance task and goal accomplishment with group members' need for feeling expression.

2. Generally short term, psychoeducational groups nevertheless can touch on issues that are usually addressed in longer-term counseling and psychotherapy groups. Although they are not explored in-depth, the group leader should be prepared to deal with transference, family-of-origin issues, intense emotions, and the like.

3. Task groups are varied and usually target adolescents and adults. These groups are designed to improve communication, performance, and productivity.

4. Teams are a special form of task groups, and require attention to the relationships among group members. They are generally composed of members who work together and will continue to do so, whose accomplishments are both individual and group related. The focus is usually on matters that enhance team relationships as well as task accomplishment.

Chapter Activities

11.1. Consult the literature and write three team-building group activities for an adult task group in a business.

11.2. Write a plan for a children's group focused on a medical illness using the directions presented in Chapter 6.

Chapter 12

Clinical Groups

Major Topics

1. Definitions, similarities and differences for counseling and psychotherapy groups.
2. Leader tasks: screening, pre-group preparation, and collaborative goal setting.
3. Group facilitation functions, and the challenge of naturally-occurring social defenses.
4. Facilitative strategies for clinical groups.
5. Special needs and considerations for children and adolescent groups.

Introduction

The clinical groups, such as counseling and psychotherapy, described in this chapter are more intense, and more focused on self-development and healing and interpersonal relationships than the groups presented in previous chapters. The psychotherapy groups in particular are also usually long term, some of which can last for years. Currently, a shift in terminology seems to be taking place in the literature for the descriptions and definitions of these groups. The shift is blurring the distinctions between them. Whereas psychotherapy was once thought to be only descriptive of the psychoanalytic perspective, it is now descriptive of various theoretical approaches. Counseling groups were once perceived as more educationally focused, but these now also address many of the same problems and concerns as do psychotherapy groups.

This discussion begins with descriptions for counseling and psychotherapy groups, presents how these groups require a different level of leader tasks, describes facilitation functions and barriers, and discusses facilitative strategies. Clinical groups for children and adolescents will have many of the same characteristics and leader tasks as discussed in this chapter, but there are some that may have special applications for these groups. Therefore, a separate section presents material focused on these audiences.

Counseling and Psychotherapy Groups

The definitions for counseling, therapy, and psychotherapy groups do not seem to have clear differences. The Wikipedia Encyclopedia (2007) notes that the terms are used interchangeably, and when one reviews the literature about these groups this seems to be the case. Yalom & Leszcz (2005), Brabender (2002), and Rutan & Stone (2001) interchange the use of the terms *therapy* and *psychotherapy*. Readers can become confused as the groups described do not fit the titles or the definitions, such as what happens when a group that is primarily psychoeducational in format is termed a therapy group.

Counseling groups have been defined as the following:

- Oriented in equal measure to the past, present, and future as well as problem and solution focused, but less on psychopathology than is psychotherapy. (Wikipedia, 2007)
- Corey (2008) describes counseling groups as having preventive and remedial aims; having a specific focus; involving an interpersonal process that stresses conscious thoughts, feelings, and behavior; often being problem centered; having concerns related to developmental tasks of the life span; and tending to be growth oriented.
- The Association for Specialists in Group Work (ASGW, 2000) has a definition that states, "Counseling groups address personal and interpersonal problems of living and promote personal and interpersonal growth and development."

Psychotherapy groups have the following definitions:

- Wikipedia (2007) defines psychotherapy as tending to deal more with seriously disturbed individuals, such as those with depression, anxiety, or personality disorders.
- The definition by ASGW (2000) refers to therapy groups as addressing personal and interpersonal problems of living, remediation of perceptual and cognitive distortions or repetitive patterns of dysfunctional behavior, and promoting personal and interpersonal growth and development.
- Burlingame et al. (2005) notes that, "A consensually accepted definition of group psychotherapy is simply not available in the extant literature" (p. 387).

When we examine the actual practices of mental health professionals, the distinctions become even more blurred, and it is difficult to distinguish between them in important ways. Counseling and psychotherapy are evolving and learning from each other to better assist clients, and this is very positive for both professionals and consumers.

Similarities

Both counseling and psychotherapy groups have some aspects in common:

- A greater focus and emphasis on affective concerns
- Less focus and emphasis on teaching–learning
- A primary aim to change attitudes and behaviors

- Emphasis on process
- Sufficient time for group stages to develop, and be experienced
- Emerging therapeutic factors such as catharsis, the interpersonal learning loop, and existential factors
- Screening as an integral part of the selection process
- Pregroup preparation
- Groups of longer duration and smaller size
- More extensive self-exploration
- Addressing of deeper, more enduring, and complex problems

Affective concerns can be a major focus for these groups, and considerable time is spent on helping group members express and explore their feelings. Ellis (1996) has as part of his theory that it is more the feelings connected to an action that are distressing, than is the act itself. Other approaches have long accepted that an exploration and expression of feelings aids the healing and growth process. Thus, a major part of these groups attends to the emotional world of the group members.

Less focus and emphasis on teaching-learning as the main interventions can be seen for counseling and psychotherapy groups. These groups are less structured and directed than are other types of groups, such as educational, skills training, and psychoeducational groups. This does not mean that teaching and learning are not important, or are lacking for these groups, as that is not the case. It's just that there can be less of both, and teaching and instruction are not focal for the sessions.

A primary aim is to change attitudes and behavior, but these are not the only aims; there are others such as planning for expected life transitions. However, many of the issues, problems, and concerns relate to needed changes for attitudes and behaviors. Certainly, cognitive therapy (Beck, 1998), cognitive-behavioral therapy (CBT) (Corey, 2008), behavioral therapy and its variations such as dialectical behavioral therapy (DBT) (Linenhan, 1993), and psychodynamic therapy (Rutan & Stone, 2001) are examples of theories that stress attitude and behavioral change for group members.

Process is emphasized. The here-and-now interaction between group members and between group members and the leader is a critical source of information for the group leader (Brown, 2003a). These groups pay considerable attention to process, and to the constructive use for process commentary. There is sufficient time for members to develop enough trust and feelings of safety so that process commentary can be tolerated and members are not threatened by its use. This use of process is highly beneficial to group members because the behavior they display in the group reflects the behavior outside the group, and it can be easier and less threatening for them to accept the perceptions of the group leader and other group members. This allows them to more objectively examine and reflect on their behavior and its impact on others.

Sufficient time is usually available for group stages to develop, and to be experienced by group members. It can be especially important for movement through stage 2 where conflict and challenges can produce considerable discomfort. The movement through this stage to the more harmonious stage 3 is dependent on the group and the leader, but time is one of the most critical elements.

Although group leaders can expect all their groups to have the beginning and ending stages no matter how brief the group may be, there has to be sufficient time for the *group stages* to unfold, and the expected tasks accomplished. Counseling and psychotherapy groups usually have sufficient time for all, or most, of the stages to appear, and it is important that group leaders recognize these, and capitalize on them to enhance the growth and development of group members.

Therapeutic factors may also have time to emerge, and for the leader to capitalize on them for the benefit of group members. Brief groups may not have sufficient time for members to establish trust in other members and in the leader, and for feelings of safety to be sufficient so that elements such as catharsis, the interpersonal learning loop, and existential factors can be expressed. When the focus is on structured material, such as what is expected for educational, skills training, task, and psychoeducational groups, there may not be space and time for many of the therapeutic factors to emerge and be recognized by group members.

Screening potential group members and selection are important for every type of group, but may be even more so for counseling and psychotherapy groups (Piper & McCallum 1994; Riva et al., 2004). This increased importance is due to the intimate nature of these groups, the intensity of feelings that will be explored, the personal disclosures that will be shared, and the need for members to respect and care for one another. Safety and trust are critical for members, and this process of screening and selection can provide some information about how potential members will fit in, interact, and profit from the group experience. The chapters on member and group challenges provide some information about the difficulties that can arise when screening is omitted, or not adequately done.

The American Group Psychotherapy Association's Best Practice Guidelines (2007) emphasizes the importance of *pregroup preparation*, and provides evidence for its efficacy. Pregroup preparation includes informing members about expected behaviors in group, the aims of the group, and what techniques and processes the leader will use; helping members develop personal goals and integrate them with group goals; reducing anxiety about the uncertain and unknown; and starting to set the foundation for establishing the therapeutic alliance.

Counseling and psychotherapy groups are usually of *longer duration* than are other types of groups—some psychotherapy groups are open ended and continue for years. Having more time for the group processes to unfold, and for members to explore the complexities of their issues, problems, and concerns can lead to increased self-understanding as well as behavior change.

These groups can provide more extensive *self-exploration* because of the time available and the focus on feelings and more enduring issues. Although behavior change is emphasized, the inner world of the group member is emphasized as part of the change. There is less pressure to stay focused only on a prespecified goal, and more opportunities to deal with material that can emerge, such as that which is repressed or unconscious. More aspects or facets of the self can be uncovered, explored, and understood.

Because of the greater opportunities for self-exploration, *deeper and more complex issues* can be an integral part of the group. It is not very helpful to uncover an issue, only to not have enough time to address it. Deeper and more complex issues develop from family-of-origin and other important past experiences. The group can assist in uncovering and understanding the impact and influences these had (have) on members' growth and development, and in providing the corrective emotional experience (Yalom, 2005). This understanding and corrective experience is of immense benefit for healing.

Differences

It is difficult to describe the differences between counseling and psychotherapy groups because the defining lines are blurred. Corey (2008) writes that the differences are the role of the leader; the kind of people in the group; and the emphases given to prevention, remediation, treatment, and development. However, a review of the literature would reveal that these are not the defining differences, and that the terms are used interchangeably. Burlingame et al. (2005) acknowledges that there is not a consensual definition for psychotherapy, and that too makes it difficult to distinguish between the two types. Therefore, this discussion will not try to separate the two types, as they share more similarities than they do differences. The similarities between counseling and psychotherapy groups are also reflective of how they differ from other types of groups, such as skills training and educational groups.

Leader Tasks

Clinical groups have certain leader tasks that are needed in more depth than may be necessary for other groups. For example, screening is recommended for all types of groups, but is much more essential for clinical groups because of the sensitivity of personal material expected to be disclosed. There is also a need for members to be able to manage and contain their intense emotions, and to handle the possible uncovering of repressed memories and trauma. Tasks discussed here include screening and pregroup preparation, which includes attention to reducing anxiety, and informed consent.

Screening

The two most important questions that are addressed during screening are the suitability of the person for the group experience, and the possible fit with the group that is being planned, or is already formed (AGPA, 2007). The personal characteristics most closely associated with positive results for group counseling and group psychotherapy include the following:

- High motivation (Seligman, 1995)
- Attraction and commitment to the group work (Anderson et al., 2001)
- Interpersonal competency (Joyce et al., 2000; Sotsky et al., 1991)
- Valuing and desiring of personal change (Lieberman & Yalom, 1973)

It is the group leader's subjective judgment that determines if the person is a possible good fit for the group. But there are some guiding principles.

- Do the personal goals mesh with the group goals?
- Are the expectations for change realistic and reasonable given the structure of the group, such as the duration of the group?
- Can a viable therapeutic alliance be established?

Pregroup Preparation

Planned and well conducted pregroup preparation has been found to be significantly related to positive outcomes (Burlingame et al., 2002; Rutan & Stone, 2000; Yalom, 2005). This finding seems to be salient for all types of group treatment, for all theoretical models, and regardless of the duration for the group (Budman et al., 1996; MacKenzie, 2001; Rutan & Stone, 2000). Preparation can be done separately from the screening interview but, when time does not permit a separate session, and preparation for group is planned, it can be incorporated into the screening session. Preparation that focuses on three goals is most prevalent in the literature; agreement on goals, tasks, and the quality of the therapeutic attunement (Bordin, 1979; Luborsky, 1976; Horvath, 2000). These three goals can be the main focus for the pregroup preparation session.

Whereas the therapeutic alliance can be initiated during the screening session, it is during the pregroup preparation session that significant bonds can be established. Much of the success of the session depends on the quality of the leader's personal development—where his or her basic relating attributes are revealed—and on the important information the members receive. In giving this information the leader must

- Address the anxiety that is most often present due to the ambiguity and uncertainty of the new and untried group experience.
- Ensure that sufficient information is provided so that the member is making an informed consent about participation.
- Discuss collaborative goal setting so that personal goals are congruent with group goals.
- Ascertain major fears about the group, and suggest strategies to reduce these.
- Review group rules.

Reducing Anxiety. It is the unusual person who will not have some *anxiety* about the new and uncertain situation that a group experience can produce. This even applies to the group leader, who can be anxious because each group is new, and the course of the group cannot be predicted. Just imagine how much more anxious a member can be who does not have the education and experience that a group leader does. This is why it can be very important to try to address anxiety.

Members entering a counseling or psychotherapy group tend to have even more anxiety because of their personalities and the problems or issues they are bringing to the group. This anxiety can get in the way of their beginning to do therapeutic work in the group. Therefore, it is for the benefit of the group members and for the group as a whole to seek to reduce some of this anxiety.

Reduction can be accomplished by openly talking about the anxiety, the fantasies about the group and other members, and what the leader will do to assist members to deal with the anxiety. Just knowing that this is expected, and will be shared by others, can be somewhat relieving.

Informed Consent. *Informed consent* is not only ethical, but is a guide for members' expectations. The leader can describe the theoretical perspective, techniques that will be used, and potential outcomes. This is also the place where members can be assured that the leader is available for support and encouragement and to intervene to prevent members from harm or becoming overwhelmed, and where members are given permission to decide on the extent and level of personal self-disclosure. It can be comforting to members to hear out loud that they will not be forced to do anything, or that disclosure will be demanded in the face of resistance. Confidentiality concerns and documentation needs should be discussed at this time, and are a part of the informed consent.

Groups for children, adolescents, or adults who have guardians should have a separate session for the parents and guardians where the procedures, techniques that will be used, and ethical constraints, such as confidentiality, are fully explained. Minors and impaired adults cannot give consent; this is obtained from their parents or guardians.

Collaborative Goal Setting. *Collaborative goal setting* can be accomplished during the pregroup preparation session. Group leaders will find it useful to help clients set realistic and achievable goals that are more likely to be accomplished. It is not unusual for group members to have unrealistic goals and expectations for the group experience. This can be especially true for counseling and psychotherapy groups where initial goals may focus on symptom relief, changes for others in their personal relationships, and general confusion about what they want to have happen or change for them.

It can seem easier for mutual goals to be developed when the group is focused on a specific problem or condition because it is clear from the beginning what the group is supposed to be about, and members know this from the very start. This may or may not be the case; many people have only fuzzy personal goals even when they bring similar conditions or issues to the group. It is important for members to understand that the initial goals can be changed as more knowledge and understanding emerge. But even then these new personal goals should be consistent with group goals. This is one reason why it is important that group leaders be careful when setting group goals, so that they can accommodate changes in members' personal goals without changing the direction for the group.

Goals and progress will be easier to assess if the goals are stated in behavioral terms. Be as specific as possible about expectations for changes. For example, it is not helpful to set a goal of "improved" relationships, unless observable or measurable behavior will define "improved." Some members may be in such turmoil that the most they are able to express is some variation of wanting to stop hurting. This is where the expertise of the group leader is most useful: to help that person better define what "stop hurting" means, to determine what he or she can realistically expect from the group to accomplish this outcome, and to provide reassurance that the leader will assist and support the member's working to get this outcome.

Addressing Fears. The pregroup preparation session is an excellent opportunity to begin the discussion on *fears* that members bring to the group, and this continues during the first stage of group. Some members will feel that they alone have these fears, most will not openly admit them, and others will try to suppress them in order to appear less anxious than they are. However, it is not unusual for every member to have one or more of the following fears: the fear that they will not be helped by the group experience, that they will be forced to disclose shameful secrets, that the group will enable them to "catch" problems from other members, that other group members and/or the leader will ridicule or reject them, that conflict will surface and get out of control, and that they will be subject to manipulation and control by other group members and/or the leader. An open discussion about these and other fears can do much to relieve the anxiety.

Group Rules. These are initially formed by the group leader, presented to group members for their review and acceptance during the pregroup preparation, and reviewed again at the first session. It can be helpful to keep these to a bare minimum, go over them with group members to clarify what is meant, and to discuss commitment. Pregroup preparation is also the time when group members can propose modifications and other rules that will help ensure safety for group members and provide some structure for expected behaviors.

Group Facilitation Functions and the Challenges of Social Defenses

Many of the basic facilitation functions were discussed in previous chapters, but clinical groups can have more intense and deeper needs for some of these. Functions presented are:

- Therapeutic attunement that calls for a higher level of the group leader's emotional presence
- Prevention of narcissistic injury, which can more easily happen because of the greater intimacy, deeper disclosures, and uncovering of shame-producing material
- The building of a group culture that encourages self-exploration, acceptance and giving of constructive feedback, and allows therapeutic factors to emerge.

The challenges presented by social defenses are pervasive, significant, and important in building the group culture. We will discuss the effects of socialization and culture, manifestations of defenses, and communication patterns signaling the use of these defenses.

Therapeutic Attunement

Therapeutic attunement is a necessary part of establishing the therapeutic alliance, and is central for identifying, preventing, and intervening with problems. Aron (1996) proposes that healing is facilitated when there is optimal therapeutic attunement to the other's experiencing. Livingston and Livingston (1998) use the term *empathic attunement* to describe how the group leader can become aware of members' vulnerability during those times when the member's self is unprotected and may be in danger of experiencing shame, humiliation, or fragmentation (p. 382). Wright (2000) uses silent countertransference in much the same way when he writes, "The assumptions are that, first, countertransference can be induced by the client and, second, by examining it the therapist may better understand the patient's internal experience" (p. 185). Others, such as Stolorow (1993), and Cohen (2000), describe therapeutic attunement and its deepening and curative aspects.

Central to therapeutic attunement is the therapist's ability to remain accessible and aware of what members and the group are experiencing at the particular time. Ormont (1990) illustrated the benefits of therapeutic attunement in his description of how this emotional involvement state led to his understanding of the cause of the group's impasse. However, in order for this to be constructive, group leaders must be able to trust that their internal experiencing is not related to their personal unresolved issues but is a real or metaphorical reenactment of what is taking place in the group.

When members experience vulnerable moments, this presents an opportunity for positive learning experiences for the affected member(s) and for the entire group (Livingston, 1999). Vulnerable moments are the fleeting times when defenses are lowered and the person is open, available, and tender (p. 23). They are the moments when the group leader can deepen the experience to promote a genuine understanding of the member's pain and vulnerability and promote "empathic resonance" (p. 26). This is one way that the corrective emotional experience occurs, and empathic failures are repaired (Yalom, 1995). The responsiveness and emotional availability of the group leader is critical to this process.

Therapeutic attunement can be particularly useful in understanding difficult groups where the problem remains obscure for the leader. Something is disquieting, but nothing leaps out as a viable explanation. For example, the group discussions are circular, and a group process comment suggesting that there are suppressed negative feelings does not interrupt the circle discussion. Or, trying to identify a member's behavior that is troubling and may be contributing to the feeling of being stuck leads to a resolution. There can be various reasons for this situation, and the group leader who can use the therapeutic attunement process will generally find an understanding of the cause, either directly or through the understanding of a metaphor.

Therapeutic attunement requires the following for the group leader:

- Attention to both individual members and to the group as a whole
- The emotional presence of the group leader
- A consciousness about the need to prevent members' narcissistic wounding
- A commitment to recognizing empathic failures, and to repairing these
- Deep caring and understanding of the group and its members
- A sensitivity to the possibility of narcissistic injury

Prevention of Narcissistic Injury

Sensitivity to the possibility of narcissistic injury for members is also part of therapeutic attunement; these can be prevented in some instances, explored when appropriate, or used constructively to help the healing and understanding process. Narcissistic injury occurs when the essential self of the person is hurt, shamed, humiliated, or in danger of becoming destroyed. These situations cannot always be anticipated, nor are all debilitating, but the sensitive group leader stays aware of the possibility of these injuries.

Rutan and Stone (2001) perceive the group setting as a place where numerous and constant injuries such as these can occur as members feel ignored, excluded or left out, insulted, and misunderstood. For some members, the perceived slights are mild and can be overlooked or assimilated, whereas for others they constitute major blows to their self-esteem. Examples for group conditions and situations that may (can) result in narcissistic injury include:

- Frustration of dependency needs
- Receiving no response to a disclosure, comment, question, or remark
- The leader's decision to explore one member's issues when there are two or more competing ones (the leader cannot win this one)

- Emphasizing cultural and diversity differences among members instead of perceiving members as individuals
- Empathic failures
- Overt or direct suggestions that a member is "wrong"
- The leader becomes distracted and "out of the group"

Reactions to narcissistic injuries are generally rage or withdrawal (Kernberg, 1990; Livingston & Livingston, 1998; Rutan & Stone, 2001). There are some narcissistic injuries that cannot be prevented because neither you nor the group members are aware of all of their sensitivities, group members do not share this personal vulnerability readily for fear that others will misuse this information, and there are individual differences for vulnerability. Stone (1992) proposes that group leaders be especially attentive to potential narcissistic injuries in the beginning stages of group where members are fearful, tentative, and less expressive or open about the little hurts. The need to be included and a desire to not experience shame and humiliation can allow narcissistic injuries to be denied, repressed, or overlooked. Then, too, the leader's need to protect his or her essential self can produce defenses that may contribute to narcissistic injury. They can be so focused on this self-protection that empathy for a member or members is not possible (Horwitz, 2000).

Stone (1992), in describing self-psychology in groups, asserts that "Psychopathology results from narcissistic injuries" (p. 337), and that repeated or intense narcissistic injuries can produce symptoms used to restore the fragmented self. He gives Kohut and Wolfe's (1978) examples of symptoms of obsessive-compulsive behaviors, alcoholism, and chronic empty depression-like states. Stone also states that narcissistic injuries are "commonplace in everyday life" (p. 338).

It is also possible that the difficult behaviors of the group and of individual members are their responses to narcissistic injury. It could be helpful for group leaders to consider this possibility whenever they think that the whole group or individual members are acting out or being difficult. The stage of group development and the stage of member development play crucial roles in the decision to explore the injury in the group. When injuries are recognized and explored in the group after safety and trust are established, that process can be a valuable experience for all group members and for the leader. It is unlikely that the group or members feel safe and trusting enough for this exploration in the beginning stage. And, it may be that until the second stage is navigated—where the leader is challenged and does not react defensively, and where conflicts emerge and are constructively resolved—group members are confident that their innerselves are not in danger of being deliberately attacked, shamed, or humiliated, and narcissistic injury can be explored and understood (Cohen, 2000). The most effective strategies for effecting identification and repair of narcissistic injury are empathy and empathic failure repair.

Build the Group's Culture

Building a group culture where members are able to accept open, honest, and direct communication and process commentary is critical to the group's movement through stages of development as well as fostering the psychological growth and development of members. Almost all textbooks on group counseling and group development have a section related to group culture, but few address building the culture. Agazarian (1997), Posthuma (2000) and Yalom (1995) do address the topic but do not provide specific information that will help group leaders. Central to building the group's culture is an understanding of naturally occurring barriers, such as the social convention that considers it rude to openly comment on another person's nonverbal behavior. Understanding the barriers can guide group leaders to make constructive use of process and process commentary.

Major barriers to developing the desired culture are social conventions, rules, norms, and taboos established early in life and acted on unconsciously. These social defenses can prevent establishing the desired group culture, and have a negative impact on process commentary. This discussion will describe social defenses, the impact of culture on their development, how social defenses are manifested, the effects on group process commentary, and the leader's role and strategies.

Socialization and the Impact of Culture

Socialization begins at birth and continues throughout life. Some social conventions, norms, and the like are specifically taught whereas others are unconsciously interjected, internalized, and become part of the self. This is partly how we become acculturated and use the culture's definition for who is acceptable and "in," and who is not acceptable and "out." The unconscious conventions, rules, norms, and taboos are more important than are the conscious ones; the conscious ones can be verbalized and observed, whereas the unconscious ones are acted on without thought and may not even be capable of being verbalized. Both overt and covert social conventions, rules, norms, and taboos are significant antigroup attitudes and behaviors (Nitsun, 1996). A group leader must overcome much of this socialization and acculturation to be effective in encouraging self-disclosure, using the interpersonal learning feedback loop, and in making process commentary and having it nondefensively accepted by group members.

In this discussion, *culture* is both macro and micro: macro in the sense of the person's larger environment, such as the community, city, or country; micro in the sense of one's family or social group. Social conventions, rules, and norms are present in our environment when we are born and significantly influence our beliefs, attitudes, and behaviors. Verderber and Verderber (1992) consider these cultural conventions, rules, and norms to be mandates that guide our understanding of acceptable and unacceptable behavior—what is appropriate to say and how to say it in various contexts, and what messages are appropriate for certain people.

Cultural normative influences cause the individual's thoughts, actions, and feelings to be in concert with what was internalized as appropriate norms. (Forsyth, 1999). These standards are accepted by the person as legitimate; there are negative consequences, such as ridicule or punishment, for failure to conform; and when behavior deviates from the norm, guilt and shame ensue as the person has failed to live up to personal expectations. Each group member brings a unique set of cultural influences to the group, and needs time to adjust to the group's culture. Group culture can have very different expectations, especially for actions such as direct feedback. Members have to learn what can be communicated in the group, how their thoughts and feelings can be delivered so as to be acceptable, and what personal information to disclose.

Effect on Process Commentary

Yalom (1995) describes three process commentary taboos that are a direct result of socialization and acculturation: Do not closely monitor or stare at another person, do not constantly make observations or comments about others' behavior, and do not allow reciprocal process observation and commentary. These taboos work against teaching group members to accept process commentary, which is a critical task for the group leader. However, members generally are not ready for or knowledgeable about it and must be gently and sensitively led to doing and accepting something that turns their conventional ways of behaving and thinking upside down. The taboos are deeply ingrained.

Close monitoring or staring at another person is perceived as rude and threatening, forcing intimacy and generally making others uncomfortable. However, group leaders need to monitor members to gauge their needs, intensity of feeling, cues for intervention, and so on. This is a vital task for the leader because members do not always speak out for what they want or need, and may expect the group leader to intuit it. Monitoring allows the group leader to observe members, and comments on those observations can be a check on their validity.

Members may and do become self-conscious when open *comments are made about their behavior*. For example, if a leader were to notice and comment about a member jiggling his foot, that member is likely to stop and to consciously refrain from foot jiggling instead of reflecting on the internal state that is reflected in the nonverbal behavior. The leader is not trying to get the member to stop the behavior; the leader wants the member to examine the behavior and its implications. It would be more productive if the member could accept the comment and reflect on it rather than becoming self-conscious about it and trying to suppress it.

The third taboo refers to the relationship of members with the leader. Members will not be accustomed to observing and commenting about *authority figures*. Such behavior is perceived as undermining the arbitrary authority stance, which can trigger anxieties and fears. Anxieties around relationships with parents can become particularly acute and troubling when some members challenge the leader. These are very strong taboos that must be overcome if members are to accept process commentary, and this learning takes time to develop.

Manifestation of Social Defenses

Agazarian (1997) presents a description of social defenses and categorizes them as cognitive, somatic, masochistic, and sadistic. Social defenses are defined as those that are stereotypical social interactions designed to avoid authenticity, deflect members from the real task, establish members' status in the group, define the rules of relationships among and between members, and maintain boundaries.

Social defenses are employed to keep the real self from being seen by others for fear of rejection, destruction, or other fantasized negative consequences. "Others won't like me." "They'll ignore or avoid me." "They may hurt me." Making self-statements such as these is a way to rationalize why a social persona is necessary, and is a common way to avoid authenticity. Further, it leads to an assumption that everyone else is doing the same and, as a consequence, not recognizing genuineness or being taken aback by genuineness and authenticity. The person who is genuine and authentic runs more of a risk of being rejected at first, than does the person who puts on a social face. The real person is not believed to be so, and can be perceived as very threatening.

Deflecting from the real task allows members to avoid intimacy, preserve their false persona, suppress important feelings, keep the group from being present–centered, and refrain from self-exploration and self-reflection. Common strategies for deflecting include intellectualizing, talking about feelings, introducing there-and-then topics or "goblet" topics (Yalom, 1995), giving advice, and having an identified patient.

Every group has a pecking order and social defenses are employed to establish and maintain one's *status*. The status each member has in the group determines, in part, the extent to which he or she is included or excluded, the deference expected or received from others, the affection he or she attracts, and the quality of acceptance and approval received from other members. Social defenses are an unconscious dance among members that select and protect each member's place in the group.

Unconscious *rules of relationship* or engagement are also established and maintained via social defenses. Verbal and nonverbal messages are sent and received about the degree of intimacy that is desired or can be tolerated; about a member's willingness to let himself or herself be known, and to whom he or she is open or closed; about appropriate and acceptable personal topics for verbalizing; and if input from others will be valued. Every relationship has its rules, and the most important rules may be on the unconscious level. That is, the expectations and needs for interactions are both sent and received on an unconscious level and social defenses are used as a means of sending these messages.

Boundaries are very important and their usefulness is not to be underestimated. Boundaries allow us to protect our self from the potential threats in the everyday world. Social defenses contribute to maintenance of boundaries. People without sufficient boundaries or boundary strength run risks of becoming enmeshed, overwhelmed, or destroyed by others who, unconsciously, have needs of power and control, underdeveloped narcissism, or other unresolved issues that do not recognize the rights of others. For example, individuals with a borderline personality disorder do not have strong and appropriate boundaries, nor do they recognize those of others. Social defenses allow us to stay safe until we can better gauge the potential threat to our self.

Recognizing Social Defenses. Agazarian (1997) mentions two main ways that social defenses are manifested—social talk and social flight. Social talk allows us to appear friendly without being a friend. This is talk that conveys no personal or factual information. For example, talking about your job does not give the person information about your perceptions, feelings, or relationships relative to the workplace. The most meaningful and significant information is kept concealed.

The other manifestation is social flight. Flight defenses are seen in the following behaviors:

- Answering a question with a question
- Changing the subject
- Interrupting a speaker
- Discounting what someone says
- Making insinuations
- Using sarcasm
- Gossipping

- Telling funny stories and victimizing jokes
- Using monologues
- Pontificating (acting like a "know it all")

Considerable effort can be expended on keeping others from becoming close, intimate, and in a position to know one's secrets.

Social Defenses and Group Communication Patterns

Observing communication patterns in group sessions reveals what social defenses are used. Agazarian (1997) describes seven communication patterns. Patterns of communication are emphasized so that unwarranted conclusions are not drawn from a single, or even two incidents. Behaviors that signal use of a social defense can include as-if statements, emotional inferiority, emotional superiority, intellectual superiority, moral righteousness, self-protection, leader defenses, and status defense.

"*As if*" statements are fogging statements that are intended to convey involvement but, in reality, are used to remain safe and protected. These are yes-but responses that start out as agreeing and end up as disagreeing. These communications are ambiguous and full of redundancies. Examples of as-if statements include the following: "I don't know what you want." "I want to do what you suggest but_____." The first statement implies that the person would do what you wanted if only you were clearer in making your desires known. In actuality, what the person is saying is that as long as he or she can claim confusion, he or she does not have to act or become involved. The second statement is a disguised way of saying that he or she has no intention of doing what was suggested but does not want to run the risk of offending, or of appearing uncooperative by saying so openly.

Emotional inferiority occurs when the speaker assumes an inferior stance compared to others. Putting oneself down and discounting self in direct or hidden ways reflects this defense. Some behaviors are complaining, becoming more needy, expecting others to read your mind, and being the scapegoat or identified patient. There always seems to be someone in the group who rushes to take care of this person either for self-soothing reasons or because that is his or her characteristic behavior. All involved are using social defenses to maintain distance and superficiality.

Intellectual superiority seeks to use social expectations to exert power and influence without openly seeming to do so. This social defense puts others on the defensive and allows the focus to be shifted to the cognitive, the impersonal, or to put the person on the defensive. The communication pattern for this defense is one of challenge, persuasion, argument, interruption, interpretation, advice giving, or asking leading questions. In all these instances, the speaker not only avoids revealing any personal information or feelings, but he or she also refocuses the spotlight on other topics or people.

Moral righteousness is not the same as taking a stand or supporting personal moral and ethical values. Either or both of those would be honest and genuine. Moral righteousness is fingerpointing that is intended to produce shame and guilt in the other person and to shore up personal feelings of superiority. "I'm better than you are" is the theme of the moral righteousness social defense communication pattern. Verbal interactions contain words such as *should* and *ought*, and *always* and *never*, applied to the other person(s). This communication taps wishes, fears, old parental messages, and the receiver's deep-seated fear that the self is not good enough and may be fatally flawed.

Some people can *keep your attention and interest* with funny stories, jokes, gossip, and so on. They always seem to know how to keep the session flowing and their social skills can make them the "life of the party." However, this behavior also functions to protect them from intimacy and from revealing their true selves. As long as the conversation is on another topic or person, they are satisfied. The interest and excitement engendered by telling jokes is icing on the cake. They will now be sought out and perceived as having something interesting or funny to say. You never get to see the real people behind the smokescreen.

Leaders, too, can mount social defenses. The most common *leader defense* is termed *one up–one down* by Agazarian (1997). Behaviors such as dissonance between what is said and what is done, avoidance of contact by not emotionally connecting with members, and double-bind messages are examples of this defense. The leader uses the position to maintain power, control, and anonymity.

The *status defense* is extremely difficult to avoid because both the leader and group members use it, although for different reasons. Members arrive at the group expecting the leader to be an authority and to take care of them. Indeed, the leader has to fulfill both functions to some extent. These functions become a defense when members continue their dependency over a period of time, refuse to accept responsibility for their own treatment, and are threatened by the leader's attempts to promote separation and individuation. Leaders use the defense to maintain power and control, and to meet personal dependency needs. Leaders who do not empower members to take responsibility for their treatment and progress will thereby encourage dependency. Leaders who want to be the "expert" and make brilliant interpretations and interventions are using the status defense.

Strategies to Address Social Convention and Defenses

Agazarian (1997) and Posthuma (2003) agree that there are limited strategies that can be used to overcome these strongly ingrained social norms. They may be capable of modification so that communication among members becomes more direct, genuine, and authentic, and so that members can accept and make use of process commentary. Agazarian (1997) proposes that the group culture be built to encourage more functional and therapeutic relationships. Posthuma (1999) proposes that an open discussion be held about the social norms, rules, and taboos that are exhibited by group members.

There are few strategies that can be used to modify social defenses and norms in the short term. Long-term therapy groups may have more success with members understanding and accepting of more open and honest communication, but that takes time to develop and lifelong practices and attitudes are well entrenched. The group leader must make extensive use of the therapeutic relationship by modeling desired communication and sensitivity to the impact of process commentary, and by providing instruction on effective communication.

The quality of *the therapeutic relationship* is a crucial component in the members' willingness to modify social defenses and promote a group culture that encourages open and honest communication, and their willingness to accept and use process commentary. Members will have to believe that your communication and process commentary are not designed to blame them for being or doing something wrong, nor are they intended to trigger feelings of guilt and shame. You have to first establish a therapeutic relationship where members believe that you care for them, have their best interests at heart, and are not seeking to hurt them. This relationship develops over time and cannot be rushed.

The behaviors *modeled* by the group leader are much more powerful than those that are discussed or taught. If the goal is to have members be open, honest, and direct in their communications, then the leader must also exhibit those characteristics. Keeping in mind the stage of group, the emotional status and well-being of group members, and the quality of the established relationship, leaders can immediately model desired communications. For example, if strength building is done in the first session(s), the leader can make open and honest comments about how members are perceived by him or her.

Sensitivity to the impact of comments, reactions, and process commentary is important, as the leader's comments can be very insightful and powerful, which is threatening and fearful for some members. Leaders' reactions require sensitivity to members' denial, silence, resistance, anger, easy agreement with what the leader says, and when the focus is shifted to the leader or when members make changes designed to please the leader.

Leaders must be especially careful when using process commentary for either individual member's personal use or for the whole group's development. They must not push for acceptance or agreement, and accept that resistance to process commentary is there for a purpose and respect it. Work with the feelings triggered by the process comment. That procedure can accomplish what the comment intended without attacking the resistance.

Group leaders can use a variety of methods to *teach* open and honest communication and an acceptance of process commentary. Modeling is essential and was previously discussed. Other modes of instruction include encouraging members to make "I" statements, to respond to others by expressing personal feelings, to constantly respond, to explore possible transference and projections, and to examine feelings triggered by responses of others and in response to process commentary. Provide written guidelines with examples for effective communication. Role-play how an ineffective communication could be redone to be more effective. These instructional strategies have to become an integral part of what you do and are as the leader.

Facilitative Strategies for Clinical Groups

There are numerous strategies that are facilitative for these groups, and most of them are discussed in previous chapters. Two facilitative strategies are presented here as having special applications for clinical groups: process commentary and teaching group members to accept this, and constructive use of the leader's countertransference.

Group leaders also have some learning and developing to do to be able to make and use process commentary and more open communication. The basic steps are as follows:

1. Become more comfortable with dropping social defenses and using open communication and process commentary.

2. Identify social defenses used by members and the support provided by the group culture that encourages or discourages open and genuine communication.

3. Cultivate patience and acceptance of social defenses, but also emphasize the positive aspects of more open and honest communications.

4. Initiate discussions of the defenses used by the group, with particular attention to feelings generated about not using them.

5. Recognize and accept the feelings of guilt and shame that can be triggered, and do not push for immediate modification of these defenses.

6. Teach more open and genuine communication.

7. Encourage members to practice *in the group.*

8. Make process commentary with sensitivity and attention to triggered feelings.

These strategies are presented as sequential steps, but some can be done out of order. For example, you may wish to make process commentary from the very beginning, or before teaching members how to make their communication more open and honest. However, the first step is essential if any of the others are to be successful.

Increase your comfort with dropping social defenses by recognizing that the therapeutic relationship is different from relationships outside the group. You can adopt the following attitudes: that members are responsible for their feelings; that the leader has a responsibility to be sensitive and caring and incorporates faith in members' abilities to care for themselves; that the leader's comments must be examined prior to verbalization for personal motives, transference, and projections; and that the therapeutic relationship is different from other relationships in that the leader is both intimate with members but also remains detached. To be effective, group leaders must learn to manage and contain their personal anxiety, not take members' comments as criticisms or attacks, deeply understand what members' concerns are no matter how indirectly they are phrased, and demonstrate faith in members' ability to participate in their treatment.

Social defenses are present from the initiation of the group and persist for some time. They are identified by observing members' behavior, their discussions of fears about group, and the communication patterns in the group. What is avoided is also a clue. For example, if members avoid responding to each other when emotionally intense material is introduced, the leader can solicit responses as to why members are not responding. These responses will help identify social defenses.

There are some defenses that are almost always present, such as fear of offending or being offended, the possibility of hurting someone, and fear of being rejected. Members will speak of these fears both directly and indirectly. Thus, identification is not usually difficult, but it is helpful if you can be specific about which ones are being used in the particular group, especially when initiating step 4.

Although process commentary can be made throughout the group's life, it is best done after establishing the therapeutic relationship. Remember that members are not accustomed to observing, monitoring, and commenting directly to others about their behavior, and will be surprised and threatened when the leader does. Leaders should *cultivate patience* so that they do not indirectly convey criticism that members should be accepting of process commentary. The same is true for teaching members to use and accept more open and honest communication.

Before initiating a *discussion about social defenses* it is important that the leader understand the whole group's communication pattern, identify individual and group social defenses, and identify or have a hunch about what is being defended against and be able to verbalize this with behavioral examples. The discussion should be about behaviors that are observable and specific. Care should be taken to ensure that there is no criticism or chastisement of members for the behavior. It is being brought to their attention so that they can become aware of their ineffective communication and modes of relating in order to begin to learn more effective ways of communicating and relating.

There can be profound *feelings of guilt and shame triggered* by the discussion. Some members will fear offending others or being rejected so much that they cannot conceive of acting any other way. Leaders should remember that they are asking members to act in dissonance with their socialization and acculturation. It takes time to even accept that there are more effective ways to communicate, and that everything does not have to be taken personally. Leaders who are aware and sensitive about the difficulty can do much to allay fears and encourage members to experiment with new behavior.

Teaching acceptance of process commentary and more open and honest communication is a continuing process. The methods previously listed, such as responding to the input of others, are a good beginning. It may be helpful to try and modify, or teach, only a few behaviors at a time rather than trying to make many changes too quickly. Leaders will want to reinforce progress by commenting on attempts to change, and to point out the positive outcomes and lack of negative outcomes for experimenting with the new behaviors.

Encourage members to *practice* new ways of behaving, relating, and communicating *in the group*. These new ways are not always appropriate or appreciated in other settings. There will be some transfer to outside the group relationships and situations as members learn how to be more direct and honest. However, until they are comfortable with this communication in the group, they should recognize and accept that it is only for use in the group.

Encouragement to practice can take the form of reminding members to make "I" statements; take ownership and responsibility for personal feelings by verbalizing them in the group; allow others the opportunity to take responsibility for their triggered feelings and not withhold input; care for others and not minimize their input by changing the topic or seeking to soothe their intense feelings; and by highlighting that their worse fears about open and direct communication are not being realized. When members do some or most of these, then they will feel closer and be more accepting of one another, and trust and safety will increase.

Process commentary is very threatening to some members and it is important that the group leader stay in touch with its impact on members. This commentary is not helpful to members if initiated before a therapeutic relationship is established because process commentary speaks of those things that socialization, norms, rules, and taboos have taught are improper to openly verbalize. The most important outcome for process commentary is that members accept and make constructive use of it, either for the individual or for the entire group. If members are busy mobilizing their defenses, they will not be able to hear the real message nor to make use of it. If the desired outcome is to be attained, then process commentary should be made with sensitivity, an understanding of the strength and level of the established therapeutic relationship, and always with attention to the impact on the individual and on the group.

Constructive Use of the Leader's Countertransference

There are various definitions for countertransference and all include the group leader's reaction to the client. The most current definitions emphasize constructive use for countertransference rather than considering it as something to be avoided at all costs. Both past and current views consider countertransference to be internal, even when feelings are induced by the client, unconscious or nonconscious, and that they are also carriers of information about the therapist, the client, and the relationship. Leaders of counseling and psychotherapy groups may have more opportunities to constructively use their countertransference because of the duration of the group; the severity and intensity of members' issues, concerns, and problems; and because of the emphasis on self-exploration in depth.

Interactional theorists consider the therapist to be an integral part of the relationship and interaction. Wright (2000), Aron (1996), and Jordan (1991) emphasize the importance of a genuine and mutual relationship, and Yalom (1985) points out how the altruistic interactions of leaders and members, and those among members, can be curative. These theorists consider the therapist's self to be a valuable resource for therapy because the feelings, fantasies, associations, dreams, and so on can be rich sources of information about group members. Countertransference is not to be avoided; it is to be understood and exploited. However, there are some countransference behaviors and attitudes that can be destructive. Examples are presented in Table 12.1.

Many current therapists have moved to a definition for countertransference that considers it as all of the following: nonpathological, a potentially useful tool, both conscious and unconscious responses, and as feelings from both the therapist's inner experiencing and projection identifications from clients (Kernberg, 1965; Segal, 1979). Countertransference has come to mean something that is not to be minimized or avoided, but something to be used as a rich source of information to assist in therapy. However, accompanying this definition and use is the assumption that the therapist will have done the necessary inner work on identifying and working through personal issues. The new definition does not mean that countransference is no longer dangerous; rather, what it intends is that there be informed countertransference. There is still an essential need for the therapist not to allow his or her unresolved issues to negatively impact therapy.

Leaders will have to contain and manage the many personal feelings that can be triggered by these behaviors and attitudes. Indeed, it may appear that group members are profoundly dissatisfied with the leader and are not shy about letting their feelings be known. Insecure leaders who are unaware of their personal issues that need work, or of their countertransference, will take these members' behaviors as personal attacks. Depending on their needs, these leaders will either go on the offensive and become aggressive and sadistic, or will work harder to get members to like them.

Table 12.1
Clues to Countertransference and Negative Leader Behaviors

Hugging clients	Fearing or avoiding sexual feelings
Behaving seductively	Suppressing conflict with a member
Demeaning or discounting the client	Becoming defensive
Putting the client on the defensive	Overprotecting
Being contemptuous	Fearing abandonment by the client
Criticizing or blaming the client	Being a perfectionist
Mind-wandering when the client is talking	Daydreaming
Becoming anxious during a session	Prolonging a session or ending early
Forgetting a client's name	Dreaming or fantasizing about a client
Being repeatedly late to sessions	Socializing outside the office
Using clients to highlight skills and power	Encouraging dependency
Insisting that clients accept your interpretations	

Group leaders can make use of their subjective experiences by attending to these and analyzing them. The experiences induced by members, such as projections, are clues for interventions. The experiences that arise from personal needs and unresolved issues should be explored in supervision or personal therapy, not in the group.

Clinical Groups for Children and Adolescents

Although many of the problems, issues, and concerns that affect children and adolescents are the same as those for adults, counseling and psychotherapy groups with these audiences must be constructed somewhat differently. Chapter 6 on planning groups describes some basic and general needs when creating groups for children and adolescents. This section discusses categories of childhood and adolescents stressors, resistance styles and how these can be handled, group facilitation strategies and techniques that will be helpful, and how the self of the group leader is used in clinical groups.

Children and adolescents of today face myriad stressors, and many do not have the internal resources or the external support to help them effectively cope. These stressors can be categorized as intraindividual—those occurring within the individual—and external. Examples for intraindividual stressors include the following:

- Physical health, including nutrition, disease, and disability
- Extent of cognitive development
- Sexual identity
- Emotional difficulties such as depression, suicide ideation, and mood disorders
- Developmental factors and expectations
- Acting out, bullying, or violence against others

Examples for external stressors include these:

- Homelessness
- Victimization
- Abuse
- Parental alcohol or drug addiction
- Parental unemployment, frequent moves, and the like
- Violence at home or in the community
- School-related problems
- Parental physical and emotional problems or disability
- Physical and emotional neglect
- Death

The intraindividual and external problems can be intertwined, with one contributing to the other. For example, cognitive development delay (intraindividual) could be due to external concerns such as violence, or parental drug addiction. They cannot always be separated.

The group leader needs to have a good understanding of the physical, emotional, cognitive, and other developmental issues that all children and adolescents encounter, and to understand when the course of development has been delayed, interrupted, or otherwise unexpected. Formal assessment can be a critical need when planning treatment, and in the decision to use group counseling or group psychotherapy.

Intraindividual stressors can affect the developing self, which may have significant implications for the child and adolescent's self-esteem, self-confidence, and self-efficacy. In effect, children and adolescents are helpless to understand just how they are supposed to develop, or how they did not get what was needed for appropriate development. Hartman (2005), in reviewing a current book on evidence-based psychotherapy treatment for children and adolescents, noted that the book did not address the intraindividual stressors, or provide the counselor with information to help understand these. Because the development of the self is basic and affects other areas of development, this is a serious omission. The same can be said for many other books covering counseling and psychotherapy for children and adolescents. This is a major and serious gap in presentation of major topics that would help the group leader plan effective groups for these audiences.

External stressors are caused and impacted by parental and familial factors, environmental, community, and even global situations and events such as military deployment, and affect the developing child and adolescent. Stressors, such as those listed, can have negative effects on adults who have some understanding of and control over many of them. These negative effects are transmitted to the child and adolescent who have less, if any, understanding and fewer coping mechanisms and resources.

Leaders may want to consider forming groups around specific issues and concerns related to external stressors to promote universality among the children or adolescents, and lessen feelings of isolation and alienation (Aronson & Kahn, 2004; Scheidlinger, 2004). Indeed, counseling and psychotherapy groups described in the literature tend to be focused on a particular issue, concern, or problem (Malekoff, 1997; Sommers-Flanagan & Sommers-Flanagan, 2007; AGPA, 2004).

Resistance Styles

Individual and group resistance was described in previous chapters. The suggestion was made that the resistance is there to protect the individual or the group, and that it is best to leave the resistance alone until the group member or the group feels sufficiently safe to lower the resistance. Children and adolescents may tend to have styles of resistance (Sommers-Flanagan & Sommers-Flanagan, 2007) that can be constructively used to understand what they are defending against, and to help them express their concerns more openly. The styles are:

- Externalizing blame, off-loading responsibility, and being unduly influenced by others
- Denial of action, or responsibility
- Nonverbal gestures that show frustration, distain, and the like
- Silence that lasts until it is uncomfortable and seems stubborn
- Verbal attacks, especially those on the leader
- Apathy, zoning out, and other indifferent acts

Externalizing blame, responsibility, and source of influence can be used to avoid punishment, disapproval, and disappointment by self and by others. Whatever happened wasn't their fault, and they should not have to bear any penalty for what was done. This resistance style can be easily supported when the events, situations, and people surrounding the child and adolescent did not protect or prepare the child or adolescent properly, or were out of control. However, this puts the child or adolescent in the position of being a victim, and of not learning to take care of himself or herself.

It is inadvisable to use direct confrontation for this resistance because it will seem to be critical of the child or adolescent group member (Glasser, 2001; Miller & Rollnick, 2002). More useful strategies would be to hear and respond to the underlying feelings and fears. Fears of experiencing, or of others seeing, their guilt, shame, and inadequacy could underlie the tendency to externalize blame and to protect the self.

Denial is not the simple act of refusing to admit something; it is a defense mechanism where the person using it does not perceive something, is not willing to accept it, and can be threatened by having it appear in his or her awareness. Thus, it is dangerous for the person to have others, such as the group leader, try to get through the defense and bring the material to conscious awareness.

A useful strategy with denial, when there is evidence that the denial is not consistent with reality or facts, is to join with the person and let him or her explain the perception. For example, if a child were to deny that he or she was sad and there were reported behaviors that indicated sadness such as crying every day over nothing that seemed to justify tears, the group leader could ask the child to talk about what was positive or happy about his or her life. As they talk, the child can become more comfortable with sharing other parts of his or her life, including the not-so-positive ones.

Nonverbal gestures of frustration, disdain, and so on include eye rolling, heavy sighs, and voice intonations that indicate disgust, disbelief, and barely controlled anger. It's like they can barely tolerate your presence, and are having difficulty with what you are saying. These gestures are an attempt to prevent being controlled by others, of needing to assert their superiority, or to keep others at a distance for fear they will not be understood or appreciated. It's easy to become offended by some of these gestures.

A strategy that may be of help is to first ignore the gestures and continue to relate to the group member as if the gestures were absent. But, if they continue, and they usually will, the leader can ask the member if it is difficult for him or her to be in the group at that time, and if he or she has some concerns about how he or she is being treated. Listen carefully, and you may pick up some clues about the real difficulty in his or her life. Empathize with the feelings expressed, and also ask if these feelings are shared by other members in the group, even if other members have different reasons for their feelings.

Silence, especially prolonged silence, can be a signal of discomfort, of deep reflection, or of needing more power and control. It can be difficult to discern the motive for the silence, because that member will not talk about it. It is not helpful to push for the group member to talk, or other verbal interaction as the silence may have its cause in physical or sexual abuse, and the member may not yet be ready to disclose this (Sommers-Flanagan & Sommers-Flanagan, 2007).

One suggestion for silence is to initiate an exercise or other activity that will encourage and support verbal responses. Art activities can be especially useful, and there are many that could be focused on something positive and relevant for the purpose of the group. Some activities are described in chapter 15.

Verbal attacks, whether toward other group members or toward the leader, should be quickly and firmly blocked. The group leader must take care to not become defensive or blame or criticize. The resistance is to prevent being seen by others, having others get too close or intimate, or to prevent being hurt or destroyed by a perceived danger. The group member is playing keep away.

Blocking these attacks should be done sensitively with awareness of the impact of what is said on the attacking member, and on other members. Whatever is done at this point will be seen by the group as a model for what can happen to others. Word choice, voice tone, and facial expression are a part of blocking, and group leaders should be aware of how they are coming across to the group. A procedure for blocking would be to look at that group member, tell him or her that you are intervening because you think that it would be helpful for the group at this point, describe the behavior without labeling it as bad or wrong, and hypothesize a possible goal for the attack. Goals to be openly hypothesized are to prevent a perceived attack (real or fantasized), to make the group feel safe, to show that the member isn't sure about trust in the group, or to avoid talking about the feelings they are experiencing at the time.

Apathy and other forms of indifference are difficult to tolerate. These fogging behaviors obscure and deflect very well so that the child or adolescent does not have to engage, and can keep others at a distance. A useful strategy is to join the group member and reflect the feelings that the apathy or indifference convey. Some empathic statements could also be of assistance. Another strategy is to use an activity that calls for some input on the member's part. Even if he or she does not say much, the activity itself will probably be enjoyable and produce some learning. If this attitude continues, the group leader can see if other members share the feelings, or if the feelings affect them in some way. The leader can also express his or her desire for the person to join the group. It is important to not criticize, blame, or label the behavior and attitude as wrong, or to ignore the member continuously. Do not allow other members to attack him or her; it can be easy for the indifferent member to be scapegoated.

Group Facilitation

When leading groups for children and adolescents it is important that the group leader be prepared, structure the group and individual sessions, explain the techniques and processes, address confidentiality and reporting concerns, set collaborative goals and group rules, and attend to the safety and trust needs for group members. So far, this is not too different from creating adult groups, except that for children and adolescents there needs to be more precise structure that is carefully explained. The same should be done for the parents or guardians.

For children and adolescents, however, it is also important to plan to do only as much as the group members can tolerate; there is a greater need for flexibility. It is also helpful for group leaders to have selected exercises and other activities consistent with group and individual goals. These may be used more frequently than would be the case for adult groups.

Leaders who use many reflective and empathic statements will most likely find that group members become more responsive as they feel more understood. This is also good modeling, and can be used as a teaching tool for members to learn how to give more empathic responses. Other facilitation strategies include supporting their feelings even when the behavior cannot be supported, providing specific symptom relief techniques and actions, doing frequent goal checkups, and encouraging member-to-member interactions and responses. Children and adolescents can be of assistance to each other, and when leaders recognize this, they can point out the helpfulness and how altruism benefits both the giver and the receiver.

The Group Leader's Self

Group leaders can bring a great deal of empathy to the problems of children and adolescents, but must be careful to monitor their negative countertransference as this is easy to get triggered. One of the most important group factors is the emotional presence of the group leader. It is refreshing and helpful to have an adult listen, reflect, and understand and validate their feelings because this may not occur anywhere else in their lives. The leader's developed self will allow him or her to better tolerate behaviors that can be distressing under other circumstances, to provide encouragement and support even in the face of considerable adversity, and to reassure group members about the commonality of expected developmental concerns and other issues.

Summary

1. Leaders of clinical groups should give special attention to screening, pregroup preparation, and the therapeutic relationship to promote the creation of a group that can address members' deeper needs, foster disclosure and self-exploration, and guide members in learning new ways to behave and relate.

2. The group leader's understanding of the challenges of naturally occurring social defenses will increase the therapeutic attunement, moderate their negative influences, and permit the judicious use and acceptance of process commentary.

3. The group experience can be enhanced when group leaders constructively use their countertransference as a guide for understanding what is taking place in the group and with individual members at the current moment.

4. Clinical groups for children and adolescents can be enhanced through leaders' understanding of their developmental needs and processes, intra and interindividual stressors, and through the use of the leader's developed self.

Chapter Activities

1. Divide the class into small groups or triads and have them develop a list of screening questions to elicit prospective group members' motivation, commitment, interpersonal competency, and desire for change. Discuss the lists with the entire class.

2. Using the lists developed in # 1, have dyads practice screening. Both the interviewer and the interviewee should report on the experience to the class.

3. Practice making group process commentary to the following group situations. Be sure to focus these comments on the group as a whole.

   a. Late in the ninth meeting a man talks about his marital problems. The members offer numerous suggestions, he listens to each of them, and then explains why the particular suggestions will not work.

   b. The group has met for several months. At this meeting, a woman who is unusually silent for the first half of the session makes a brief attempt to fight back tears, and then begins to cry. No one says anything to her or about the crying.

Chapter 13

Challenges, Difficulties, and Interventions: Member Level

Major Topics

1. Definitions for difficult groups and difficult members, and possible goals for the behaviors.

2. Leader's contributions to the emergence of difficulties.

3. Descriptions for member behavior for three categories: taking charge, hopeless or helpless, and indirect attack and defense. Each category has several descriptive behaviors, possible goals for the behavior, and suggested leader responses.

4. Leader interventions and strategies for prevention of difficult behaviors, counterproductive interventions, and suggested interventions and strategies.

5. A model and strategy for confrontation/enlightenment.

Introduction

This chapter redefines problem members as displaying behaviors that are difficult to manage, and are troubling to the group's process and progress (Brown, 2006). This redefinition takes away blame and criticism, and directs the focus to understanding the possible goal for the behavior so that leaders can reflect and choose more effective and constructive interventions.

Specific suggestions are provided that can assist the leader in preventing some behaviors, including certain leader behaviors that can be counterproductive. In addition, actions to address specific difficult behaviors are discussed, and a reconceptualization of confrontation to reduce its perceived negative qualities. Leaders are encouraged to perceive difficult member behaviors as information about the member or the group.

Definitions and Descriptions

The difficult group or difficult member is defined here in terms of the group leader's experiencing of the situation or person as disruptive, unhelpful, and in some cases even destructive. Rutan and Stone (2001) define difficult groups as those where the leader has "trouble making and sustaining emotional contact" and experiences the group as stuck, confusing, boring, frustrating, or even unresponsive. Gans and Alonso (1998) use the concept of *intersubjectivity*—that is, the mutual experiencing of one another's world at the same time—to explain how the group leader or other members contribute to the construction of the difficult member, the need that role or difficulty fulfills, and its value to the group. They propose that the difficult member can best be understood in terms of the need he or she fulfills, and that the difficult member is partly a "construction of the whole system" (p. 312). Rutan and Stone (2001) propose that members identified as difficult, such as the monopolizer and help-rejecting complainer, do not exist as such from the self-psychology perspective.

This self-psychology perspective would redefine the behavior as the functions that it serves for the person, and for the group. For example, Rutan and Stone (2001) write, "The so-called help-rejecting complainer probably does not exist!" (p. 302). They redefine the behavior for this person as a fundamental failure to communicate what help they are looking for, and as empathic failures for both the leader and members.

This shift to a self-psychology perspective depends on the leader

- Understanding the goal of the behavior
- Having a strong connection to the group member
- Possessing an ability to empathize with the member
- Providing the member with encouragement and support to facilitate self-exploration
- Having a deep understanding of how that member perceives him or herself and his or her emotional fragility

The focus is on hearing what the member needs, wants, and desires that is not being communicated appropriately or effectively.

Goals for troubling behaviors generally fall into one or more of the following categories: attention, power, control, revenge, protection of the self, yearning for connection or intimacy, fearing connection or intimacy, avoidance of emotions or emotional intensity, a need for being heard and understood, and as a way to prevent disintegration or fragmentation. Leaders, by virtue of their training, experience, and personal development, can uncover the possible goal the troubling behavior fulfills, make an empathic connection, and be emotionally present so that an empathic response and experience could provide reassurance of caring and safety. Thus, the members exhibiting the troubling behaviors will be deeply understood, the possibility of scapegoating can be reduced, and other group members will learn that the group is a safe place and that the leader is prepared to handle conflict, aggression, and other disquieting behaviors.

The Leader's Contributions to Difficulties

Gans and Alonso (1998) feel that the leader can contribute to fostering the "construction" of the difficult group member in several ways: faulty selection of group members where unsuitability for the group is not identified; incompetent or inappropriate management of group norms, scapegoating, and boundary violations; an inability to admit to mistakes; defensiveness when challenged or a refusal to let the members express negative feelings about the leader; and failure to recognize personal limitations. Many of these can be the result of underdeveloped narcissism (Horwitz, 2000), or unresolved narcissistic needs (Gans Alonso, 1998). Several leader attitudes and behaviors are indicative of underdeveloped narcissism (Horwitz, 2000).

- Being unable to tolerat or accept negative criticisms or devaluation
- Being overly nurturing
- Ignoring the behaviors of members who are difficult or act out
- Working hard to avoid doing or saying anything that might provoke a negative response
- Encouraging scapegoating
- Consciously or unconsciously seeking flattery from members
- Responding favorably only to those members who are able to meet the leader's self-perception of being talented, having expertise, and of being very effective
- Using emotionally abusive behavior
- Saying things and expecting them to be accepted without question
- Refusing to admit or disclose self-doubts, uncertainty, or lack of knowledge
- Boasting about personal lives
- Becoming angry or hurt when a member rejects intervention
- Lacking empathy

The discussion that follows identifies three categories for these challenging behaviors, describes possible goals for the behaviors, presents some suggestions for prevention, and describes some effective leader interventions.

Categories for Difficult Member Behavior

Challenges and difficulties at the member level are placed into three categories that are descriptive for the behavior—taking charge, hopeless or helpless, and indirect attack and defense. Categorized as taking charge are advice-giving, the expert, monopolizing, and storytelling. Hopeless or helpless categories include sullenness, becoming withdrawn or silent, and yes–but behavior. Indirect attack and defense categories are sarcasm, teasing, taunting, provoking, and the like. Each behavior will be briefly described and possible goal(s) identified. The goals give the group leader some clues for intervention, and can help him or her understand the behavior.

Taking Charge Category

The taking charge category has behaviors that commonly occur in the beginning stage of group when members are very anxious, do not know each other well, and are wondering if they can be helped. Many are not accustomed to working in a group environment, and are unfamiliar with expectations for members. Although these expectations are minimal and simple, they can be difficult to practice in the group, and members easily revert back to their usual ways of relating and communicating.

Members are likely to engage in considerable *advice-giving* to try and be helpful. However, the usual outcome is that the receiver can feel bombarded, as if he or she is being told what should or ought to be done, or even that he or she is inadequate for not having solved the situation or problem. Further, advice is usually presented from that member's personal perspective, which is unlikely to fit the other person. If the advice is rejected, not acted on, or even does not have the expected outcome, the advice giver and receiver can have negative feelings about the attempt to be helpful.

The *expert* member may have experience, knowledge, and expertise but is more likely to just be a know-it-all who is not shy about sharing thoughts, ideas, solutions, and so on. These members want to be helpful but are also, consciously or unconsciously, wanting to show off their superiority, especially when they repeatedly give their expertise without being asked. Leaders can expect expert members to be attacked if they often engage in this behavior.

The *monopolizing* member may be unaware of the impact of this behavior on other members. Their anxiety can lead him or her to talk a lot, give unnecessary details, and so on in an effort to not experience the anxiety that can emerge during silence in the group. These members often talk because others are not talking, or are slow to begin talking. There are different reasons for this behavior. For example, they could be trying energize the group. They may not know how to present their concerns or input concisely, or be unable to constructively contain and manage their anxiety.

The *storytelling* behavior is often appreciated in the beginning stage of the group because other members can focus on this member instead of on their personal concerns. The story gives an illusion that the group is working, and group members only have to listen. At some point during the group's development, the storytelling becomes distracting and may be irritating. Where before members asked questions and for more details, they are now impatient and want these storytelling members to get to the point. The storyteller is also anxious, and is engaging in some social convention behavior by providing extensive details. This person is so focused on the story and its details that he or she may not be able to adequately access the feelings connected to the story. It can be a way to cognitively separate from feelings.

The possible goals for the take charge category of behaviors are to "fix it," to show superiority, to gain attention, or to relieve anxiety. Group leaders can consider these goals for the particular person and stage of group as part of formulating an intervention. Depending on the group, and the members, an intervention could be to speak of the possible goal in tactful terms. For example, the goal for a particular behavior could be presented as follows:

> *Advice-giving.* "You really want to be helpful to _____, and this is what you would recommend."

> *Expert member.* "You want to show _____ how to solve the problem (not make a mistake, and so on) based on your knowledge and expertise."

Monopolizing. "You are taking care of the group, and trying to do something you think would reduce anxiety."

Storytelling. "You want to make sure you are fully understood."

Hopeless or Helpless Category

The behaviors in this category are indirect ways of communicating feelings of despair about the person, his or her self-efficacy, the situation, and so on. The person can nonverbally communicate discouragement and depression, but not openly speak of these feelings, or may even deny having them.

The *sullen* member is often an involuntary member, such as a court order participant. Some adolescents may also exhibit this behavior, and participants of all ages whose life experiences were traumatic, neglectful, and unsatisfying can also be sullen.

The sullen member is present in body, and brings negativity, hostility, and suppressed anger to the group. He or she may not be openly defiant, but is not pleased or open to being in the group. There can be resentment for the circumstances, a grudge for life's experiences, or for a particular person's unfairness, which can be displaced on the leader and other group members, and a lack of commitment or participation in the group.

Withdrawing or prolonged silence can signal a need to protect oneself from something that is dangerous or threatening, either in the group or emerging from within the person that is triggered by group events, or by group members as part of transference. The person "flees" cognitively and affectively, but maintains a physical presence. This person is not confident of his or her efficacy at self-protection, can fear being abandoned by the leader or destroyed by other members, has learned from experience that he or she cannot rely on others for support or protection, and thus leaves the threatening situation.

Yes–but behavior generally results from frustration at self or others. This person is seeking answers or solutions, has a particular desired outcome in mind, cannot generate actions or alternatives that would seem to be feasible, or that would guarantee the desired outcome, and is closed to the possibilities suggested by others. The person who engages in yes–but behavior has given up on some level, and is despairing of ever finding a satisfactory answer or solution. The frustration is transmitted to other group members whose best efforts are rebuffed.

The goals for the helpless or hopeless category are revenge for real or imagined injuries, protection of the self, and prevention of the impoverished self from being seen by others. These behaviors can generate negative reactions by other group members, and leaders must be alert to block them and protect the member exhibiting the behavior. It can be easy for the group to let these members carry or hold the negative feelings for the group, and then to deny that they, too, have some measure of the same feelings, or to criticize these members for not being more positive. It has been my experience that group members first try to "fix" these members, and when that does not work, the member becomes a target for the other members' frustration and even anger.

Examples for possible leader interventions include the following:

Sullen. Ask other group members to report on their feelings about unfair treatment, being forced to do something they do not want to do, feeling trapped, and so on. Generate a discussion about the universality of these experiences and the resulting feelings. Be sure to have each member speak for himself or herself, and to block advice-giving.

Withdrawn/silent. Prolonged silence or withdrawal when challenged usually brings the response that the person is thinking about what is happening, or is a very private person who does not usually share a lot with others, or just that he or she cannot relate to what is taking place in the group at that time. Group leaders have to act quickly to block attacks on this person, either when initially challenged or before the challenge accelerates. Ask group members to talk about their feelings, fantasies, musings, and the impact on them when the person is silent. It could also be helpful if they were to report on what it is that they want from the person, along with what benefit it would bring to them, not to the silent member.

Yes–but. Leaders must intervene before frustration levels become too high or intense because group members will not be shy about letting the yes–but person know of their displeasure. The leader can empathize with the speaker about the frustration of not being able to generate viable answers or solutions on his or her own, and when suggestions from others don't seem to fit. It could be helpful to ask group members if this also describes their experiencing, after the yes–but person has responded to the leader. After this process, the leader could suggest that some of the frustration may be the result of an inadequately defined problem, or unrealistic outcome expectations, and lead a discussion about how to define a problem and develop realistic expectations for outcomes.

Indirect Attack and Defense Category

Behaviors in this category are indirect communications for hostile feelings and thoughts that are unacceptable to that person, or used to prevent retaliation for an indirect attack. These actions are used to hurt others, show superiority, and to keep that person safe from others' attacks, and from seeing personal inadequacies. Many of these behaviors, such as teasing, are also accepted social convention behavior, and the speaker has the protection of being humorous, whereas the receiver can appear to be overreacting or acting inappropriately if he or she objects to what was said.

Sarcastic remarks can be very hurtful to the receiver who has few effective responses available. The speaker is fearful of the results, such as an attack, if he or she should voice real feelings or thoughts, and so hides these with sarcasm. When a receiver protests the inaccuracy, spitefulness, or inappropriateness of the sarcastic comment, the speaker usually shows the goal for that behavior by noting that the comment was supposed to be funny and that something must be wrong if he or she could not see the humor (superiority). The receiver has then been hit twice.

Teasing can be fun, flirty, or a way to help relieve tension, but in reality it is a put-down of the other person. It puts the receiver in a position where the only acceptable response is an agreement with the put-down. Other responses can elicit the comeback by the teasing person that it was an attempt at humor, there was no intent to hurt or injure, and that the speaker thought the other person could "take it." The receiver is then put in the position of having to soothe the teasing person, accept the intent, but not be able to address the negative aspects of the teasing.

Taunting, like teasing and sarcasm, is a sadistic act. Others' perceived mistakes, imperfections, flaws, and other inadequacies are highlighted, emphasized, and revealed in public. The taunting person is trying to show just how inferior the receiver is under the guise of humor that is inappropriate. Sometimes the taunts are about physical characteristics, errors, or other factors over which the receiver has no control or cannot change, thus frustrating him or her.

Provoking behavior is a deliberate attempt to elicit a particular response from someone, usually a response that puts the receiver in a negative light or position. The behavior pushes the receiver's known buttons, and is also a sadistic action. Goals can be to show the receiver's inferiority, to demonstrate the speaker's superiority and control over the receiver, and to protect the self by a preemptive strike. The receiver may be perceived as dangerous, so he or she is kept busy with defending, and the speaker is then safe.

The discussion on interventions will start with strategies that can be used as prevention, present some counterproductive interventions or what not to do, and end with suggested interventions.

Prevention

It may be helpful to discuss some strategies the leader can take that may prevent some of the behaviors, such as monopolizing and withdrawn silence. The suggested strategies fall into two categories; guidelines for participation and teaching. Guidelines for participation describe member behaviors that are enhancing to the group's process, that will help them gain the maximum benefit from the group experience, and that can reduce the need for other leader interventions to block and redirect nonconstructive behaviors. The teaching category has suggestions for leader interventions to present new ways to behave, relate, and respond at appropriate times in the group, such as when a nonconstructive behavior first appears.

Central to the success of the group, and prevention of difficult behaviors, are the behaviors, attitudes, and self-understanding of the leader (Gans Alonso, 1998; Horwitz, 2000; Yalom, 1995). Gans and Alonso (1998) propose that the leader can contribute to fostering the emergence of the difficult group member in several ways: through faulty selection of group members where unsuitability for the group is not identified during the screening process; by incompetent or inappropriate management of group norms, scapegoating, and boundary violations; when the leader is unable to admit to mistakes and becomes defensive when challenged; when the leader refuses to let the members express negative feelings about him or her; and when the leader fails to recognize personal limitations. Many of these can be the result of underdeveloped narcissism (Horwitz, 2000), or unresolved narcissistic needs (Gans Alonso, 1998). Working to develop this part of self is part of the needed personal development for any therapist, and may be especially so for the group therapist.

Counterproductive Leader Interventions

We begin with some interventions that are unlikely to produce outcomes that are beneficial for the group, for particular members, and for the group's process. These counterproductive leader interventions apply in both whole-group and individual member situations.

Dismiss the behavior as unimportant or trivial. There are times when it is too early in the life of the group to use the intervention, but the leader should note the behavior and intervene when it appears again. Nothing in the group is trivial or unimportant, but may be of lesser priority at that time.

Express anger or annoyance. The leader's anger, in whatever form it appears, is very threatening to group members and can arouse intense fears. Old situations where parents or other authority figures became angry can be triggered: Members tend to personalize the leader's anger and react in terms of the old situation rather than being objective about the present situation.

Make sarcastic comments or responses. Although some people think that sarcasm is readily understood by others to be a joke or tension reliever, it is not generally perceived as such, and the emotional state of group members can reduce their ability to see the humor. Sarcasm is disguised hostility, and is received as such. Members can be wary of leaders who use sarcasm.

Lecture. Some leaders may erroneously think that the group or person needs to be informed about their behavior and what it means, and deliver a lecture. The leader may have the conscious intent of dissemination of information, but his or her unconscious intent of asserting expertise and authority, of showing superiority, or of maintaining control are more likely. Again, using lecturing, just like expressing anger and annoyance by the leader, can trigger old parental situations.

Label the group or member. This action is not likely to produce the desired outcome as being labeled is perceived by the receiver as criticizing, blaming, and pejorative. The group or person can feel shamed, humiliated, inadequate, and inferior. Labeling can produce fear that this action will reoccur, which has a negative effect on the quality of participation.

Place Blame. Blame is corrosive to any relationship, and can be especially so in the group. Any intervention that produces feelings of being blamed, whether intended or not, is not likely to foster connections by that member, but can have a negative impact on disclosure by him or her and for other members, and the quality of their participation may be reduced.

Other counterproductive leader behaviors that affect the group are the leader misusing his or her role with the intent to intimidate, becoming defensive, or failing to monitor his or her countertransference to ensure that unresolved personal issues are not influencing the choice of action (Alonso and Rutan, 1996; Cohen, 2000; Gans and Alonso, 1998; Horwitz, 2000; Livingston and Livingston, 1998; Schermer, 2000; Wright, 2000).

Constructive Prevention Strategies

Preparing members to maximize the group experience for personal benefit will do much to reduce undesirable behaviors. Informing members of expected behaviors, and guidelines for relating and participating, is part of the preparation process, even when it has to be delayed until the first group session. Following are some suggestions on what to tell members, or what to put in written materials.

Set goals. Goals that are realistic, logical, and achievable provide a framework for your work in the group, and a basis for assessing accomplishments.

Have a positive attitude. How you perceive the experience can make an enormous difference in the learning you accomplish, the personal satisfaction you derive, and in your inner growth and development.

Express important feelings. It is important to distinguish between thoughts and feelings, although both can be important. Learn to verbalize your feelings and you will find that your communications are clearer.

Take responsibility for your progress. The leader can only present information and ideas; you are in charge of what you learn and apply.

Make personal statements. Your communication will be much clearer and more concrete when you make personal statements instead of general and vague ones. For example, it is clearer what is meant when the speaker says, "I have something important I want to discuss" rather than "I feel we are talking about trivia."

Express thoughts and ideas. Make declarative statements instead of asking questions as a way to express your thoughts and ideas. It can be helpful for other group members, as well as for yourself, to speak of what you are thinking and imagining.

Interventions

Whereas the best intervention is prevention, leaders can expect some or all of these kinds of behaviors because group members have been using them for many years and they are part of their usual patterns of behavior. It's hard to change them, and it may even be difficult for members to accept that their behaviors have negative effects. Effective interventions take into consideration the goal or goals for the behavior, the impact on other group members, and the emotional state of the person exhibiting the behavior.

The overall perspective for deciding on an intervention should incorporate trying to understand the goals for the particular behavior. You probably will not have enough information about each group member to predict his or her goals, and will have to act on the basis of insufficient data. Here are some possible general goals that you can use.

- Gain attention
- Need for admiration
- To show-off expertise or superiority
- Highlight others' inferiority and thereby appear to be superior
- To hurt others as he or she has been hurt
- Defend against a possible or feared attack
- Prevent being abandoned
- Fear of being destroyed
- To prevent the real self from being seen by others

Understanding the goal or goals can suggest interventions. For example, the quest for superiority can be countered with an intervention that highlights other members' positive attributes.

Six strategies can be employed that capitalize on understanding the goals for the behavior, and also take into consideration the possible emotional states and needs of the speaker and of other group members, and are encouraging, supportive, and constructive. The six strategies are:

- Block and link
- Empathize and reframe
- Provide alternative ways to achieve the goal
- Do nothing
- Teach more constructive strategies
- Confront/Enlighten

Block and Link

These strategies are intended to halt the particular behavior before it becomes destructive or more destructive for the person and for the group, and to demonstrate how the behavior is meeting the needs of the group, or how group members demonstrate other forms of the behavior. Let's take blocking first. The group leader intervenes promptly to stop the behavior. This can take the form of the leader saying to the member, "I want to stop you for a moment," or even interrupting and saying, "I feel a need to stop you at this point." Notice that the leader is making "I" statements and taking responsibility for the action. Once the behavior is blocked, the leader can try linking: bringing other group members into the interaction so that the member does not feel isolated. Linking, in this instance, connects the speaker's personal goals for his or her behavior to similar goals other members have, or to how the behavior fulfills a need the group has, or with concerns shared by one or more other group members. Let's use storytelling as an example.

> Marie is once more telling group members about her frustration with the search for a job. She is relating details about what she wore to the interview, thoughts and feelings experienced in the reception room, and her initial impressions of the interviewer. Because Marie has done the same thing in the previous two sessions, the group leader decides to intervene. She interrupts Marie by saying, "Marie, I want to stop you right here before you provide any more details, and ask group members to give you their reactions as they listened to you." Group members report on their reactions, including feeling impatient and inadequate. The leader then lists the reactions and asks Marie if any of these reactions mirror what she was feeling. Marie admits to having almost all of the feelings. Other members chime in and disclose having similar feelings in their job searches.

Empathize and Reframe

This leader intervention begins with an empathic response even when the speaker is interrupted, and then the leader reframes the behavior so that its goal is more open and acceptable. It is important to first acknowledge the feelings of the speaker before doing anything else as this establishes a connection. The person and his or her behavior are not being criticized, blamed, put down, or minimized, and this can reduce defensiveness and promote openness to hearing the intervention. The reframing of the behavior can take a little effort, but the results may be well worth it. Reframe the behavior to highlight a positive aspect, or to acknowledge how the behavior takes care of the group. Some possible reframes follow.

Behavior	Reframe
Monopolizing	Try to get need met (unspecified), and hope members will help.
Storytelling	Want to be fully understood, and think that details are important for this.
Silent, withdrawn	Like to think things through before speaking; so much is going on that it's hard to focus on or determine what is most important.
Yes–but	It can be very discouraging to try alternatives that are not successful, and sometimes that leads to giving up because it seems futile.
Sarcasm	Joking is your way of trying to connect or to relieve the tension in the group.

Provide Alternative Ways

A positive leader intervention is to provide alternative ways that members can achieve the goal for the difficult behavior. You do not have to label the behavior out loud, such as saying to a member that he or she is seeking attention; but you have identified the possible goal for yourself. Some leader lead-in statements include:

- It may be more effective to . . .
- You may find it helpful to . . .
- I think you would get the response you're look for when you . . .
- It may be useful to . . .

Let's match each leader lead-in statement with a behavior, and present an alternative.

Monopolizing	It may be more effective to try and connect by speaking of your thoughts, ideas, and feelings you are having in the group.
Yes–but	You may find it helpful to ask group members if they have or have had similar feelings to yours.
Storytelling	I think you would get the response you're looking for when you provide extensive details if you would focus on your feelings instead.
Silence, withdrawal	It may be useful to let group members know when you want time to think things through rather than remaining silent or withdrawn.

Do Nothing

There are times when the most appropriate intervention is to do nothing. These times include the beginning of the group, when a member is in crisis, when someone is emotionally fragile, when the leader does not know enough about possible trauma in members' backgrounds, and when there is insufficient time to adequately work with the member(s) in that session. Note the behavior, and when it seems appropriate, or when the behavior is repeated, initiate an intervention.

Teach Constructive Strategies

Behaviors described in this chapter can also present opportunities to teach more effective ways to relate, communicate, connect, and so on. This can be especially effective when the material is integrated into the work of the group, and when all group members can become involved. For example, one goal for several difficult behaviors is to manage anxiety. Rather than just focusing on a member who is using an ineffective way to manage anxiety, such as storytelling, the leader can encourage each group member to speak of his or her anxiety, and then teach some techniques that can help manage and contain it. Techniques such as concentrating on deep breathing, short meditation, conscious progressive relaxation, and imaging a place of peace have been found to be helpful to calm and reduce anxiety.

Some suggested strategies include the following:

Behavior	Teach
Yes–but	Realistic goal setting, more precise goals, give up fantasies of having the other person change
Sarcasm, teasing, inappropriate jokes	Become genuine, speak of personal thoughts, feelings, and ideas
Intellectualizing	Distinguish between thoughts and feelings; identify feelings openly
Monopolizing	How to identify and speak about one's current experiencing, especially personal feelings

Confront/Enlighten

Another strategy that can be helpful is generally termed *confrontation*, but here we also call it *enlightenment*. One reason we call it enlightenment is that *confrontation* has negative connotations for many people, and raises fears associated with attacks and conflict. The other reason is that many leaders dread this task. However, when properly used it can be very helpful and constructive. So, to reduce some of the negative associations the term arouses, and to redirect the focus in a more positive path, the term *enlightenment* (Brown, 2006) is used in this discussion.

Enlightenment can be helpful when dealing with troubling behaviors that are disruptive to the group's progress and process, can retard members' learning and development, and work against the focus and purpose for the group. Situations where enlightenment can be helpful include all of the identified difficult behaviors, when members seem to have strengths that are unrecognized by them, when the group as a whole appears to be unaware of what they are doing, and when conflict is being suppressed or denied.

A Model for Enlightenment. The major components for understanding and carrying out enlightenment are the relationship between the illuminator and the receiver, the internal states for both, and the process. The model is illustrated in Figure 13–1. Essential to enlightenment is

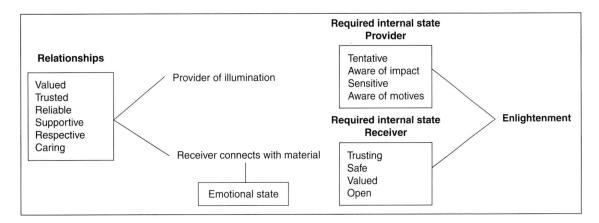

Figure 13–1 Enlightenment

the relationship between the illuminator and the receiver, where trust and safety are established so that the receiver can be open to hearing what the illuminator has to say. This is why it is inadvisable to initiate enlightenment in the beginning stage of group, before some measure of trust and safety are established, and before the leader has an opportunity to demonstrate caring, concern, respect, and genuineness. Group members are more likely to be receptive after these attitudes and inner states of the leader have emerged and are seen. It is important for the receiver to feel that the leader values, trusts, respects, has caring and concern, and is reliable and supportive. The most supportive and constructive uses for enlightenment include:

- Encouraging someone to notice a strength he or she is overlooking or minimizing
- Inviting someone to examine a less than constructive behavior
- Pointing out the unrealized impact of behavior on others
- Describing outcomes of inaction or failure to make a decision

The leader's internal state prior to initiating enlightenment is critical in that he or she should be aware of his or her motive(s) for initiating the process. This is not as simple as it sounds because there can be an unconscious component to the leader's motives of which he or she is unaware. Unacceptable motives include the following:

- To put someone down, or in his or her place
- To show the leader's superiority or expertise
- To highlight that a member is wrong, inappropriate, or shameful
- To get even
- To tell him or her off, or vent anger or annoyance
- To make sure that he or she knows what you think of him or her

These motives can cause even the most accurate information to be rejected, the receiver to become defensive, or even to negatively affect the leader's relationship with other group members.

The internal state of the receiver is also important because the information in the enlightenment process cannot be absorbed and used when the receiver is experiencing intense emotions, or feels attacked, or cannot trust that the illuminator has the receiver's best interest in mind and will take care of him or her. For example, when a receiver is angry, he or she is wary and rejecting of what others are saying, and his or her emotional state leads to inaccurately hearing what is said.

The process for enlightenment includes preparation by the leader for initiating enlightenment: what the focus should be; how the information should be conveyed to the receiver; the importance of limiting the amount of information; and the continual awareness of the impact of the exchange on the receiver and on other group members. Preparation for the leader was discussed previously and includes motive check, relationship establishment, and an awareness of the internal state of the receiver.

How enlightenment is initiated and conducted is also very important. Group leaders should be tentative and genuine, must show caring and concern for the member, and be ready to stop the process if it becomes evident that the information is not being received accurately, or is producing defensiveness or distress for the receiver. It is best done by either waiting for an invitation from the member, or by asking if you can share some information with him or her. Do not impose enlightenment because you think the person needs to hear the information. Monitor your emotional reactions so that, if you have negative feelings such as anger, these do not become part of the process.

It cannot be overemphasized that the focus for enlightenment should be on behavior that is *observable*, and that it is possible for the person to change. It is not helpful to identify attitudes, thoughts you fantasize the other person has, or other inferred intangibles, nor is it helpful to focus on characteristics about which the person can do nothing. An example for the latter would be telling someone he or she is intimidating because of his or her size. Other examples for an inappropriate focus include telling someone:

- You need to work on your attitude.
- You are monopolizing the floor.
- You are so sarcastic.
- You seem withdrawn and uncaring.
- You aren't appreciative.
- You always pull away when someone talks to you.

These labels or charges are vague, which leaves the receiver in a position where he or she is uncertain about what specific action or behavior is causing the reaction. That can be very frustrating to the receiver who then is more likely to become defensive, be hurt, angry, and attack or withdraw. Two-way communication ceases. A focus on behavior for the previous items listed as inappropriate would look something like this:

- You've said several things that indicate or suggest that you are resentful about having to attend these sessions. (The leader should be prepared to give specific examples.)
- You're doing your best to make sure that the group has something to consider and work on.

- You try to use humor to get your point across.
- I notice that you haven't said anything for some time.
- You don't respond or acknowledge the support and encouragement members are giving you.
- I've noticed several times that you shift in your chair and lean back when other members talk directly to you.

Another important consideration is to limit the amount of information presented to the receiver. If there are several behaviors that could use attention and monitoring, address only one during this process; save the others for subsequent sessions. Don't bombard the person with numerous complaints, criticisms, needed changes, and the like. Too much information can be overwhelming.

For example, let's suppose that you have an adolescent male in the group who is sullen, withdrawn, and when he does talk, makes inappropriate comments. Think about the priority for initiating the enlightening procedure, and the impact on him. What behavior would you focus on first? Or, would you think that if he changed his attitude, the other problem behaviors would be resolved? Although a change in attitude would probably work, what is the likelihood that he would be receptive to hearing that he needed an attitude change, and changing it? Probably the chances are slim to none. What might work is to bring the inappropriate remarks to his attention first by acknowledging that his participation is desired and valued, and that his comments would be more helpful to the group if he phrased them in a way that members could use his thoughts ideas, and feelings. This would be the point where you could reframe some of his inappropriate remarks to illustrate how these could be more acceptable and usable.

Whenever enlightenment is conducted for one member, it has an impact on that person, and on other group members. Leaders must take care to monitor the reactions for both throughout the process. This is essential because you are challenging someone, and others may be identifying with him or her, and also feel challenged. The process could trigger old experiences where the person felt blamed and criticized; or being the focus could be scary or shaming for the person, and other such reactions. Be prepared to check in with the receiver and with group members, and ask what is emerging for them, what feelings are being experienced, and the intensity for the feelings. Pay particular attention to nonverbal signs of distress.

Leaders must be emotionally prepared when, or if, the enlightenment does not produce the desired results. When this happens, it can feel like failure, but it is more constructive to think of it as a setback, capable of being improved. Do not blame the member for not being responsive. Review what was done to see if there is room for improvement in your motives, timing, focus, delivery, the relationship, and so on. Another possibility is that the person needs time to take it in and act on it.

The Challenge of Transference

Group members can increase their awareness and understanding of their transference. A side benefit can be a reduction in their judgmental attitudes, fingerpointing, defensive reactions, and so on. Examining their transference, or possible transference, allows them to step back from making quick judgments about others by constantly examining their own responses and possible past associations that are producing the reactions to the new person, or to what that person is doing. Members can also reduce any tendency to blame others for personal reactions as they increase their awareness and acceptance that others are not causing the reactions, but that other past relationships may be contributing. They can also become less defensive for the same reason.

How do you detect transference? It is unconscious, buried in past relationships; positive and negative attributes are involved; whole or past objects are involved; it does not have to be real but can be around an imaginary event or misperception of an event; and it is not limited to the parental relationship. Adding to the complexity is that it is dynamic, ever shifting in order to remain unknown to the person. That is, the unconscious works to keep the material unconscious.

Yet, all the leader has to work with are members' behaviors, their patterns of interactions and communication, the leader's knowledge about transference, and his or her feelings and past experiences. Leaders are confronted with defense systems mounted to keep the material in the unconscious, other group and individual dynamics, and members' personal issues, all of which can make the task of recognizing transference more difficult.

The first step is the group leader's acceptance that transference is a naturally occurring phenomenon and is not limited to members' reactions to you alone. That is, transference is also taking place between and among members. The second step is the connection that transference is not "wrong" or pathological, but that it is expected and a rich source of information about the impact of members' past experiences on their current relationships. This alone can be beneficial for group members.

Identification

What can the leader observe that could indicate transference? This is not easy to specify; recognition of possible transference develops with experience and an understanding of the leader's personal transference. However, there are some group events or member behaviors where transference can be inferred, such as out-of-sync responses, a push for a particular response, fight or attack behavior, erotic responses, idealization or rejection, and the inability to resolve a conflict. There are others, but these can serve as examples.

When a reaction or response is *out of sync*, it is not congruent with the stimulus, and it may be that what the person is hearing or receiving are old messages instead of current reality. Examples are when a member reacts or responds more intensely than would be expected, or his or her response is off target. What the person is hearing is different from what other members heard, his or her reaction is at odds with both the intent and content of the stimulus remark, and the reaction has intense affect *or* a noticeable lack of affect.

Clinical Vignette: Out of Sync

A female group member enters the room for the sixth session and sits between two male group members. When another member notes that she changed her usual seat, she jokes that she wanted to "sit with her men." She laughs, but one of the men reacts angrily to her comment saying he does not like her characterization of him.

What is out of sync is the man's anger. Even if there was a hidden agenda in her comment, a more reasonable response would be an expression of discomfort, or a question about intent and meaning, or a joking response in kind. His intensity did not match the offense.

When members, or the leader, continue to *push for a particular response*, transference may be at work. In this instance, it seems as if no matter what anyone says, it is not sufficient. It is even more frustrating for everyone concerned because that member cannot articulate what response he or she is seeking. The exchange goes in circles.

The person seeking a particular response may be experiencing transference at the preverbal level. The person knows that he or she wants something, expects the other person to know what is wanted and provide it, and is frustrated when it is not forthcoming. Doesn't that description sound like infants or toddlers who lack the words to make their wishes clearly known, and parents and other caretakers are expected to fulfill their unspoken wishes? Have you ever tried to deal with an infant or child in this sort of situation where you had to try over and over again to intuit what they wanted or were screaming for? Both of you end up frustrated. This is similar to what can take place in the group.

Fighting or attacking behavior, especially when it persists in spite of efforts to retreat, may signal transference. Another instance is when a member takes quick offense at a seemingly innocent remark and goes on the offensive. This is new behavior for this person in that he or she does not generally act this way. Members who are aggressive and prone to attacking or fighting will have multiple reasons for their behavior, one of which may be transference. However, their behavior is consistent, but the reason may vary. Sometimes it will be transference, but many times the principle reason for their behavior is something else. Do not be too quick to label their behavior as transference.

Members who use attacking and fighting where transference is involved become so mired in their past relationships that they are unable to perceive the other person realistically. That person may retreat, apologize, or try to work out the conflict, but will be unsuccessful. The attacking member cannot respond to present reality, only past experience. It is troubling for the group when a member goes on an attack against someone who is perceived as weaker, more emotionally fragile, or is well liked by members. The attacking member may in turn be attacked by other group members, or can even be excluded. The group members are perplexed at this member's attacking behavior, and are also angered and frustrated that all attempts to remedy the problem meet with failure. Transference in this instance is being destructive. A group leader has to quickly intervene, stop all attacks, and institute repair work.

Reference to *sex and other erotic responses* should always be taken seriously, even when in the form of a joke. Sexual implications in metaphors are also important. These can carry much important information about members' issues. However, all such comments are not necessarily transference; they could be a signal of flirting or interest among members, and although important to address, may require other interventions. When directed to the leader, these comments are almost always transference.

Group leaders must have strong boundaries, a deep understanding of their personal issues, and a dedication to upholding professional standards and ethics when confronted with erotic comments directed to them. Group leaders must accept that they are powerful authority figures and that group members will want to ally or merge with them or seduce them. There can be a strong desire to identify with the group leader. Some members who have sexual issues, such as incest, molestation, rape, and so on, will respond to the leader in overtly or subtly erotic ways because of their lingering unresolved issues around sex. It is important that the group leader recognizes the basis for these erotic responses.

Too often, and I maintain that once is too often, mental health professionals who lack sufficient personal development, have weak boundaries, or are not fully dedicated to professional standards and ethics will respond in kind to erotic overtures. This leader response is not helpful at the least and can be very destructive. Even mild flirting with a member is destabilizing to the group.

When members *idealize a member or the leader,* this can be an instance of positive transference whereas rejection can indicate transference of negative qualities. Either way, the response is not based on the person as he or she really is, but reflects the transferring person's past relationships. Group leaders must learn how to adequately respond to either idealizations or rejection and, above all, not take either personally.

There is a tendency for members to consider the leader as an authority or expert in the beginning stage of a group and to mount the attack in the second stage. These events can confound identifying what part is transference, and what may be due to other explanations. When members idealize or reject one another it can be a reflection of parental relationships, sibling relationships, or other relationships. Sometimes it is a mixture of all three. What can add to the confusion for the beginning group leader is that transference is not limited to one member at a time. In any exchange among members, transference may affect all, including members not involved in the exchange. Not everything is transference, but it sure seems that way at times.

Idealization and rejection comments and behaviors may provide an opportunity to bring possible transference to awareness. Having members explore their reactions in the group at that time can be fruitful. When done in a nonthreatening way, and the person is given the freedom to stop at any time, group leaders will find that members are more apt to be willing to engage in self-exploration. They can more easily see that their reactions and responses are tied to past experiences. This exploration should be done only after the group develops safety and trust and the therapeutic relationship is established. Group leaders should not push members to explore possible transference toward them. Instead, leaders should be open to exploring and allowing members to decide when exploration would be beneficial.

Transference and Unresolved Group Conflict. Conflict in the group is very uncomfortable and threatening to members. Some may work hard to deny, avoid, ignore, or minimize conflict. Although others may seem to thrive on stirring things up so that there is conflict, these conflicts are usually capable of being resolved, or the agitator becomes known for his or her behavior and members refuse to play the game. Some conflicts, however, seem to be fueled by attempts at resolution, and intensify and escalate.

Following is an example of how the leader can work with possible transference between two members who are unable to resolve a conflict, and whose reactions are out of sync. This example presents how to work with the entire group—not just the two involved in a conflict.

The group was composed of five women and four men, all enrolled in a graduate class that required a process group as part of the experience. The conflict was between two of the men and happened at the fifth session. The topic for the conflict is not important to presenting the process. Both became very angry and were still visibly upset during the fishbowl processing after the session.

The leader made some attempts to intervene and reduce some of the negative affect, but neither would let go of the anger and both continued to insist that the other one was wrong. After a couple of attempts at resolution that failed, the leader asked the two if something else could be tried. They both agreed.

The leader began by asking each of the other members to report what feelings he or she experienced during the conflict and give those feelings an intensity rating. Every member was affected intensely by the conflict and wanted very much to have it resolved. Intensity was rated on a scale of 1 to 10 with 10 being the most intense. No member rated his or her feelings below a 7.

The next step was to have each man in the conflict state what he heard the other person saying. They did so and a check with the speaker revealed that both were accurate in what they heard the other person say. In spite of the emotional intensity, each was accurate in his paraphrasing.

The leader then asked each to describe the feelings aroused when he heard the speaker and to rate the intensity. Each also estimated the intensity of feelings then versus the intensity experienced as they talked. The intensity was reduced, although it was still very high.

Each was asked to tell what he wanted from the other person that would resolve the conflict or reduce the intensity. This is where it became obvious to the participants that there was a definite possibility of transference. The leader highlighted transference by asking each if the feelings and what they wanted from each other was associated with past relationships. Both said yes, and one man began to describe past relationships with his father and uncles that produced some of the same feelings as did the current conflict. The other man also verbalized some recognition of transference.

The leader asked each man to again rate the level of his emotional intensity. Levels for both men had dropped significantly and additional support for the drop could be observed by their voice tones, postures, facial expressions, and ability to maintain eye contact. At this point, other group members began to volunteer the levels of their emotional intensity that had also been significantly reduced. Both men explored their new awareness of transference in subsequent sessions.

These conflicts generally begin with an innocuous remark to which another member takes offense. The speaker may apologize and clarify that the meaning was not directed at the other member, all to no avail. Neither an apology nor an explanation seems to make any difference. That member is still angry and offended. The speaker then becomes angry. The members can exchange remarks back and forth very quickly, making it difficult or impossible to intervene. Both are angry, keep repeating the same thoughts, other members are emotionally affected, and no resolution is in sight. This sort of conflict can be rooted in transference.

Even though transference can play a role in other types of conflicts, my experience is that transference is a major contributor in conflicts that flare up, and both members become more emotionally intense when they try to work it out. The effect on them and on other group members is potentially inflammatory and destructive. What is probably happening is that both members in the conflict are hearing old relationship messages and reacting and responding to these rather than to the other member as he or she currently is.

How can you tell if this is transference? One way is to have each member in the conflict repeat what he or she heard the other person saying. Paraphrasing is acceptable, as that can be checked out with the speaker for accuracy. What was found in the vignette was that both members heard what was said accurately, there was no distortion or misunderstanding, and they were even able to verbalize each other's intent. Apologies were offered, and acceptance that the apology was sincere was recognized. Affirmation of the relationship between the members and acknowledgment of respect for each other can be noted by each. However, none of that seems to make a difference in either member's emotional intensity, or in resolving the conflict. In short, reasonable measures do not work.

They do not work because members are stuck in those old relationships that have unfinished business. They have not, or cannot, get beyond this because they have not come to terms with residual feelings associated with those relationships. Until some of this is worked out they will continue to have these old feelings triggered and be unable to respond to the here and now appropriately because of transference.

Understanding Transference

As you can see, transference is complex, abstract, and obscure. Once identified, the task becomes even more complicated because group leaders are not working with just one member, they are working with the entire group. Even when the focus is on one member, other members are affected and the leader must remain sensitive and open to what is being experienced by all members.

The leader has three main tasks and responsibilities when guiding group members to explore their transference. The first is to remain sensitive to the emotional impact for them of some of their early experiences that are leading to their transference. The second is to recognize members' possible roles in their families of origin. The third is to highlight and help them recognize the continuing impact of transference on their current experiencing and relationships.

The impact of early experiences on an individual is considerable. Regardless of what theoretical approach is favored, the group leader can still be faced with the outcomes of these early experiences for group members as they manifest themselves in transference, even if addressing it is not part of the intended approach. Group leaders should be familiar with physical, psychological, and emotional growth and development theories. What is even more important is to know something about each member's early experiences, and about some of the relationships from members' pasts that are significant. It is not possible to know everything because members themselves may not be aware of this material—some of the most significant material remains in the unconscious. However, even limited information can be valuable in identifying potential transference.

Unfinished business and issues with parents are also important. These tend to emerge during the course of therapy, and group leaders need to be patient and not try to rush the process. After all, members are being asked to experience pain, and that is not comfortable. No wonder they resist. Pay attention to members' behavior toward one another in the group. These behaviors provide cues to their roles in their families of origin, other significant relationships, and unfinished business.

Leaders will have numerous opportunities to highlight possible transference. Once started, members become more sensitive to their possible personal transference, and will begin to wonder out loud if their reactions and responses are more connected to past relationships than present ones. Members will begin to explore why they become angry in certain situations, can be hurt by remarks, tend to immediately become defensive at times, feel guilty or shamed, and so on. Further exploration of the impact of transference on current relationships outside the group is another positive outcome.

Summary

1. Member challenges are a way to describe behaviors and attitudes group members exhibit that are detrimental to the group, and to that person's relationships. Attitudes and behaviors such as monopolizing, continual silence or nonparticipation, and so on can lead to that member being attacked or scapegoated.

2. Reconceptualizing member challenges as inadequate communication of conscious and unconscious needs, wishes, and the like can permit the leader to make more effective interventions. The behavior has a goal, and it is important that the group leader understand the goal for that member.

3. The challenging group member may also be carrying and expressing something for the group, but other members are either not aware of what it is, or are unwilling to speak about it. The group leader has an opportunity to determine if the challenging member's behavior is a reflection of something for the group, or is a personal ineffective communication style.

Chapter Activities

1. Form a group of 6–8 volunteers. Have one member as the leader, and another to play a monopolizer. Role play enlightenment (confrontation) with a monopolizer. After the role play, explore what was difficult about the process with the leader and with each of the group members.

2. Brainstorm possible member goals for the following behaviors: prolonged silence, jokes, erotic suggestions, denial of having concerns and issues, and suppressing conflict in the group.

3. Give each person a sheet of paper with three columns. In column 1, instruct them to make a list of behaviors and attitudes that irritate, annoy, hurt, arouse resentment, or anger them. Label column 2 as Mother or Mother Figure, and put a check by the behaviors and attitudes that are like or similar to mother. Label column 3 as Father or Father Figure and repeat the procedure used for column 2. Instruct them to write a summary statement about their transference.

Chapter 14

Group-Level Challenges and Interventions

Major Topics

1. Group-level difficulties and suggested strategies for conflict, group resistance, group "think," scapegoating a member or the leader, competition, and seduction.
2. Group destructive members: when the leader is powerless.
3. A conflict analysis and resolution procedure.
4. Group-level resistance.
5. Intangible and unseen group influences.

Introduction

There are group-level challenges that occur when the entire group is involved in the action(s), or a significant number of group members are involved, or the effects of the action(s) bring other members into the situation to the extent that the intervention needs to be for the group as a whole. Behaviors that fall into this category include the following:

- Conflict among members
- Group resistance
- Group "think"
- Scapegoating
- Competition among and between members
- Seductive behavior
- Group destructive members, such as narcissistic personalities, and the potentially explosive member

The most effective interventions can be at the group level. These call for a higher level of leader skill and expertise than would be used when working with individuals in a group setting, as these group-level interventions use the resources of the group as a whole. Individual members are helped during the process of group intervention by learning new ways to respond to problematic behaviors and situations, being a participant in working through problems and challenges, realizing that their fears and anxiety about situations such as conflict can be contained or need not be denied, and understanding their contributions to the problem and to the constructive resolution. This chapter presents descriptions for some group-level challenges, a process for diagnosing and selecting intervention(s), and possible leader strategies.

Conflict

The open emergence of conflict in the group can be threatening for some group members, and for some group leaders who have life experiences that predispose them to fear conflict because of possible unpleasant and negative outcomes. Thus, any disagreement arouses their fear and dread, and they work hard to maintain harmony, ignore the conflict, or withdraw. They have not learned or accepted the value of working through conflicts to reach constructive and acceptable solutions, or in being comfortable with a decision by all to disagree on this particular point or issue and move on without negative impact on the relationship(s). When leaders fear conflict they work hard to ensure that conflict does not emerge in the group, or they ignore conflict, suppress it, and use a wide variety of strategies to keep from having to deal with it. This seldom works because conflicts are a natural part of life, are always present in some form in every group and, when not openly acknowledged and addressed, work on a nonconscious level to negatively affect the group and individual members.

The first step for leaders is to become more comfortable with a higher level of conflict. The second step is to identify open and disguised conflict among members. Becoming more comfortable with conflict is part of the leader's personal development, which is addressed in previous chapters. The focus here is on working with conflicts as they emerge in the group, and presenting of material that can be used with groups whose focus is on conflict resolution.

Redefining your thoughts about the nature of conflict can aid in identification. All conflicts are not battles, attacks, and the like; they are also disagreements, differences of interests, opinions, or values; as well as disputes, and dissentions. Conflicts range from mild to intense, and are best dealt with as they emerge. The leader and members may also need to redefine their expectations about the outcomes for conflict to move away from a win–lose perspective to a negotiating–problem solving one where each person's perspective is valued and respected, and the relationship is strengthened.

When a conflict emerges and is identified as such, leaders should listen and gauge the intensity of feelings for each participant openly expressing the disagreement, and observe the nonverbal intensity for those group members who are not actively involved at the present time. First, acknowledge your recognition of the conflict and either ask about the intensity of feelings, or make a reflective response that identifies the intensity. It can be especially important and helpful to immediately continue to work with conflicts that have strong and intense feelings triggered. This can be more important than continuing to work on the other goals for the session. Also, leaders may want to ask other group members about their feelings and intensity as they listen to the members having a conflict.

There are some ground rules that can facilitate the process. The leader must

1. Appear to be in control, and should guide and facilitate the process
2. Intervene to keep members from choosing sides
3. Refrain from name calling or making demeaning comments
4. Include the whole group in the process, as indicated in the following procedure

Table 14.1 presents an overview for suggested strategies leaders can use when both parties have low emotional intensity, one party has high emotional intensity and the other has low intensity, and when both parties have high emotional intensity. The goals for the following procedure are to reduce emotional intensity to the level where it is manageable by all involved, and to set the stage for resolution.

A Procedure for Addressing Conflict in the Group

A. Both members have low emotional intensity

1. Assess the emotional intensity for each person involved in the conflict. Note body positions, gestures, voice tone and quality, word choice, facial expression, and the leader's reactions.
2. Acknowledge the disagreement, differences, or conflict.
3. Ask each person to describe his or her feelings at the moment; you could also have them rate the intensity of the feelings using the range from 0—no intensity, to 10—extreme intensity.
4. Ask other group members to report their feelings. These could be rated by using the same scale as in step 3.
5. Judge whether to continue or not. If the emotional intensity is rated 3 or below, the conflict may not need addressing at this time.
6. Ask members in the conflict if they want to work through the conflict.
   a. If both say yes—continue by using the procedure that follows.
   b. If both say no—stop at this point.
   c. If one member says yes, and the other says no, then work with the member who says no to get a better understanding of the resistance.

Table 14.1
Conflict, Intensity Levels, and Leader Strategies

Member States	Leader Tasks and Strategies
A. Mutual low emotional intensity for both	Use negotiation process, delay, or ignore
B. High emotional intensity for one member	Acknowledge the intensity and difference for the other member, explore the intensity, affirm
C. High emotional intensity for both or many members	Reduce intensity, affirm all positions

B. One member has high emotional intensity (After completing steps A. 1–6, proceed as follows.)

1. Ask him or her to define the conflict as he or she perceives it.

2. Listen carefully and assess if the conflict is one of the following:

   a. A clash of opinions

   b. A clash of values

   c. Any misunderstandings or errors of fact

   d. A clash of interests where the member with high emotional intensity could potentially lose something of importance to him or her

3. Repeat steps a and b for the other person(s) in the conflict.

4. Label the conflict as 1, 2, or 4; correct misunderstandings and errors if 3.

5. Get agreement, or not, to work on the conflict from all involved.

6. Continue to work with the high-intensity member(s).

7. Ask him or her to describe what it is like to have a different perspective with the feelings he or she reported earlier.

8. Ask him or her to rate the intensity of his or her feelings at the moment. (There can be some reduction from the previous rating. If there is no reduction, proceed on a hypothesis that there could be some transference or projection present, and be very tentative.)

9. Reflect the feelings and perspective. Ask the other person if these mirror his or hers, or if they are different, even when the emotional intensity was lower for him or her from the beginning.

10. If the member's emotional intensity is still high (above 3), ask what it would take to bring it down.

11. Try a short breathing exercise for self-calming, and do another check-in with the person.

12. Ask if there is an association with a previous experience where he or she had similar feelings. Listen to the story and reflect content and feelings.

13. Ask if there might be some residual feelings from the previous experience that may be influencing his or her perception of the current experience. The answer will probably be yes, but even if the member does not see the association, he or she will start to reflect on that possibility. Do not push for acceptance of the possible association.

14. Do a check-in with the other person in the conflict, and with other group members. Reassess the high-intensity member's rating. It should be low enough at this point to cease this procedure. If the emotional intensity is still too high, use breathing or meditation for further calming.

15. It is probably best to stop working on the conflict at this point, and initiate a discussion about the procedure. This will introduce a cognitive focus that also helps reduce residual intensity and tension.

16. If both have reduced intensity, proceed with the negotiation process.

C. Both members have high emotional intensity (Initiate steps A.1–6. Work with both members, switching back and forth during the process, but pay particular attention to step 4 as other group members may have "caught" the high intensity, or because of their own past experiences. The steps described in B can be followed, again switching between members in the conflict. After that, proceed as follows.)

1. Assess each member's emotional intensity.

2. Acknowledge each member's position for the conflict—paraphrase or restate what each said, and ask him or her to describe and rate his or her emotional intensity at this time.

3. Begin with the member who has the most emotional intensity, or choose one to work with first. Be sure to tell the other member that he or she will also have a chance to work.

4. Check in with other group members and ask them to describe and rate their feelings and reactions.

5. Keep working if any member's emotional intensity is above 3.

6. Ask the members in the conflict if they want to work on the conflict.

7. If the answer to step 6 is yes, implement steps in B.

When conflicts produce highly intense feelings that are linked to projections, transference, or fears, the leader can expect the issue to remain unresolved for the time being, and to reemerge in some form in later sessions. When it does reemerge, the intense feelings will be reduced, and the negotiation process can be used. One or more members will also have reflected on the conflict, and can help provide a more objective perspective. It is detrimental to the group to suppress or deny that there is still work to be done on the conflict, or that there are residual feelings that may need attention.

Conflict and Group Stage

Conflict, no matter how mild, is usually present in all groups from the beginning, and the stage of group development is an important consideration in the leader's decision about managing it. Some suggested leader strategies follow for each stage.

Stage 1	Quick intervention; sell members on expressing thoughts, feelings, and ideas. Convince them of the benefits of working through the conflict. Determine group members' dread, fear of conflict, past experiences, and need for support.
Stage 2	Expect conflict. Encourage expression and working through conflict. Frequently assess members' comfort levels with conflict.
Stage 3	Conflict is likely to be suppressed in the quest to maintain harmony. Encourage members to express and work through mild differences, and to explore their previous experiences for clues to their reactions.
Stage 4	Conflict reemerges because of impending termination. The leader's task is to connect the conflict to the impending termination of the group, and to encourage members to work through the conflict to avoid leaving the group with unfinished business.

Group Resistance

Group resistance can emerge at any time, and can be unexpected and disconcerting. The leader may not recognize the group resistance at first because each member is expressing the resistance in different ways, and there can be a tendency to focus on individual resistance. Clues to possible group resistance can include:

- The leader is puzzled or confused about what is taking place in the session.
- Interventions and suggestions are ignored, discounted, or are ineffective.
- Several members get confused or misunderstand what the leader says or means.
- Group members become irritated and snap at one another—which snap is a change from their usual behavior.
- The discussion in the session is unfocused and wide ranging, usually on outside-the-group topics.
- The session feels unsettling to the leader and to group members.
- Formerly participating members are quiet, reserved, or may appear to be withdrawn.

These situations describe an environment where individual resistance is not an adequate explanation for what is happening.

Bion (1961) and others who developed whole-group understanding termed these group actions as *fight or flight*. The group members are protecting themselves from real or imagined danger and these are the strategies they use. There is no conscious collusion among members to resist, no discussion about the real or imagined danger or an understanding of what they collectively are doing.

The group leader's task is to determine what the real or imagined danger may be, and to do it for the entire group and not focus on individual resistance except to link these in order to understand the group's resistance. The leader needs to reflect on previous group sessions and the stage of group development, and incorporate individual members' needs and issues into his or her deliberations. This is also where some attention to group process could be of assistance.

Reflecting on the present and previous sessions allows the leader to recall if there was an event, missed empathic failures, or an overlooked opportunity that could be contributing to the group's feeling of danger. For example, is conflict being suppressed, minimized, or ignored? How the group manages conflict could lead to feelings of danger, as conflict is not being worked through. The uncertainty about when and how it could or will emerge can lead to feeling unsafe. Another example could be that empathic failures occurred for several members over several sessions, and these were not repaired. Members can then wonder when they and others will be failed again, and be fearful of the impact on them.

The stage of group development can also be a factor in group resistance. For example, because conflict is a characteristic of stage 2, the group may be fearful of having conflict in the group, or of challenging the leader. Several or all group members could be fearful of intimacy and help produce group resistance for stages 1 and 3. The group could be resisting termination if the group is in the ending stage. It could be helpful for leaders to remember characteristic behaviors for each group stage to see if this is part of the explanation for the resistance.

Individual members' needs and issues may also be factors in the group resistance, especially when there are deep similarities among members. The leader can link these as part of understanding the resistance. For example, although their experiences were different, several group members could have issues around betrayal, rejection, and the resulting pain. Thus, when the group seems on the verge of becoming more intimate, connected, and involved, their fears about these previous experiences emerge, and collectively members ward off the potential danger by resistance.

Incorporating group process at this point would mean attending to the here-and-now interactions among group members, to what the group as a whole was doing or not doing when the resistance occurred or was noticed, the theme and feeling tone of the whole group for that session, and the internal experiencing of the group leader. Putting all of this information together can usually help identify what is, or what may be, resisted by all members in some form.

Some general threats to members' safety that can produce group resistance include the following:

- Resisting intimacy—members' past experiences and insecurities about tolerating closeness and connection can produce this resistance
- Resisting becoming known to others for fear of rejection
- Resisting disclosing shameful secrets or unacceptable parts of self
- Resisting for fear of being hurt, abandoned, or destroyed
- Resisting challenging the leader
- Resisting conflict emerging among members

Identifying the possible threat can provide the leader with some ideas for intervention strategies. Unlike what is recommended for resistance by individuals—which is that the resistance be noted and left alone—group resistance calls for some intervention by the leader. Leaving group resistance unaddressed can cause the group to feel even less safe for members, prevent the group from engaging in productive work, and retard group progress.

After identification of a possible threat, the leader should consider the stage of group development and the emotional state of members, such as their emotional fragility or emotional maturity. A good intervention is a group process comment about what the group is doing or not doing, but not trying to interpret the behavior or resistance. Possible reasons or hypotheses can be suggested, but the group should not be presented with an interpretation. The comment and possible reasons can be explored in the group.

However, making group process comment in the beginning stage of group is usually not advisable as members are still getting used to one another and the leader, the social convention taboo about speaking openly about observed behavior is still in effect, and group members can feel threatened or criticized by these comments. Groups in stages 2 and on can be more receptive and ready to make constructive use of group process commentary.

If the group is in stage 1 and group resistance is experienced, the leader's tasks are to help neutralize the perceived threat, and help members feel safer and more secure. Some possible interventions for stage 1 include:

Intimacy. Discuss feelings about safety in the group and making connections among members: emphasize similarities among members.

Fear of rejection. Highlight acceptance, respect, and tolerance for diverse perspectives; ask members what they need or want that will make them feel accepted; reinforce the position that members are in charge of personal decisions about self-disclosure.

Shame and unacceptable parts of self. Introduce a cognitive-oriented exercise or discussion to give members time to feel safer; don't push for disclosure or deeper self-exploration: emphasize similarities among members.

Hurt, abandoned, or destroyed. Move the group more slowly to introduce more safety and trust, model acceptance and lack of criticism or blame, encourage acceptance and support among members, and be patient.

Challenging the leader. Ask if members are in agreement or satisfied with the group experience to this point, or if there is something group members want, but haven't verbalized. Determine if there are reasonable needs that are not being met, and what can be done to make the group experience more productive for them.

Conflict. State that conflict can be upsetting and scary when it is not managed properly, but that working through conflicts in the group, with the leader's guidance, can be constructive and strengthen relationships. Ascertain members' feelings and fears about conflict, their definitions for conflict, and discuss what effects they experience when conflicts such as disagreements are suppressed.

If the group is in stage 2, the leader can be more direct, and use some group-level process commentary. The previously suggested interventions in the section on conflict can also be used in stage 2. Additionally, the leader can be more open about members' need to challenge the leader, and invite them to express thoughts, feelings, or ideas related to the leader that members have not expressed. In stage 2 there may be enough safety, trust, and therapeutic alliance established so that the leader can identify the theme of the resistance, such as fear of intimacy, and point out the behaviors exhibited. He or she may suggest that members explore their personal relations or associations with the identified theme.

In the advanced and ending stages, the leader can identify the theme and make empathic responses to members' possible feelings related to that theme. For example, in the working or productive stage, it would not be unusual for members to resist conflict for fear it would disrupt the good feelings among members, and the group harmony. The leader could state the difficulty and reluctance members may feel about bringing up differences or dissention, and the desire to keep the good feelings and harmony, but also remind them of the value of working out these differences early, and the negative effects for suppressed conflict on the group and relationships. The same process can be used for the termination stage where members can experience the reemergence of the anxiety and fears they had in stage 1. Further, there are feelings about ending the group, and the leader can note this and encourage members to express these feelings.

Group "Think"

Janis (1972, 1982) defined group think as what happens when the group pressure is for unanimity to the exclusion of consideration of assessing realistically alternative opinions, actions, options, and the like. Differences are not encouraged, tolerated, or explored, and this tends to produce less mental efficiency, less testing of reality, and less moral judgment. The emphasis is on concurrence, and there is little or no discussion in the efforts to avoid disagreements or arguments. Information from sources external to the group that is inconsistent with the favored course of action is ignored, discounted, disparaged, or minimized.

Group think can be found in highly cohesive groups, especially those where membership does not change or change is very infrequent, and the group has worked together for some time. The group is usually self-contained with little or no input or oversight from external sources, insulated from external criticism, and values harmony, agreement, and the collectiveness of feeling apart, unique, and special that membership in the group brings. The group leader is instrumental in the presence of group think. Janis (1982) proposes that the directive and dynamic leader sets the group's tone and culture that allows group think to flourish. This does not mean that all directive and dynamic group leaders will permit or encourage group think, but that there is a greater possibility that these leaders will stifle dissent and disagreement, insulate the group from external input or criticism, and will help foster a "we against them" attitude and group culture. Examples of groups in which group think may exist include the following:

- Political parties
- Teams and work groups
- Gangs and social clubs
- Committees and task forces
- Departments and other focused work units
- Fraternities and sororities

Prevention of group think is the best strategy, and the group leader can facilitate strategies that will help ensure that it does not occur. The first step for the leader is to engage in self-exploration about the personal need for harmony, to win, and to limit or stifle dissent. These are not undesirable needs unless they are so strong that the leader who has these strong needs can convey them to the group who then acts on them as well as on their similar needs. After this self-assessment, the leader can take other preventive measures.

- Address conflict in the group openly and constructively.
- Be alert to group members' suppression or denial of conflict, and help them express and work through it.
- Encourage and support expression of a variety of opinions, thoughts, and ideas, and take each seriously.
- Show members how to incorporate dissenting ideas and suggestions so that each member's input is valued; do not let members immediately reject ideas and suggestions.
- Do not encourage a win–lose attitude norm, such as allowing voting for group decisions.
- If an "us against them" attitude starts to develop, discuss this in the group to determine what caused it to appear, and the safety needs that it meets.

Scapegoating

Agazarian and Gantt (2005) note that "the group creates a scapegoat role to contain the differences that the group system is not yet ready to integrate" (p. 191). The scapegoat serves a purpose for the group, and is a role that is uncomfortable and nonconscious for that person except when the leader consciously accepts the role. This person, or the leader, becomes the repository or target for members' personal and unacceptable thoughts, fantasies, needs, projections, transference, and displacement. The person is the "identified patient" in need of fixing so that members do not have to work on their personal issues, concerns, and the like; or the person who speaks of the negative or unacceptable perceptions or perspectives that members cannot or are unwilling to openly verbalize. The scapegoat usually assumes the role unintentionally when he or she speaks the unacceptable, exhibits behavior that arouses indignation or irritation, is active or in the spotlight, or is out of sync with most other members.

Scapegoating can occur at any time and for a variety of reasons that can be different for each member. For example, some members may be projecting, others are reacting to unconscious transference, and still other members may be using this means to delay confronting their issues. Whatever the reasons for scapegoating, the leader needs to quickly intervene to stop the behavior. This can be difficult and complicated because it can be compressed or can gradually happen over time. Following are some indices that scapegoating may be present in the group.

- The group continually focuses on one member and tries to fix his or her concerns over several sessions. They keep coming back to this member's concerns.
- Group members become irritated, upset, or critical of one member or the leader, and they all, or mostly all, verbalize these feelings in the group. They act to let the person know just how they feel about him or her, and these feelings are generally negative.
- The group leader is continually challenged in the meeting, or over several sessions, and chastised for not being adequate enough.
- A member is labeled by several members. For example, he or she is charged with being uncaring, unempathic, having too many problems, monopolizing, angry, and so on. Members may use different words, but all are labels of some sort.

In general, the possibility of scapegoating exists when the group seems dissatisfied and one member or the leader becomes the target of this dissatisfaction; or when the group is content to work on one person's issues rather than each member working on his or her own issues; or when confrontation of oneself is too threatening and scary.

The leader must intervene to protect the scapegoated members, and to keep the group from being divided. Cohesion cannot be built unless all group members are accepted and valued. Leader interventions when the leader is scapegoated are discussed later. The focus here is on the scapegoated member. Interventions must take into account all parties involved, with the intent of bridging an unseen gap between them and promoting cohesion. Let's examine the four situations presented as descriptive of possible scapegoating and give some suggested interventions.

Center of Attention. This person usually has a significant problem or crisis that keeps them in the group's spotlight. This can be especially true and helpful for the group when this behavior occurs in stage 1. Group members are grateful for a focus that does not concern them personally. They want to be helpful and show caring, and do everything they can to help fix the problem, such as giving advice. However, if this continues for several sessions, or group members continue to return to it for more fixing, then the leader needs to intervene to prevent scapegoating.

Possible Intervention(s). After one or two incidents, the leader should block the behaviors. Then the leader should acknowledge the validity of the member's concern or problem, and how members want to be helpful, but also point out that it may be more helpful if group members respond empathically instead of giving advice or asking questions.

If the group is beyond stage 1, the leader can make a group process comment that describes how the members are using the scapegoated member to keep from working on their personal concerns, or to prevent self-disclosure. Phrase the comment tentatively, as if it is only a possibility. Also acknowledge members' desires to be helpful.

Cranky and Attacking. When group members become cranky, critical, or attacking, the group is probably acting on suppressed conflict, either among members or with the leader. However, if a group member becomes the target for the suppressed conflict and receives much or most of the negative comments, then that person is the scapegoat. This usually occurs when a member speaks of feeling disconnected to the group or what is taking place in the group, is bored or uninterested, or is withdrawn and silent. Other members may find it a relief to be able to engage in conflict with this member, and not have to challenge the leader.

Possible Intervention(s). Leaders must act quickly to block the attacking or criticizing behavior, and to protect the targeted member. One of the following two questions can be posed to the group: Are the feelings expressed (by the scapegoated member) shared or similar to feelings other members have but have not expressed? Could it be that this member is challenged so that members don't have to challenge the leader (me), or express dissatisfaction with him or her (me)? The exploration of these questions can change the direction and focus for the group.

Challenge to the Leader. Leaders can be scapegoated and serve as containers for the negative feelings members have about themselves. The leader is perceived as inadequate and may even be termed as intimidating, uncaring, distant, or unhelpful. What members may be trying to convey is their desire to become less dependent on the leader, some self-criticism, or what they wish the leader to be or do.

Possible Intervention(s). The leader should listen carefully to the challenges and determine what are the disguised needs, wishes, and desires that are contained in the challenge. The level of the leader's personal development can assist in understanding if he or she is serving as the group's container. Of course, the leader needs to examine his or her behavior to assess the validity of the challenges, and make changes where needed. If the challenge is not valid, the leader must respond carefully and with empathy, but should not become defensive. For example, the leader could point out how much members are accomplishing and growing with the constraints and barriers they point out about the leader. In spite of the leader's inadequacies, progress is being made.

Labeling Comments. These behaviors can be the most overt signals for scapegoating. Labels are usually pejorative or judgmental, even when stated in a manner or with a stated intent of being helpful. The hidden or unconscious intent is to place the blame, unacceptable personal feelings, and so on outside oneself and redefine the problem as the scapegoat's need to be fixed. It's much easier to work on someone else than it is to work on oneself.

Possible Intervention. The leader can set a norm and culture of asking group members to report on their thoughts, feelings, and reactions when responding to other members. If this has been established, then when labeling occurs, the leader can intervene with a statement or request that it would be more helpful to tell the labeled member the impact or reactions that emerge when experiencing the member's behavior. For example, if a member was labeled as angry, the leader could intervene and ask other group members to report on their feelings and other reactions to the labeled member's behavior instead of labeling him or her as angry.

Competition

Competition in the group is to be expected, but need not be destructive or a problem. Group members compete for attention; admiration; being the most needy; to be considered as unique and special; for power, dominance, and control; and for getting their needs met. The most common and obvious competition is for the leader's liking, approval, and as being favored, much like what happens in a family where siblings compete for parental favor. On occasion, there will be members who compete with the leader for control of the group, which is more difficult to identify and manage. The leader's countertransference, unresolved issues, unfinished business, and undeveloped narcissism all play critical roles in how competition is managed. Some member behaviors that suggest competition likely to be present in the group include:

- Frequent boasting and bragging
- Playing one-upmanship, using put-downs
- Constantly agreeing with the leader
- Complimenting and flattering the leader
- Developing greater needs and dependency
- Asking the leader for favors or special sessions outside the group
- Protecting the leader from attacks or criticism
- Becoming the leader's assistant

Boasts and brags. Members who frequently boast and brag are demonstrating their need to be thought of as superior, and are usually looking to gain the leader's and members' approval and admiration. They are particularly interested in the leader's reaction, much like siblings seeking parental approval.

One-upmanship. This is really saying, "I'm better than you are" or "I can top that." Members could also be seeking the leader's attention and approval. Put-downs are another form of one-upmanship that can have the same goals of showing the speaker's superiority, and of seeking attention and approval.

Agrees with the leader. This member can be identifying with the authority or a parental figure to be perceived as connected with him or her, and thus be perceived favorably by the leader and as having some of the leader's power and authority. This doesn't mean that every member who agrees with the leader falls into this competitive category. But members who almost always have to verbalize their agreement could have these goals.

Compliments and flattery. A possible goal for this frequent behavior could be to gain the leader's liking, and thereby be considered by him or her as unique and special, different from the other members.

Greater needs and dependency. The member who is in more need is usually the one who gains the greatest amount of attention, caring, and concern. It's expected that the leader, and even other group members, will care for and attend to the neediest group members, but some of them can unconsciously use their needs and dependency to gain more of the group and leader's time, energy, and resources.

Favors and the like. Asking for favors, special consideration, and the like is another way that some members seek to gain favored status. Granting these favors can encourage the emergence of jealousy in the group, much like what happens in a family when a sibling is perceived as being favored by a parent.

Protecting the leader. Again, this member seeks approval and admiration from the leader for being the leader's assistant. He or she seeks to rescue the leader, and to be perceived as having some of the leader's power and control.

Leader's assistant. There are many ways that members become the leader's assistant, and two have already been listed. Other ways include assuming some of the mannerisms and skills the leader uses to encourage and support members; but the member uses them to keep from working on his or her issues. These members seek to become extensions of the leader, and to be perceived as being less in need of the leader's assistance.

It is important that leaders stay aware of their possible countertransference issues so that they do not become a part of competitive behavior in the group, or unwittingly cause problems by seeming to have favorite group members. A good practice could be to ask yourself two questions when the competitive behaviors previously described appear: What could be some goals for the behavior? How may I be influenced by the behavior, or be playing a role that is encouraging the behavior? Understanding competitive needs suggests possible interventions, such as blocking and making microprocess or group process commentary.

Group leaders will like some members more than others because they, too, are human. However, all members in the group need to feel valued and that they are being treated fairly and equally. Leaders should not ask for or provide favors; hold out-of-group planned or unplanned interactions without bringing these back to the group; get mired in compliments and flattery to the extent that these have undue influences on perceptions and behavior; or allow assistants, or permit takeover of the leadership role by one or more members.

Seduction

Seduction is a form of manipulation used both consciously and unconsciously to gain control of others, to get what the person wants and desires, and to show that person's superiority. It is a sneaky and underhanded action. There can be seduction in the group setting, and is a misuse of the relationship between the seducer and the receiver.

Some seductive acts include the following:

- Flirting
- Starting to disclose and pulling back
- Encouraging or pushing to get someone to do something he or she does not want to do, or that is against his or her best interests
- Rushing to rescue or protect someone so that he or she will agree or take the person's side when needed
- Capitalizing on others' needs, weaknesses, and the like for personal gain
- Pretending to have care and concern for that person; lack of genuineness
- Trying to have a unique, special, personal, and exclusive relationship with members or the leader

It is a misuse of the power differential when leaders seduce members, and if the seduction becomes erotic or sexual, there is also an ethical violation. All ethical codes prohibit a sexual relationship, and some recognize the dangers of a romantic relationship, and for a coercive one. Although a leader may not act on sexual desires, he or she should stay aware that these are difficult to hide from group members, and that a lesser acting on those feelings, such as romance, could also be a misuse of the therapeutic relationship. When the leader experiences these kinds of feelings, he or she must seek consultation with a supervisor or explore these feelings with his or her therapist—not discuss the feelings with the group. Remember that the effects on the receiver and on the other group members can be powerful and detrimental.

What about the reverse situation where a member tries to seduce the leader? Leaders should learn to recognize seductive behavior, and have sufficient personal development to be able to resist it. Some good self-reflective questions for the leader to ask are: What could be the goal for the behavior? For example, is this seductive behavior that person's characteristic way of trying to form connections? What need does this behavior meet or suggest? What might I (the leader) be doing (unconsciously) that is attracting the behavior? The next step would be to ensure that this member receives the same amount of leader attention, care, and concern as do other group members, and to encourage all group members to speak openly and directly of their wants, wishes, and needs. The leader should continually monitor his or her feelings and actions to prevent succumbing to the seduction.

It is considerably more difficult to prevent seduction among group members because they are less likely to have the knowledge, awareness, and level of personal development that the leader has to prevent their responding to it. That is why it is the leader's responsibility to stay aware of what may be happening and to try and intervene before it becomes troublesome. The therapeutic relationship is of the most use because the quality and strength of the relationship, when positively developed, can permit the leader to make observations and microprocess comments. For example, the leader could remark that two or more members seem to be flirting, and encourage them and other members to speak of their attraction, appreciation, and liking for one another. This would block the flirting and turn the action into an opportunity for the whole group to participate in making connections.

Potentially Destructive Members

There are members who present real difficulties for the group and for the leader. These members usually have serious developmental issues that can challenge the leader, disrupt the group and its progress, be difficult to identify, and that respond to few or no interventions. Group members who have any of the following disorders fall into this category: borderline disorder, narcissistic disorder, antisocial/psychopathic disorder, or uncontrolled rage that can explode at any time. These members are considered "difficult" primarily because they were undiagnosed before putting them in the group. This can be particularly true of the narcissistic member who tends to remain unidentified as such for a long time. It is only through sustained contact over time that the group leader identifies him or her through the leader's persistent feelings and reactions (Brown, 1998a; Kernberg, 1990). These difficult group members can exert an unconscious corrosiveness on the group where the leader will not make much headway on building safety and trust, and can seem to have to constantly work through conflicts. They make the group appear to be difficult, and a group needs to have only one such member for there to be a negative impact. The group and the leader can spend a disproportionate amount of time trying to contain a difficult member, which reduces the time they can spend working on more important issues. The leader is not ineffective, but can feel so if these difficult group members go unidentified.

The most difficult thing for group leaders to accept under these circumstances is that there is little or nothing that can be done that will be effective for the group. Even if the member were to leave or be removed from the group, the damage has been done and the therapeutic alliance compromised. Screening and diagnosis prior to the group's beginning is the best solution, but this may not be possible for reasons listed in the chapter on planning.

Intangibles and Unseen Forces That Impact the Group

There are some intangible and unseen forces that impact the group's functioning, but little is available in the literature to guide beginning group leaders in identifying them or their constructive interventions. It is reasonable to accept that group members (transference) and the leader (countertransference) bring their previous life experiences to the group in some way; that these experiences influence behaviors, attitudes, feelings, and relationships; that there may not always be conscious awareness of these and how they influence personal perceptions and responses (resistance); and that their intangible and unseen nature impact the group. However these forces are termed, they should not be overlooked, discounted, or ignored. This discussion uses the terms *resistance*, *transference*, and *countertransference*.

Resistance

Resistance is not irrational or wrong. It has an important function and purpose. The definition used in this discussion is derived from the many perceptions of resistance by theorists. Some of these follow.

Sigmund Freud (1926/1936) described resistance as that used by the client to protect against the pain of recognizing unbearable ideas. Anna Freud's book *The Ego and the Mechanisms of Defense* (1946) expanded the concept of defenses used as resistance. The expansion proposed that the defenses employed are important sources of the individual's ego functions in general, and that these same defenses are used in everyday life by the person. Wilhelm Reich (1945/1972) felt that individuals use their character traits, or characterological armor, as resistance, and that the armor could be perceived by observing the client's posture, body movements, facial expression, and other nonverbal behaviors. Heinz Hartman (1958) provided a different perspective for resistance when he tied it to ego function. The resistance was there to protect the ego and its functioning and therapists could better plan treatment if they could understand the client's ability to handle frustration, bear anxiety, and relate to therapists. Ralph Greenson (1967) classified resistance according to the psychosexual stage that is the client's fixation point, the type of defenses used, the diagnostic category for the client, and if the resistance is ego alien or ego syntonic. He also proposed a sequence to be used with the client and their resistance—confrontation, clarification, interpretation, and working through. All of these definitions related to resistance by individual group members. There is also group-level resistance.

Examples of Group Resistance. Group-level resistance examples include:

- A member makes an emotional disclosure and the group falls silent.
- After the group has met for several sessions, the current session could be described as "milling around." No one topic seems to be of interest; there are numerous topics introduced that could lead to constructive work, but no one picks up on them.
- The group starts and continues social chit-chat. No one seems to be upset that no work is being done.
- A member is scapegoated.
- Every attempt the leader makes to bring the discussion to the here and now is rebuffed and members continue to focus on there-and-then topics.
- The group is relieved to have an "identified patient" and members are working hard to fix him or her.
- All suggestions from the leader are met with a yes–but response.
- Whatever the leader says is complimented and or agreed with by the members.
- Members are obviously ignoring the leader.
- There is considerable member acting-out behaviors.
- The group seems out of sorts. Members are cranky and grumpy.
- Group members make discounting and devaluing comments about the leader.
- The group reports feeling stuck.
- The leader cannot intervene successfully to move the group to another topic; they keep returning to the same topic even though members seem, or say they are, tired of rehashing the same material.

Group Level Resistance Categories. Thorensen (1972) proposed three categories for group resistance: flight defenses, fight defenses, and group manipulation defenses. Flight defenses are used to avoid dealing with intense feeling aroused in the group. Fight defenses are employed to deflect attention, generally in an attacking way. Group manipulation defenses are used to protect against deep involvement. Some examples may be helpful.

Flight defenses can be inferred when the group continues to interact with there-and-then concerns instead of being present-centered. Most, or all, group members participate in the flight, although each may use a different defense. Some member defenses that may indicate group flight defenses are intellectualization, generalizing, projecting, rationalization, and withdrawal.

Fight defenses are often employed toward the leader. Again, many or all group members participate in one form or the other in mounting a fight defense. As long as the attention is on the attacking behavior, members do not need to cope with having the attention turned to them. Some behaviors that signal fight defense are competition with the leader, open skepticism of process and progress of the group, attacking one another, or intense questioning of one another.

Group manipulation defenses can be used to protect against intimacy. The threat is that by becoming close they will likely experience rejection and betrayal, hence they must make sure this does not happen. Fight defenses can be used in this way, but the more subtle form of group manipulation is often used. Behaviors that characterize group manipulation are forming alliances, rescuing, band-aiding, and having an identified patient to fix.

Group resistance is characterized by some of the same behaviors and motives as is individual resistance. Members individually and collectively resist intimacy and being manipulated or controlled, having the "self" be known, being rejected, allowing conflict to emerge, becoming enmeshed, being abandoned, or being destroyed.

Tuning In to Group Resistance. What can the leader do to become aware of group resistance? Certainly a review of sessions will help, but that may not be sufficient. Leaders will find, through their experience leading groups, that the first sign of group resistance is they experience a general disquiet, or sense that they are missing something taking place in the group. The leader simply feels that something is awry. The review of sessions at this point could be helpful if the leader were to focus on the following:

- What are the behaviors members use to keep from joining the group?
- What are members doing to keep the leader from getting too close?
- What are members doing to keep the group harmonious?
- What are members doing to get their needs met, and what are these needs?

Behaviors to *resist joining the group* are those that continually emphasize differences, and show a reluctance to participate on any but a minimal or surface level. Examples for group resistance are the following member behaviors that, when combined for most or all group members, are indicative of this resistance.

- Failure to initiate contact with one another
- Reluctance to provide input even when solicited
- Vague comments that do not seem to reflect true feelings or thoughts
- Denial of having negative feelings
- Moral statements (should, ought)
- Absenteeism or continual tardiness

- Excuses for lack of participation by saying that others have more critical needs
- Continual emphases on surface differences between members

Strategies for recognizing group-level resistance include identifying the session's theme; noting stress points, where resistance seems to be especially strong; attending to shifts in participation, direction, and the like; recognizing behaviors related to group stages; and using free association and metaphor analysis.

The fear that the leader will see *the "real self" and reject* it can lead some members to exhibit considerable resistance to the leader. They credit the leader with powers to see through facades or masks, and are convinced on some level that if they are known, they will be found lacking. Thus, they expend effort to make sure the leader cannot perceive the real self. This fear may be common to most of the group members, and will lead to a group resistance. Some behaviors that may signal this fear and need are storytelling, especially with considerable detail; intellectualizing; deflecting; scapegoating other members or the leader; challenging the leader; questioning the efficacy of group; acting as the leader's assistant; showing dependency; and exhibiting helplessness.

It is not unusual for some group members to *resist conflict emergence* in the group. Conflict is not a pleasant situation but is very likely to emerge in the group. Some members dread and fear conflict so much that they will do anything to keep conflict at bay. They fear that they, or the group, will be destroyed by conflict. This is certainly true of some individuals, but can also be true for the group as a whole. The members collude on an unconscious level to make sure that interactions in the group remain harmonious. Some member behaviors that suggest resisting conflict are using carefully chosen words, never expressing negative emotions, rushing to soothe or "band-aid" someone who is upset, giving advice to solve the perceived problem, and using humor to cover feelings.

There are four goals for this resistance: attention, power, avoiding intimacy, and revenge. That is, most or all members are behaving in a way that collectively suggests that they all have similar goals. For example, assume the goal is attention. Some members may be withdrawn, another may be chattering but not talking about anything important, another member expresses irritation at other group members, a couple are making comments to each other or exhibiting other behaviors that will put them in the spotlight. Thus, the goal of the resistance for this group is to gain the leader's attention. You could also say that there was competition and sibling rivalry, but members may not be aware that attention is what they are seeking, and whould deny it if it were suggested.

When members have power as a goal, they are resisting the leader's power and control. They fear that they will be manipulated by the leader to do something they do not wish to do. Quite often there is considerable transference incorporated in this resistance.

The fear of intimacy can produce strong resistance and it seems to be especially strong when most, or all, group members have this fear. They will do almost anything to avoid being intimate with the leader and with one another. Underlying this resistance is the fear of rejection, betrayal, abandonment, destruction, enmeshment, and so on. Just when someone is making a connection, they collude to push the person away, or foster conflict, all with the goal of avoiding intimacy.

When the group has the goal of revenge, members are hostile, aggressive, angry, or sadistic. Not every member displays all these characteristics, but all members display some form of them almost continuously, with one another and with the leader. They are trying to get even for real, or imagined, hurts. There is considerable resentment, pain, and yearning present, but the viciousness of the behavior keeps others away to minimize the likelihood of being hurt. They go on the offensive, as they perceive that to be the best defense.

Constructive Leader Behaviors and Interventions

Once you have recognized group resistance, the next task is to decide what, if anything, to do. Before we tackle that task, a review of counterproductive behaviors can be helpful: Do not attack either the resistance or the group; do not push members to accept identification of their defenses; do not insist that the group accept your interpretation or analysis; do not challenge individual members or the entire group; do not become defensive, take their resistance personally, manipulate members to agree with your analysis, or use the established therapeutic relationship to emotionally blackmail members, such as telling them that you are disappointed. These are counterproductive behaviors because they undermine the status of safety and trust developed in the group. Members will be wary of doing or saying anything that will incur your displeasure, which is stifling to therapy. Further, the resistance is there for protection and if you take it away without putting anything in its place, members are left exposed to whatever they perceive the threat or danger to be. This is very destabilizing and can be destructive.

There are some behaviors that will, in the long run, be constructive. The leader needs to leave the resistance alone but stay in contact with the resistance, and can make group process commentary. By not trying to minimize or eliminate the resistance, the group leader teaches members that they are in charge of what they want to disclose and that they are empowered to be in charge of their safety. This can be reassuring to them that the leader will not try to push or demand that they not resist.

Staying in contact with the resistance provides leaders with information about the individual members' issues. You can gain data about their defenses, transference, and projections. The leader will learn what members consider to be dangerous, and what safety needs they have.

Making process commentary highlights the resistance without demanding that they stop resisting. They are free to consider the validity of the commentary, but they are also free to reject it. Just because they reject it does not mean it was wrong. It just means that members are not yet ready to look at the threatening material.

Once the resistance is identified the group leader could actively work to strengthen the therapeutic alliance, note the resistance but not take any further action, and make process commentary. If the resistance is taking the form of attacks on members, the leader should act to block that behavior, or demonstrate to members how to explore the resistance.

A Process to Address Resistance

If the leader chooses to demonstrate resistance exploration, here is a procedure the leader can use to guide members. This process can be used with both individual and group resistance, and is presented here for whole-group resistance.

1. Ask members to become aware of personal resistance.
2. Focus on sensations and identify feelings associated with them.

3. Identify the defense mechanism being used, such as intellectualization, deflection, and suppression.

4. Try to identify the threatening material or person who is producing the resistance.

5. Focus on what specifically seems to be threatening about the topic or person.

6. Make an association with previous situations or persons.

7. Tell members to explore their personal perceptions of how the "self" was in danger, thus producing the resistance

Members will want to know how to *recognize their resistance*. Some reactions that indicate resistance are intense feelings arise; there is blankness or no awareness of any particular feeling; there is an instant response of defiance or revulsion; or confused feelings arise. Members must become comfortable with the notion that *resisting is not wrong*, and that it is used to protect the person from danger. When first asked to become aware of their resistance some members may be puzzled. Even when you give some examples such as those in the previous section, members will report that they never had those feelings, or that they were trivial. This response is a resistance to be worked through before addressing the initial resistance. For example, they can say with some assurance that it is normal to be confused at the beginning of the group. Although this is true, it is also a rationalization to keep from self-exploration. These members need some instruction and guidance in tuning in to feelings and identifying them.

Begin with asking them to *note sensations*, such as body tenseness, feeling flushed, crossed arms, a rapid heartbeat, and so on. All these are sensations that have associated feelings. As members become more aware of these sensations, ask them to *label or describe feelings* associated with the sensations. This is an exercise that can help increase awareness of feelings around resistance.

Group leaders may wish to point out the behavior(s) they observed that indicated the defense without labeling it as a defense. Each member may have used a different defense. Behaviors that could be highlighted include:

- Deflection to another person or topic
- Suppression of feelings, especially intense feelings
- Expression of inappropriate feelings
- Intellectualizing
- Sudden silence
- Moral statements, such as should, ought
- Denial
- Displacement

When the group seems ready to explore the resistance, the following sequence can be used. Begin by having them *identify the threatening material* or person. It is possible that each member will work on a different person or material that triggered the resistance, or is the root cause for the resistance. To identify the threat members can recall the moment when they became aware of resisting, or when they employed their defense mechanism. Questions to guide the recall are:

- What was said? By whom?
- Was it directed to you, or to someone else?
- What was done in response?
- What was avoided?
- What was your personal nonverbal behavior?
- What were other's nonverbal behavior?

The next step is to try and *focus on the specific threat*, and identify what was threatening about the material or person. It will be difficult to do, but members should not make judgments about the appropriateness of their resistance. That is, they should not minimize their reaction, saying that there was no reason to react as they did. There was a good reason for their reaction, and it is important that they remain with their feelings to better understand the perceived threat. The reasons can be explored later.

Ask members to *make associations with previous situations*, relationships, or persons. These associations are generally unconscious ones and difficult to access. This is why it can be beneficial for members to talk out what they are experiencing, both thinking and feeling as they do the associations. That seems to aid the process of uncovering and understanding.

The final step is for members to decide how their personal "self" was in danger. Were they in danger of being engulfed—taken over by someone else? Were they in danger of being destroyed? Was the danger that they would be abandoned? The associations gleaned in the final step can highlight if there was transference or projection. After exploring the individual resistance, the group leader can link these to show how they were collectively used as group resistance.

Transference and Countertransference

What is transference? There are several definitions, each different from the other in slight but significant ways, and all trying to give substance to an abstract concept that cannot be directly observed, only inferred. Transference involves childhood memories that are stored, mental representations of significant others, affect, relationships with significant others in childhood, unconscious interpretations of childhood relationships and events, and application of these to new encounters.

Hoffer (1952) defines transference from an object-relations theoretical perspective that proposes that any form of object relationship—that is, images of people we experienced as infants and children—triggers transference. He considers these images to be real, imaginary, positive, negative or ambivalent. The object-relations definition extends Freud's (1912/1953) concept of transference that emphasized only childhood fantasies and conflicts with parents.

Harry Stack Sullivan (1953) proposed that the mental representations of self and others were perceived and stored in content of the interpersonal relationship, and that needs for safety, connection, nurturance, and satisfaction play significant roles in establishing these mental representations. Others propose a social-cognitive model for transference that is derived from empirical studies. These studies (Andersen & Glassman, 1996; Andersen, Reznik, & Chen, 1997) provide evidence for the notion that transference is not limited to therapy; it also occurs in everyday life. That is, we react to new encounters in terms of how we experienced and remember past relationships. Their review of studies suggests that transference should be considered normal and expected rather than pathological, and that transference occurs among group members and between group members and the leader. The social-cognitive model of transference does not discount the unconscious nature, but seems to suggest that because it is so common, a group leader should expect it to be an integral part of all relationships in the group. If you also accept that behavior and attitudes in the group are reflective of those for the members outside the group, then attending to the impact of transference in the group illustrates conditions in other parts of member's lives. It is the latter definition that is used in this presentation.

Transference occurs when group members perceive the group leader or other group members as having characteristics like someone they knew in a previous relationship, usually a relationship from the family of origin. This perception leads to their responding and reacting to them as if they were this person. This happens on an unconscious level and they are not responded to or reacted to in terms of objective reality—as they really are—but in terms of the "old" relationship.

A group leader should expect to experience transference from group members but it is not always easy to recognize it when it is happening. Identifying when and what transference is taking place are rich resources of information for understanding long-term issues members have that originated in the family of origin. It is important for the group leader to remember that both positive and negative feelings may be transferred, transference can be either the mother or the father, transference is an unconscious act, and the leader is the target for all members in the beginning stage of group. Table 14.2 presents examples for group members' behaviors and attitudes that can indicate transference, and for the leader's countertransference.

Table 14.2
Examples of Behaviors and Attitudes That Suggest Transference

---

Over- or underreacting to comments or suggestions

Being hypersensitive to perceived criticism

Using excessive efforts to try and please everyone

Seeking alliances with members perceived as influential and powerful, or with the leader

Becoming needy to obtain care and concern

Not speaking thoughts and feelings for fear of being rejected or wrong

Wanting to be considered as "special"

Being profoundly disappointed when expectations are not met

Constantly seeking advice, support, or directions

Telling others what they should or ought to do

Having fear of being perceived as inadequate or wrong

Strongly identifying with the leader

Being overly critical of the leader

Soothing and rescuing other members

Competing for the leader's attention or admiration

Keeping secrets from the leader

The last point is very important because leaders must be willing to tolerate transference from 5 to 10 members at any time. Transference may be active during the beginning stages of group before a strong therapeutic relationship is established. Much valuable information about members and their family-of-origin relationships can be gathered during this period, but leaders will not be able to work with transference during this time. Members are not likely to be at the point where they can tolerate visibility of their transference, accept it, or work through it.

Summary

1. Group-level challenges present other difficulties for the group leader, as the messages, expressed by the behavior can be expressed in different ways by each group member. The leader's expertise is needed to integrate the different expressions, and to understand the collective message.

2. Clues for group-level challenges include discussions based on circular or out-of-group topics; a feeling of being stuck or mired; crankiness or attacks among group members; a lack of progress and growth; regression to an earlier stage of group development; conflicts that resist resolution; and so on.

3. Interventions at the group level can be effective and helpful when the group leader has correctly identified the collective issue because the intervention does not single out any group member or a subgroup. All group members are involved and it will take all group members to resolve the difficulty, each in a personal way.

4. The most helpful technique for the group-level intervention is group process commentary. This is the leader's responsibility and should be conveyed in a way that members can accept the message and not become defensive.

Chapter Activities

1. Divide into small groups and develop a list of possible reasons or causes for group resistance.

2. Write a list of feelings aroused in you as you imagine being the group leader when the following occurs: a prolonged group silence, conflict among several members that produces intense feelings, no response from members when you make an intervention or suggestion, and a reluctance or refusal to participate in a planned exercise.

Chapter 15

Group Activities

Major Topics

1. A description of effective uses of group activities.

2. A five-phase process description.

3. Fourteen example exercises for six categories of activities.

Introduction

There are numerous group activities that can be helpful, and this chapter presents some that can have particular applications for nonclinical groups. The activities described here fall into the following categories: art-related, role-play and simulation, writing, fairy tales, homework, and relaxation. Art-related activities use drawing as a stimulus for the focus; role-play and simulation use acting and behavioral rehearsal; writing and story telling guide the exploration of a focus; homework refers to assignments of outside-the-group activities that address a particular focus; and relaxation refers to physical movement. Applications for children, adolescent, and adult groups will be used as illustrations. The discussion begins with some basic considerations to take into account when using group activities, potential benefits to the group and to members, and counterindications—that is, when group activities may not be helpful.

Basic Considerations

Careful thought should be given to the decision to use an activity, and to the selection of an activity. The decision to use an activity should consider

- Stage of group development
- Emotional maturity and the needs of group members
- The main purpose and goal for the activity and how this connects to the overall goal and purpose for the group

- Expected outcome(s)
- Time available, materials, and environment suitability

Stage of Group Development

Trotzer (2004) proposed three reasons for using activities—initiate, facilitate, and terminate/culminate—and these seem to be related to the stage of group development. Further, the group's stage of development suggests the appropriateness of the proposed activity. For example, during the first stage, activities that initiate discussion, disclosure, and expression of feelings would be appropriate and helpful. Activities that call for deep self-disclosure usually found after trust and safety are developed in the group would not be appropriate. Activities suitable for stage 1 should be nonthreatening, and serve to reduce tension and anxiety usually present in stage 1. Activities for stages 2 and 3 should focus on the purpose for the group along with the needs of individual members and for the group as a whole. Activities during these stages can promote learning and insight, assuming sufficient trust and safety are developed. Activities during the final stage should focus on summarization and feelings about termination.

Emotional Maturity and Needs

Although the age of participants is an important factor to consider during the decision process, much more important can be the emotional maturity and needs of group members, such as their emotional fragility and ability to manage and contain intense emotions that may emerge. The leader must allow enough time to adequately work through each member's experience and residual feelings. This is why it is important to delay using activities that have the ability to arouse emotions until there is enough information about members' emotional maturity and fragility, to use activities judiciously, and to be tentative and cautious in the exploration phase.

Each activity should have a goal and purpose—not only for its use, but also one that is connected to the goal and purpose for the group. The main question in the decision-making process focuses on a clear understanding of what the activity is supposed to accomplish, and how it fits in or is associated with the focus, goal, and purpose for the group.

Expected Outcomes

Another important question for the leader is that of expected outcome(s). What is it that you expect members or the group to gain from engaging in the activity? How will this outcome benefit the members or the group? Some possible outcomes that could be helpful include the following:

- Increased awareness of personal connections and associations
- Expression of feelings not previously known or expressed
- Recognition of possible barriers and constraints
- Acceptance of personal responsibility, and other personal behaviors and attitudes
- Highlighting and emphasis of personal concerns

- Refocus on thoughts, feelings, and ideas
- Relieved tension and anxiety
- Accentuated personal positive aspects of self, attitudes, and behaviors
- Learning of new concepts, ideas, and so on

Time and Material Available and Suitability of Environment

The leader should also consider the time available for completing and exploring the exercise and members' products, if appropriate and sufficient materials are readily available, and the suitability of the environment. There should be sufficient time to guide group members through the exercise, and to permit each member to explore his or her product and its personal associations for him or her. Waiting until the next session is not advised because the impact is considerably lessened, as is the possible personal learning for group members.

Careful consideration should be given to the availability of appropriate and sufficient materials. This can be particularly important when using art-related exercises that involve drawing. There should be sufficient materials so that members don't have to share because the wait or unavailability of the desired material or color can modify the members original thought, idea, or feeling. Sometimes the modification is mild and less important, but this cannot be anticipated in advance, and it is best to prevent it from happening.

The environment suitability is also of concern. For example, it is probably not advisable to do a movement exercise in a small room where there are also tables and chairs. In this situation, members may be more focused on avoiding bumping or being bumped, rather than on the purpose for the exercise. If tables or hard surface are needed for writing or drawing, these should be readily available and should not intrude on the group's seating, nor should the group sessions be held around tables. If products are to be posted on walls or boards, there should be sufficient space for posting all the products.

Selection Process

The decision to use an activity also involves the selection process. This process includes matching the kind of activity to the needs of the group and its members, with the leader's expertise and training for use as fundamental. The particular activity choice is made after the first two steps are complete.

Because this presentation is limited to five general activity categories, we will use them as illustrations. There are other categories, such as music, dance, and imagery, that are not presented here, but the same general process can be used for them.

Matching Decisions

Match the choice of activity to the needs of the group and its members by reflecting on the purpose and potential benefits, the level and stage of development for participants, and members' skill and expertise for the activity. It is very important that the group leader have a rationale for the activity to present to the group when introducing the activity.

The level and stage of development of members also play roles in matching, and care must be taken to not introduce an activity that is beyond the capabilities of group members, as their inability to complete the exercise can itself produce frustration and feelings of inadequacy. Here is an example.

A counseling intern student decided to complete her internship in a nursing-assisted living facility for seniors. She designed a reminiscence group because the literature showed its effectiveness with this population. The director of the facility was encouraging, and approved the group plan. One of the first activities was art related, but what she encountered made the activity impossible to complete. One or more group members could not understand the directions, some could not manage to draw and became frustrated, and medication or illness effects caused one or two members to nod off during the activity.

Matching choice of activity can also mean assessing members' emotional states and emotional strength. It is not advisable to use an exercise that has the potential for increasing emotions or intensifying present emotions when members may be unable to contain and manage them. For example, suppose you were leading a group of managers who were facing the task of handling cuts in their budgets and possible dismissal of staff. Even though their emotions may be subdued, there is still the likelihood that the impending situation that is still uncertain and ambiguous has aroused their anxiety. Using an energizing exercise would not be advisable, as there is a definite possibility that simmering anger and resentment could become too intense to be adequately contained.

Leader Expertise and Training

The final basic topic presented in selection of an activity is the leader's expertise and training. Ethical guidelines have cautions and prohibitions about using techniques and strategies that require specialized training. That caution is echoed here, and such specialized training is encouraged. However, there are activities that can be used that do not require specialized training when used as described here. The main purpose for these activities is to stimulate discussion and thought, not for interpretation or other psychotherapy reasons. The group leader serves as a guide to provide the framework, and group members derive their own unique personal associations and meaning. Leaders are encouraged to receive training in use of these categories of activities, even when they plan to use them as described here, just as stimuli without interpretations.

Procedures and Phases

There are also general procedures to be followed, and phases to be completed. These overlap and form the structure and direction for activities. The procedure will focus on the sequence to be followed, and related primarily to the work done before introducing the exercise. Phases are developmental and build on each other. There are several procedures in each phase. The phases are conceptual, introductory, productive or working, reporting, and expansion.

Conceptual Phase

This phase incorporates the decision making and selection of activities discussed earlier in the chapter, plus the additional procedures of adapting and modifying, writing a short plan and directions, and gathering materials. The time and effort spent in this phase will contribute significantly to the effectiveness of the chosen activity.

After completing the fundamental decision-making and selection process, the next task is to adapt and modify the activity to better fit your group. There can be minor adjustments such as the time frame for a relaxation exercise, to major adjustments such as adjusting the topic for a role-play that incorporates personal material disclosed by group members. Another example of adapting and modifying is what I do for a favorite art-related activity: four colors, four emotions. The basic activity asks participants to divide a sheet of paper into four quadrants, select one color for each of the four designated emotions, and draw a symbol with that color for each—one emotion and one color for each quadrant. This is an exercise suitable for all age groups, and for all types of groups. I've modified it for use as an icebreaker where members are asked to identify four emotions they are experiencing in the moment—their choice; these are undesignated. Another modification is when members seem to have difficulty expressing a particular emotion. I then designate four emotions, one of which is the emotion that is difficult to express.

Written Plan. It is recommended that a short plan be written. The plan need not be long or comprehensive, but it will help organize thoughts and ensure that the procedures are followed. It can also include the purpose and objectives. It also allows for identification of potential areas for clarification and anticipated questions. Also included in the plan should be the following:

- The estimated time for each phase, with ample time provided for the reporting and expansion phases
- Materials that will be used for the exercise
- Expansion phase focus questions

The estimated time is flexible, but can serve as a guide for when to move to the next phase, and when to adjust the time for a particular phase. Because group members will most likely complete some activities at different rates, such as art-related exercises, the time allowed should be sufficient for most to complete the product, but not necessarily every member. Completion is not always necessary to gain some benefit, and completion is not the goal for the activity. It is much more important to have sufficient time for the reporting and expansion phases than it is for every member to complete the product to his or her satisfaction. Some guides for estimating the time for different activities are provided later in the chapter.

There is more time available during the conceptual phase to think about what materials will be needed than there will be after the group begins and other things intervene. How members report their experiencing can be the basis for deciding on materials for other than art-related exercises. For example, if a role-play is used, how will the role-play participants and other members report and expand what emerged for them in the experience?

Talking is not always the best method for reporting. Drawing and writing could better allow the individual experiencing to remain uncontaminated from hearing about others' experiences. If drawing or writing are used, materials are also needed. Planning provides an opportunity to determine if materials are available or need to be purchased, if they are available in sufficient quantity for the size of the group, and if the planned materials are appropriate for the abilities of members. For example, you may not want to use oil pastel crayons with children, as these can be messy and cleanup is more difficult.

Plan the general questions to be asked during the expansion phase, and also write these on a card. Some topics can be anticipated, whereas others will emerge during the activity. Make the questions general so that the member's individual experiencing is not lost or misdirected. For example, instead of asking if a particular feeling was experienced, the general question would be, "What feelings were experienced?"—which is much less restrictive and directive. General questions such as the following can be facilitative.

- What was easy about the activity for you?
- What was most difficult for you?
- What feelings emerged as you completed the activity, during the reporting phase, and now?
- Was there anything you experienced that was surprising?
- Did any awareness or new learning emerge for you?
- What was most focal for you about this activity?

Introductory Phase

The introductory phase refers to presenting and introducing the activity to the group. The leader presents the rationale for the activity, a short description, and the opportunity for members to agree to participate or to decide to not participate. What you say and do when introducing the activity sets the tone and framework for how the activity will proceed, and can affect group members' attitudes.

Pay particular attention to the following:

- Word choices for the introduction
- Nonverbal reactions of group members
- Types of questions
- Skeptical and other resistant comments

Choose words that fit the group members' capacities, that are jargon free, and do not form a "sales pitch." Simple and clear language is best, even if there are jargon words that present concepts more concisely. And, yes you are trying to sell members on the value of participating in the activity, but they should not feel coerced, pushed, or manipulated. They should feel that they freely chose to participate.

Note the nonverbal reactions, as these can provide clues to members' feelings about what you are proposing. Some members will verbalize their feelings, but others will try to conceal them for many reasons. If someone appears to be reluctant, it can be helpful to point this out by saying something like, "Sue, you seem reluctant about the activity. Is there something about it that doesn't appeal to you?"

The types of questions members ask can also be clues to their feelings. Are the questions focused on facts, or are they focused on possibilities, inferences about the activity, possible hidden motives, or the degree of disclosure required? The factual questions are most likely for clarification, but the others are disguised resistance, and for other feelings about the activity.

Not hidden are the resistance and negative feelings found in members' skeptical and other resistant comments. They may be reluctant to openly say that they do not want to participate, but these comments communicate just that. They can be a signal to explore the resistance instead of proceeding with the exercise.

Productive or Working Phase

The productive or working phase starts with the distribution of materials, or at the end of the directions for activities that do not involve the distribution of materials. This is the phase where members are involved in action of some kind. Leaders should fade into the background and be minimally involved. They should observe, answer individual's questions, and provide clarification. Members should be encouraged to "do it their way" and to not get hung up on there being a wrong or right way. The major task for leaders is to observe members' reactions as they work, perform, and act. Note comments, nonverbal behavior, and interactions or their lack. Pay particular attention to facial signs of distress and pleasure as these can be indications of sensitive and significant personal material emerging for that person. Do or say nothing at that time; save it for possible comment during the expansion phase.

Reporting Phase

The goal for the reporting phase is a simple one of giving group members an opportunity to talk about their product or experience. Directions for this phase include:

- Disclose only what is comfortable, or choose to not disclose at all.
- Provide no interpretations, motives, or deeper meanings.
- Try to identify important feelings both during the activity, and as you speak.
- Note your reactions when others are reporting on their products (both the leader and members should do this).
- Listen, make reflective or empathic responses, and ask few if any questions.
- Keep this phase short and call time, if a specific time was part of the initial directions, but allow every member to report.
- If the group is divided into dyads or triads for reporting, bring the entire group back together for all to comment or to share a small part of what was disclosed.

Expansion Phase

The expansion phase is where the experience of the activity is integrated and associated, and an effective understanding can occur. Personal connections and exploration help group members derive personal meaning, and help the group leader get clues for additional issues to be addressed, get feedback on the efficacy of the activity, learn where members may be blocked or unable to access material, and where they can help members gain new awarenesses.

Keep the questions general, and resist temptations to deepen the exploration and pursue the material for one member. If a member seems to be open and ready for this as a result of the activity, note this and comment that it will be explored in the future if that member wants to do so; or the member can explore it himself or herself. It is much more important that all group members have an opportunity to do some expansion than it is to work with only one member.

Let members talk, and encourage them to note similarities and make empathic responses. Leaders will find it more beneficial to provide the stimulus questions, and then refrain from input as much as possible. Leaders, too, can comment on similarities among members, make empathic responses, and disclose some of their here-and-now reactions. Keep the focus on group members and their experiencing. Let's turn now to descriptions and applications for the different types of activities: art-related activities, role-play and simulation, writing, fairy tales, homework, and relaxation activities.

Art-Related Activities

Art-related activities have some evidence to support the efficacy of their use with all ages, and a wide variety of conditions. Examples include:

- Macrame with rehabilitation clients (Halasz-Dees, 1986)
- Scrapbooks with chemically dependent women (Washington & Moxley, 2004)

These art-related activities can be used with clinical and nonclinical groups to facilitate learning, understanding, insight, and member-to-member interaction.

Uses for art-related activities include icebreaker exercises to relieve tension and to facilitate expression of feelings. They can be relatively nonthreatening, except in cases where participants have concerns about their drawing or artistic ability. It is very important for all ages that the group leader speak specifically to this concern, and to assure group members that artistic ability is neither a requirement nor is it expected. Following are five art-related exercises that can be adapted for different ages and for different types of groups: icebreaker, a focus on feelings, getting better, symbols of hope, and collaborative team-building exercise.

Exercise 15.1

Icebreaker

Materials. For each participant, a set of crayons, felt markers or colored pencils, and a 5×8-inch unruled index card.

Directions. Draw three symbols to represent the following:

- An important personal value
- A prized possession
- A favorite activity

Expansion Questions:

What similarities did you notice with other members?

What was hard to do about the exercise?

What was easy about the exercise?

Exercise 15.2

A Focus on Feelings

Materials. For each participant, a set of crayons, felt markers or colored pencils, two sheets of paper, and a pen or pencil.

Directions. Ask participants to list 8 to 10 feelings they are bringing into the session. (The number of feelings can be adjusted.) Select a different color for each feeling and make a line with it beside the feeling on the list. Take the other sheet of paper and draw a big shape that covers most of the page. The shape should symbolize them at this time, such as a square, abstract shape, rectangle, and so on. Fill in the shape with the feelings colors in proportion to their importance and intensity. For example, if sadness was the most important immediate feeling, then the space for it would be the largest and filled in with the color selected for it.

Expansion Questions:

Did any feelings change from when you began the exercise to now?

Are there any similarities among members?

What associations do you have for your color choices?

Exercise 15.3

Getting Better

Materials. For each participant, 1 or 2 sheets of paper, pencils, and crayons or felt markers.

Directions. Introduce the exercise by saying that all members' goals involve "getting better." It may be feeling better about oneself, improving one or more relationships, letting go of feelings around an old issue or unfinished business, or coping with an illness. The intent of the exercise is to clarify that goal.

1. Ask members to list all the thoughts, feelings, and ideas they have concerning their personal goals, and the situation. These can be a combined list, or two separate lists.

2. Once the lists are complete, ask members to sit back with their hands free, close their eyes, and concentrate on their breathing to try and make it deep and even. Allow at least 30 to 60 seconds.

3. After the breathing period, ask members to visualize what getting better would be like, and how they or the situation would change. Ask them to note the feelings they would have when they are "better," and the feelings they experience as they do the visualization. Allow 2 or 3 minutes.

4. Tell members to open their eyes and draw a scene or symbol that captures the essence of what they experienced. This step may take some time, and leaders should allow sufficient time for members to complete all or most of their drawings. However, it is much more important to leave sufficient time for the next step.

5. Regroup and ask members to share their drawings and experiences. Every member must have an opportunity to share.

Expansion Questions:

Did any new awareness about you or the situation emerge?

What feelings emerged as you thought about getting better? As you drew your picture? Now?

What was easy or difficult about the exercise?

How will you know that you are making progress toward "getting better"?

(**Exercise 15.4**)

Symbols of Hope

Materials. For each participant, a 5 × 8-inch index card without lines, and a set of crayons or felt markers.

Directions:

1. Distribute materials.

2. Ask members to mentally divide their card into four sections. They will be given a concept or word for each section one at a time, and they are to select one color for that word or concept, and draw a symbol for it.

3. Present the following words or concepts one at a time, allowing sufficient time for members to draw before presenting the next one.

   Hope

   Optimism

   Self-efficacy (how competent do you feel you are)

   Inspiration

4. Regroup and ask members to share their symbols. Call attention to similarities, especially similar symbols.

Expansion Questions:

Which symbols were easy to create, and which were difficult?

What feelings did you experience during the exercise, and what feelings do you have now?

What could increase hope for you?

(**Exercise 15.5**)

Collaborative Team-Building

Materials. For each group, blank folded cards, enough for each small group to have two; a set of felt markers or colored pencils; several sheets of paper and pens or pencils for writing; images cut out of magazines; scrap pieces of different colors and patterns of card stock and memory paper; three pennies and three buttons; glue sticks and double-faced tape; and sample cards made in advance to show as examples.

Directions. The leader should make two or three sample cards using the same materials that will be provided to the group. The goal is to produce a card that captures the combined thoughts, ideas, images, or values, of the particular group. Members should portray this as a collage on a card that the small group will use for correspondence.

1. The collage must have representation from and for each participant.
2. The card must also contain a poem, saying, or stylized written description of the group on the inside.
3. All group members must contribute.

Present the goal, directions, and time frame to the small groups of three to five members each. They are to first use the sheets of paper and individually write thoughts, ideas, and so on about the group and the representative collage. Next, they will be shared in the small group and a focus will be selected, such as a focus on our ideas. The small group then brainstorms for about 5 minutes for suggestions that incorporate the focus, and the group decides how to proceed. The leader may want to suggest a division of labor, such as separating the tasks of constructing the collage and writing on the inside of the card. Remind the groups that each member's contribution must be identifiable.

Role-Play and Simulation

Role-play and simulation have applications for many groups.

- Practicing for a job interview
- Practicing social skills for a particular event or in general
- Anticipating conflict and how to defuse it
- Listening and responding communication skills
- Acting out a dilemma, a fantasy, or the like
- Assuming the other person's perspective
- Asking the boss for a raise

Children, adolescents, and adults can all participate, benefit, and learn from the behavioral rehearsal and dramatic portrayal of real, imagined, past, or future events. New learning and awareness emerge, anxiety over the unknown can be reduced, and skills can be enhanced.

Examples of research using role-play include improving cognitive functioning and impulse control of preschool children (Saltz, Dixon, & Johnson, 1977), assertiveness (Kipper, 1992), rehearsal and modeling with male alcoholics (Nelson & Howell, 1982-1983), couples (O'Farrell, Choquette, & Cutter, 1998), psychiatric patients (Hersen, Kazdin, Bellack, & Turner, 1979), adults with disabilities (Glueckauf & Quittner, 1992), and high school students (Rotheram & Armstrong, 1980).

Limitations for role-play and simulation include:

- Time available usually permits only one or two members to actively assume the role or practice the behavior.
- There needs to be more extensive debriefing of the participants *and* the observers.

- Setting the stage takes more time, especially when several people have to be prepared.
- Role-play exercises can produce intensive and hard-to-control feelings for some participants and even for some observers, such as the Gestalt exercises of empty chair and top dog–under dog. Special training is needed when these are used.

Although role-play and simulation can have limitations, they are also very helpful for a variety of group learning, and can assist group members to gain understanding through feedback and self-analysis.

There are four phases: warm-up and introduction, preparation, production, and debriefing. The warm-up and introduction phase is where the leader proposes the exercise; describes what will be done; discusses group members' reactions, either for or against, or reluctance; and solicits volunteers. Take time to fully explore anxieties and resistance, as these can signal sensitivities and possible intense emotions. The preparation phase focuses on coaching participants for their roles and giving suggestions for what the observers should attend to during the action.

The production phase is where the acting or reenacting occurs. It may be helpful to have a specific time limit for the action, and to stop at that point. Allow enough time for the scenario to unfold, and for the actors to get into the roles. Stop the action if or when an actor starts to become too intense, or when you judge that enough information has been revealed.

The debriefing phase can be the most important for all group members. This phase is like the expansion phase described for all activities. Take care to first fully debrief the actors. Ask the following:

What was the experience like for you?

What feelings emerged as you portrayed the role?

Did any awareness, learning, or insight emerge?

Was any portion difficult? Easy?

Be sure to debrief the observers. They, too, had thoughts, feelings, and ideas emerge during the production. Some may even have some personal associations with the material, and it can be important that they have an opportunity to verbalize this.

Writing

Writing is included with group activities, although it is an individual, and sometimes a solitary, action. The writing described here is intended to be a stimulus activity with the products shared in the group complete with the expansion phase. Thus, all such activities in the group should be short, with writing that takes longer—such as journals—assigned as homework.

Advantages for writing activities include the following:

- Focuses members' thoughts, ideas, and imagination
- Allows for expression of feelings, some of which may be too threatening to the person to verbalize
- Can be personal and private, uncontaminated by others' comments

Disadvantages include the time needed, not only to write, but also to report and explore. In addition, some members may not have the facility of expression through writing, and, may become frustrated. However, writing activities can be designed to overcome these limitations.

Examples of the efficacy of writing activities from the literature include these studies:

- Improvement in emotional and mental health (King, 2001; Pennebaker, 1997a; Pennebaker, Mayne, & Francis, 1997)
- Poetry—multicultural and multilingual (Asner-Self & Feyeisa, 2002; Smyth, Store, Hurewitz, & Kaell, 1999)
- Job loss (Spera, Buhrfeind, Pennebaker, 1994)
- Adjustment to college (Pennebaker, Colder, Sharp, 1990)
- Life goals (King, 2001)
- Improved self-regulation (Richards et al., 2000)
- Increased self-confidence (Lomonaco, Scheidlinger, & Aronson, 2000)

The types of writing activities are varied and include essays, letters, poetry, cinquains, journals, and guided writing. The age and ability of the target audience guide the selection of the writing activity. Use short writing activities to complete within the session time, such as poetry and cinquains. Essays, letters, and journals can take more thought and time, and may be best assigned as homework. Some example activities follow.

(Exercise 15.6)

Poems

Target Audience. Children 8 years and older, adolescents, and adults.

Materials. A large sheet of newsprint to post, and for each participant, a sheet of paper and a pen or pencil.

Directions. Select a concept, term, or feeling that is relevant for the group and write it on the newsprint. Ask group members to create a poem that describes their reaction to the posted word(s). It may be helpful to write a couple of poems and read them aloud or post them on the newsprint, as examples. Announce the time for writing. After writing, have members read their poems. Note similarities of word choices, images, and so on.

Expansion Questions:

Was it difficult to write the poem?

Were you more concerned about the product than accurate expression of your thoughts and feelings?

Did you change or reject any images or thoughts?

What were your most prominent feelings as you wrote or read your poem?

What thoughts and feelings do you have now?

Exercise 15.7

Thoughts, Feelings, and Ideas

Target Audience. Any age that has the verbal skills to write thoughts, feelings, and ideas.

Objective. This is a brainstorming activity that can be used for a variety of topics ranging from tasks such as study skills, to feelings about a medical condition. Whatever concept is used, it should be a common one for the group.

Materials. For each participant, a sheet of paper and a pen or pencil.

Directions. Distribute the materials and tell group members to quickly write all thoughts, images, feelings, and ideas that come to mind when they think about the selected concept. For example, if the concept was "procrastination," what thoughts emerge as they think about it. Don't edit or change what emerges. Give 5 or 10 minutes to complete the writing portion. It is not necessary for everyone to finish, just to have some thoughts written. Ask group members to read aloud what they wrote.

Expansion Phase. Try to link the various thoughts to show similarities and listen for a theme that shows similarities, and reveals feelings to report to the group. Focus the expansion phase on feelings that accompany the term, and personal associations.

Exercise 15.8

Cinquains for Expanded Understanding

Target Audience. Possibly third grade through adult.

Materials. Two large sheets of newsprint, one with the directions, and one with an example of a cinquain; for each participant, at least two sheets of paper and a pen or pencil.

Directions. Explain that a cinquain is a way to describe, expand, and understand thoughts, ideas, feelings, and images. Post the two sheets of newprint and review the directions.

Line 1	Names the thought, etc.
Line 2	Two words that tell what it is or does
Line 3	Three adjectives that describe it
Line 4	Two words that describe your feelings about it
Line 5	Renames it

Expansion Questions:

What changed about your image?

Did you gain a new awareness or more understanding?

How do you feel about your image now?

(**Exercise 15.9**)

My Inner Resources

Materials. For each participant, a sheet of paper and a pen or pencil.

Directions. Introduce the exercise by telling members that people (all humans) can ignore, overlook, or lack awareness of personal inner resources. This exercise is intended to focus their thoughts and self-reflection on the inner resources they are not using that could be helpful.

1. Distribute materials and ask member to list 10 to 12 adjectives that describe themselves.

2. Share these lists in the group.

3. Next, ask members to evaluate these characteristics as positive or negative in their view, and note if they listed more positive or negative characteristics.

4. Ask members to read their lists silently, and then list how each positive characteristic could be increased or enhanced. For each negative characteristic, list a possible embedded strength. For example, if "stubborn" was listed as a negative characteristic, a possible embedded strength could be "steadfastness" or "loyalty." If members have difficulty thinking of a possible embedded strength, either the leader or other members could provide suggestions.

5. Regroup and have members share the characteristics that could be increased or enhanced, and the possible strengths embedded in what they perceive as weaknesses.

Expansion Questions:

What feelings did you experience while doing the exercise?

What thoughts, feelings, and ideas emerged when you looked for strengths?

What other possible personal inner resources might you be overlooking?

Fairy Tales

What is interesting about fairy tales is that few contain any fairies. Fairy tales are stories to illustrate that everyone encounters difficulties in life, difficulties are unavoidable, and continue throughout one's life, and are a part of the human condition. This is what makes fairy tales useful for everyone, children through adults. Myths and other such stories have their value, but do not tap the existential and developmental issues that fairy tales can (Bettelheim, 1976).

The usefulness of fairy tales lies in their ability to stimulate imagination; to help identify underlying and continuing problems, concerns, and underdeveloped parts of self; and to suggest possible solutions and illustrate how one can gain confidence.

The value of these tales when used with adults is similar in many ways to their value for children. Many stories deal with psychological problems encountered when growing up, and for adults, these can be unresolved, incomplete, or recurring. Problems, issues, and concerns, such as narcissistic wounding, sibling rivalry, fears of destruction or abandonment, dependency issues, and others can continue throughout life, reemerging when they once again assume prominence for the person. Fairy tales can highlight what underlying developmental and existential issues are central in the person's lives at the present time.

Some people resist using fairy tales because of how most depict women, either as passive or as mean and cruel, and this is a legitimate concern. Males, on the other hand, are depicted as strong action takers. However, the reported use of fairy tales in the therapeutic literature for children and adults seems to support the notion of universality for the characters regardless of gender. The stories speak of human concerns, dilemmas, and situations, and people seem to respond to these and not to role identification such as kings or peasants, age identification, or gender identification. The deeper significance seems to be accessed by just about everyone. It can be helpful to not let your adult, logical, and rational self prevent you from seeing the more universal symbols embedded in fairy tales.

Dieckmann (1997) describes the use of fairy tales as a way to provide better access to the problems, and to identify the central concerns and personal ways of relating. He also presents a case where a fairy tale was used and related to the symptoms of an adult male. Stevens-Gruille & Boersma (1992) propose that fairy tales can be used therapeutically with adults to help clients reframe existential issues. Lubetsky (1989) describes how these stories can expose inner thoughts and feelings, expose conflicts and frustrations, reduce anxiety, and help master developmental tasks. Brandt's (1983) work with adolescents with borderline personality disorder found that fairy tales seemed to reflect childhood developmental issues, especially separation and individuation. The tales were used to mirror these struggles and to present strategies for resolution. Saltz and colleagues (1977) used fairy tales with preschool children to improve cognitive development and impulse control.

From an object-relations perspective, fairy tales are a safe way to reexperience early object relations, to externalize conflicts with the self, and to show how personality integration can be accomplished (Bettelheim, 1976; Cashdan, 1988).

Themes and Symbols

Every fairy tale has several developmental and existential symbols, and the leader should identify these before using the tale as a way to understand current concerns for the group as a whole, and to use as clues to members' suppressed or ignored concerns. Many fairy tales have symbols for existential concerns such as death (turned to stone), assuming responsibility (protecting a person or animal), and loneliness (traveling alone). There are also symbols for developmental concerns such as unrealized or unused parts of self (jewels), destructive parts of self that are not adequately controlled (wild animals or people acting destructively), and separation and individuation (leaving home). The symbols listed here are only suggestions, as the intent is to have group members identify and analyze their own symbols. However, the leader can use these to identify group themes, link members' underlying concerns, and to better understand their developmental and existential issues. Suggestions for symbols as metaphors for some fairy tales can be found in Bettleheim (1987) and Brown (1996).

Instructions

Select a fairy tale to use based on your (the leader's) understanding of members core needs; for example, achieving separation, developing a personal identity, and fulfilling security needs. Just any fairy tale is not sufficient. Bettleheim (1987) notes that safe stories that do not mention existential issues such as death, have ambivalent figures, or use trickery to win are not suitable. Neither are myths and fables. These have their uses, but do not serve the same purpose as does a fairy tale. Bettleheim (1987) and Brown (1996) suggest that the Grimm Brothers fairy tales be used.

It is advisable to understand some of the core issues your group members may be struggling with as part of the tale selection process. Select fairy tales that speak to a human condition, but are not likely to trigger emotional expressions that are too intense for a particular member. For example, Jack and the Beanstalk may not be useful for a member who has deep, intense feelings of hatred for his or her father, or one who was sexually abused by the father, or by a grown male figure. On the other hand, it could be just the mechanism for that person to safely explore unexpressed feelings about that father or male figure. Knowing your members is a very important part of this exercise.

There are some counterindications for use of fairy tales. Members who are unable to follow directions, are physically disruptive, or who cannot sit still long enough to listen to the story may not gain much of anything from the exercise. However, even anxious members can usually profit from listening to the tale.

Materials. Materials will be used for drawing. Suggested for each participant are 2 sheets of 11 × 7-inch (or larger) newsprint, and a set of oil pastels, colored felt markers, or crayons. Tables or other hard surfaces for drawing are needed. Paper can be taped on the walls, if they are smooth enough for drawing.

Directions:

- Introduce the activity.
- Distribute materials.
- Read the fairy tale.
- Ask members to draw pictures, and give them titles.
- Have each member describe their pictures without questioning; comments are okay.
- Expand and enhance the experience.

Introduce the activity by telling members that you want to try a fairy-tale exercise. Tell them that you will read the fairy tale and then ask them to draw one or two pictures about it. Ask if anyone has objections or questions. Some may ask what it is supposed to reveal. A good answer is that sometimes it can aid in clarifying deeper issues or concerns, or highlight existential issues. It could be different for each member.

Distribute materials and have members find a place to draw. Ask them to first sit in silence and to close their eyes and listen as you read the story.

Read the story with inflections, emphases, and excitement. When finished, ask members to open their eyes and draw one or two scenes from the story that seem important or focal for them. Allow sufficient time for drawing. As members finish their pictures, tell them to give the pictures titles.

The first stage of expansion and enhancement is to have a go-around where every member describes his or her drawing. Do not allow comments about lack of artistic talent, as this can be shaming for some members. Emphasize that artistic talent is not necessary. Try and block questioning, especially that which is designed to take the person deeper or to have him or her explain more. It is important that there be sufficient time for every member to share his or her product; questions can be saved until everyone has finished sharing. As the leader, you will want to comment on each person's, work, such as noticing colors used. Keep your comments factual and somewhat neutral. As members describe their pictures, note commonalties—these can be the basis for your comments.

Once the go-around is complete, the second phase of expansion and enhancement begins. This is where the group leader can take the experience to a deeper level. Start by asking general questions such as: Was it difficult to get started? What feelings emerged as you listened to the story, drew your pictures, and described them? What feelings or awareness emerged as you heard and saw what other members drew?

From this you can move to making the questions more focused. For example, ask members what associations and other connections they see between what they drew, the titles given the drawings, and their current life circumstances. Many times this information comes out in the first phase.

It is very important that you allow members to interpret or make associations for the symbols in their drawings rather than you giving an interpretation. The leader can ask, "What does _____ mean for you?" or "What feelings emerge for you as you think about this symbol?"

Homework

Homework can be helpful for practicing new behaviors and empowering group members to facilitate their progress. Burns and Spangler (2000) found that homework helped ameliorate depressive symptoms. Kazdin and Mascitelli (1982) used homework to help teach social skills, and found that self-reports, global ratings, and behavioral measures all showed improvement. A meta-analysis by Morgan and Flora (2002) provides evidence for the efficacy of homework with inmates.

The primary benefits for homework include:

- Time can be available for personal thought and exploration without interruptions and distractions.
- Skills can be practiced in the "real world," and this can be reinforcing.
- More material can be covered, or topics explored in more depth to enhance learning and understanding.
- Group members can become more active participants in their own learning.

The limitations and disadvantages include members' resistance to outside-the-group activities and failure to complete assignments, so that there is uneven reporting exploration. Some activities may arouse intense emotions and there is no safety net outside the group. Members may be skeptical about the reason(s) and benefits for completing homework. The group leader will have to weigh the advantages and disadvantages for the particular group.

Basic guidelines for using homework include the following:

- Develop the goal, objective, and rationale in advance.
- Keep the assignment brief, focused, and show a direct connection to the purpose of the group.

- Describe the personal benefits for members.
- Provide both written and oral directions.
- Clarify the reporting expectations.

Members may need to be "sold" on completing the assigned homework, and the first three guidelines are designed to accomplish this. What is trying to be accomplished, how the assignment relates to this, and why it could be helpful are necessary to encourage members' participation and compliance. What can seem evident and obvious to the leader may not seem so to group members. It can be very helpful to be able to describe potential personal benefits for members, and this is a major selling point. Whatever the assignment, it should be brief, focused, and connected to the purpose for the group. An example of homework that is not brief, but can be helpful, is bibliotherapy, where the reading material can be long. In these cases, break down the assignment into smaller units. Provide both written and oral directions. Written directions can help refresh memories, and oral directions provide an opportunity to answer questions, reduce anxiety, and provide clarification. The final guideline is to define, describe, and clarify expectations for reporting back to the group. What will members be asked about, what information is most important and focal, and what other things such as feelings are of interest? Following are three examples of homework activities.

Exercise 15.10

Beauty and Wonder

Target Audience. All ages.

Materials. For each participant, sheet of paper with each day of the week between sessions recorded on it, with the numbers 1 to 5 listed vertically for each day.

Directions. Record three to five beauty or wonder items for each day. More can be recorded if desired.

Expansion Questions:

Was it hard to find three items each day?

What happened when you saw something that fit?

Were you happy? Pleased? Surprised?

Did seeing beauty or wonder affect your mood?

Exercise 15.11

Empathic Responding (Assumes this was taught as part of the group)

Target Audience. Adolescents and adults.

Materials. None needed.

Directions. Instruct group members to select one person with whom they interact on a regular basis, such as a friend, parent, and the like. Sit down with that person and listen to them for 5 minutes and give only empathic responses. They are to orient their bodies to the person, maintain eye contact as much as their comfort allows, refrain from asking questions, and refrain from telling their stories, giving advice, and the like. Ask them to note the other person's reactions, and their personal feelings during the exercise.

Expansion Questions:

What was the experience like for you?

What did you notice about the other person?

What feelings did you experience during and after the empathic responding?

What was difficult? Easy?

(Exercise 15.12)

Skill Practice

Target Audience. All ages.

Materials. None needed.

Directions. Select a skill related to the purpose for the group that can be practiced outside the group, such as a communication skill that was taught in the group. For example, you could use a time management activity, or a study skill activity. Ask group members to use the skill twice or more between group sessions. For example, the communication skill of making statements instead of asking questions could be practiced.

Expansion Questions:

Did it become easier the more you used the skill?

Did using the skill have the desired results?

Is there something you need to do differently, or that you need more information on?

Are you feeling more confident about your ability to effectively use the skill?

Relaxation

Group leaders will find it helpful to know some relaxation exercises that can be used at any time, with all ages, and that can be part of the plans for the group—for example, a psychoeducational group for a medical illness. Examples of conditions and audiences where relaxation was used or taught include the following:

Anger treatment (DiGiuseppe, Deffenbacher, & Oetting, 2002)

Aggressive behavior (Olweas & Limber, 2002)

Team management (Driskell & Johnston, 1998)

Medical illness (Baum, Gatchel, & Krantz, 1997; Fawzy, Fawzy, Hyun, & Wheeler, 1997)

Vetraus (Green et al., 2004)

Workplace stress management (Bruning & Frew, 1987; Wheelan, 2006)

Life skills

For some group situations and individual members, using a relaxation exercise could be helpful such as during conflict resolution, to prevent a member from becoming overwhelmed by intense emotions, to relive tension, when a group seems mired, or to help members better focus their energies. Indeed, some group leaders routinely use a short meditation at the start of every group session.

Relaxation exercises need not be long, and the leader is the best judge of how much time to use. It's best to tell members what you propose to do and why before conducting a relaxation exercise. Ask afterward if it was beneficial, and note when members did not find it so. Also, give permission to not participate.

Presented is an example for a breathing exercise for calming. It can be helpful for group leaders to personally experience and to receive instruction about relaxation exercises to use them to their fullest extent. These can be used without having specialized training, and are relatively easy to implement.

Exercise 15.13

Breathing (Calming)

Target Audience. All age levels.

Materials. None needed.

Directions. Ask member or members to concentrate on their breathing and consciously try to make it deep and even. Allow 5 to 10 seconds for this. Then, ask them to note if they are breathing from the top of their chest or lungs, or if they are able to breathe from their diaphragm. Use a quiet, calm voice, and pace your directions. Allow 30 to 40 seconds. Observe and note who seems to be breathing shallowly, and repeat the instructions to consciously make the breath deep and even. Remind them to concentrate on their breathing. Continue for 2 to 3 minutes.

Expansion Questions:

> Did anyone find it difficult to concentrate on your breathing?
>
> Are you calmer? Or are you about the same as when we began the exercise?

Exercise 15.14

Focusing on or Identifying feelings

Target Audience. All age levels.

Materials. None needed.

Directions:

1. Ask members to close their eyes and concentrate on their breathing. Give permission for eyes to remain open if one or more members choose to do so. Give them 5 to 10 seconds.

2. As members sit in silence, direct them to become aware of their body and how each part feels at this moment—the head and neck, shoulders, arms and hands, chest, stomach, back, thighs and legs, and feet. Pause briefly after each named body part.

3. Ask members to note where they feel tension, discomfort, or pain and to try to rate its intensity: 0—none, 10—extreme. Tell them to pay particular attention to the parts of their body where the ratings are 5 or above.

4. Next, have them focus on the most uncomfortable part of their body and the location of the tension, discomfort, or pain. Guide them to silently describe it, pausing briefly after each.

   a. What shape is the tension—round, abstract?

   b. What color is it?

   c. Is it still or moving?

   d. Does it change as you focus on it? If so, how does it change?

5. Instruct members to remain with the sensation until they are ready to open their eyes and return to the room. Wait in silence until the last member opens his or her eyes. Ask each member to report on the experience.

Expansion Questions:

Was it difficult or easy to identify the sensations?

Putting together all your sensations at the beginning of the exercise, can you name or label a feeling that expresses what you were experiencing at that time?

What happened with the tension, discomfort, or pain as you focused on it?

What are you feeling right now?

Other Types of Activities

Presented here were some of the many and varied activities that can be used to teach, experience, and facilitate the group. There are many more that are also effective but are not included, such as the following,

Short stories (Van Lone, Kalodner, & Coughlin, 2002)

Movement such as dance (Williams, Frame, & Green, 1999)

Puppetry (Schmidt & Biles, 1985)

Sculpture (Groves, 2006)

Photography

Drama (Dansky, 1980)

Masks (Groves, 2006)

Music

Imagery (Ray, 2004)

These activities and others can be used as stimulus to accomplish a particular goal. While participation in art activity alone can be rewarding, pleasurable, and exciting, the real goal must relate to the purpose for the group. Further, the group leader is not likely to know enough about participants to fully understand what basic and enduring issues may be tapped by experiencing the activity, but must be prepared to deal with whatever emerges. Activities can be valuable, but should not be the main focus for the group.

Summary

1. Exercises and other activities can be of great value in group. For example, they are used to promote new learning and new awareness, to highlight difficulties, to produce solutions, to make unknown parts of self visible, and to relieve tension.

2. Group leaders should plan in advance of using an exercise or activity so that the choice is consistent with the goals or topic for the group, appropriate for the target audience, and so that sufficient materials are available.

3. Most exercises are relatively easy to use, but group leaders must be judicious in their use to avoid overusing them. They tend to lose their effectiveness through overuse and overreliance.

4. Group leaders should select exercises and other activities for which they have training and expertise. These are stimuli that are designed to promote thoughts, feelings, and ideas. The exploration of the products is the phase where the reactions are discussed, and the leader's expertise in guiding the exploration is critical and essential.

Chapter Activities

Select one exercise described in the chapter and write an adaptation for each of the following:

1. A children's group
2. A group of male adolescents
3. Elderly people in an assisted living facility
4. A group of Korean War veterans

References

Acuff, F. (1993). *How to negotiate anything with anyone anywhere around the world.* New York: American Management Association.

Adler, A. (1969). *The practice and theory of individual psychology.* Patterson, NJ: Littlefield, Adams.

Agazarian, Y. (1997). *Systems-centered therapy for groups.* New York: Guilford Press.

Agazarian, Y., & Gantt, S. (2005). *The systems perspective.* In S. A. Wheelan (Ed.), *The handbook of group research and practice* (pp. 187–200). Thousand Oaks, CA: Sage.

Alonso, A., & Rutan, J. S. (1996). Separation and individuation in the group leader. *International Journal of Group Psychotherapy, 46,* 149–162.

Alvidrez, J., Azocar, F., & Miranda, J. (1996) Demystifying the concept of ethnicity for psychotherapy researchers. *Journal of Consulting and Clinical Psychology, 64*(5) 903–908.

American Association of University Women's Educational Foundation. (1993). *Hostile hallways: The AAUW survey on sexual harassment in America's schools.* Washington, DC: Author.

American Group Psychotherapy Association. (2007). *Practice guidelines for group psychotherapy.* New York: Science to Service Task Force, AGPA.

American Psychiatric Association. (2000). *Diagnotstic and statistical manual of mental disorders* (fourth ed., text revision). Washington, DC: Author.

Andersen, S. M., & Glassman, N. S. (1996). Responding to significant others when they are not there: Effects on interpersonal inference, motivation and affect. In R. M. Sorrentino & E. T. Higgens (Eds.), *Handbook of motivation and cognition* (pp. 262–321). New York: Guilford Press.

Andersen, S. M., Reznik, I., & Chen, S. (1997). The self and others: Cognition and motivational underpinnings. In J. G. Snodgrass & R. L. Thompson (Eds.), *The self across psychology: Self-recognition, self-awareness, and the self-concept* (pp. 233–275). New York: New York Academy of Science.

Anderson, C., John, O. P., Kelter, D., & Kring, A. M. (2001). Who attains social status? Effects of personality and physical attractiveness in social groups. *Journal of Personality & Social Psychology, 8,* 116–132.

Aron, L. (1996). Symposium on the meaning and practice of intersubjectivity in psychoanalysis. *Psychoanalytic Dialogues, 6,* 591–597.

Aronson, S. & Kahn, G. (2004) Group interventions for treatment trauma in adolescents. In American Group Psychotherapy Association, *Group Interventions for Psychological Trauma.* New York: American Group Psychotherapy Association.

Arredondo, P., Toporek, R., Brown, S., Jones, J., Locke, D., Sanchez, J., et al. (1996). Operalization of multicultural counseling competencies. *Journal of Counseling and Development, 24,* 42–78.

Asner-Self, K. K., & Feyissa, A. (2002). The use of poetry in psychoeducational groups with multicultural-multilingual clients. *Journal for Specialists in Group Work, 27*(2), 136–160.

Association for Specialists in Group Work (2000). Professional standards for the training of group workers. *Journal for Specialists in Group Work, 25,* 327–342.

Avants, S. K., Margolin, A., Kosten, T. R., Rounsaville, B. J., & Schottenfeld, R. S. (1998). When is less treatment better? The role of social anxiety in matching methadone patients to psychosocial treatments. *Journal of Consulting and Clinical Psychology, 66,* 924(8).

Baca, L., & Koss-Chioino, J. (1997). Development of a culturally responsive group counseling model for Mexican American adolescents. *Journal of Multicultural Counseling & Development, 25,* 130–141.

Baile, W. F., Kudelka, A. P., Beale, E. A., Glober, G. A., Myers, E. G., Greisinger, A. J., et al. (1998). Communication skills training in oncology: Description and preliminary outcomes of workshops on breaking bad news and managing patient reactions to illness. *Cancer, 86,* 887–897.

Balwin, T. (1997). Effects of alternate modeling strategies on outcomes of interpersonal skills training. *Journal of Applied Psychology, 2,* 147–154.

Bandura, A. (1977). *Principles of behavior modification.* New York: Holt, Rinehart & Winston.

Barlow, J., & Stewart-Brown, S. (2000). Behavior problems and group-based parent education programs. *Journal of Developmental & Behavioral Pediatrics, 21*(5): 356–370.

Barnett, J., Rosenthal, S., & Koocher, G. (2007). In care of ethical dilemma, break glass: Commentary on ethical decision making in practice. *Professional Psychology: Research and Practice, 38*(1), 7–12.

Baum, A., Gatchel, R., & Krantz, D. (1997). *An introduction to health psychology* (3rd ed.). New York: McGraw-Hill.

Bauman, S. (2008) *Essential topics for the helping professional.* Boston: Allyn & Bacon.

Beck, A., & Weishaar, M. (2005) Cognitive therapy. In R. J. Corsini & D. Wedding (Eds.), *Current psychotherapies* (4th ed., pp. 285–320). Itasca, IL: F.E. Peacock.

Beck, J. (2000). Cognitive therapy. New York: Guilford Press.

Beck, R. (1998). Trauma and the group therapists: Group psychotherapy with male incest survivors. *Issues in Group Psychotherapy, 2*(1), 7–7.

Bednar, R. L., Corey, G. , Evans, N. J., & Gazda, G. M. (1987). Overcoming obstacles to the future development of research on group work. *Journal for Specialists in Group Work, 12,* 98–111.

Benjamin, L. S. (1987). Use of the SASB dimensional model to develop treatment plans for personality disorders. I: Narcissism. *Journal of Personality Disorders, 1,* 43–70.

Bennett, B., Bricklin, P., Harris, E., Knapp, S., VandeCreek, L., & Younggren, J. (2006). *Assessing and managing risk in psychological practice.* Rockville, MD: The Trust.

Bennis, W., & Shepard, H. (1956). A theory of group development. *Human Relations, 9,* 415–437.

Berg, R., Landreth, G., & Fall, K. (1998). *Group counseling: Concepts and practices* (3rd ed.). Philadelphia: Accelerated Development.

Bernstein, J. M. (1999). Development of the here-and-now in training groups for prospective group counselors. *Dissertation Abstracts International: Section B. The Sciences and Engineering, 60* (1-B), 357.

Bettleheim, B. (1976). *The uses of enchantment: The meaning and importance of fairy tales.* New York: Knopf.

Bettleheim, B. (1987, March). The importance of play. *Atlantic Monthly,* 40.

Bion, W. (1959). *Experiences in group.* Tavistock: London.

Bion, W. (1961). *Experiences in groups.* New York: Basic Books.

Boland, G. M., & Davidson, M. (2001). Intensive diabetes management plus coping skills training improved metabolic control and quality of life in adolescents. *Evidence-Based Nursing, 4*(1), 11.

Bombardier, C. H., D'Amico, C., & Jordan, J. S. (1990). The relationship of appraisal and coping to chronic illness adjustment. *Behaviour Research and Therapy, 28*(4), 297–298.

Booth, R. (1990). A short-term peer model for treating shyness in college students: A note on a exploratory study. *Psychological Reports, 66*(2), 417.

Bordin, E. (1979). The generalizability of the psychoanalytic concept of the working alliance. *Psychotherapy: Theory, Research and Practice, 16,* 252–260.

Botvin, G., Schinke, S., & Orlandi, M. (Eds.). (1995). *Drug abuse prevention with multiethnic youth.* Thousand Oaks, CA: Sage.

Braaten, L. J. (1974/1975). Developmental phases of encounter groups: A critical review of models and a new proposal. *Interpersonal Development, 75,* 112–129.

Brabender, V. (2002). *Introduction to group therapy.* New York: Wiley.

Brammer, L., & MacDonald, G. (2003). *The helping relationship: Process and skills* (8th ed.). Needham Heights, MA: Allyn & Bacon.

Brandt, L. M. (1983). A fairy tale as paradigm of the separation-individuation crisis: Implications for treatment of the borderline adolescent. *Adolescent Psychiatry, 11,* 75–91.

Brown, M. B. (2000). Diagnosis and treatment of children and adolescents with attention-deficit/hyperactivity disorder. *Journal of Counseling and Development, 78,* 195–203.

Brown, N. (1996). *Expressive processes in group counseling.* Westport, CT: Praeger.

Brown, N. (1998a). *The destructive narcissistic pattern.* Westport, CT: Praeger.

Brown, N. (1998b). *Psychoeducational groups.* Philadelphia: Accelerated Development.

Brown, N. (2002). *The group culture and the curative factors of hope and altruism.* American Group Psychotherapy Association Conference.

Brown, N. (2003a). Conceptualizing process. *International Journal of Group Psychotherapy, 53*(2), 225–243.

Brown, N. (2003b). *Psychoeducational groups: Process and Practice.* New York: Brunner-Routledge.

Brown, N. (2005). Psychoeducational groups. In S. A. Wheelan (Ed.), *The handbook of group research and practice* (pp. 511–530). Thousand Oaks, CA: Sage.

Brown, N. (2006). Reconceptualizing difficult groups and difficult members. *Journal of Contemporary Psychotherapy. 36*(3), 145–150.

Brown, N. (2007). *Coping with infuriating, mean, critical people.* Westport, CT: Praeger.

Browne, A. (1993). Violence against women by male partners: Prevalence, outcomes, and policy implications. *American Psychologist, 48,* 1077–1087.

Bruning, N. S., & Frew, D. R. (1987). Effects of exercise, relaxation, and management skills training on physiological stress indicators: A field experiment. *Journal of Applied Psychology, 72,* 515–521.

Budman, S. H., Demby, A., Soldz, S. & Merry, J. (1996). Time limited group psychotherapy for patients with personality disorders: Outcomes and dropouts. *International Journal of Group Psychotherapy, 46,* 357–377.

Bultz, B., Speca, M., Brasher, P., Geggie, P., & Page, S. (2000).A randomized controlled trial of a brief psychoeducational support group for partners of early stage breast cancer patients. *Psycho-Oncology, 9*(4), 303–313.

Burlingame, G. M., Fuhriman, A., & Johnson, J. E. (2001). Cohesion in group psychotherapy. *Psychotherapy, 38,* 373–379.

Burlingame, G. Kapetanovic, S. & Rose, S. (2005). Group psychotherapy. In S. Wheelan, (Ed.), *The Handbook of Group Research and Practice* (pp. 387–406). Thousand Oaks, CA: Sage Publishers.

Burns, D. D., & Spangler, D. L. (2000). Does psychotherapy homework lead to improvements in depression in cognitive-behavioral therapy or does improvement lead to increased homework compliance? *Journal of Consulting and Clinical Psychology, 68*(1), 46–56.

Capuzi, D., & Gross, D. (1998). *Introduction to group counseling* (2nd ed.). Denver, CO: Love.

Carroll, M., Bates, M., & Johnson, C. (1997). *Group leadership: Strategies for group counseling leaders* (3rd ed.). Denver, CO: Love.

Carter, R. T. (1995). *The influence of race and racial identity in psychotherapy: Toward a racially inclusive model.* New York: Wiley.

Cashdan, S. (1988). *Object relations therapy.* New York: Norton.

Chapman, J. L. (1971). Development and validation of a scale to measure empathy. *Journal of Counseling Psychology, 18*(3), 281–282.

Chase, J. L. (1991). Inpatient adolescent and latency-age children's perspectives on the curative factors in group psychotherapy. *Group, 15*(2), 95–108.

Chase, J. L., & Kelly, M. M. (1993). Adolescents' perceptions of the efficacy of short-term, inpatient group therapy. *Journal of Child and Adolescent Group Therapy, 3*(3), 155–161.

Chen, M. Y., & Han, Y. S. (2001). Cross-cultural group counseling with Asians, a stage specific interactive approach. *Journal for Specialists in Group Work, 25,* 369–382.

Cheung, G., & Chan, C. (2002). The Satir model and cultural sensitivity: A Hong Kong reflection. *Contemporary Family Therapy, 24,* 199–215.

Cohen, B. D. (2000). Intersubjectivity and narcissism in group psychotherapy: How feedback works. *International Journal of Group Psychotherapy, 50*(2), 163–179.

Colijn S., Hoencamp, E., Snijders, H., Van Der Spek, M., & Duivenvoorden, H. (1991). A comparison of curative factors in different types of group psychotherapy. *International Journal of Group Psychotherapy, 41,* 365–378.

Collins, N. M., & Pieterse, A. L. (2007). Critical incident analysis based training: An approach for developing active racial/cultural awareness. *Journal of Counseling and Development, 85*(1), 14–23.

Colmant, S., & Merta, R. (1999). Using the sweat lodge ceremony as group therapy for Javajo Youth. *Journal for Specialists in Group Work, 24,* 55–73.

Conway, K. M. (2005). An evaluation of social skills training for youth with learning disabilities. *Dissertation Abstracts International: Section B. The Sciences and Engineering, 65 (9-B),* 4822.

Cooper, A. M. (1987). Changes in psychoanalytic ideas: Transference interpretation. *Journal of the American Psychoanalytic Association, 35,* 77–98.

Corey, G. (2000). *Theory and practice of group counseling* (5th ed.). Belmont, CA: Wadsworth/Thomson.

Corey, G. (2004). *Theory and practice of group counseling.* Pacific Grove, CA: Brooks/Cole.

Corey, G. (2008). *Theory & practice of group counseling.* (7th ed.) Belmont, CA: Thompson, Brooks/Cole.

Corey, G., Corey, M. S., & Callanan, P. (2003). *Issues and ethics in the helping professions* (6th ed.). New York: Brooks/Cole.

Corey, M. S., & Corey, G. (1997). *Groups: Process and practice* (5th ed.). Pacific Grove, CA: Brooks/Cole.

Cornish, P. A., & Benton, D. (2001). Getting started in healthier relationships: Brief integrated dynamic group counseling in a university counseling setting. *Journal for Specialists in Group Work, 26,* 129–143.

Corrigan, P. W. (1991). Social skills training in adult psychiatric populations: A meta-analysis. *Journal of Behavior Therapy and Experimental Psychiatry, 22,* 203–210.

Corsini, R., & Rosenberg, B. (1955). Mechanisms of group psychotherapy: Process and dynamics. *Journal of Abnormal and Social Psychology, 51,* 406–411.

Coyne, R. K. (2004). Prevention groups. In J. L. DeLucia-Waack, D. A. Gerrity, C. R. Kalodner, & M. T. Riva (Eds.), *Handbook of group counseling and psychotherapy,* (pp. 621–629). Thousand Oaks, CA: Sage.

Coyne, R. K., & Horne, A. M. (2001). Special issue: The use of groups for prevention. *Journal for Specialists in Group Work, 26*(3).

Crouch, E., Bloch, S., & Wanlass, J. (1994). Therapeutic factors: Interpersonal and Interpersonal mechanisms. In A. Fuhriman & G. Burlingame (Eds.), *Handbook of group psychotherapy: An empirical and clinical synthesis.* New York: Wiley.

Cuijpers, P., & Stam, H. (2000). Burnout among relatives of psychiatric patients attending psychoeducational support groups. *Psychiatric Services, 51*(3), 375–379.

Cunningham, A. J., & Tocco, E. K. (1989). A randomized trial of group psychoeducational therapy for cancer patients. *Patient Education and Counseling, 42*(2), 101–114.

Dansky, J. L. (1980). Make-believe: A mediator of the relationship between play and associative fluency. *Child Development, 51*(2), 576–579.

Davis, N. (1999). *Resilience: Status of the research and research based programs* (Draft working paper). Bethesda, MD: Substance Abuse and Mental Health Services Administration, Center for Mental Health Services, Division of Program Development, Special Populations & Projects, Special Programs Development Branch.

DeLucia-Waack, J. L., & Kalodner, C. R. (2005). Contemporary issues in group practice. In S. A. Wheelan (Ed.), *The handbook of group research and practice.* Thousand Oaks, CA: Sage.

Devan, S. G. (2001). Culture and the practice of group psychotherapy in Singapore. *International Journal of Group Psychotherapy, 51*(4), 571–577.

Devine, E. (1996). Meta-analysis of the effects of psychoeducational care in adults with asthma. *Research in Nursing & Health, 19*(5), 367–376.

Dieckmann, H. (1997). Fairy-tales in psychotherapy. *Journal of Analytical Psychology, 42*(2), 253–268.

Dies, R. R. (1977). Group therapist transparency: A critique of theory and research. *International Journal of Group Psychotherapy, 27*, 177–200.

Dies, R. R. (1994). Therapist variables in group psychotherapy research. In A. Fuhriman and G. Burlingame (Eds.), *Handbook of group psychotherapy: An empirical and clinical synthesis* (pp. 114–154). New York: Wiley.

Dies, R. R. (1997). Comments on issues raised by Slavson, Durkin, and Scheidlinger. *International Journal of Group Psychotherapy, 47*, 169–174.

DiGiuseppe, R. A., Deffenbacher, J. L., & Oetting, E. R. (2002). Principles of empirically supported interventions applied to anger management. *Counseling Psychologist, 30*(2), 262–280.

Dilk, M. N., & Bond, G. R. (1996). Meta-analytic evaluation of skills training research for individuals with severe mental illness. *Journal of Consulting and Clinical Psychology, 64*, 1337–1346.

Dirks, K. (1999). The effects of interpersonal trust on work group performance. *Journal of Applied Psychology, 84*(3), 445–455.

Douglas, M. S., & Mueser, K. T. (1990). Teaching conflict resolution skills to the chronically mentally ill: Social skills training groups for briefly hospitalized patients. *Behavior Modification, 14*, 519–547.

Driskell, J. E., & Johnston, J. H. (1998). Stress exposure training. In J. A. Cannon-Bowers & E. Salas (Eds.), *Making decisions under stress: Implications for individual and team training* (pp. 191–217). Washington, DC: APA Press.

Dunphy, D. C. (1964). Social change in self-analytic groups. In P. J. Stone, D. C. Dunphy, M. S. Smith, & D. M. Ogilvie (Eds.), *The general inquirer: A computer approach to content analysis.* Cambridge, MA: MIT Press.

Dunphy, D. C. (1968). Phases, roles, and myths in self-analytic groups. *The Journal of Applied Behavioral Science, 4*, 195–225.

Durkin, R. (1964). Attitudes concerning the etiology of mental illness. *Dissertation Abstracts, 26*(1), 518.

Durlak, J. A., & Wells, A. M. (1997). Primary prevention mental health programs for children and adolescents: A meta-analytic review. *American Journal of Community Psychology, 25*, 115–152.

Dyck, D., Hendryx, M., Short, R., Voss, W., & McFarlane, W. (2002). Service use among patients with schizophrenia in psychoeducational multiple-family group treatment. *Psychiatric Service, 53*(6), 749–754.

Edmondson, A. (1999). Psychological safety and learning behavior in work teams. *Administrative Science Quarterly, 44*, 350–383.

Edmondson, A., Bohmer, R., & Pisano, G. (2001). Disrupted routines: Team learning and new technology implementation in hospitals. *Administrative Science Quarterly, 46*, 685–716.

Eitel, S. (1996). *Examining outcomes of sexual harassment in high school and college students.* Unpublished doctoral dissertation (UMI No. 9627313), University of Rochester, NY.

Elliott, D. M. (1997). Traumatic events: Prevalence and delayed recall in the general population. *Journal of Consulting and Clinical Psychology, 65*, 811–820.

Elliott, J. M. (1999). Feminist therapy. In C. Capuzzi & D. Gross (Eds.), *Counseling and psychotherapy: Theories and Interventions* (2nd ed., pp. 201–230). Columbus, OH: Merrill.

Elliott, T. R., Rivera, P., & Tucker, E. (2004). Groups in behavioral health and medical settings. In J. L. DeLucia-Waack, D. A. Gerrity, C. R. Kalodner, & M. T. Riva (Eds.), *Handbook of group counseling and psychotherapy.* Thousand Oaks, CA: Sage. pp. 338–350.

Ellis, A. (1993). RET becomes REBT. *IRETletter,* 1, 4.

Enns, C. Z. (1993). Twenty years of counseling and therapy: From naming biases to implementing multifaceted practice. *The Counseling Psychologist, 21*(1) 3–87.

Evans, K., Seem, S., & Kincade, E. (2005). In G. Corey (Ed.), *Case approach to counseling and psychotherapy* (6th ed., pp. 212–246). Belmont, CA: Wadsworth.

Farrell, K. (1976). *Shakespeare's creation: The language of magic and play.* Amherst: University of Massachusetts Press.

Fawzy, I., Fawzy, N., Hyun, C., & Wheeler, J. (1997). Brief coping-oriented therapy for patients with malignant melanoma. In J. Spira (Ed.), *Group therapy for medically ill patients* (pp. 133–164). New York: Guilford Press.

Fleckenstein, L. B., & Horne, A. M. (2004). Anger management groups. In J. L. DeLucia-Waack, D. A. Gerrity, C. R. Kalodner, & M. T. Riva (Eds.), *Handbook of group counseling and psychotherapy.* (pp. 547–562). Thousand Oaks, CA: Sage.

Forester-Miller, H., & Davis, T. (1996). *A practitioners guide to ethical decision making.* Alexandria, VA: American Counseling Association.

Forsyth, D. (1999). *Group dynamics* (3rd ed.). Pacific Grove, CA: Brooks/Cole.

Fossage, J. (1995). Self psychology and its contributions to psychoanalysis. *International Forum of Psychoanalysis, 4,* 238–246.

Fowler, S. (2006). Training across cultures: What intercultural trainers bring to diversity training. *Mumford; International Journal of Intercultural Relations, 30*(3), 401–411. (Original journal article)

Fowers, B. J., & Davidov, B. J. (2006). The virtue of multiculturalism: Personal transformation, character and openness to the other. *American Psychologist, 61*(6), 581–594.

Fredrickson, B. L. (2001). The role of positive emotions in positive psychology: The broaden-and-build theory of positive emotions. *American Psychologist, 56*(3), 218–226.

Freud, A. (1946). *The ego and the mechanisms of defense.* New York: International Universities Press.

Freud, S. (1936). Inhibitions, symptoms and anxiety. In J. Strachey (Ed. & Trans.), *The standard edition of the complete psychological works of Sigmund Freud* (Vol. 20, pp. 77–175). London: Hogarth Press. (Original work published 1926)

In Freud, S. (1953). The dynamics of transference. In J. Strachey (Ed. & Trans.), *The standard edition of the complete psychological works of Sigmund Freud* (Vol. 12, pp. 97–108). London: Hogarth Press. (Original work published 1912)

Frost, J., & Alonso, A. (1993). On becoming a group therapist. *International Journal of Group Psychotherapy, 17*(3), 179–184.

Frydenberg, E., Lewis, R., Bugalski, K., Coota, A., McCarthy, C., Luscombe-Smith, N., et al. (2004). Prevention is better than cure: Coping skills training for adolescents at school. *Educational Psychology in Practice, 20*(2), 117–118.

Fuhriman, A. (1997). Comments on issues raised by Slavson, Durkin, and Scheidlinger. *International Journal of Group Psychotherapy, 47,* 169–174.

Fuhriman, A., & Burlingame, G. (1994). (Eds.), *Handbook of group psychotherapy: An empirical and clinical synthesis.* New York: Wiley.

Gans, J. S., & Alonso, A. (1998). Difficult patients: Their construction in group therapy. *International Journal of Group Psychotherapy, 48*(3), 311–326.

Gazda, G., Ginter, E., & Horne, A. (2001). *Group counseling and group psychotherapy.* Needham Heights, MA: Allyn & Bacon.

Gehan, J. P., Toomey T. L., & Jones-Webb, R. (1999). Alcohol outlet workers and managers: Focus groups on responsible service practices. *Journal of Alcohol and Drug Education, 44*(2), 60–71.

Gibbard, G., & Hartman, J. (1973). The Oedipal paradigm in group development: A clinical and empirical study. *Small Group Behavior, 4,* 305–354.

Gill, K. M., Carson, J. W., Sedway, J. A., Porter, L. S., Orringer, E., & Wilson Schaeffer, J. J. (2000). Follow-up of coping skills training in adults with sickle cell disease: Analysis of daily pain and coping practice diaries. *Health Psychology, 19*(1), 85–86.

Gladding, S. (1991). *Group work: A counseling speciality* (2nd ed.). Upper Saddle River, NJ: Merrill/Prentice Hall.

Gladding, S. (1999). *Group Work: A counseling specialty.* (3rd ed.) Upper Saddle River, NJ: Merrill/Prentice Hall.

Gladding, S. (2003). *Group work: A counseling specialty* (4th ed.). Upper Saddle River, NJ: Merrill/Prentice Hall.

Gladding, S. T. (2004). *Counseling: A comprehensive profession* (5th ed.). Upper Saddle River, NJ: Prentice Hall.

Glasser, W. (1965). *Reality therapy: A new approach to psychiatry.* New York: Harper and Row.

Glasser, W. (2001) *Counseling with choice theory: The new reality therapy.* New York: HarperCollins.

Gloria, A. M. (1999). Apoyando estudiantes Chicanas: Thereapeutic factors in chicana college student support groups. *Journal for Specialists in Group Work, 20,* 33–39.

Glueckauf, R. L., & Quittner, A. L. (1992). Assertiveness training for disabled adults in wheelchairs: Self-report, role-play, and activity pattern outcomes. *Journal of Consulting and Clinical Psychology, 60*, 419–425.

Green, L. R., Meisler, A. W., Pilkey, D., Alexander, G., Cardella, L. A., Sirois, B. C., et al. (2004). Psychological work with groups in the veterans administration. In J. L. DeLucia-Waack, D. A. Gerrity, C. R. Kalodner, & M. T. Riva (Eds.), *Handbook of group counseling and psychotherapy.* Thousand Oaks, CA: Sage.

Greenson, R. R. (1967). *The theory and practice of psychoanalysis.* New York: International Universities Press.

Grey, M., Boland, E., Davidson, M. A., Li, J., & Tamborlane, W. (1999). Coping Skills Training (CST) for youth on intensive treatment has long-lasting effects on control and quality of life. *Diabetes, 48*(5), SA8.

Grey, M., Urban, A., Lindemann, E., Insabella, G., Berry, D., & Tamborlane, W. (2003). Can coping skills training for school-aged youth and their parents improve psychosocial well-being and metabolic control? (Pediatrics—Type 1 Diabetes). *Diabetes, 52*(6), A562.

Groves, J. E. (2006). Art as a behavior modification tool. *Multicultural Education, 13*(4), 55–57.

Grus, C. L. (2001). Daily coping practice predicts treatment effects in children with sickle cell disease (Journal article reviews: chronic illness). *Journal of Developmental & Behavioral Pediatrics, 22*(5), 340.

Hafen, B. Q., Karren, K. J. Frandsen, K. J., & Smith, N. L. (1996). *Mind/Body health.* Boston: Allyn & Bacon.

Hahn, W. (1994). Resolving shame in group psychotherapy. *International Journal of Group Psychotherapy, 44*(4), 449–461.

Halasz-Dees M., & Cuvo, A. J. (1986). Teaching a functional leisure skill cluster to rehabilitation clients: The art of macrame. *Applied Residential Mental Retardation, 7*(1)79–93.

Halstead, R. (1998). Academic success support groups. *Journal of College Student Development, 39*(5), 507–508.

Hansson, H., Zetterlind, U., Aberg-Orbeck, K., & Berglund, M. (2004). Two-year outcome of coping skills training, group support and information for spouses of alcoholics: A randomized controlled trial. *Alcohol and Alcoholism, 39*(2), 135–136.

Hartman, H. (1958). *Ego psychology and the problem of adaptation.* New York: International Universities Press.

Hartmann, L. (2005). Psychotherapy for children and adolescents: Evidence-based treatments and case examples [Book review]. *American Journal of Psychiatry, 162*, 1231–1232.

Heikkinen, C. A. (1975). Another look at teaching experience and close-mindedness. *Journal of Counseling Psychology, 22*(1), 79–83.

Herbert, R., Levesque, L., Vezina, J., Lavoie, J., Ducharme, F., Gendron, C., et al. (2003). Efficacy of a psychoeducative group program for caregivers of demented persons living at home: A randomized controlled trial. *Journal of Gerontology, 58*(1), S58–S67.

Hersen, M., Kazdin, A. E., Bellack, A. S., & Turner, S. M. (1979). Effects of live modeling, covert modeling and rehearsal on assertiveness in psychiatric patients. *Behaviour Research and Therapy, 17*(4), 369–377.

Hersey, P., & Blanchard, K. (1977). *Management of organizational behavior: Utilizing human resources* (3rd ed.). Englewood Cliffs, NJ: Prentice Hall.

Hill, M., Glaser, K., & Harden, J. (1995). *A feminist model for ethical decision making.* New York: Guilford Press.

Hobbs, M., Birtchnell, S., Harte, A., & Lacey, H. (1989). Therapeutic factors in short-term group therapy for women with bulimia. *International Journal of Eating Disorders, 8*, 623–633.

Hoffer, W. (1952). The mutual influences in the development of ego and id: Earliest stages. *Psychoanalytic Study of the Child 7*, 31–41.

Hoge, M. A., & McLoughlin, K. A. (1991). Group psychotherapy in acute treatment settings: Theory and technique. *Hospital & Community Psychiatry, 42*(2), 153–158.

Holladay, C. L., & Quinones, M. A. (2003). Practice variability and transfer of training: The role of the self-efficacy generality. *Journal of Applied Psychology, 88*, 1094–1103.

Honey, K., Bennett, P., & Morgan, M. (2002). A brief psycho-education group intervention for post-natal depression. *British Journal of Clinical Psychology, 41*(4), 405–409.

Hopper, E. (2001). On the nature of hope in psychoanalysis and group analysis. *British Journal of Psychotherapy, 18*(2), 1–21.

Horwitz, L. (2000). Narcissistic leadership in psychotherapy groups. *International Journal of Group Psychotherapy, 50*(2), 219–235.

Horvath, A. O. (2000). The therapeutic relationship: From transference to alliance. *Journal of Clinical Psychology, 56*, 163–173.

Howatson, K. (2005). Problem postcards: Social, emotional and behavioural skills training for disaffected and difficult children aged 7 to 11. *Educational Psychology in Practice, 21*(3), 246–248.

Ison, M. (2003). Training in social skills: An alternative technique for handling disruptive child behavior. *Psychological Reports, 88*(3), 903.

Ivey, A., Pedersen, P., & Ivey, M. (2001). *Intentional group counseling.* Belmont, CA: Wadsworth.

Ivey, A. E., & Ivey, M. B. (2003). Intentional interviewing and counseling (5th ed.). Pacific Grove, CA: Thompson Brooks/Cole.

Jackson, L. C., & Greene, B. (Eds.). (2000). *Psychotherapy with African American women.* New York: Guilford Press.

Jacobs, E. E., Harvill, R. L., Masson, R. L. (1988). *Group counseling: Strategies and skills.* Pacific Grove, CA: Brooks/Cole.

Janis, I. L. (1972). *Victims of groupthink: A psychological study of foreign-policy decisions and fiascoes.* Boston: Houghton Mifflin.

Janis, I. L. (1982). *Groupthink: Psychological studies of policy decisions and fiascoes* (2nd ed.). Boston: Houghton Mifflin.

Janocko, K. M. (1995). Client perceptions of therapeutic factors in an inpatient sexual abuse survivor's group. *Dissertation Abstracts International: Section B. The Sciences & Engineering, 56* (2-B), 1110. (UMI).

Jauregui, M. I. P. (2004). Training group for operators in violent contexts. *Interdisciplinaria Revista de Psicologia y Ciencias Afines, 21,* 173–181.

Johnson, D. (2003). *Reaching out* (8th ed.). Boston: Allyn & Bacon.

Johnson, D., & Johnson, F. (2003). *Joining together* (8th ed.). Boston: Allyn & Bacon.

Johnson, D., & Johnson, F. (2006). *Joining together,* (8th ed.). Boston: Allyn & Bacon.

Johnson, D. W., & Johnson, R. (1989). *Cooperation and competition: Theory and research.* Edina, MN: Interaction Book.

Jordan, J., Walker, M., & Hartling, L. M. (Eds.). (2004). *The complexity of connection.* New York: Guilford Press.

Jordan, J. V. (1991). The meaning of mutuality. In J. Jordan, A. Kaplan, J. Miller, I. Stiver, and J. Surrey (Eds.), *Women's growth in connection* (pp. 81–96). New York: Guilford Press.

Joyce, A. S., McCallum, M., Piper, W. E., Ogrodniczuk, J. S. (2000). Role behavior expectancies and alliance change in short-term individual psychotherapy. *Journal of Psychotherapy Practice & Research, 9,* 213–225.

Jung, C. (1959). *The archetypes and the collective unconscious.* Princeton, NJ: Princeton University Press.

Kagan, N. I., Kagan, H., & Watson, M. G. (1995). Stress reduction in the workplace: The effectiveness of psychoeducational programs. *American Psychological Association, 42*(11), 71–78.

Kalodner, C. R., & Coughlin, J. W. (2004). Psychoeducational and counseling groups to prevent and treat eating disorders and disturbances. In J. L. DeLucia-Waack, D. A. Gerrity, C. R. Kalodner, & M. T. Riva (Eds.), *Handbook of group counseling and psychotherapy.* (pp. 481–496). Thousand Oaks, CA: Sage.

Katzenbach, J. R., & Smith, D. K. (1993). *The wisdom of teams: Creating the high-performance organization.* Boston: Harvard Business School Press.

Kazdin, A. E., & Mascitelli, S. (1982). Covert and overt rehearsal and homework practice in developing assertiveness. *Journal of Consulting and Clinical Psychology, 50*(2), 250–258.

Keefe, F. J., Beaupre, P. M., & Gil, K. M. (2002). Group therapy for patients with chronic pain. In D. C. Turk & R. J. Gatchel (Eds.), *Psychological approaches to pain management: A practitioner's handbook* (2nd ed., pp. 234–255). New York: Guilford Press.

Kellerman, H. (1979). *Group psychotherapy and personality: Intersecting structures.* New York: Grune & Stratton.

Kernberg, O. (1965). Counter transference in social research: Beyond Georges Devereux. *Public Opinion Quarterly, 40,* 165–181.

Kernberg, O. (1990). *Borderline and narcissistic conditions.* New York: Aronson.

King, L. A. (2001). The health benefits of writing about life goals. *Personality and Social Psychology Bulletin, 27,* 798–807.

Kipper, D. A. (1992). The effect of two kinds of role playing on self-evaluation of improved assertiveness. *Journal of Clinical Psychology, 48*(2), 246–250.

Kivlighan, D., Coleman, M., & Anderson, D. (2000). Process, outcome and methodology in group counseling research. In S. D. Brown & R. W. Lent (Eds.), *Handbook of counseling psychology* (3rd ed., pp. 767–796). New York: Wiley.

Kivlighan, D., & Holmes, S. (2004). The importance of therapeutic factors. In J. DeLucia-Waack, D. A. Gerrity, C. R. Kalodner, M. T. Riva (Eds.), *Handbook of group counseling and psychotherapy.* Thousand Oaks, CA: Sage.

Kivlighan, D., Jr., & Goldfine, D. C. (1991). Endorsement of therapeutic factors as a function of group development and participant interpersonal attitudes. *Journal of Counseling Psychology, 38,* 150–158.

Kivlighan, D. M. (1990). Career group therapy. *Counseling Psychologist, 18*(1), 64–79.

Kivlighan, D. M., Jr., & Mullison, D. (1988). Participant's perception of therapeutic factors in group counseling. The role of interpersonal style and stage of group development. *Small Group Behavior, 19,* 452–468.

Klein, G. A. (1999). *Sources of power: How people make decisions.* Cambridge, MA: MIT Press.

Klein, M. (1952). The origins of transference. In *Envy and gratitude and other works 1946–1963.* New York: Delta Books.

Kline, W. (2005). *Interactive group counseling and therapy*. Upper Saddle River, NJ: Merrill/Prentice Hall.

Kline, W. B. (2003). *Interactive group counseling and therapy*. New York: Merrill/Prentice Hall.

Klose, P., & Tinius, T. (1992). Confidence builders: A self-esteem group at an inpatient psychiatric hospital. *Journal of Psychosocial Nursing, 30*, 5–9.

Kobak, K. A., Rock, A. L., & Greist, J. H. (1995). Group behavior therapy for obsessive-compulsive disorder. *Journal for Specialists in Group Work, 20*(1), 26–32.

Kohut, H. (1975). *The restored self*. New York: International Universities Press.

Kohut, H. (1977). *The restoration of the self*. Madison, CT: International Universities Press.

Kohut, H. (1984). *The nature of the psychoanalytic cure*. Chicago: University of Chicago Press.

Koocher, G. (2007). Twenty-first century ethical challenges for psychology. *American Psychologist, 62*(5), 375–384.

Kottler, J. (2002). *Theories in counseling and therapy*. Needham Heights, MA: Allyn & Bacon.

Kottler, J. A. (2001). *Learning group leadership: An experiential approach*. Boston: Allyn & Bacon.

Kruesi, M. J., Grossman, J., Pennington, J. M, Woodward, P. J., Duda, D., & Hirsch, J. G. (1999). Suicide and violence prevention: Parent education in the emergency department. *Journal of the American Academy of Child & Adolescent Psychiatry, 38*(3), 250–255.

Landry-Dattee, N., Gauvain-Piquard, A., & Cosset-Delaigue, M. (2000). A support group for children with one parent with cancer: Report on 4-year experience of a talking group. *Bulletin of Cancer, 87*(4), 355–362.

Larson, C. E., & LaFasto, F. M. J. (1989). *Team work: What must go right/what can go wrong*. Newbury Park, CA: Sage.

Lavallee, K. L., Bierman, K. L, & Nix, R. L. (2005). The impact of first-grade 'friendship group' experiences on child social outcomes in the Fast Track Program, Conduct Problems Prevention Research Group. *Journal of Abnormal Child Psychology, 33*(3), 307–324.

Lese, K., & MacNair-Semands, R. (2000). The therapeutic factors inventory: Department of a scale. *Group, 24*, 303–317.

Lewin, K. (1944). Dynamics of group action. *Educational Leadership, 1*(4), 195–200.

Lewin, K. (1948). *Resolving social conflicts*. New York: Harper.

Liberman, R. P., Wallace, C. J., Blackwell, G., Eckman, T. A., Vaccaro, J. V., & Kuehnel, T. G. (1998). Innovations in skills training for the seriously mentally ill: The UCLA social and independent living skills (SILS) modules. *Innovations and Research, 2*(2), 43–59.

Liberman, R. P., Wallace, C. J., Blackwell, G., Kopelowicz, A., & Mintz, J. (1998). *American Journal of Psychiatry, 155*, 1087–1091.

Lieberman, M. & Yalom, (1973). *Encounter groups: First facts*. New York: Basic Books.

Linenhan, M. (2001). *Cognitive-behavioral treatment of borderline personality disorder*. New York: Guilford Presss.

Linenhan, M. M. (1993) *Skills training manual for treating borderline personality disorder*. New York: Guilford Press.

Linenhan, M., Litt, M. D., Kadden, R. M., Cooney, N. L., & Kabela, E. (2003). Coping skills and treatment outcomes in cognitive-behavioral and interactional group therapy for alcoholism [Abstract]. *Journal of Consulting and Clinical Psychology, 71*(1), 118.

Little, C., Packman, J., Smaby, M. H., & Maddux, C. D. (2005). The skilled counselor training model: Skills, acquisition, self-assessment, and cognitive complexity. *Counselor Education and Supervision, 44*(3), 189–200.

Little, L. (2005). Program trains families to address addiction. *Family Practice News, 35*(22), 43.

Livingston, M., & Livingston, L. L. (1998). Conflict and aggression in group psychotherapy: A self psychological vantage point. *International Journal of Group Psychotherapy, 48*, 381–391.

Livingston, M. S. (1999). Vulnerability, tenderness, and the experience of selfobject relationship: A self psychological view of deepening curative process in group psychotherapy. *International Journal of Group Psychotherapy, 49*(1), 19–40.

Lomonaco, S., Scheidlinger, S., & Aronson, S. (2000). Five decades of children's group treatment: An overview. *Journal of Child and Adolescent Group Therapy, 10*, 77–96.

Lott, B. (2002). Cognitive and behavioral distancing from the poor. *American Psychologist, 57*, 100–110.

Lubetsky, M. J. (1989). The magic of fairy tales: Psychodynamic and developmental perspectives. *Child Psychiatry and Human Development, 19*(4), 245–255.

Luborsky, L. (1976). Helping alliances in psychotherapy. In J. L. Claghorn (Ed.) *Successful psychotherapy*. (pp. 92–116). New York: Brunner/Mazel.

Luft, J. (1969). *Of human interaction*. Palo Alto, CA: National Press.

Luks, A. (1988, October). Helper's high. *Psychology Today*, 39–42.

Lundgren, D., & Knight, D. (1978). Sequential stages of development in sensitivity training groups. *Journal of Applied Behavioral Science, 14*, 204–222.

MacKenzie, K. (1990). *Introduction to time-limited group therapy*. Washington, DC: American Psychiatric Press.

MacKenzie, K. R. (2001). Group psychotherapy. In W. J. Livesley (Ed.) *Handbook of Personality Disorders* (pp. 497–526). New York: Guilford Press.

MacKenzie, K. R. (2002). Group psychotherapy. In W. J. Livesley (Ed.), *Handbook of personality disorders.* (pp. 497–526) New York: Guilford Press.

MacLennan, B. W. (1975). The personalities of group leaders: Implications for selection and training. *International Journal of Group Psychotherapy, 25*(2), 177–183.

MacNair-Semands, R. R., & Lese, K. P. (2000). Interpersonal problems and the perception of therapeutic factors in group therapy. *Small Group Research, 31,* 158–174.

Magen, R., & Mangiardi, E. (2005). *Groups and individual change.* Thousand Oaks, CA: Sage.

Mahler, M. (1968). *On human symbiosis and the vicissitudes of individuation.* New York: International Universities Press.

Mahler, M., Pine, F., & Bergman, A. (1975). *The psychological birth of the human infant.* New York: Basic Books.

Mahler, M. S. (1975). On the current status of the infantile neurosis. *Journal of the American Psychoanalytic Association, 23*(2), 327–333.

Malekoff, A. (1997). *Group work with adolescents, principles and practice.* New York: Guilford Press.

Mann, J. (1966). Evaluation of group psychotherapy. In J. Moreno (Ed.), *International handbook of group psychotherapy.* New York: Philosophical Library.

Mann, R., Gibbard, G., & Hartman, J. (1967). *Interpersonal style and group development.* New York: Wiley.

McFall, R. M., & Lillesand, D. B. (1971). Behavior rehearsal with modeling and coaching in assertion training. *Journal of Abnormal Psychology, 77*(3), 313–323.

McFarland, P., & Sanders, S. (2000). Educational support groups for male caregivers of individuals with Alzheimer's disease. *American Journal of Alzheimer's Disease, 15*(6), 367–373.

McFarlane, W., Link, B., Dushay, R., Marchal, J., & Crilly, J. (1995). Psychoeducational multiple family groups: Four-year relapse outcome in schizophrenia. *Family Process, 34*(2), 127–144.

McFarlane, W., Lukens, E., Link, B., Dushay, R., Deakins, S., Newmark, M., et al. (1995). Multiple-family groups and psychoeducation in the treatment of schizophrenia. *Archives of General Psychiatry, 52*(8), 679–687.

McFarlane, W. (2002). *Multifamily groups in the treatment of severe psychiatric disorders.* New York: Guilford Press.

McGillicuddy, N. B., Rychtarik, R. G., Duquette, J. A., & Morsheimer, E. T. (2001). Development of a skill training program for parents of substance-abusing adolescents. *Journal of Substance Abuse Treatment, 20*(1), 59–68.

McIntosh, P. (1992). White privilege and male privilege: A personal account of coming to see correspondences through work in women's studies. In M. L. Anderson & P. H. Collins (Eds.), *Race, class, and gender: An anthology* (2nd ed., pp. 70–81). Belmont, CA: Wadsworth.

McIntosh, P. (1998). "White privilege and male privilege: A personal account of coming to see correspondences through work in women's studies." Excerpt from Working Paper 189. Wellesley, MA: Wellesley College Center for Research on Women.

Meichenbaum, D. (1977). *Cognitive-behavior modification: An integrative approach.* New York: Plenum.

Meichenbaum, D. (1986). Cognitive behavior modification. In F. H. Kanfer & A. P. Goldstein (Eds.), *Helping people change: A textbook of methods.* (pp. 346–380). New York: Pergamon.

Meyers, L. (2006). Asian-American mental health. *Monitor on Psychology, 37*(2), 44–46.

Meyerson, D., Weick, K., & Kramer, R. (1996). Swift trust and temporary groups. In R. Kramer (Ed.), *Trust in organizations* (pp. 166–195). Thousand Oaks, CA: Sage.

Miles, M. (1971). *Learning to work in groups.* New York: Teachers College Press.

Miller W. & Rollnic, K. S. (2002). *Motivational interviewing.* New York: Guilford Publishers.

Mills, T. (1964). *Group transformations: An analysis of a learning group.* Upper Saddle River, NJ: Prentice Hall.

Monti, P. M., Abrams, D. B., Binkoff, J. A., Zwick, W. R., Liepman, M. R., Nirenberg, T. D., et al. (1990). Communication skills training, communication skills training with family and cognitive behavioral mood management training for alcoholics. *Journal of Studies on Alcohol, 51,* 263–270.

Monti, P. M., & Rohsenow, D. J. (1999). Coping-skills training and cue-exposure therapy in the treatment of alcoholism. *Alcohol Research & Health, 23*(2), 107.

Morgan, R., & Flora, D. (2002). Group psychotherapy with incarcerated offenders: A research synthesis. *Group Dynamics, 6*(3), 203–218.

Morran, D., Stockton, R., & Whittingham, M. (2004). Effective leader interventions for counseling and psychotherapy groups. In J. L. DeLucia-Waack, D. A. Gerrity, C. R. Kalodner, & M. T. Riva (Eds.), *Handbook of group counseling and psychotherapy* (pp. 91–103). Thousand Oaks, CA: Sage.

Morrison, T. (1992). *Playing in the dark: Whiteness and the literary imagination.* Cambridge, MA: Harvard University Press.

Munsey, C. (2006). A family for Asian psychologists. *Monitor on Psychology, 37*(2), 60–62.

Mussell, M., Binford, R., & Fulkerson, J. (2000). Eating disorders: Summary of risk factors, prevention programming, and prevention research. *Counseling Psychologist, 28,* 764–796.

Myers, D. (2000). The funds, friends and faith of happy people. *American Psychologist, 55*(1), 56–67.

Neighbors, H. W., Jackson, J. S., Campbell, L., & Williams, D. (1989). The influence of racial factors on psychiatric diagnosis: A review and suggestions for research. *Community Health Journal, 25,* 301–309.

Nelson, J. E., & Howell, R. J. (1982–1983). Assertiveness training using rehearsal and modeling with male alcoholics. *The American Journal of Drug and Alcohol Abuse, 9*(3), 309–323.

Nitsun, M. (1996). *The anti-group: Destructive forces in the group and their creative potential.* London: Routledge.

Nystul, M. (2006). *Introduction to counseling: An art and science perspective* (3rd ed.). Boston: Allyn & Bacon.

O'Farrell, T. J., Choquette, K. A., & Cutter, H. S. (1998). Couples relapse prevention sessions after behavioral marital therapy for male alcoholics: Outcomes during the three years after starting treatment. *Journal of Studies on Alcohol, 59*(4), 357–370.

O'Leary, C. A. (2000). Reducing aggression in adults with brain injuries. *Behavioral Interventions, 15*(3), 205–216.

Olweus D., & Limber, S. (2002). *Bullying Prevention program* (Rep. No. Book nine). Boulder: Center for the Study of Prevention and Violence, Institute of Behavioral Science, University of Colorado at Boulder.

Orasanu, J., & Connolly, T. (1995). The reinvention of decision making. In G. A. Klein, J. Orsanu, R. Calderwood, & C. E. Zsambok (Eds.), Decision making in action: Models and methods (pp. 3–20). Norwood, NJ: Ablex.

Ormont L. (1990). The craft of bridging. *International Journal of Group Psychotherapy, 40,* 3–17.

Osgood, E. E., Tannenbaum, P. H., & Suci, G. J. (1957). *The measurement of meaning.* Urbana: University of Illinois Press.

Ousdigian, S. K. A. (2001). Relationship of perceived social support to school adjustment for children in special and regular education programs. *Dissertation Abstracts International: Section A. Humanities and Social Sciences, 61* (12-A), 4674.

Palazzoli, M. S., Boscolo, L., Cecchin, G. F., & Prata, G. (1974). The treatment of children through brief treatment of their parents. *Family Process, 13*(4), 429–442.

Paunonen, S., Keinonen, M., Trzebinski, J., Forsterling, F., Grishenkoroze, N., Kouznetsova, L., et al. (1996). The structure of personality in six countries. *Journal of Cross-Cultural Psychology, 27*(3), 339–353.

Pavkov, T. W., Lewis, D. A., & Lyons, J. S. (1989). Psychiatric diagnoses and racial biases: An empirical investigation. *Professional Psychology: Research & Practice, 6,* 364–368.

Pavlov, I. P. (1927). *Conditional reflexes: An investigation of the physiological activity of the cerebral cortex.* Oxford, England: Oxford University Press.

Pekkala, E., & Merinder, L. (2002). Psychoeducation for schizophrenia. *Cochrane Database System Review, 2,* CD002831.

Pennebaker, J. W. (1997a). *Opening up: The healing power of expressing emotion.* New York: Guilford Press.

Pennebaker, J. W. (1997b). Writing about emotional experiences as a therapeutic process. *Psychological Science, 8,* 162–166.

Pennebaker, J. W., Colder, M., & Sharp, L. K. (1990). Accelerating the coping process. *Journal of Personality and Social Psychology, 58,* 528–537.

Pennebaker, J. W., Mayne, T. J., & Francis, M. E. (1997). Linguistic, and therapeutic implications. *Behavior Research and Therapy, 31,* 520–533.

Perls, F. (1969) *Gestalt therapy verbatim.* Moab, UT: Real People Press.

Peterson, C. (2000). The future of optimism. *American Psychologist, 55*(1), 44–55.

Phillips, J. H. (2005). An evaluation of school-based cognitive-behavioral social skills training groups with adolescents at risk for depression. *Dissertation Abstracts International: Section A. Humanities and Social Sciences, 65*(7-A), 2768.

Pincus, D., & Friedman, A. (2004). Improving children's coping with everyday stress: Transporting treatment interventions to the school setting. *Clinical Child and Family Psychology Review, 7*(4), 223–240.

Piper, W. E., & Marrache, M. (1981). Selecting suitable patients: Pretraining for group therapy as a method of patient selection. *Small Group Behavior, 12,* 459–476.

Piper, W. E., & McCallum, M. (1994). Selection of patients for group interventions. In H. S. Bernard & K. R. MacKenzie (Eds.), *Basics of group psychotherapy* (pp. 1–34). New York: Guilford Press.

Piper, W. E., McCallum, M., Joyce, A. S., Rosie, J. S., & Ogrodniczuk, J. S. (2001). Patient personality and time-limited group psychotherapy for complicated grief. *International Journal of Group Psychotherapy, 51,* 525–552.

Piper, W. E., & Perrault, E. L. (1989). Pretherapy preparation for group members. *International Journal of Group Psychotherapy, 39,* 170–194.

Polster, E., & Polster, M. (1973). *Gestalt therapy integrated.* New York: Vintage.

Posthuma, B. (2002). *Small groups in counseling and therapy.* Boston: Allyn & Bacon.

Posthuma, B. (2003). *Small groups in counseling and therapy* (4th ed.). Boston: Allyn & Bacon.

Price, R. H., Cowen, E. L., Lorion, R. P., & Ramos-McKay, J. (1988). *14 ounces of prevention: a casebook for practitioners.* Washington, DC: American Psychological Association.

Prinz, R. J., Blechman, E. A., & Dumas, J. E. (1994). An evaluation of peer coping-skills training for childhood aggression. *Journal of Clinical Child Psychology, 12*(2), 193–203.

Ray, D. (2004). Supervision of basic and advanced skills in play therapy. *Journal of Professional Counseling: Practice, Theory, and Research, 32,* 28–41.

Reddon, J. R., Payne, L. R., & Starzyk, K. B. (1999). Therapeutic factors in group treatment evaluated by sex offenders: A consumers' report. *Journal of Offender Rehabilitation, 28*(3–4), 91–101.

Reich, W. (1972). *Character analysis.* New York: Simon and Schuster. (Original work published 1945)

Rice, A. H. (1996). *Structured group treatment of depression: An integrated social work model.* Ann Arbor MI. (UMI)

Richards, P. S., Baldwin, B. M., Frost, H. A., Clark-Sly, J. B., Berrett, M. E., & Hardman, R. K. (2000). What works for treating eating disorders? Conclusions of 28 outcome reviews. *Eating Disorders: The Journal of Treatment and Prevention, 8,* 189–206.

Ridley, C. R. (1995). *Overcoming unintentional racism in counseling and therapy.* Thousand Oaks, CA: Sage.

Riva, M. T., Wachtel, M., & Lasky, G. B. (2004). Effective leadership in group counseling and psychotherapy. In J. L. DeLucia-Waack, D. A. Gerrity, C. R. Kalodner, & M. T. Riva (Eds.), *Handbook of group counseling and psychotherapy* (pp. 37–48). Thousand Oaks, CA: Sage.

Robertiello, R. C., & Schoenewolf, G. (1987). *101 common therapeutic blunders: Countertransference and counterresistance in psychotherapy.* Northvale, NJ: Jason Aronson.

Rogers, C. (1951). *Client-centered therapy.* Boston: Houghton Mifflin.

Rogers, C. (1970). *On encounter groups.* New York: Harper and Row.

Rogers, R. W. (1975). A protection motivation theory of fear appeals and attitude change. *Journal of Psychology, 91,* 93–114.

Rohsenow, D., Monti, P., Rubonis, A., Gulliver, S., Colby, S., Binkoff, J., et al. (2001). Cue exposure with coping skills training and communication skills training for alcohol dependence: 6 and 12 month outcomes. *Addiction, 96,* 1161–1174.

Romano, J., & Hage, S. (2000). Prevention and counseling psychology: Revitalizing commitments for the 21st century. In J. Romano & S. Hage (Special Section Eds.), The *Counseling Psychologist, 28,* 733–763.

Roth, B. E., Stone, W. N., & Kibel, H. D. (1990). *The difficult patient in group.* Madison, CT: International Universities Press.

Rotheram, M. J., & Armstrong, M. (1980). Assertiveness training with high school students. *Adolescence, 15*(58), 267–276.

Rugel, R. P., & Barry, D. (1990). Overcoming denial through the group: A test of acceptance theory. *Small Group Research, 21*(1), 45–58.

Rutan, J. S. (1993). Psychoanalytic group psychotherapy. In H. I. Kaplan & B. J. Saddock (Eds.), *Comprehensive group therapy* (3rd ed.), pp. 98–150). Baltimore: Williams & Wilkins.

Rutan, J. S., & Rice, C. A. (1981). The charismatic leader: Asset or liability. *Psychotherapy: Theory, Research, Practice, 18,* 12–24.

Rutan, S., & Stone, W. (2001). *Psychodynamic group psychotherapy* (3rd ed.). New York: Guilford Press.

Rutan, S. J., & Stone, N. W. (2000). *Psychodynamic groups psychotherapy* (3rd ed.). New York: Guilford Press.

Ryan, R. M., & Deci, E. L. (2000). Self-determination theory and the facilitation of intrinsic motivation, social development and well-being. *American Psychologist, 55*(1), 68–78.

Rychtarik, R. G., & McGillicuddy, N. B. (2005). Coping skills training and 12-step facilitation for women whose partner has alcoholism: Effects on depression, the partner's drinking, and partner physical violence. [Brief article]. *Journal of Consulting and Clinical Psychology, 73*(2), 249.

Salovey, P., Rothman, A. J., Detweiler, J. B., & Steward, W. T. (2000). Emotional states and health. *American Psychologist, 55* (1), 110–121.

Saltz, E., Dixon, D., & Johnson, J. (1977). Training disadvantaged preschoolers on various fantasy activities: Effects on cognitive functioning and impost control. *Child Development, 48*(2), 367–380.

Salvendy, J. T. (1999). Ethnocultural considerations in group psychotherapy. *International Journal of Group Psychotherapy, 49*(4), 429–464.

Sandahl, C., & Ronnbers, S. (1990). Brief group therapy in relapse prevention for alcohol dependent patients. *International Journal of Group Psychotherapy, 40*(4), 453–476.

Santarsiero, L. J., Baker, R. C., & McGee, T. F. (1995). The effects of cognitive pretraining on cohesion & self-disclosure in small groups: An analog study. *Journals of Clinical Psychology, 51,* 403–409.

Scharff, J. (1992). *Projective and introjective identification and the use of the therapist's self.* Northvale, NJ: Aronson.

Schectman, Z., Levy, M., & Leichtentritt, J. (2005). Impact of life skills training on teachers' perceived environment and self-efficacy. *Journal of Educational Research, 98*(3), 144–154.

Scheidlinger, S. (2004) Group interventions for treatment of trauma in children. In American Group Psychotherapy Association, *Group Interventions for Psychological Trauma.* New York: American Group Psychotherapy Association.

Schermer, V. (2000). Contributions of object relations theory and self psychology to relational psychology and group psychotherapy. *International Journal of Group Psychotherapy, 50*(2), 199–217.

Schmidt, J. J., & Biles, J. W. (1985). Puppetry as a group counseling technique with middle school students. *Elementary School Guidance & Counseling, 20*(1), 67–73.

Schwartz, J. P., & Waldo, M. (1999). Therapeutic factors in Duluth model spouse abusers group treatment. *Journal for Specialists in Group Work, 24,* 197–207.

Scott, C. D. (1989). Coping with stress. *Journal of the American Medical Association, 262*(17), 2466.

Segal, M. W. (1979). Varieties of interpersonal attraction and their interrelationships in naturally occurring groups. *Social Psychology Quarterly, 42,* 253–261.

Seligman, M.E.P. (1995). The effectiveness of psychotherapy: The Consumer Report Study. *American Psychologists, 50,* 965–974.

Selvini-Palazzoli, A. (1974). *From the intrapsychic to the transpersonal approach: to anorexia nervosa.* (A. Pomranz, trans.) London: Human Context Books.

Shapiro, J. (1978). *Methods of group psychotherapy and encounter: A tradition of innovation.* Itasca, IL: F. E. Peacock.

Sharma, M. (2004). Tapping into the potential of focus groups for research in alcohol and drug education [Editorial]. *Journal of Alcohol & Drug Education, 48*(3), 3.

Sherif, M. (1936). *The psychology of group norms.* New York: Harper.

Shulman, L. (1994). Group work method. In A. Gitterman & L. Shulman (Eds.), *Mutual aid groups, vulnerable populations, and the life cycle* (2nd ed., pp. 29–58). New York: Columbia University Press.

Simms, D. E., Salas, E., & Burke, C. S. (2005). Promoting effective team performance through training. In S. A.

Wheelan (Ed.), *The handbook of group research and practice* (pp. 407–425). Thomson Oaks, CA: Sage.

Singer, G. H. S., Glang, A., & Nixon, C. (1994). A comparison of two psychosocial interventions for parents of children with acquired brain injury: An exploratory study. *Journal of Head Trauma Rehabilitation, 9*(4), 38–49.

Skinner, B. (1953). *Science and human behavior.* New York: Macmillan.

Skinner, B. (1968). *The technology of teaching.* New York: Appleton-Century-Crofts.

Slater, P. (1966). *Microcosm.* New York: Wiley.

Smead, R. (1995). *Skills and techniques for group work with youth.* Champaign, IL: Research Press.

Smyth, J. M., Stone, A. A., Hurewitz, A., & Kaell, A. (1999). Effects of writing about stressful experiences on symptom reduction in patients with asthma or rheumatoid arthritis: A randomized trial. *Journal of the American Medical Association, 281,* 1304–1309.

Snijiders, K., Vlaeyen, M., Goossens, M., Heuts, P., van Molken, R., Bruekelen, G., & van Eek, H. (1999). Chronic low back pain: What do cognitive coping skills add to operant behavioral treatment? *Journal of Consulting and Clinical Psychology, 67*(6), 931–944.

Snyder, C., Cheaveus, J., & Sympson, S. (1997). Hope: An individual motive for social commerce. *Group Dynamics: Theory, Research, and Practice, 1*(2), 107–118.

Sobel, D. (1993). Rx: Helping others. *Mental Medicine Update,* 6.

Sommers-Flanagan, R., & Sommers-Flanagan, J. (2007). *Becoming an ethical helping professional.* New York: Wiley.

Sotsky, S. M., Glass, D. R., Shea, M.T., Pilkonis, P. A., Collins, J. F., Elkin, I., Watkins, Imber, S. D., Lebr, W. R., & Moyer, J. (1991) Patient predictors of response to psychotherapy and pharmacotherapy: Findings in the NIMH treatment of depression collaborative research program. *American Journal of Pyschiatry, 148*(8), 997–1008.

Spera, S. P., Buhrfeind, E., & Pennebaker, J. W. (1994). Expressive writing and coping with job loss. *The Academy of Management Journal, 37*(3), 722–733.

Steele, C. M. (1997). A threat in the air: How stereotypes shape intellectual identity and Performance. *American Psychologist, 52,* 613–629.

Stephenson, J., & Staal, M. (2007). An ethical decision making model for operational Psychology. *Ethics & Behavior, 17*(1), 61–82.

Stevens-Guille, M. E. & Boersma, F. J. (1992). Fairy tales as trance experience's possible therapeutic uses. *American Journal of Clinical Hypnosis.* 34(4), 245–254.

Stock, D., & Thelen, H. (1958). *Emotional dynamics and group culture.* New York: New York University Press.

Stolorow, R. (1986). Toward a functional definition of narcissism. In A. Morrison (Ed.), *Essential papers on narcissism (pp. 197–210)*. New York University Press.

Stolorow, R. (1993). Thoughts on the nature and therapeutic action of psychoanalytic interpretation. In A. Goldberg (Ed.), *Progress in self psychology* (pp. 49–84). Hillsdale, NJ: Analytic Press.

Stone, W. N. (1992). The place of self psychology in group psychotherapy: A status report. *International Journal of Group Psychotherapy, 42,* 335–350.

Strakowski, S. M., Hawkins, J. M., Keck, P. E., Jr., McElroy, S. L., West, S. A., Bourne, M. L., et al. (1997). The effects of race and information variance on disagreement between psychiatric emergency service and research diagnoses in first-episode psychosis. *Journal of Clinical Psychiatry, 58,* 457–463.

Sue, D., Capodilupo, C., Torino, G., Bucceri, J., Holder, A., Nadal, K., et al. (2007). Racial microaggressions in everyday life: Implications for clinical practice. *American Psychologist, 62*(4), 271–286.

Sue, D. W., Bucceri, J., Lin, A. I., Nadal, K. L., & Torino, G. C. (2007). Racial microaggressions and the Asian American Experience. *Cultural Diversity and Ethnic Minority psychology, 13,* 72–81.

Sue, S. (2006). Cultural competency: From philosophy to research and practice. *Journal of Community Psychology, 34*(2), 237–245.

Sue, S., Akutsu, P. D., & Higashi, C. (1987). Training issues in conducting therapy with ethnic minority-group clients. In P. Pederson (Ed.), Handbook of cross-cultural counseling and therapy (pp. 275–280). New York: Praeger.

Sullivan, H. (1953). *The collected works of Harry Stack Sullivan.* New York: Norton.

Sullivan, H. S. (1968). *The interpersonal theory of psychiatry.* New York: Norton.

Sundstrom, E., DeMeuse, K. P., & Futrell, D. (1990). Work teams: Applications and effectiveness. *American Psychologist, 45,* 120–133.

Tapert, S. F., Ozyurt, S. S., Myers, M. G., & Brown, S. A. (2004). Neurocognitive ability in adults coping with alcohol and drug relapse temptations. *American Journal of Drug and Alcohol Abuse, 30*(2), 445.

Taylor, K., Lamdan, R., Siegel, J., Shelby, R., Moran-Klimi, K., & Hrywna M. (2003). Follow-up results of a randomized psychoeducational group intervention. *Health Psychology, 22*(3), 316–323.

Taylor, R., Reeves, B., Ewings, P., Binns, S., Keast, J., & Mears, R. (2000). A systematic review of the effectiveness of critical appraisal skills training for clinicians. *Medical Education, 34,* 120.

Taylor, S. E., Kemeny, M. E., Reed, G. M., Bowers, J. E., & Gruenwald, T. L. (2000). Psychological resources, positive illusions and health. *American Psychologist, 55*(1), 99–109.

Thibaut, J. W., & Kelley, H. H. (1959). *The psychology of groups.* New York: Wiley.

Thorenson, P. (1972). Defense mechanisms in groups. In J. W. Pheiffer & J. E. Jones (Eds.), *The 1971 annual handbook for group facilitators.* LaJolla, CA: University Associates.

Toth, P. L., Stockton, R., & Erwin, W. J. (1998). Application of skill-based training model for group counselors. *Journal for Specialists in Group Work, 44,* 185–208.

Toumbourou, J. W., & Gregg, M. E. (2002). Impact of an empowerment-based parent education program on the reduction of youth suicide risk factors. *Journal of Adolescent Health, 31*(3), 277–285.

Tracey, M. D. (2006). Cultural worlds intersect. *Monitor on Psychology, 37*(2), 48–51.

Trimble, S. K., Nathan, B. R., & Decker, P. J. (1990). The effect of positive and negative models on learning in behavior modeling and training: Testing for proactive and retroactive interference. *Journal of Human Behavior & Learning, 7,* 1–12.

Trotzer, J. P. (1989). *The counselor and the group: Integrating theory, training and practice* (2nd ed.). Muncie, IN: Accelerated Development.

Trotzer, J. P. (2004). Conducting a group: Guidelines for choosing and using activities. In J. L. DeLucia-Waack, D. A. Gerrity, C. R. Kalodner, & M. T. Riva (Eds.), *Handbook of group counseling and psychotherapy* (pp. 76–90). Thousand Oaks, CA: Sage.

Tschuschke, V., & Dies, R. (1994). Intensive analysis of therapeutic factors and outcome in long-term inpatient groups. *International Journal of Group Psychotherapy, 44,* 185–208.

Tuckman, B. (1965) Developmental sequence in small groups. *Psychological Bulletin, 63,* 384–399.

Tuckman, B., & Jensen, M. (1977). Stages of small group development revisited. *Group and Organizational Studies, 2,* 419–427.

Uehaqra, T., Kawashima, Y., Goto, M., Tasaki, S., & Someya, T. (2001). Psychoeducation for the families of patients with eating disorders and changes in expressed emotion: A preliminary study. *Comprehensive Psychiatry, 42*(2), 132–138.

Vaillant, G. (2000). Adaptive mental mechanisms. *American Psychologist, 55*(1), 89–98.

Vallina-Fernandez, O., Lemos-Giraldez, S., Roder, V., & Gutierrez-Perez, A. (2001). Controlled study of an integrated psychological intervention in schizophrenia. *European Journal of Psychiatry, 15*(3), 167–179.

Van Lone, J. L., Kalodner, C. R., & Coughlin, J. W. (2002). Using short stories to address eating disturbances in groups. *Journal for Specialists in Group Work, 27*, 59–77.

Verderber, R., & Verderber, K. (1992). *Interact* (6th ed.). Belmont, CA: Wadsworth.

Waller, C. S. (1996). Art therapy with adult female incest survivors. *Art Therapy, 9*(3), 135–138.

Washington, O. G., & Moxley, D. P. (2004). Using scrapbooks & portfolios in group work with women who are chemically dependent. *Journal of Psychosocial Nursing and Mental Health Services, 42*(6), 42–53.

Watzlawick, P., Weakland, J., & Fisch, R. (1974). *Change: Principles of problem formation and change.* Palo Alto, CA: Science & Behavior Books.

Weinberg, N., Uken, J. S., Schmale, J., & Adamek, M. (1995). Therapeutic factors: Their presence in a computer mediated support group. *Social Work With Groups, 18*(4), 57–69.

Weitlauf, J. C., Smith, R. E., & Cervone, D. (2000). Generalization effects of coping- skills training: Influence of self-defense training on women's efficacy beliefs, assertiveness, and aggression. *Journal of Applied Psychology, 85*(4), 625–33.

Welfel, E. (2002) *Ethics in counseling and psychotherapy: Standards, research, and emerging issues.* (2nd ed.). Pacific Grove, CA: Brooks/Cole.

Wexel, R., & Brown, N. (2000). *Student generated sexual harassment in secondary schools.* Westport, CT: Bergin & Garvey.

Whaley, A., & Davis, K. (2007). Cultural competence and evidence-based practice in mental health services. *American Psychologist, 62*(6), 563–574.

Whaley, A., & Geller, P. (2007). Toward a cognitive process model of ethnic/racial biases in clinical judgment. *Review of General Psychology, 11*(1), 75–96.

Wheelan, S. (1994). *Group processes: A developmental perspective.* Boston: Allyn & Bacon.

Wheelan, S. A. (1990). *Facilitating training groups: A guide to leadership and verbal intervention skills.* New York: Praeger.

Wheelan, S. A. (2005a). The developmental perspective. In S. A. Wheelan (Ed.), *The handbook of group research and practice.* Thousand Oaks, CA: Sage.

Wheelan, S. A. (2005b). Groups in the workplace. In S. A. Wheelan (Ed.), *The handbook of research and practice* (pp. 401–413). Thouand Oaks, CA: Sage.

Wheeler Q., & Bertram, B. (2008). *The counselor and the law* (5th ed.) Alexandria VA: American Counseling Association.

Whitaker, D., & Lieberman, M. (1964). *Psychotherapy through the group process.* New York: Atherton Press.

Wiggins, J. S. (1996). *The five-factor model of personality: Theoretical perspectives.* New York: Guilford Press.

Wikipedia Encyclopedia (2007) Group psychotherapy. http://en.wikipedia.org/wiki/Group-psychotherapy.

Williams, C. B., Frame, M. W., & Green, E. (1999). Counseling groups for African American women: A focus on spirituality. *Journal for Specialists in Group Work, 24*, 260–273.

Williams, J. E., & Best, D. L. (1983). The Gough-Heilbrun Adjective Checklist as a cross-cultural research tool. In J. E. Derogowski, S. Dziurawiec, & R. C. Annis (Eds.), *Expiscations in cross-cultural psychology.* Netherlands: Swet & Zeitlinger B.V.

Williams, B. & Rutan, J. S. (1999). Psychodynamic therapy. In J. Donigan & D. Huse-Killacky (Eds.), *Critical incidents in group therapy.* (2nd ed., pp. 57–65. Pacific Grove, CA: Brooks/Cole.

Winerman, L. (2006). The culture-cognition connection. *Monitor on Psychology, 37*(2), 64–65.

Winnicott, D. (1964). *The maturational process and the facilitating environment.* New York: International Universities Press.

Wolpe, J. (1958). *Psychotherapy by reciprocal inhibition.* Stanford, CA: Stanford University Press.

Wong, D., Chau, P., Kwok, A., & Kwan, J. (2007). Cognitive-behavioral treatment groups for people with chronic physical illness in Hong Kong: Reflections on a culturally attuned model. *International Journal of Group Psychotherapy, 57*(3), 367–386.

Wright, F. (2000). The use of the self in group leadership: A relational perspective. *International Journal of Group Psychotherapy, 50*(2), 181–198.

Yalom, I. (1980). *Existential psychotherapy.* New York: Basic Books.

Yalom, I. (2006). *The Schopenhaur cure.* New York: HarperCollins.

Yalom, I. (with Leszcz, M.). (2005). *The theory and practice of group psychotherapy* (5th ed.) New York: Basic Books.

Yalom, I. D. (1985). *The theory and practice of group psychotherapy.* New York: Basic Books.

Yalom, I. D. (1995). *The theory and practice of group psychotherapy* (4th ed.). New York: Basic Books.

Zetterlind, U., Hansson, H., Aberg-Orbeck, K., & Berglund, M. (2001). Effects of coping skills training, group support, and information for spouses of alcoholics: A controlled randomized study. *Nordic Journal of Psychiatry, 55*(4), 257(6).

Index